Teacher Companion

MyMaths

for Key Stage 3

2B

Powered by **MyMaths**.co.uk

OXFORD
UNIVERSITY PRESS

OXFORD
UNIVERSITY PRESS

Great Clarendon Street, Oxford, OX2 6DP, United Kingdom

Oxford University Press is a department of the University of Oxford.
It furthers the University's objective of excellence in research, scholarship,
and education by publishing worldwide. Oxford is a registered trade mark of
Oxford University Press in the UK and in certain other countries.

First published in 2014

British Library Cataloguing in Publication Data
Data available

978-0-19-830460-9

10 9 8 7 6 5 4 3 2

Paper used in the production of this book is a natural, recyclable product made
from wood grown in sustainable forests. The manufacturing process conforms to
the environmental regulations of the country of origin.

Printed in Great Britain by Bell and Bain Ltd., Glasgow

Acknowledgements

The editors would like to thank Gwen Wood, Katie Wood and Ian Bettison
for their excellent work on this book.

Contents

This Teacher Companion is part of the MyMaths for Key Stage 3 series which has been specially written for the new National Curriculum for Key Stage 3 Mathematics in England. It accompanies Student Book **2B** and is designed to help you have the greatest impact on the learning experience of middle ability students at the start of their Key Stage 3 studies.

The author team brings a wealth of classroom experience to the Teacher Companion making it easy for you to plan and deliver lessons with confidence.

The structure of this book closely follows the content of the student book so that it is easy to find the information and resources you need. These include for each

Lesson: objectives; a list of resources – including MyMaths 4-digit codes; a starter, teaching notes, plenary and alternative approach; simplification and extension ideas; an exercise commentary and full answers; the key ideas and checkpoint questions to test them; and a summary of the key literacy issues.

Chapter: National Curriculum objectives; any assumed prior knowledge; notes supporting the Student Book introduction and starter problem; the associated MyMaths and InvisiPen resources – including those offering extra support to weaker students; questions to test understanding; and how the material is developed and used.

The accompanying CD-ROM makes all the lesson plans available as Word files, so that you can customise them to suit your students' needs. Also on the CD are full sets of answers for Homework Book **2B**.

The integrated solution

This teacher guide is part of a set of resources designed to support you and your students with a fully integrated package of resources.

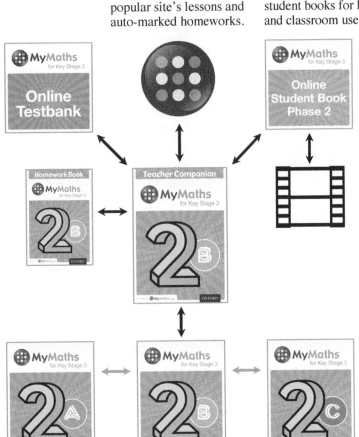

MyMaths
Direct links to the ever popular site's lessons and auto-marked homeworks.

Online Student Book
Digital versions of the student books for home and classroom use.

Online Testbank
A complete suite of assessment tests: good to go, formative (including feedback), auto-marked and print based.

InvisiPen solutions
Student friendly videos explaining just what is needed to solve a sample problem.

Homework Book
Handy, pocket-sized books, tailored to the content of each student book lesson.

Student Book
The three books in a phase are organised to cover topics in the same order but at three ability levels.

Learning outcomes

N1 Understand and use place value for decimals, measures and integers of any size (L5)

N2 Order positive and negative integers, decimals and fractions; use the number line as a model for ordering of the real numbers; use the symbols $=, \neq, <, >, \leq, \geq$ (L5)

N3 Use the concepts and vocabulary of prime numbers, factors (or divisors), multiples, common factors, common multiples, highest common factor, lowest common multiple, prime factorisation, including using product notation and the unique factorisation property (L5)

N4 Use the 4 operations, including formal written methods, applied to integers, decimals, proper and improper fractions, and mixed numbers, all both positive and negative (L5)

N7 Use integer powers and associated real roots (square, cube and higher), recognise powers of 2, 3, 4, 5 and distinguish between exact representations of roots and their decimal approximations (L6)

Introduction

The chapter starts by revising ordering negative decimals and arithmetic with negative integers. The main focus is working with multiples, factors, prime numbers, prime factor decomposition and finding LCMs and HCFs. Finally square and cube numbers are discussed together with the corresponding roots found either by calculator or trial-and-improvement.

The introduction discusses sending sensitive information, such as credit card details, over the internet where there is a risk that it can be intercepted. The first step is to convert any message into a number, say using ASCII codes. The number is then encrypted to turn it into apparent gibberish that can only be decrypted using a secret key. The difficulty is in giving enough information to encrypt a message without making it obvious how to decrypt the message.

One solution called public key encryption is RSA, named after Rivest, Shamir and Adleman. This involves sending, via the internet, two numbers, e and N, to allow a message to be encrypted. The trick is that the decryption requires N to be factored into two primes. N is typically 100 digits long and factorising such large numbers is ferociously difficult making the encryption practically unbreakable if you don't already know the two primes.

The technical details involve modulo arithmetic and Fermat's little theorem. A discussion is available here http://www.claymath.org/publications/posters/primes-go-forever

Prior knowledge

Students should already know how to...

- Use place value with integers and decimals
- Interpret negative numbers
- Do basic integer arithmetic
- Use a calculator for simple sums

Starter problem

The starter problem leads naturally to discussing factorisation and prime numbers. In testing n for primality, $\sqrt{n}$ provides a cut-off on numbers to test.

All primes (after 2 and 3) fall into the pattern $6n + 1$ or $6n - 1$ (or $6n + 5$). These are the numbers that remain in the sieve of Eratosthenes after striking out multiples of 2 and 3. (Numbers of the form $6n$, $6n + 2$, $6n + 3$ and $6n + 4$ have obvious factors of 2 or 3.)

The formula $n^2 - n + 41$, was proposed by Euler in 1772. It works for all values of n from 1 to 40. (Thought of as a finite quadratic sequence the differences between the primes generated, 41, 43, 47, 53, 61..., are 2, 4, 6, 8...)

Primes of the form $2^n - 1$, where n must itself be prime, are named after the French friar Marin Mersenne who studied them in the seventeenth century. The formula works for $n = 2, 3, 5, 7, 13, 17, 19$ and 31 but not for, say, $n = 11$ when it gives $2047 = 23 \times 89$.

The current largest prime is a Mersenne prime $M_{57\,885\,161} = 2^{57\,885\,161} - 1 = 5.81887266... \times 10^{17\,425\,170}$. How many digits does it have? (17 425 170)

Resources

MyMaths

Factors and primes	1032	LCM	1034	Multiples	1035
HCF	1044	Squares and cubes	1053	Negative numbers 2	1068
Ordering decimals	1072				

Online assessment

Chapter test	2B–1
Formative test	2B–1
Summative test	2B–1

InvisiPen solutions

Place value	111	Negative numbers	113
Mental multiplication	122	Mental division	123
Multiples and factors	171	HCF and LCM	172
Primes and prime factors	173	Prime factor decomposition	174
Powers and roots	181		

Topic scheme

Teaching time = 8 lessons/3 weeks

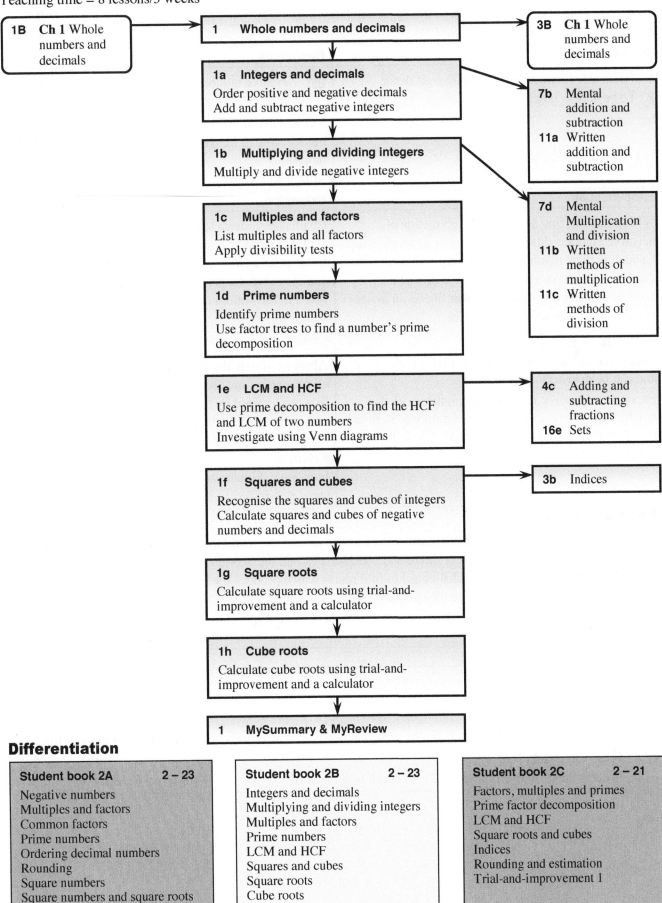

1B **Ch 1** Whole numbers and decimals

1 **Whole numbers and decimals**

3B **Ch 1** Whole numbers and decimals

1a **Integers and decimals**
Order positive and negative decimals
Add and subtract negative integers

7b Mental addition and subtraction
11a Written addition and subtraction

1b **Multiplying and dividing integers**
Multiply and divide negative integers

7d Mental Multiplication and division
11b Written methods of multiplication
11c Written methods of division

1c **Multiples and factors**
List multiples and all factors
Apply divisibility tests

1d **Prime numbers**
Identify prime numbers
Use factor trees to find a number's prime decomposition

1e **LCM and HCF**
Use prime decomposition to find the HCF and LCM of two numbers
Investigate using Venn diagrams

4c Adding and subtracting fractions
16e Sets

1f **Squares and cubes**
Recognise the squares and cubes of integers
Calculate squares and cubes of negative numbers and decimals

3b Indices

1g **Square roots**
Calculate square roots using trial-and-improvement and a calculator

1h **Cube roots**
Calculate cube roots using trial-and-improvement and a calculator

1 **MySummary & MyReview**

Differentiation

Student book 2A   2 – 23
Negative numbers
Multiples and factors
Common factors
Prime numbers
Ordering decimal numbers
Rounding
Square numbers
Square numbers and square roots

Student book 2B   2 – 23
Integers and decimals
Multiplying and dividing integers
Multiples and factors
Prime numbers
LCM and HCF
Squares and cubes
Square roots
Cube roots

Student book 2C   2 – 21
Factors, multiples and primes
Prime factor decomposition
LCM and HCF
Square roots and cubes
Indices
Rounding and estimation
Trial-and-improvement 1

Objectives

- Order decimals (L4)
- Understand negative numbers as positions on a number line (L5)
- Add and subtract integers (L5)

Key ideas	Resources
1 To be able to order decimals with confidence 2 To be able to order negative numbers in context	Negative numbers 2 (1068) Ordering decimals (1072) Vertical and horizontal number lines (a vertical number line as image of thermometer would be helpful) Mini whiteboards

Simplification	Extension
Where students find addition and subtraction of negative numbers difficult make use of a number line. Using a vertical number line may help students to see that when you have a negative you go down that number of steps. Having the number line as an image of a thermometer can also be helpful.	Challenge students to make up their own addition and subtraction number pyramids together with answers. Swap puzzles with a partner. Together with a partner can they invent a puzzle where values are not just given in the bottom row?

Literacy	Links
Check that the notation $<$; $>$; $\geq$; $\leq$; is fully understood and can be read accurately. Encourage other vocabulary to strengthen both the notation and the concept of directed numbers, such as: rise; fall; increase; decrease; + as and; – as difference between.	Absolute zero is the temperature at which (classically) all molecules and atoms stop moving. The idea was first put forward by the brilliant mathematical physicist and engineer William Thomson, later Lord Kelvin, in the 19th century. There is more information about Lord Kelvin at http://en.wikipedia.org/wiki/William_Thomson,_1st_Baron_Kelvin

Alternative approach

Contextualise a variety of values as temperatures of places around the world that are typical of the current season. Students may work in twos or threes and consider a Round the World tour, looking for temperature changes on route. Students can be challenged to find routes which produce the largest/smallest changes in temperatures; or maximise/minimise the overall change of the whole journey. Number lines can be used to support the work. Differentiation may take place by selecting an appropriate variety of values for certain groups of students.

Checkpoint

1 Which of these statements is true and explain why:
   a   -6 is less than -4 (True)
   b   -36 is greater than -31? (False)

   (Explanations may include demonstrating with a visual aid such as a number line.)

2 a   Is the value -2.3 closer to -3 or to -2? (Closer to -2)
   b   What is the difference between -2.3 and each of these values? (+0.7 from -3; and -0.3 from -2)

Starter – Guess my number

Choose a number between -15 and 115.

Invite students to guess the number. After each guess say whether the next guess should be higher or lower.

This can be extended by using numbers with one decimal place.

Teaching notes

Use students' prior knowledge of negative numbers, place value and ordering to get them to explain how they solve the various types of problems. The number line provides a visual aid to reasoning and common misconceptions should be discussed. Ask how they remember how to use the '<' sign: 'the small end points to the smaller number', 'the crocodile eats the bigger number', etc. Point out that -2 < -1 'less than' carries the same information as -1 > -2 'greater than' and both are right. However, when ordering several numbers they should keep the signs aligned: -3 < -2 < -1 rather than -2 > -3 < -1

Ask students to sum three temperature changes + 3° + 4° + (-5)° = 2°. Illustrate this on the number line: go to +3, the first number, and move up +4 units then move down +(-5) = -5 units. What would you get if you took away -5 from +2? (2 – (-5) = 2 + 5 = 7). Illustrate this as start at +2, the first number, and go up 5 units. Lead students towards recognising that:

- adding a negative number is the same as subtracting a positive number
- subtracting a negative number is the same as adding a positive number

by posing contextualised scenarios illustrating these equivalences and asking them what they notice. Contexts may include bank balances or temperatures.

Plenary

Students should be challenged, in pairs, to explain their workings to question **5** and appreciate that there were a number of different ways to get to the answer. For example, in part **a**, who added £13 and £8.50 and then wrote the answer as owed £21.50? Who wrote -£13 – £8.50 = -£21.50?

Exercise commentary

Encourage students to use a number line to help them think through what they are doing.

Question 1 – This is similar to the example. Check that students understand the significance of place value: a larger decimal does not have to be longer 0.024 > 0.0235. (But -0.024 < -0.0235)

Question 2 – Remember that the 'largest' negative number is always the smallest.

Question 3 – Emphasise that, when a positive number is taken away from a negative number, the answer will be a more negative number. Using a number line helps to emphasise this point.

Question 4 – Remind students to consolidate two signs together into one before they complete the question. (A plus and a minus together make a minus, two plusses make a plus, two minuses make a plus.)

Question 5 – Students must write down the equivalent arithmetic calculation, not just an answer.

Question 6 – Number pyramids are common but some students may need further explanation of how to proceed. In part **b**, the order is important, -4 – -2 ≠ -2 – -4. It may help to write out the calculations separately.

Answers

1 a -8 < 6   b -7 < -5
   c -5 < -4.5   d -3.2 < -3
   e -1.5 < -1.49   f -2.7 > -2.8
   g -0.37 > -0.39   h -0.0235 > -0.024

2 a -12, -8, -6, 3, 5   b -8, -3.5, -1.5, 0.5, 1.4
   c -2.9, -1.6, -1.4, 3.2, 4.7   d -3, -2.9, -2.5, -2.3, 1.35

3 a 15   b 8   c -4   d -9
   e -20   f -1   g 4   h -4
   i 6   j 12

4 a 0   b 0   c 3   d -11
   e -14   f 11   g 14   h 0
   i 3   j 4   k -5   l -25
   m 5   n -21

5 a £21.50   b 6 m

6 a

```
              -34
          -25   -6
       -15  -13   7
     -6   -9   -4   11
   -4   -2   -7   3   8
```

b

```
              -42
          -22   20
        -7   15   -5
     -2   5   -10   -5
   -4   -2   -7   3   8
```

c

```
            -6
          -8   2
        3   -5   7
      4   7   2   5
    7   -3   -4   6   -1
```

Objectives	
• Multiply and divide (negative) integers	(L5)

Key ideas	Resources
1 Have a good sense of combining negative and positive numbers and their position on any number line 2 Beginning to be able to link the concept of multiplication and division to directed numbers	Negative numbers 2 (1068) Number lines Directed number puzzles: http://nrich.maths.org/secondary-lower

Simplification	Extension
Supply short practice questions without negative signs and then take the next step and follow the three stage solution shown in the examples, that is, multiply (divide) the numbers, check the sign, write the answer.	Ask students to make up their own grid question involving multiplication of positive and negative numbers as in question **6**, together with an answer. Then, exchange grids with someone else in the class. Students may also be asked to consider multiplying and dividing with more than two values, helping them extend their understanding by linking signs to whether there are an odd or even number of them.

Literacy	Links
Reading and saying the operations from a recorded problem will help establish and communicate the concepts, e.g. -3×2 'two lots of minus 3' $-6 \div -2$ 'how many minus 2s are in minus 6?' Linking the verbal statements to one or more visual images, including a number line, will also assist in consolidating these concepts.	The Ancient Babylonians used a number system based on 60. The large number of multiplication facts (60×60) made multiplication difficult, so the Babylonians developed multiplication tables. The tables were written in cuneiform script on clay tablets and then baked. There is a picture of a Babylonian multiplication tablet for the 35 times table at http://it.stlawu.edu/~dmelvill/mesomath/tablets/36Times.html

Alternative approach
Use a game such as 'Up, Down, Flying Around' or 'Connect Three', both from the nrich maths website, to rehearse addition and subtraction with directed numbers. Explore student knowledge of the +/– button on the calculator, how to use it and its effects on values. Students may be required to complete a grid similar to that in question **2**, but using integers such as -97, -41, -15, -3, 0, 7, 13, 25, 52 with the help of a calculator. Ask the students if they can generalise results for multiplying and dividing any 2 numbers in terms of the sign result, then test their statement(s). Students might be asked to devise a partly completed grid similar to the puzzle for completion by another student, thus encouraging both multiplication and division practice.

Checkpoint

1 **a** Write a short situation that is described by the problem $-12 \div -3$, and give the answer.
                     (4 or +4; any appropriate scenario illustrating the number of -3s that make up -12)
    b Give the three further related facts that follow from this statement:
     $-3 \times 4 = -12$ ($4 \times -3 = -12$, $-12 \div -3 = 4$, $-12 \div 4 = -3$)

Starter – Tables bingo

Ask students to draw a 3 × 3 grid and enter numbers from the 6, 7 and 8 times tables.

Give questions, for example, 7 × 9. The winner is the first student to cross out all their numbers.

The game can be differentiated by the choice of tables.

Teaching notes

To motivate and gain a feel for the signs of the various products, consider calculating the area of a rectangle 8 × 6 whose sides are shortened to 5 × 4. (A very quick reminder about areas might be needed.)

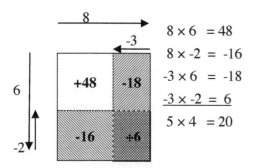

$$8 \times 6 = 48$$
$$8 \times -2 = -16$$
$$-3 \times 6 = -18$$
$$-3 \times -2 = 6$$
$$5 \times 4 = 20$$

Its area is given as the starting area, 8 × 6 = 48, take away a narrow horizontal strip, 8 × -2 = -16, take away a narrow vertical strip, -3 × 6 = -18, but this double counts so we must add back in the overlap area, -3 × -2 = 6, which totals 5 × 4 = 20.

This can be used to motivate the multiplication grid in the text, whose three-step use can be explained with some examples. Use a number of very simple examples to test understanding of multiplication and then try division.

Plenary

Put up a multiplication grid, as in question **6**. Go around the class asking students to tell you how to solve it. First they must say what is the corresponding calculation, for example, 3 × 4 = ? or -6 × -? = 12. If any students have produced their own you could use one of these.

Exercise commentary

Question 1 – Ask students to explain the patterns that occur in their answers.

Question 2 – The grid developed should be used to find the answers. Require students to write out both the calculation and their answer, for example, 3 × -4 = -12.

Question 3 – A basic practice question testing students' ability to apply the rules without scaffolding.

Question 4 – Links to inverse operations. Encourage the students to write down the calculation they do to arrive at the answer, rather than just writing solutions down in a list.

Question 5 – Insist that students write down their explanations: it may be necessary to suggest some possible responses. It may also help to go around the class and ask students to read out their answers.

Question 6 – Suggest proceeding in two steps, first, find the number, second, decide its sign.

Answers

1 a 21, 14, 7, 0, -7, -14, -21, -28
  b -15, -10, -5, 0, 5, 10, 15, 20

2

×	-4	-3	-2	-1	0	1	2	3	4
4	-16	-12	-8	-4	0	4	8	12	16
3	-12	-9	-6	-3	0	3	6	9	12
2	-8	-6	-4	-2	0	2	4	6	8
1	-4	-3	-2	-1	0	1	2	3	4
0	0	0	0	0	0	0	0	0	0
-1	4	3	2	1	0	-1	-2	-3	-4
-2	8	6	4	2	0	-2	-4	-6	-8
-3	12	9	6	3	0	-3	-6	-9	-12
-4	16	12	8	4	0	-4	-8	-12	-16

  b i -6   **ii** 6   **iii** 3   **iv** -3
    v What is 4 × -3 or 3 × -4 or -3 × 4 or -4 × 3?
    vi What is 2 × 4 or 4 × 2 or -2 × -4 or -4 × -2?

3 a -12   **b** -10   **c** 12   **d** 35
  e -40   **f** 24   **g** -25   **h** 81
  i -121   **j** 150   **k** 4   **l** -3
  m 13   **n** 11   **o** -3   **p** -44
  q -60   **r** 90   **s** 6   **t** -16

4 a -4   **b** 5   **c** -7   **d** -5
  e 7   **f** 9   **g** -36   **h** 36
  i -100   **j** -8   **k** -17   **l** 3

5 a -6   **b** -5   **c** 5   **d** -8
  e -28   **f** -4

6 a

×	4	5	-6	8
-2	-8	-10	12	-16
3	12	15	-18	24
-7	-28	-35	42	-56
-9	-36	-45	54	-72

  b

×	2	-1	-3	-4
-1	2	1	3	4
-6	-12	6	18	24
2	4	-2	-6	-8
5	10	-5	-15	-20

1c Multiples and factors

Objectives

- Use simple tests of divisibility   (L5)
- Recognise and use multiples and factors   (L5)

Key ideas	Resources
1 Know and use a few simple factor tests 2 Have a clear sense of the difference between a multiple and a factor	Multiples (1035) Dictionaries Factors & Multiples puzzle from http://nrich.maths.org/5448

Simplification	Extension
For students who find this work difficult there is a need to find factors for smaller numbers, such as 12 or 16, and to practise divisibility testing for 2, 3, 4, 5, 6 and 8 to develop confidence.	Ask students to make their own productogon as in question **7**, together with a solution, and ask others to solve it.

Literacy	Links
Make use of the opportunities here to use the words multiple and factor frequently, requesting that the students also do this, together with giving a simple reason why it is one and not the other. These two words are commonly alternated in meaning by students and helping to expose this will also help to avoid the problem.	Bring in some dictionaries for the class to use. The word *divisibility* has five i's, the word *indivisibilities* has seven. Ask the class to find other words with at least four i's. Some examples include *infinitesimal* (4), *impossibilities* (5), *invisibility* (5) and *indistinguishability* (6). The dictionary will probably not include *supercalifragilisticexpialidocious* (7)!

Alternative approach

Challenge students to find as many integers as possible that will go into, say 12 375. (NB: $3^2 \times 5^3 \times 11$) Encourage the use of calculators as well as mental approaches here. This lends itself to paired work. Ask students to explore and share how they approached this problem and their actions, including any reforms they made. Common divisibility tests will arise from this work, and then can be extended to include others. This activity can be extended to decomposing into prime factors for the most able, but this is not the intention. By providing a list of numbers divisible by and not divisible by, say 9, students may be encouraged to search for a possible test themselves. The game on Factors and Multiples from nrich will provide further consolidation.

Checkpoint

1 Which of these numbers are divisible by 2, 3, 5?
   11, 15, 16, 22, 24, 25, 30, 33, 34   (2: 16, 22, 24, 30, 34; 3: 15, 24, 30, 33; 5: 15, 25, 30)

2 Is 124 divisible by 4? Explain how you know.   (Yes, because 24 is a multiple of 4)

Starter – The answer is -12

Ask students to write down questions where the answer is -12. Score 1 point for an addition question, 2 points for a subtraction question, 3 for a multiplication or division question.

Teaching notes

Finding multiples is straightforward, if tedious, whilst finding factors requires students to be systematic; students should be encouraged to write factors in pairs.

Students may already know some divisibility tests (for 2, 5, 10, …) and should be encouraged to explain these themselves. Others will need clarifying or introducing with examples.

- 2, 5 and 10: only the last digit is looked at since $10 = 2 \times 5 = 1 \times 10$.
- 3: the test can be applied repeatedly: 854 622 sum of digits 27, sum of digits $9 = 3 \times 3$ is a multiple of three ($854\,622 = 3 \times 284\,874$).
- 4: only the last two digits need to be tested as $100 = 4 \times 25$.
- 7: must still be checked even if there is no simple test.
- 8: only the last three digits need to be tested as $1000 = 8 \times 125$.
- 9: this test can also be applied repeatedly: 854 622 sum of digits 27, sum of digits 9 is a multiple of 9 ($854\,622 = 9 \times 94\,958$).
- 11: this must be explained: 5291 alternating sum $= 5 - 2 + 9 - 1 = (5 + 9) - (2 + 1) = 14 - 3 = 11$ is a multiple of 11 ($5291 = 11 \times 481$).

Plenary

Pose a series of missing digit questions, as in question 5, and challenge students to find the possible values for the digit to make the number a multiple.

Exercise commentary

Question 1 – Students may find it easier to keep adding the first term rather than do multiplications.

Question 2 – Encourage students to be systematic in order to get all factors. It will help to write them as a list in pairs, one column increasing, and the other decreasing in size. They should stop when the columns 'swap over'.

Question 3 – Follows on from question 1.

Question 4 – This could be done as a whole-class activity.

Question 5 – Follows on from question 4g and 4j.

Question 6 – In part **c**, hint that factor pairs are the key to this question. Remind students that three groups of eight is different from eight groups of three.

Question 7 – Part **a** can be done by looking at the equations associated with each side, for example, $9 \times ? = 63$. Part **b** will require students to find common factors.

Question 8 – In part **b**, there is more than one answer. Ask why divisible by 2 and 3 is insufficient.

Answers

1
- a 5, 10, 15
- b 14, 28, 42
- c 21, 42, 63
- d 35, 70, 105
- e 48, 96, 144
- f 115, 230, 345
- g 45, 90, 135
- h 90, 180, 270

2
- a 1, 2, 4, 5, 10, 20
- b 1, 2, 4, 7, 14, 28
- c 1, 3, 5, 9, 15, 45
- d 1, 2, 4, 13, 26, 52
- e 1, 2, 3, 6, 11, 22, 33, 66
- f 1, 2, 3, 4, 6, 7, 12, 14, 21, 28, 42, 84
- g 1, 2, 4, 8, 16
- h 1, 2, 4, 8, 16, 32

3 a 120 b 135 c 9 d 0 e 89

4 a Yes b Yes c No d Yes
   e Yes f Yes g Yes h No
   i Yes j Yes

5 a 5 b 8

6
- a No, because the sum of the digits is not divisible by 9
- b Yes, because 540 is divisible by both 3 and 4
- c There are 6 ways

2 groups of 12	3 groups of 8
4 groups of 6	6 groups of 4
8 groups of 3	12 groups of 2

- d 23 is prime, so only as 1 group of 23

7 a 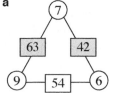 b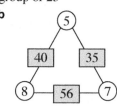

8
- a Yes
- b ÷ 9 and ÷ 2, ÷ 6 and ÷ 3

Objectives

- Recognise and use primes (L5)
- Find the prime factor decomposition of a number (L5)

Key ideas	Resources
1 Have an understanding that primes are the building blocks of all numbers 2 Be able to decompose simple numbers into prime factors	Factors and primes (1032) Mini whiteboards Prime number activities: http://nrich.maths.org/public/leg.php?group_id=1&code=9#results

Simplification	Extension
Some students may need further consolidation of tests of divisibility from the previous spread. A useful method of reinforcement is to ask students to design an additional 'textbook example' of their own to show how they would explain to another student.	Challenge students to design an interesting question (with answer!) of their own along the lines of question **8** and to swap with another student to offer a solution. This offers an opportunity to develop the process skill of communicating and reflecting through discussing and reflecting on different approaches to solving a numerical problem.

Literacy	Links
Take the opportunity to examine other uses of the key word PRIME in everyday language. Compare this usage and the implied definitions with the mathematical one.	Eratosthenes lived from about 276 BC to 194 BC. He was born in Cyrene, North Africa (now Libya) and became not only a mathematician but also a poet, athlete, geographer and astronomer. One of his achievements was to use geometry to estimate the circumference of the Earth. There is more information about Eratosthenes at http://en.wikipedia.org/wiki/Eratosthenes

Alternative approach

Request students find any two factors of one of these numbers: $780, 215, 90$, and record that value as a product of the two factors. Students choosing a similar number should now compare their findings. Now they should be encouraged to break these two values into two others if possible, and so on until primes are achieved. The students can then compare results with their group. Ask students to explain what has resulted from this and why it might be useful. Pose questions such as 'did it matter which two factors were the initial choice?'. This helps to widen starting points for decomposing a number so that all students can call on their own number knowledge confidently, and not necessarily starting with the first prime, and using a systematic approach. Ask students to investigate 'Stars' from nrich. More able students may be encouraged to work on 'Why 24' from nrich.

Checkpoint

1 Which of these values are not prime $1, 2, 3, 5, 11, 13, 15, 21, 23, 27, 29, 31$? $(1, 15, 21, 27)$

2 Write the number 54 as a product of primes. $(2 \times 3 \times 3 \times 3$ or $2 \times 3^3)$

Starter – Make 1 to 15

Throw three dice and ask students to make one number between 1 and 15 inclusive using all three scores and any operation(s). Throw again; students make another number between 1 and 15. Repeat a further 13 times. The winner is the student who makes the most different numbers.

Teaching notes

To make links with students' prior knowledge, initiate a paired discussion and then take feedback to agree a whole class definition of what is a prime number. Consolidate understanding by inviting students to account for why 1 is not defined to be a prime number and why 2 is the only even prime number.

When developing discussion of factors, choose a number and use mini whiteboards to invite students to contribute the factors of that number and ensure all are involved. Pose the question 'why should factors be used in pairs?' and tease out that it is helpful to make sure no factors are missed and to know when the list is exhausted.

When discussing factor trees, ask different groups of students to use the same number but use a different factor pair as the starting point. Take feedback on the prime factors to illustrate that they will always be the same.

Plenary

Refer back to the lesson objectives and ask students to identify for themselves what they have done during the lesson that shows they understand and can use their knowledge of prime numbers, tests of divisibility and factors. Introduce this initially as an opportunity to think for themselves, then to discuss with a friend and finally to share as a whole group to encourage engagement with moving learning forward.

Exercise commentary

This exercise gives an opportunity to develop classroom dialogue via an emphasis on explanation and justification.

Question 1 – Encourage students to memorise the early primes.

Question 2 – Insist on explanations.

Question 3 – Relates to the text. Ask why you don't need to test 4 or 6.

Question 4 – Develops question **3**. Discuss efficient approaches: 75 is clearly a multiple of 5, therefore no need to test for divisibility by 2 and 3. Why does this not undermine using a systematic approach?

Question 5 – Encourage the use of factor trees. Point out that one can start the tree with any factor pair, a unique answer is guaranteed.

Question 6 – Students should continue the working out rather than copy out what has already been done.

Question 7 – This investigation could be extended for other numbers.

Question 8 – There is no shortcut way to do part **b**.

Answers

1. **a** $1, 2, 3, 5, 6, 10, 15, 30$
   b $1, 2, 3, 4, 6, 8, 12, 16, 24, 48$
   c $1, 67$
   d $1, 2, 29, 58$
   e $1, 53$
   f $1, 3, 37, 111$
   67 and 53 are prime

2. **a** Yes, as number ends in 5
   b Yes, as digits add up to 15, a multiple of 3
   c Yes, as number is even
   d Yes, as $1 + 3 = 4$
   e Yes, 2 is a factor and 3 is a factor

3. **a** 59 is prime   **b** 67 is prime

4. **a** 3×5 **b** Prime   **c** Prime   **d** 3×29
   e 2×27 **f** Prime   **g** 5×17 **h** Prime
   i 2×48 **j** 3×35 **k** Prime   **l** 7×19

5. **a** 3×5 **b** $2 \times 2 \times 2 \times 3$
   c $2 \times 2 \times 2 \times 5$ **d** $3 \times 3 \times 3$
   e $2 \times 2 \times 2 \times 2 \times 2 \times 2$ **f** $2 \times 2 \times 2 \times 7$
   g $2 \times 2 \times 2 \times 2 \times 3$ **h** $2 \times 2 \times 2 \times 3 \times 3$
   i $2 \times 2 \times 2 \times 2 \times 5$ **j** $2 \times 2 \times 2 \times 2 \times 2 \times 3$
   k $2 \times 2 \times 2 \times 5 \times 5 \times 5$ **l** $2 \times 3 \times 5 \times 7$

6. **a** 211   **b** Yes

7. **a** $11 + 11$ **b** $13 + 17$
   c $3 + 29$ **d** $29 + 31$

8. **a** Multiple answers   **b** $102 (= 2 \times 3 \times 17)$

Objectives	
• Use multiples, factors, common factors, highest common factors, lowest common multiples and primes (L5)	

Key ideas	Resources
1 Begin to understand that numbers are all composed of primes **2** That finding common prime factors of values is a useful tactic in problem solving	⊞ LCM (1034) HCF (1044) Mini whiteboards

Simplification	Extension
This exercise is supportive of a range of abilities of student as the more able will use prime factors readily whilst the weakest will still be able to achieve using a method that may be more familiar and can be encouraged to make connections at their own pace. For students who are experiencing difficulty with this work, give additional practice with smaller numbers and encourage them to become confident with the table method as illustrated in question **1** before introducing the use of prime factors.	Ask pairs to work together to create their own productogon with answer, using question **5** as a model, which they can then swap with another pair.

Literacy	Links
Include the word product when using and writing factors to reinforce the connection with the operation. Check that any recording makes correct use of equals signs e.g. LCM of 20 and 25 = 100 HCF of 20 and 25 = 5 Discourage recording such 20 & 25 = 100, etc.	Periodical cicadas live for years underground as grubs, emerge from their burrows for a few weeks to breed and then die. The population is synchronised so that they all become adults and emerge together. This can result in huge populations, up to 1.5M/acre. The males make a distinctive drumming or singing noise. There is more information about cicadas at http://magicicada.org/magicicada.php and at http://biology.clc.uc.edu/steincarter/cicadas.htm

Alternative approach
Show the two statements, for example 14 is the highest common denominator (HCF) of 56 and 70   280 is the lowest common multiple (LCM) of 56 and 70   saying that both are correct. Allocate pairs of students one of the statements, and other pairs the second, with the task of trying to explain what is given and how and why the result occurs. If necessary, offer the hint that thinking about prime factors, as in previous lesson, may be helpful. Group into fours with one pair as 'HCF experts' and the other 'LCM experts' in order for them to demonstrate and explain their findings to each other. Include new examples, or use questions from the exercise for the fours to work on as a team.

Checkpoint	
1 What is the LCM of 9 and 12?	(36)
2 What is the HCF of 12 and 15?	(3)

Ask students questions involving prime numbers less than 20. For example,

Two prime numbers that have a difference of 9? (2, 11)

Two prime numbers that have a total of 22? (5, 17)

Two prime numbers with a product of 65? (5, 13)

Sum of first four prime numbers? (17)

Make a list of prime numbers on the board if necessary.

Teaching notes

Help students to make connections by linking back to the earlier spreads in this chapter and establish, through questioning, that they are certain of the definitions of factor and multiple. Suggest a number and ask, for example, for half of the students to suggest a factor of that number and the other half to suggest a multiple of the same number. Discuss the responses. Mini whiteboards could be used for easy whole-class involvement and assessment.

Develop this idea, giving half the group one number and the other half another number, enter student suggestions into two Venn diagrams, one for factors and one for multiples, as a way to find the HCF or LCM of pairs of numbers. Ensure that students are confident with this before moving on to discuss how prime factors can be used to find these in a more efficient way: a single Venn diagram with far fewer entries will be needed. A diagrammatic approach will help to support some students who struggle.

Plenary

As a very brief assessment overview, give two numbers and ask students to draw a Venn diagram themselves, using the student book example as a model, to demonstrate how they have used prime factors to find the HCF and LCM. Additional support is provided by offering a selection of pairs of numbers and inviting students to share their responses with others with a different number pair.

Exercise commentary

Question 1 – This is the simplest way to find the HCF and LCM.

Questions 2 and **3** – Suggest the prime factor method as a more efficient approach to that in question **1**.

Question 4 – The approaches used in questions **1** and **2** are both options, though moving to the prime factor method should be encouraged.

Question 5 – For students who have struggled with the previous questions, it may be necessary to revisit the word 'product' and suggest a method.

Question 6 – Applied problems that use LCM/HCF. Encourage students to write down their methods carefully and clearly.

Answers

1

Numbers	Factors	HCF	First five multiples	LCM
4	1, 2, 4	2	4, 8, 12, 16, 20	12
6	1, 2, 3, 6		6, 12, 18, 24, 30	

2 **a** 4 **b** 7 **c** 8
  d 13 **e** 8 **f** 7

3 **a** 24 **b** 42 **c** 160
  d 156 **e** 120 **f** 196

4 **a** 14, 84 **b** 7, 728 **c** 36, 216
  d 24, 720 **e** 45, 1350 **f** 64, 384

5 **a**

```
          (20)
        /      \
    [360]     [480]
     /           \
  (18)—[432]—(24)
```

b

```
          (25)
        /      \
    [375]     [750]
     /           \
  (15)—[450]—(30)
```

6 **a** 378 seconds **b** 16 cm by 16 cm

Objectives

• Use squares, positive and negative square roots and cubes	(L6)
• Use index notation for small positive integer powers	(L5)

Key ideas	Resources
1 Begin to understand squares and cubes 2 Begin to understand use index notation	Squares and cubes (1053) Multilink cubes Digat http://nrich.maths.org/619 Square routes http://nrich.maths.org/589 Forgotten number http://nrich.maths.org/508

Simplification	Extension
Allow students to develop their understanding of square and cube numbers using a kinaesthetic approach, building the numbers with cubes, sketching or drawing.	Ask students to investigate the relationship between square numbers and odd numbers. Encourage them to use visual images to explain their thinking.

Literacy	Links
Examine the difference in everyday usage of the words root and route. Ask students to link this knowledge to the use of the word root in mathematics. Similarly explore the word power. Examine the conventions of recording using index numbers linking it with reading values e.g. 4^3 or '4 cubed' or ' 4 to the power of 3'	The sugar cube was invented in 1841 by Jakub Kryštof Rad in Dacice, Bohemia (now the Czech Republic). At this time, sugar was produced in a large, solid cone shape and had to be cut for the customer. Rad invented the sugar cube after his wife cut her finger slicing the sugar. Sugar cubes first appeared in shops in Vienna in 1843. A granite memorial of a sugar cube stands in the Town Square in Dacice.

Alternative approach

Ask students to explore and record the prime factors of some non-square numbers and some square numbers, drawing on the students own knowledge of such numbers. Ask them what is different about these two groups of values. Encourage students to hypothesise and test their results. Those grasping this quickly may be encouraged to try to explain why square numbers have an odd number of prime factors, but non-square numbers have an even number of prime factors. This activity can be extended to examine known cube numbers in a similar way.

While encouraging as much estimation as possible while using square and cube numbers, include and explore the use of the calculator by the variety of approaches with the available calculators, e.g. square or cube button, x^y or y^x button, or the constant multiply feature. Students may consolidate work through these activities from nrich: 'Digat', 'Square Routes' and/or 'Forgotten Number'.

Checkpoint

1 Which is bigger, 3^2 or 2^3?	(3^2)
2 Which of these is likely to be bigger, 21^2 or 14^3? Explain why, and then check your answer.	
(14^3 is likely to be bigger because it is $14 \times 14 \times 14$, whereas 21^2 is only 21×21. $21^2 = 441$, $14^3 = 2744$)	

Starter – Prime bingo

Ask students to draw a 3 × 3 grid and enter 9 prime numbers less than 100.

Give calculations yielding prime numbers, for example, half of 82, 7 × 5 + 2, 39 ÷ 3.

The winner is the first student to cross out all their primes.

The game can be differentiated by the choice of calculations.

Teaching notes

Make links with students' prior knowledge of number patterns as a way of introducing this work. Refer to the visual representations of square and cube numbers in the student book to reinforce concepts. This offers the opportunity to develop the process skill of analysing – using appropriate mathematical procedures, visualising images to support mental methods.

When developing the use of index notation, it is important to remember that a common misconception amongst students is that, for example, 3^2 means 3×2, rather than 3 multiplied by itself. Again, referring to the use of the visual images in the student book will provide support in overcoming this.

The first example offers the opportunity to discuss what happens when two negative numbers are multiplied together.

Plenary

Ask students to write a definition of a square and a cube number and to discuss how they would explain to someone who didn't understand, what the small number (index) means.

Exercise commentary

Question 1 – Students may need support with parts **e** and **f**.

Question 2 – Similar to the first example; some students may need a calculator.

Question 3 – Check that students try to match as many pairs as they can without defaulting to using a calculator.

Question 4 – Similar to the second example. Check that students can use their calculator correctly.

Question 5 – Inverse problems requiring the mathematics to be identified: students may use 'guess work' or the 'square root' key .

Question 6 – Suggest trying numbers close to the square root.

Question 7 – Here, work on prime numbers is revisited. For some students, a brief reminder of the meaning of 'sum' may be appropriate. For the square of an even number this is a special case of the (presently unresolved) Goldbach conjecture.

Question 8 – This is actually an investigation into Pythagorean triples.

Answers

1	a	36	b	81	c	144	
	d	225	e	216	f	1000	
2	a	196	b	324	c	576	d 2197
	e	4913	f	49	g	2744	h 6.25
	i	1000	j	3.375	k	421.875	l -125
	m	1.21	n	1.331	o	0.81	p 0.729

3 a
A–d	B–g	C–a	D–b
E–h	F–c	G–f	H–e

b
A = 12.25	B = 60.84	C = 123.21
D = 28.09	E = 193.21	F = 42.88
G = 185.19	H = 24.39	

4 a 343   b 289   c 1, 64, 729

5 a 11 cm   b 56   c 32 m

6   $\sqrt{2070} = 45.5$
    $45 \times 46 = 2070$

7   Only 1 and 121 cannot be written as the sum of 2 primes.

8   There are infinitely many solutions, for example
    $13^2 = 12^2 + 5^2$ $(169 = 144 + 25)$
    $10^2 = 8^2 + 6^2$ $(100 = 64 + 36)$
    $17^2 = 15^2 + 8^2$ $(289 = 225 + 64)$

Objectives

- Recognise the squares of numbers to at least 12×12 and the corresponding roots (L5)
- Use squares and positive (and negative) square roots (L5)
- Use ICT to estimate square roots (and cube roots) (L6)

Key ideas	Resources
1 To have knowledge of some of the simple square numbers and their roots 2 To have a sufficient understanding of square numbers to be able to estimate some non-integer roots	● Square and cubes (1053) Calculators – basic if available, and scientific Mini whiteboards A1, A2, A3, A4, A5 size paper Powers and roots puzzles http://nrich.maths.org/8466

Simplification	Extension
Some students will need to use the number line to get a clearer picture when looking at numbers with square roots that are not whole numbers and will need support with trial-and-improvement.	The most able students could begin to look at Pythagoras' theorem and how this uses square roots.

Literacy	Links
Check the notation for roots, and make it explicit that $^2\sqrt{\ }$ is acceptably written as $\sqrt{\ }$ as a 'shorthand' or abbreviation. Check also that inclusion of this symbol is read carefully and interpreted correctly by comparing for example, these two statements: Find $\sqrt{25} + 4 + 7$ Find $\sqrt{(25 + 4 + 7)}$	Bring in some sheets of A3, A4 and A5 paper and other ISO sizes if available. Ask the class to measure the paper and calculate the ratio of the length to the width for each size. The ratio is $\sqrt{2} : 1$ or $1.4142 : 1$ in all cases. Now fold a sheet of A4 in half and compare with a sheet of A5 (same size). ISO paper sizes are designed so that A0 has an area of 1 m^2 but with a length to width ratio of $\sqrt{2} : 1$. When a sheet of A0 is cut in half, it makes two smaller sheets size A1, each with a length to width ratio of $\sqrt{2} : 1$, etc. There is a chart illustrating ISO paper sizes at http://en.wikipedia.org/wiki/Image:A_size_illustration.svg

Alternative approach

After rehearsing some knowledge facts of both square and cube numbers, a mini challenge could be set up where groups of three students try to estimate square roots of some values resulting in non-integer values. This could be set against a time limit requiring the use of only mental tools. If basic calculators only are available, the challenge can be extended to finding close root estimates of more complex values. When using only basic calculators, trial-and-improvement systems will evolve naturally, but if scientific calculators are available then this technique will appear cumbersome and unnecessary for most students. Trial-and-improvement is not the purpose of this lesson, however, so is best not pursued here. If basic calculators are provided, then discussion over whether an answer of say 2.3 is a closer estimate than 2.4 will arise naturally, allowing the work to be extended into accuracy to, say, one decimal place. Speed use of scientific calculators can help establish efficient use of the appropriate buttons.

Checkpoint

1 a Between which two whole numbers is the square root of 160? (12 and 13)

   b Which of these two values is the closest to the actual answer? Explain how you know.

(13, with any appropriate explanation about it being over half way between 12 and 13)

Key outcomes	Quick check
Order and compare decimals. L5	**a** Which is larger, 3.45 or 3.4? (3.45) **b** Order these decimals, smallest first: $0.1, 0.11, 1.1, 1.01, 0.01$ $(0.01, 0.1, 0.11, 1.01, 1.1)$
Add, subtract, multiply and divide integers. L5	Calculate: **a** -5×6 (-30) **b** $-5 + 7$ (2) **c** $-3 - -5$ (2) **d** $30 \div -2$ (-15)
Recognise and use multiples and factors. L4	Which of these numbers are **a** multiples of 8 **b** factors of 8? $1, 4, 8, 16, 20, 24$ (Multiples: 8, 16, 24; Factors: 1, 4, 8)
Use divisibility tests. L5	**a** Is 3 a factor of 456? (Yes) **b** Is 9 a factor of 678? (No) **c** Is 53 prime? (Yes)
Find the prime factor decomposition of a number. L5	Write the following as a product of prime factors: **a** 60 $(2^2 \times 3 \times 5)$ **b** 150 $(2 \times 3 \times 5^2)$
Find the lowest common multiple and highest common factor of two numbers. L5	**a** Find the LCM of 12 and 20 (60) **b** Find the HCF of 60 and 150 (30)
Recognise and use cube and square numbers, cube and square roots. L6	Write down: **a** $\sqrt{81}$ (9) **b** 6^2 (36) **c** $\sqrt{144}$ (12) **d** 11^2 (121)

⊞ MyMaths extra support

Lesson/online homework			Description
Rounding decimals	1004	L5	Rounding numbers to the nearest whole number and to 1 decimal place
Negative numbers 1	1069	L3	Understanding and ordering negative numbers
Decimal place value	1076	L4	Reading and writing decimal numbers

1 MySummary

Check out
You should now be able to ...

			Test it ➡ Questions
✓	Order and compare decimals.	⑤	1, 2
✓	Add, subtract, multiply and divide integers.	⑤	3, 4
✓	Recognise and use multiples and factors.	④	5
✓	Use divisibility tests.	⑤	6
✓	Find the prime factor decomposition of a number.	⑤	7, 8
✓	Find the lowest common multiple and highest common factor of two numbers.	⑤	9, 10
✓	Recognise and use cube and square numbers, cube and square roots.	④	11–13

Language	Meaning	Example
Decimal	A number which has digits after the decimal point	3.25 and 4.13 are decimal numbers
Multiple	A number which is part of a number's times table	12 and 18 are both multiples of 6
Factor	A number which exactly divides another number	4 and 6 are both factors of 12
Product	Another word for multiplication	The product of 3 and 4 is 12
Factor tree	A method for finding the prime factor decomposition of a number	See page 10
Highest common factor (HCF)	The biggest number which divides both of two other numbers	6 is the highest common factor of 12 and 18
Lowest common multiple (LCM)	The smallest number which is in the times tables of two other numbers	30 is the lowest common multiple of 5 and 6
Square number Cube number	A number which is found by multiplying an integer by itself twice or three times	$9 = 3 \times 3 = 3^2$ is the square of 3 and $27 = 3 \times 3 \times 3 = 3^3$ is the cube of 3
Square root Cube root	The opposite of a square number or a cube number	$3 = \sqrt{9}$ is the square root of 9 $3 = \sqrt[3]{27}$ is the cube root of 27

1 MyReview

1 Write < or > between these pairs of numbers to show which number is the larger.
a -16 and -16.5   b 0.457 and 0.52
c 0.043 and 0.34   d -0.56 and -0.055

2 Put these numbers in order from smallest to largest.
a 6   - 3   0   -5
b 1.3   - 2.4   -2.6   -0.9

3 Calculate
a -8 + -7   b -9 – 5
c 5 – -4   d -11 – -19

4 Calculate
a 5 × -3   b -7 × -4
c 30 ÷ -6   d -50 ÷ -5

5 Which of these numbers are
a factors of 6
b multiples of 6?

1 3 4 6 12 14 15 18

6 Use divisibility tests to say if these statements are true or false and explain your answer.
a 3 is a factor of 965
b 9515 is divisible by 11
c 770 is a multiple of 8
d 143 is a prime number

7 Which of the following numbers are prime numbers?

1 2 3 4 5

8 Write each of these numbers as a product of its prime factors.
a 63   b 385

9 Find the highest common factor of each pair of numbers.
a 25 and 75   b 11 and 17

10 Find the lowest common multiple of each pair of numbers.
a 28 and 84   b 16 and 24

11 Which of the following numbers are square numbers?

1 2 4 6 8

12 Write down the value of these square roots.
a $\sqrt{64}$ b $\sqrt{25}$
c $\sqrt{121}$ d $\sqrt{1}$

13 Calculate
a 2^3 b $\sqrt[3]{64}$
c 4^3 d $\sqrt[3]{216}$

What next?

Score		
0 – 4	Your knowledge of this topic is still developing. To improve look at Formative test: 2B-1; MyMaths: 1032, 1034, 1035, 1044, 1053, 1068 and 1072
5 – 11	You are gaining a secure knowledge of this topic. To improve look at InvisiPen: 111, 113, 122, 123, 171, 172, 173, 174 and 181
12 – 13	You have mastered this topic. Well done, you are ready to progress!

Question commentary

The term 'minus' can be confusing; try to use 'negative' to describe numbers and 'subtract' to describe the operation.

Questions 1 to **4** – Students could draw or visualise a number line to do these questions.

Question 5 – Students can confuse factors and multiples. Students should understand that the number 1 is a factor of all other integers and that any number will be both a factor and a multiple of itself.

Questions 6 and **7** – Students must be able to explain their reasoning clearly.

Question 8 – Encourage the use of index notation.

Question 9 – Students should understand that the HCF can sometimes be 1 (coprime numbers).

Question 10 – Students should realise that a LCM can be one of the two original numbers.

Questions 11 – Common misconceptions include 2 and 6 being square numbers and 1 not a square number.

Question 12 – Students should recognise without a calculator.

Question 13 – Part **a** should be straightforward to do mentally (although a common wrong answer is 6); a calculator could be allowed for parts **b** and **d**. Part **c** should follow directly from part **b**.

Answers

1	a	-16 > -16.5		b	0.457 < 0.52		
	c	0.043 < 0.34		d	-0.56 < -0.055		
2	a	-5, -3, 0, 6		b	-2.6, -2.4, -0.9, 1.3		
3	a	-15	b -14		c 9		d 8
4	a	-15	b 28		c -5		d 10
5	a	1, 3, 6	b 6, 12, 18				
6	a	False	b True		c False		
	d	False (11 × 13)					
7	2, 3, 5						
8	a	$3 \times 3 \times 7$	b $5 \times 7 \times 11$				
9	a	25	b 1				
10	a	84	b 48				
11	1, 4						
12	a	8	b 5		c 11		d 1
13	a	8	b 4		c 64		d 6

Write the following five calculations on the board:
99×999, 99^3, $\sqrt{999\,999}$, $9(99 + 999)$, $\sqrt{99 \times 99^2}$.

Ask students to estimate the answers and arrange them in order of size, smallest first.

Challenge students to explain their methods.

Correct order:

$\sqrt{999\,999}$, $\sqrt{99 \times 99^2}$, $9(99 + 999)$, 99×999, 99^3.

Teaching notes

Make links here with work on squares and square roots. Assess understanding using the first two questions in the exercise as whole-class interactive activities using mini whiteboards.

This spread offers the opportunity to consolidate finding a solution by trial-and-improvement, a skill that students will use elsewhere.

Make effective links with work in geometry and measures involving volume and use this opportunity to consolidate understanding.

It is important to support the efficient use of a calculator. Many students are caught out by the fact that not all calculator functions are found in the same place on all calculators. This is a good time to look at more than one model/make of calculator to locate the cube root button. Students need to be familiar with their own model of calculator.

Plenary

Provide a word-based problem involving cubes and/or cube roots along similar lines to the examples in the exercise. To support analysis, discuss the problem as a whole class, highlighting key information.

Exercise commentary

Not all calculators are the same so students may need help finding/using the $[\sqrt[3]{\ }]$ key which may require the use of [shift] or [2nd fn].

Question 1 – All have whole number answers; students should be encouraged to learn to recognise the first few cubes.

Question 2 – Students may need reminding how to calculate the volume of a cube.

Question 3 – A chance to confirm that students can use their calculators properly.

Question 4 – Make links here to prior experience of trial-and-improvement. The example can be used as a model.

Question 5 – A simple example but in a text-based problem; check that units are given.

Question 6 – A word problem involving solution by trial-and-improvement.

Question 7 – Part **a** may require a hint. Part **b** has similar solutions but is more difficult.

Question 8 – Shows that the order of index operations can be changed.

Question 9 – Encourage students to try a few examples first and then proceed systematically.

Answers

1 a 64, 4   b 8, 2   c 125, 5
   d 27, 3   e 216, 6   f 1000, 10
2 a i $64\,\text{cm}^3$ ii $216\,\text{cm}^3$
   b i 2 cm   ii 5 cm
3 a 3.68   b 3.91   c 3.98   d 4.02
   e 4.99   f 5.01   g 2.96   h 4.64
   i -4.00
4 a 3.36   b 4.31   c 4.06   d 4.12
   e 4.56   f 5.08   g 2.15   h 4.72
   i 5.19
5 3 cm
6 2.1 m
7 a 0 and 1 (and -1)
   b 3.16 (also -3.16 and 0, of course)
8 a 4 and 4   b 2.92 and 2.92
   c Cube root of the square is equal to the square of the cube root
9 2

Key outcomes	Quick check
Order and compare decimals. L5	**a** Which is larger, 3.45 or 3.4? (3.45) **b** Order these decimals, smallest first: $0.1, 0.11, 1.1, 1.01, 0.01$ $(0.01, 0.1, 0.11, 1.01, 1.1)$
Add, subtract, multiply and divide integers. L5	Calculate: **a** -5×6 (-30) **b** $-5 + 7$ (2) **c** $-3 - -5$ (2) **d** $30 \div -2$ (-15)
Recognise and use multiples and factors. L4	Which of these numbers are **a** multiples of 8 **b** factors of 8? $1, 4, 8, 16, 20, 24$ (Multiples: 8, 16, 24; Factors: 1, 4, 8)
Use divisibility tests. L5	**a** Is 3 a factor of 456? (Yes) **b** Is 9 a factor of 678? (No) **c** Is 53 prime? (Yes)
Find the prime factor decomposition of a number. L5	Write the following as a product of prime factors: **a** 60 ($2^2 \times 3 \times 5$) **b** 150 ($2 \times 3 \times 5^2$)
Find the lowest common multiple and highest common factor of two numbers. L5	**a** Find the LCM of 12 and 20 (60) **b** Find the HCF of 60 and 150 (30)
Recognise and use cube and square numbers, cube and square roots. L6	Write down: **a** $\sqrt{81}$ (9) **b** 6^2 (36) **c** $\sqrt{144}$ (12) **d** 11^2 (121)

MyMaths extra support

Lesson/online homework	Description
Rounding decimals 1004 L5	Rounding numbers to the nearest whole number and to 1 decimal place
Negative numbers 1 1069 L3	Understanding and ordering negative numbers
Decimal place value 1076 L4	Reading and writing decimal numbers

MyReview

Check out
You should now be able to ...

		Test it Questions
✓	Order and compare decimals.	⑤ 1, 2
✓	Add, subtract, multiply and divide integers.	⑤ 3, 4
✓	Recognise and use multiples and factors.	④ 5
✓	Use divisibility tests.	⑤ 6
✓	Find the prime factor decomposition of a number.	⑤ 7, 8
✓	Find the lowest common multiple and highest common factor of two numbers.	⑤ 9, 10
✓	Recognise and use cube and square numbers, cube and square roots.	⑥ 11–13

Language	Meaning	Example
Decimal	A number which has digits after the decimal point	3.25 and 4.13 are decimal numbers
Multiple	A number which is part of a number's times table	12 and 18 are both multiples of 6
Factor	A number which exactly divides another number	4 and 6 are both factors of 12
Product	Another word for multiplication	The product of 3 and 4 is 12
Factor tree	A method for finding the prime factor decomposition of a number	See page 10
Highest common factor (HCF)	The biggest number which divides both of two other numbers	6 is the highest common factor of 12 and 18
Lowest common multiple (LCM)	The smallest number which is in the times tables of two other numbers	30 is the lowest common multiple of 5 and 6
Square number Cube number	A number which is found by multiplying an integer by itself twice or three times	$9 = 3 \times 3 = 3^2$ is the square of 3 and $27 = 3 \times 3 \times 3 = 3^3$ is the cube of 3
Square root Cube root	The opposite of a square number or a cube number	$3 = \sqrt{9}$ is the square root of 9 $3 = \sqrt[3]{27}$ is the cube root of 27

1 Write < or > between these pairs of numbers to show which number is the larger.
 a -16 and -16.5   b 0.457 and 0.52
 c 0.043 and 0.34   d -0.56 and -0.055

2 Put these numbers in order from smallest to largest.
 a 6   - 3   0   -5
 b 1.3   - 2.4   -2.6   -0.9

3 Calculate
 a -8 ÷ -7   b -9 × 5
 c 5 – -4   d -11 – -19

4 Calculate
 a 5 × -3   b -7 × -4
 c 30 ÷ -6   d -50 ÷ -5

5 Which of these numbers are
 a factors of 6
 b multiples of 6?

  1 3 4 6 12 14 15 18

6 Use divisibility tests to say if these statements are true or false and explain your answer.
 a 3 is a factor of 965
 b 9515 is divisible by 11
 c 770 is a multiple of 8
 d 143 is a prime number

7 Which of the following numbers are prime numbers?

  1 2 3 4 5

8 Write each of these numbers as a product of its prime factors.
 a 63   b 385

9 Find the highest common factor of each pair of numbers.
 a 25 and 75   b 11 and 17

10 Find the lowest common multiple of each pair of numbers.
 a 28 and 84   b 16 and 24

11 Which of the following numbers are square numbers?

  1 2 4 6 8

12 Write down the value of these square roots.
 a $\sqrt{64}$ b $\sqrt{25}$
 c $\sqrt{121}$ d $\sqrt{1}$

13 Calculate
 a 2^3 b $\sqrt[3]{64}$
 c 4^3 d $\sqrt[3]{216}$

What next?

Score		
0 – 4		Your knowledge of this topic is still developing. To improve look at Formative test: 2B-1; MyMaths: 1032, 1034, 1035, 1044, 1053, 1068 and 1072
5 – 11		You are gaining a secure knowledge of this topic. To improve look at InvisiPen: 111, 113, 122, 123, 171, 172, 173, 174 and 181
12 – 13		You have mastered this topic. Well done, you are ready to progress!

⊙ **MyMaths**.co.uk

Question commentary

The term 'minus' can be confusing; try to use 'negative' to describe numbers and 'subtract' to describe the operation.

Questions 1 to 4 – Students could draw or visualise a number line to do these questions.

Question 5 – Students can confuse factors and multiples. Students should understand that the number 1 is a factor of all other integers and that any number will be both a factor and a multiple of itself.

Questions 6 and 7 – Students must be able to explain their reasoning clearly.

Question 8 – Encourage the use of index notation.

Question 9 – Students should understand that the HCF can sometimes be 1 (coprime numbers).

Question 10 – Students should realise that a LCM can be one of the two original numbers.

Questions 11 – Common misconceptions include 2 and 6 being square numbers and 1 not a square number.

Question 12 – Students should recognise without a calculator.

Question 13 – Part **a** should be straightforward to do mentally (although a common wrong answer is 6); a calculator could be allowed for parts **b** and **d**. Part **c** should follow directly from part **b**.

Answers

1	a	$-16 > -16.5$			b	$0.457 < 0.52$	
	c	$0.043 < 0.34$			d	$-0.56 < -0.055$	
2	a	$-5, -3, 0, 6$			b	$-2.6, -2.4, -0.9, 1.3$	
3	a	-15	b	-14	c	9	d 8
4	a	-15	b	28	c	-5	d 10
5	a	$1, 3, 6$	b	$6, 12, 18$			
6	a	No	b	Yes	c	No	
	d	No (11×13)					
7		$2, 3, 5$					
8	a	$3 \times 3 \times 7$	b	$5 \times 7 \times 11$			
9	a	25	b	1			
10	a	84	b	48			
11		$1, 4$					
12	a	8	b	5	c	11	d 1
13	a	8	b	4	c	64	d 6

1a

1 Put these numbers in order from smallest to largest.

a -5	4	-3	2	-1
b 1.5	-2.4	-3.1	-0.9	-2
c 3.2	-1.4	-2.6	2.7	-1.1
d -1.5	0.15	-2.1	-1.6	-0.5

2 Calculate

a $8 + -4$	**b** $6 + -9$	**c** $4 + -8$	**d** $-3 + -7$	**e** $-11 + -2$
f $9 - -2$	**g** $3 - -12$	**h** $1 - -5$	**i** $-8 - -4$	**j** $-6 - -11$
k $-9 - -3$	**l** $-6 - -12$	**m** $-13 + -21$	**n** $12 + -15$	**o** $17 - -12$
p $11 + -21$	**q** $13 - -24$	**r** $28 + -23$	**s** $35 - -21$	**t** $-17 + -31$

1b

3 Calculate

a 2×-5	**b** -4×3	**c** -6×-4	**d** -8×-5	**e** -9×6
f -7×-9	**g** 9×-9	**h** -12×-3	**i** -14×5	**j** -15×-6
k $-40 \div -8$	**l** $-35 \div 7$	**m** $-36 \div -9$	**n** $-56 \div -8$	**o** $45 \div -9$
p -13×5	**q** -25×4	**r** -11×-15	**s** $-84 \div -7$	**t** $-96 \div 8$

4 Copy and complete these calculations.

a $8 \times \square = -72$	**b** $-54 \div \square = -6$	**c** $-7 \times \square = 49$
d $-104 \div \square = 8$	**e** $\square \times -12 = -48$	**f** $-6 \times \square = -72$
g $\square \div -4 = 64$	**h** $\square \div -9 = -14$	**i** $128 \div \square = -16$

1c

5 Write all the factors of

a 30	**b** 48	**c** 65	**d** 72	**e** 96	**f** 100
g 130	**h** 108	**i** 120	**j** 132	**k** 144	**l** 150

6 Use the divisibility tests to answer each of these questions. In each case explain your answer.

a Is 2 a factor of 98?	**b** Is 3 a factor of 93?
c Is 4 a factor of 112?	**d** Is 5 a factor of 157?
e Is 6 a factor of 184?	**f** Is 8 a factor of 196?
g Is 9 a factor of 289?	**h** Is 10 a factor 362?
i Is 12 a factor of 200?	**j** Is 11 a factor of 385?

1d

7 Use the divisibility tests for prime numbers to see which of these numbers are prime. In each case explain your answer.

a 35	**b** 38	**c** 37	**d** 47	**e** 51	**f** 53
g 75	**h** 79	**i** 76	**j** 85	**k** 93	**l** 91

1d

8 Write each of these numbers as the product of its prime factors.

a 18	**b** 28	**c** 45	**d** 57	**e** 63	**f** 76
g 88	**h** 92	**i** 108	**j** 115	**k** 130	**l** 132
m 144	**n** 160	**o** 170	**p** 175	**q** 188	**r** 240

1e

9 Use an appropriate method to find the HCF (highest common factor) of

a 6 and 10	**b** 12 and 16	**c** 18 and 27
d 15 and 20	**e** 24 and 32	**f** 25 and 30
g 28 and 40	**h** 56 and 80	**i** 54 and 90

10 Use an appropriate method to find the LCM (lowest common multiple) of

a 6 and 10	**b** 12 and 16	**c** 18 and 27
d 15 and 20	**e** 16 and 24	**f** 24 and 30
g 28 and 32	**h** 50 and 56	**i** 7 and 13

> Write each number as the product of its prime factors.

11 In these productogons the number in each square is the product of the numbers in the circles on each side of it. Find the missing numbers in each of these productogons.

a

(productogon: 450, 432, 600)

b

(productogon: 960, 768, 720)

1f

12 Work out these using a calculator where appropriate.

a 7^3	**b** 13^2	**c** 21^2	**d** 9^3	**e** 15^3	**f** $(-3)^2$
g 24^3	**h** 0.5^2	**i** 0.1^2	**j** 0.1^3	**k** $(-2)^2$	**l** $(-2)^3$

1g

13 Write the values of these square roots.

a $\sqrt{36}$	**b** $\sqrt{169}$	**c** $\sqrt{40}$	**d** $\sqrt{30}$	**e** $\sqrt{77}$

14 Find two consecutive numbers with the product 2162.

1h

15 Use trial and improvement to find these cube roots to 1 decimal place.

a $\sqrt[3]{27}$	**b** $\sqrt[3]{125}$	**c** $\sqrt[3]{89}$	**d** $\sqrt[3]{56}$	**e** $\sqrt[3]{90}$

16 Find three consecutive numbers with the product 10626.

MyMaths.co.uk

Question commentary

Questions 1 and 2 – Basic practice at ordering and then calculating with negative numbers.

Questions 3 and 4 – Basic practice at calculating with negative numbers. Students should use inverse operations for question **4**.

Questions 5 and 6 – Listing factor pairs is useful for question **5**. Discourage calculation for question **6**.

Question 7 – Students are directed to use divisibility tests for only prime numbers. Check students understand why this is the case.

Question 8 – Prime factor trees are expected.

Questions 9 to 11 – Factor trees should again be encouraged.

Question 12 – Suggest students try and do some calculations without the calculator first.

Questions 13 and 14 – Use of calculators is expected except on Question 13 parts **a** and **b**.

Questions 15 and 16 – Students may spot that question **15** parts **a** and **b** are cube numbers. A hint may be required for question **16**.

Answers

1
a	$-5, -3, -1, 2, 4$	**b**	$-3.1, -2.4, -2, -0.9, 1.5$
c	$-2.6, -1.4, -1.1, 2.7, 3.2$	**d**	$-2.1, -1.6, -1.5, -0.5, 0.15$

2
a	4	**b**	-3	**c**	-4	**d**	-10
e	-13	**f**	11	**g**	15	**h**	6
i	-4	**j**	5	**k**	-6	**l**	6
m	-34	**n**	-3	**o**	29	**p**	-10
q	37	**r**	5	**s**	56	**t**	-48

3
a	-10	**b**	-12	**c**	24	**d**	40
e	-54	**f**	63	**g**	-81	**h**	36
i	-70	**j**	90	**k**	5	**l**	-5
m	4	**n**	7	**o**	-5	**p**	-65
q	-100	**r**	165	**s**	12	**t**	-12

4
a	-9	**b**	9	**c**	-7	**d**	-13
e	4	**f**	12	**g**	-256	**h**	126
i	-8						

5
- **a** $1, 2, 3, 5, 6, 10, 15, 30$
- **b** $1, 2, 3, 4, 6, 8, 12, 16, 24, 48$
- **c** $1, 5, 13, 65$
- **d** $1, 2, 3, 4, 6, 8, 9, 12, 18, 24, 36, 72$
- **e** $1, 2, 3, 4, 6, 8, 12, 16, 24, 32, 48, 96$
- **f** $1, 2, 4, 5, 10, 20, 25, 50, 100$
- **g** $1, 2, 5, 10, 13, 26, 65, 130$
- **h** $1, 2, 3, 4, 6, 9, 12, 18, 27, 36, 54, 108$
- **i** $1, 2, 3, 4, 5, 6, 8, 10, 12, 15, 20, 24, 30, 40, 60, 120$
- **j** $1, 2, 3, 4, 6, 11, 12, 22, 33, 44, 66, 132$
- **k** $1, 2, 3, 4, 6, 8, 9, 12, 16, 18, 24, 36, 48, 72, 144$
- **l** $1, 2, 3, 5, 6, 10, 15, 25, 30, 50, 75, 150$

6
a	Yes	**b**	Yes	**c**	Yes	**d**	No
e	No	**f**	No	**g**	No	**h**	No
i	No	**j**	Yes				

7
a	Not	**b**	Not	**c**	Prime	**d**	Prime
e	Not	**f**	Prime	**g**	Not	**h**	Prime
i	Not	**j**	Not	**k**	Not	**l**	Not

8
a	$2 \times 3 \times 3$	**b**	$2 \times 2 \times 7$
c	$3 \times 3 \times 5$	**d**	3×19
e	$3 \times 3 \times 7$	**f**	$2 \times 2 \times 19$
g	$2 \times 2 \times 2 \times 11$	**h**	$2 \times 2 \times 23$
i	$2 \times 2 \times 3 \times 3 \times 3$	**j**	5×23
k	$2 \times 5 \times 13$	**l**	$2 \times 2 \times 3 \times 11$
m	$2 \times 2 \times 2 \times 2 \times 3 \times 3$	**n**	25×5
o	$2 \times 5 \times 17$	**p**	$5 \times 5 \times 7$
q	$2 \times 2 \times 47$	**r**	$2^4 \times 3 \times 5$

9
a	2	**b**	4	**c**	9	**d**	5
e	8	**f**	5	**g**	4	**h**	8
i	18						

10
a	30	**b**	48	**c**	54	**d**	60
e	48	**f**	120	**g**	224	**h**	1400
i	91						

11 **a** **b**

12
a	343	**b**	169	**c**	441	**d**	729
e	3375	**f**	9	**g**	13 824	**h**	0.25
i	0.01	**j**	0.001	**k**	4	**l**	-8

13
a	6	**b**	13	**c**	6.32	**d**	5.48
e	8.77						

14 $46, 47$

15
a	6.3	**b**	5.8	**c**	9.4	**d**	3.8
e	4.5						

16 $21, 22, 23$

Learning outcomes

N1 Use standard units of mass, length, time, money and other measures, including with decimal quantities (L5)

R1 Change freely between related standard units (for example time, length, area, volume/capacity, mass) (L5)

G1 Derive and apply formulae to calculate and solve problems involving: perimeter and area of triangles, parallelograms, trapezia, volume of cuboids (including cubes) and other prisms (including cylinders) (L6)

G2 Calculate and solve problems involving: perimeters of 2D shapes (including circles), areas of circles and composite shapes (L5)

Introduction

The chapter starts by reviewing which metric units to use to measure everyday lengths, weights and capacities. It then covers how to convert between metric units, between metric and imperial units and how to read scales. After reviewing how to calculate perimeters and areas of rectangles and simple composite shapes the main focus becomes using the formulae for the area of a triangle, parallelogram and trapezium.

The introduction discusses the origin of geometry. The word itself is Greek for *measuring the earth* and the Greek historian Herodotus claimed it developed in Egypt from the need to re-measure fields after the annual river Nile floods. As a practical subject for surveying and building, geometry is certainly very old. An early Egyptian geometry textbook the Rhind (Ahmes) papyrus is about 4000 years old. Formal geometry, involving proofs and deriving results from first principles, developed later around 500 BC with the ancient Greeks and is associated with the name Euclid.

Students could be asked for examples of real-life areas and how they could be broken down into definite mathematical shapes. For example, the floor of a classroom might be broken down into different sized rectangles.

Prior knowledge

Students should already know how to...

* Multiply and divide by 10, 100 and 1000
* Do basic arithmetic with decimals
* Understand perimeter and area by counting edges and squares

Starter problem

The problem requires an understanding of perimeter, area, how to calculate areas and appropriate units.

You might wish to start with a smaller example such as 24 m of fencing which the students can then represent as rectangles, squares and possibly right-angled triangles. Encourage them to record their results in an ordered table so that they can spot the relationship between the side lengths and the area.

For rectangles the maximum area, 3600 m^2, occurs for a square of side 60 m. Allowing for different length perimeters, p, the maximum area $p^2/16$ occurs for a square of side $p/4$.

For a right-angled triangle the maximum area is 2470.7.3 m^2 and occurs for an isosceles right angle triangle with sides, 70.3 m, 70.3 m and 99.4 m. (An equilateral triangle has area 2771.3 m^2.)

Students could investigate regular and irregular shapes, perhaps using a string of fixed length, and subdividing their shapes into approximations of regular shapes.

This is the classic isoperimetric problem associated with queen Dido and the founding of Carthage. The optimum solution is a circle (area 4583.7 m^2). It might be worth asking why fields are not circular.

Resources

MyMaths

Metric conversion	1061	Area of rectangles	1084	Area of a parallelogram	1108
Perimeter	1110	Area of a triangle	1129	Imperial measures	1191

Online assessment

Chapter test	2B–2
Formative test	2B–2
Summative test	2B–2

InvisiPen solutions

Perimeter	312	Area of a triangle	314
Area of shapes made from rectangles			313
Area of a parallelogram and a trapezium			315
Metric measures			332
Metric and imperial measures			333

Topic scheme

Teaching time = 5 lessons/2 weeks

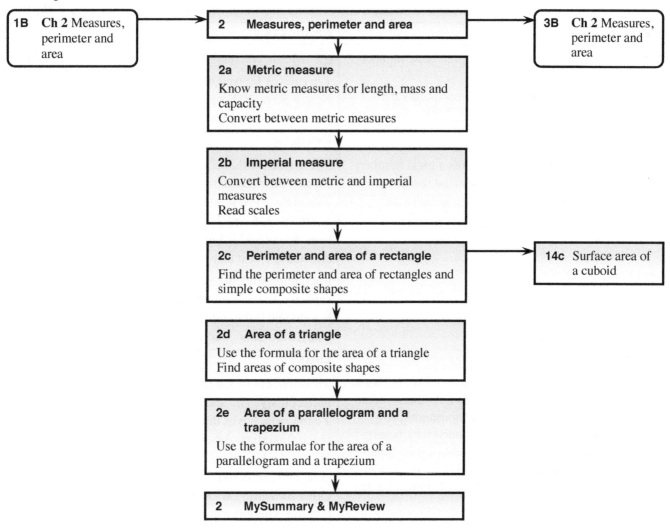

1B **Ch 2** Measures, perimeter and area

2 **Measures, perimeter and area**

3B **Ch 2** Measures, perimeter and area

2a **Metric measure**

Know metric measures for length, mass and capacity
Convert between metric measures

2b **Imperial measure**

Convert between metric and imperial measures
Read scales

2c **Perimeter and area of a rectangle**

Find the perimeter and area of rectangles and simple composite shapes

14c Surface area of a cuboid

2d **Area of a triangle**

Use the formula for the area of a triangle
Find areas of composite shapes

2e **Area of a parallelogram and a trapezium**

Use the formulae for the area of a parallelogram and a trapezium

2 **MySummary & MyReview**

Differentiation

Student book 2A	24 – 43
Metric measure
Metric and money conversions
Other units of measure
Reading scales
Perimeter and area
Area of a rectangle
Shapes made from rectangles

Student book 2B	24 – 39
Metric measure
Imperial measure
Perimeter and area of a rectangle
Area of a triangle
Area of a parallelogram and a trapezium

Student book 2C	22 –39
Metric measure
Imperial measure
Area of a rectangle and a triangle
Area of a parallelogram and a trapezium
Circumference of a circle
Area of a circle

Objectives

- Convert one metric unit to another (L5)
- Choose and use units of measurement to measure and estimate in a range of contexts (L5)

Key ideas	Resources
1 Have a sense of size about the three basic units of length, mass and capacity 2 Be able to write a measure in simple equivalent ways, such as 24 mm or 2.4 cm	Metric conversion (1061) 1 m ruler, 1 kg weight, (empty) 1 litre bottle Box of 50 or 100 paper clips Some scales, tape measures, and measuring cylinders

Simplification	Extension
This type of work on measures mixes a great number of different topics – where students find the work challenging it is appropriate to practise questions involving only one of length or mass or capacity.	It is important that competent students are able to explain their mathematical thinking and these students should be asked to justify their choices and answers for questions 5, 6 and 7. What if the fence lengths had been 80 cm and 1.5 metres – how would this have affected the best answer to the problem? Encourage students to make links, particularly with capacity, to cm^3 and ml. Addressing the common term weight and linking it to mass can be valuable by asking what is the same, and what is different about them.

Literacy	Links
Emphasise the generic nature of key prefixes in metric measure and their meanings: kilo as a thousand, centi as one hundredth and milli as one thousandth. A further three prefixes might be included for interest: deci as one tenth; deca as ten and hecta as one hundred. Encourage students to read the prefixes and replace them with the appropriate meaning to help consolidate the knowledge. Use ruler labelling to facilitate communication. Weaker students over rely on the units printed on a ruler, which may well be mm, for instance, thus causing concern when using rulers to measure cm.	Measurement of length was originally based on the human body. The ancient Egyptians used a unit called a cubit, which was the length of an arm from the elbow to the fingertips. As everybody's arm was a different length, the Egyptians developed the standard Royal cubit and preserved this length as a black granite rod. Other measuring sticks were made the same length as this rod. There is a picture of a cubit rod at http://www.globalegyptianmuseum.org/detail.aspx?id= 4424

Alternative approach

As an introductory task ask students to sort a list of specific measures into length, mass or capacity. It is useful to include both metric and imperial units with this task. Check all students are clear about the basic units: metre, gram and litre. Having produced three lists, these can now form the basis of a discussion about what context each measure might occur, enabling comparisons to be made about the relevance of the unit to the size in context; for example 2.4 km might be a distance of a walk to school while 20 cm might the length of a ribbon. A circuit of practical activities for small groups of students can be used to encourage estimation, followed by actual measuring and checking. If both metric and imperial units are introduced in this session, take the opportunity to explore and establish rough equivalents between the units. Request that students make themselves a small flashcard reminder of the rough equivalents that they may keep and refer to. If this introductory alternate approach is taken the questions from 2b may be used for consolidation or homework.

Checkpoint

1	What is 12.8 m in centimetres?	(1280 cm)
2	What is 3520 millilitres in litres?	(3.52 litres)

Starter – Powers of ten

Write 10.7 on the board.

Ask students what answer you will get if you multiply the number by 1000, 100, 10.

Repeat using different starting numbers.

This can be extended by using division.

Teaching notes

Ask three or four questions in context, for example, how much liquid is in a 2 litre bottle about a quarter full? How heavy is a large textbook (over 1 kg)? What is the length of the teacher's desk? Lead into a discussion of metric measures and common conversions: the desk is 1.5 m = 150 cm, etc. It is now appropriate to supply a table for the different conversions and measures or the families of measures: tonne, kilogram, gram, milligram, etc.

Questions **1** and **2** lend themselves to whole-class discussion.

A worked example, such as given, of how to convert between units will provide students with a template for setting out their answers to questions **3** and **4**.

Wider issues are relevant to questions **5** and **6** where more than one solution might exist. Can a student convince the class that they have all the solutions or why they have the best solution: are four small bottles better than one large one?

Plenary

Give students working in pairs – five lengths (heights), five weights and five animals (blue whale, giraffe, large python, lion, Labrador dog). Can they match the appropriate animal with their mass and length?

Exercise commentary

Questions 1 and **2** – Students could be encouraged to work in pairs to identify relevant information, agree on appropriate units and good approximations.

Questions 3 and **4f–4i** involve conversion from large to small units while parts **4a–4e** require conversions from small to large units.

Question 5 – Students must use a consistent set of units and can be encouraged to find more than one solution.

Question 6 – It will be easiest to compare the prices of 1 litre = 4 × 250 ml of shampoo. The suitability of the solution as well as value for money may be introduced as a consideration.

Question 7 – A larger number is involved in the conversion; for the comparison only an estimate of the student's mass is necessary. In part **b** a consideration should be the paper clip's bulk as well as mass.

Question 8 – Students could research the distance involved and this would make a good homework task.

Answers

1 **a** cl   **b** m   **c** litres
   d g   **e** mm

2 **a** 6 m   **b** 10 litres   **c** 2 tonnes   **d** 3 min
   e 15 kg   **f** 3 m

3 50 000 m

4 **a** 7.5 kg   **b** 65 cm
   c 8.5 litres   **d** 0.5 km
   e 2.5 tonnes   **f** 0.085 m
   g 0.007 litres   **h** 19 500 g
   i 400 000 cm   **j** 10 cl
   k 1 km

5 5 Type A and 1 Type B

6 The 250 ml bottle as this costs £4 × 0.99 = £3.96 per litre

7 **a** 1 million paper clips weighs 500 kg and is therefore heavier
   b Depends on how strong they are and the way the paper clips are packaged, but should be able to carry about 10 kg, i.e. 20 000 paper clips

8 1400 km walk at 4 km/hr would take 14 days and 14 hours (so about 30 days walking 12 hours a day)

Objectives

- Know rough metric equivalents of imperial measures in common use (L5)
- Read and interpret scales on a range of measuring instruments (L5)

Key ideas	Resources
1 Being able to use and interpret a variety of measuring instruments 2 Confidently link rough equivalent measures to a few key common everyday items	Imperial measures (1191) Rulers with centimetres and inches A 1 metre rule also showing inches (builder/dressmaker's tape) Scales with both kg and lb/oz weights Reference booklets or diaries that include conversion data in the form of a multiplier

Simplification	Extension
Many students find this difficult because they just try to apply the different rules without a context to check their answers against. For question **2** real-life examples with these measurements may help. Also measure items in the classroom in both imperial (ft and in and lb and oz) and in metric (m and kg). For example, weigh a 2 litre bottle in kilograms (2 kg) and then in pounds and ounces (4 lb 6 or 7 oz); also measure length of books, tables, etc.	For those who have mastered the idea of conversion, develop more problem solving activities. At a market the cost of potatoes is given as 40p a pound and also £1 per kilogram – is this acceptable? A leg of lamb weighs 2.4 kg and costs £10, how much is this per pound? Using conversion multipliers found from reference sources or a diary is useful for establishing real multiplicative relationships for more able pupils.

Literacy	Links
The key imperial units to include for vocabulary are feet, miles, pounds, pints and gallons, though these may be extended, especially if introduced by the students themselves. It is worth examining notation for approximates here such as ≈ or ≅. While recognising that common use is made of the = symbol, strictly speaking it should not be used. Approximation notation is used inconsistently within mathematics. Shorthand notation for each of the imperial units should also be made explicit.	The United States has its own system of weights and measures that is largely similar to the imperial system. Yards, feet, inches and pounds are all in everyday use in the US, however, the US pint and US gallon are both smaller than the imperial pint and gallon. There is more information about the differences between the two systems at http://home.clara.net/brianp/usa.html and at http://en.wikipedia.org/wiki/Imperial_units

Alternative approach

Following a first lesson examining and exploring both metric and imperial measures, the second lesson can focus on converting between metric units, and the importance of checking units when problem solving. Making this a practical session with a variety of objects to measure and record results in two or three different ways will help, so for example weighing an item and recording the result in kg, and g; or measuring a piece of string and recording the length in mm, cm and m. This can be carried out as a circuit of activities with small groups. For consolidation here exercise **2a** may be used, together with checkpoint **2a**.

Checkpoint

1 The average man is 6 feet tall – what is this roughly in metres? (2 m)

2 Which is the shorter distance 10 km or 5 miles? (5 miles)

Starter – Metric pairs

Write the following measurements on the board:

0.01 g, 0.1 g, 0.1 kg, 1 g, 1 kg, 1 t, 10 mg, 10 g, 100 mg, 100 g, 1000 mg, 1000 g, 1000 kg, 10 000 mg.

Ask students to find the equivalent pairs (1000 mg = 1 g).

This can be extended by asking students to make their own equivalent pairs for capacity or length.

Teaching notes

Ask students to name units used in everyday life: miles on roads, litre bottles and pint glasses, etc. Make lists, grouping the units for length, mass and capacity and within each group split them into metric and imperial units. Invite students to match comparable units: inch ~ centimetre, yard ~ metre, mile ~ kilometre, etc. and give examples of objects with these sizes. A ruler/tape with inches and centimetres can be used to confirm the examples. Likewise scales can be used to confirm that 1 kg = 2 lb + 3 oz.

Introduce the formal conversion factors and show how these can be used to convert between units by multiplication or division.

A wider discussion may involve which system of units is better. Metric is more systematic but what is 1/3, 1/6 or 1/9 of a metre or a yard? What is the role of the European Union in promoting the metric system? How is international business organised, for example America uses (a version) of imperial units.

A demonstration of how to read a scale should focus on establishing what a sub-interval is worth and not to assume that it is a tenth of the interval unit.

Plenary

The most widely used imperial measures are for length. Miles are used exclusively on UK roads and students will probably only be able to give their height in feet and inches. Ask all students to convert their height from feet and inches to metres. On average are the boys taller than the girls? Ask students to estimate the average, then in small groups work out the averages.

Exercise commentary

Question 1 – Helps develop an intuition for comparable units.

Questions 2 and **3** – Conversions as in the first example. question **2** generally involves multiplications and question **3** divisions.

Questions 4 and **5** – Students will need to be clear how much a sub-division is worth: 50 miles, 2 °C, etc.

Questions 6 and **7** – Real-life situations requiring conversion of units.

Question 8 – Students could first make an estimate based on 400 days before multiplying by 365; answers should be converted to appropriate units.

Question 9 – An interesting investigation could be developed into whether there are other differences between standard imperial units and their American equivalents.

Answers

1 a inch   b kg   c litre
   d mile   e metre
2 a 11 lb   b 4.8 litres c 30 cm
   d 154 lb   e 90 cm   f 176 lb
   g 84 litres   h 1.1 lb   i 60 cm
   j 5.5 kg
3 a 6 inches   b 45 kg   c 20 pints
   d 0.5 pints   e 16 inches   f 60 kg
   g 20 inches   h 40 pints   i 50 inches
   j 18 litres
4 a 100 miles, 350 miles   b 4 °C, 18 °C
   c 50 ml, 175 ml   d 60 m, 120 m
   e 40 cm, 80 cm
5 750 g
6 Manchester   48 km
   Stoke   104 km
   Birmingham   176 km
   Bath   320 km
7 a £5.85
   b i 10.7 miles per litre
      ii 17.1 kilometres per litre
8 a i 14.6 kg
      ii after 1250 days (3 years 155 days)
   b 76 pints
9 3.84 litres

2c Perimeter and area of a rectangle

Objectives

- Know and use the formula for the area of a rectangle   (L5)
- Calculate the perimeter and area of shapes made from rectangles   (L5)

Key ideas	Resources
1 Be able to recognise the difference between perimeter and area including the units for each 2 Confidently explain what perimeter and what area actually measures	Area of rectangles (1084) Perimeter (1110) Squared paper Calculator

Simplification	Extension
Using an accurate scale diagram on grid paper and counting squares can be used to give confidence in the numerical approach to finding perimeters and areas.	Challenge students with a problem like – A rectangle has a perimeter of 28 cm, what different areas might this rectangle have? You are told that the area of this rectangle is 30 cm² to the nearest square cm. What could the dimensions be? (Remember the perimeter is still 28 cm.) Students may need a calculator as this will bring in decimal lengths.

Literacy	Links
Emphasise the importance of including correct units when recording values for perimeter and/or area. Make links to the notation used when measuring area in terms of squares, so that the concept has a concrete visual basis.	An area of 10 000 m² is called a hectare and is a common unit used to measure an area of land. Measure or estimate the size of the classroom. What fraction is this of a hectare? Estimate how many hectares the school field or other local open space covers. The O2 arena in Greenwich has a ground area of over 80 000 m². How many hectares is this? There is a picture of the O2 arena at http://en.wikipedia.org/wiki/Image:Canary.wharf.and.d ome.london.arp.jpg

Alternative approach

Students will already have some pre-knowledge of area and perimeter and it is worth exploring this together with their perceptions. Use a list of a variety of units for students to sort into perimeter, area or volume, then ask them to explain how they identify each. Extend this into pairs of students deriving their own definitions for perimeter and area, then combine two pairs for reviewing, sharing and improving upon the definitions before sharing. Set up challenges for the students where they are encouraged to find a rectangle with the maximum or minimum perimeter for a given area and also maximum or minimum areas for a given perimeter. Students may be encouraged to examine only integer values or to extend this into decimals as appropriate. Pairs of students may be asked to decide whether a statement such as: 'if a rectangle is cut reducing its area, its perimeter is also reduced'; or 'the numerical value of the area of a rectangle is greater than that of its perimeter' is true (always, sometimes, never) showing their results with justification as a poster. This can be extended to include statements involving other shapes, or indeed generally to any shape.

When consolidation work from the given exercise is used, question **3** offers opportunities for students to share and evaluate the different ways that may have been used. The different methods can open up discussions about efficiency of calculation as well as accuracy, and exposes the often more efficient subtraction method to students who may not otherwise have considered its use.

Checkpoint

1 Draw a rectangle that has an area of 42 cm² and a perimeter of 26 cm.   (7 cm by 6 cm)
2 Find the area and perimeter of a rectangle that is 3.4 m by 10 cm.   (7 m or 700 cm; 0.34 m² or 3400 cm²)

Starter – Estimation

Draw lines on the board.

Ask students to estimate the length of the lines in cm.

Ask how much this would be in inches.

Use a scoring system for the estimations, for example, within 10% score 3 points, within 20% score 1 point. Bonus points for correct metric to imperial conversion.

Teaching notes

It is important for students to be aware of the units used and convert where necessary.

A good introduction to the lesson would be to give students the area of a rectangle, say 36 cm², and ask them what the dimensions could be. Why are there more than two possible answers? Do the lengths have to be whole numbers? Which lengths and widths give the largest and smallest perimeters? This could form the basis of a paired activity. It also relates directly to question **2**.

When dealing with composite shapes, strongly recommend that students make their own sketch first. This is especially important if the original drawing is not to scale. To find the perimeter, carefully identify any missing lengths and work them out before adding up all the lengths. To find the area divide the shape into simpler rectangles. It may help to label these as A and B, work out their areas and then compute A + B.

Plenary

Ask students to work in pairs on a problem like: A rectangular towel is folded in half four times and the dimensions are now 20 × 30 cm. What is the area of the towel and what could the dimensions of the towel be?

Exercise commentary

Question 1 – Areas and perimeters, similar to the first example.

Question 2 – An 'inverse' problem, an example of which could be discussed in the lesson.

Question 3 – Composite shapes as illustrated in the second example. There is more than one way to decompose the shapes; it is also possible to use subtraction.

Questions 4 and **5** – There are several ways to find the area of the yellow cross by dissection or subtracting four blue rectangles from the flag. The cross in the Swiss flag is made up of five 10 cm by 10 cm squares.

Answers

1 a 42 cm, 90 cm²   b 40 cm, 75 cm²
   c 23 m, 33 m²   d 18.8 mm, 22 mm²
2 a 30 cm   b 46 m   c 64 m   d 21 cm
3 a 28 cm, 23 cm²   b 32 cm, 28 cm²
   c 60 cm, 125 cm²   d 62 cm, 72 cm²
4 a 500 cm² and 900 cm²   b 1200 cm²
5 a 500 cm²   b 200 cm²

2d Area of a triangle

Objectives	
• Derive and use the formula for the area of a triangle	(L5)
• Calculate areas of compound shapes	(L5)

Key ideas	Resources
1 Have a sense of a triangle evolving from halving a rectangle 2 Confidently explore shapes by seeing them as made up of other basic shapes (rectangles and triangles)	Area of a triangle (1129) Squared paper Mini whiteboards Y8 Shape & Space assessment materials Lesson 1 (Area) : http://teachfind.com/node/96336?quicktabs_1=0#quicktabs-1

Simplification	Extension
As in question **1**, accurately drawing shapes on squared paper will allow a 'square counting' approach to be used. This can be used to give confidence in the use of the formula. This approach will also work for the more complex shapes in question **5**.	To challenge the more able students, draw a 3, 4, 5 right- angled triangle with the base as 5 cm. Show the right angle and draw in the height h. Ask them to find the area ($\frac{1}{2} \times 3 \times 4$) cm² and then to find the given height. You can add a similar question with a 5, 12, 13 triangle.

Literacy	Links
It will be necessary to include the key word perpendicular in this lesson. Combine this with the standard language of height and base, and make sure that students do not assume that a base is always horizontal by using a variety of orientations. Continue to ensure that students accurately use and label measurements with the appropriate units.	The area of the sail of a yacht affects its performance, the greater the area, the greater the force that the wind can exert on the yacht. However, if the sail is too large, the boat will become unstable.

Alternative approach
Lesson notes and resources provided by the National Strategies (link given via Teachfind) is a secure and active way of helping students to develop and embed the notion of triangular area. It includes IWB visuals, as well as worksheets and assessment advice. It also extends into examining area of parallelograms.

Checkpoint	
1 How do you find the area of a triangle? (Equivalent explanation to half base × perpendicular height)	
2 A triangle has base 8 cm and perpendicular height 10 cm. Find its area. (40 cm²)	

Starter – Calculating length

Give the area and width of rectangles and ask students for the lengths, for example,

Area = 39 cm² and width = 3 cm

Area = 48 cm² and width = 6 cm

Area = 125 cm² and width = 25 cm

This can be extended by using numbers that will generate decimal lengths.

Teaching notes

A natural introduction would be to demonstrate why the area of a triangle is given by half the area of the 'bounding' rectangle. The case of an 'overhanging' triangle should be treated with some care and an emphasis placed on deciding what is the perpendicular height of the triangle. Doing a worked example, as supplied in the student book, will show students how to set out their written answers.

Question **2** could be used as the basis of a paired activity to find multiple solutions. Classroom discussion can then be used to see what features groups of answers have in common and why the formula gives the same answer for each triangle.

It may be helpful to provide a worked example involving a composite shape, such as those in question **5** and question **6**. Emphasise being methodical and careful setting out of workings: make your own sketch, dissect it into more basic shapes, apply formula to calculate these sub-areas and sum the results and add units.

Plenary

Tell all students that you have drawn a triangle of area 18 cm² – they can ask questions but only with a yes or no answer. Their target is to work out what your triangle looks like and sketch it (mini whiteboards are very useful here). Questions could be: Are the height and base of the triangle equal? Is the height greater than the base?, etc.

Exercise commentary

Question 1 – This question can be answered using the formula or by counting squares; students could be asked to use both methods and confirm agreement. If counting squares, encourage students to group part squares to make whole squares.

Question 2 – Students could be asked to find several solutions and note what they have in common.

Question 3 – Similar to the first example. Part **d** may cause confusion over what is the height of the triangle. Make sure that students know how to set out their working.

Question 4 – Similar to the second example. Students may need reminding to include the factor ½ and should be encouraged to check their answers by using the formula.

Question 5 – Encourage students to draw the shapes and break them down into triangles and rectangles.

Question 6 – The challenge is to give a clear explanation for the area of the kite being half of that of the rectangle. It may help to split the kite further into four right-angled triangles.

Answers

1 **a** 6 cm² **b** 4 cm² **c** 8 cm² **d** 4.5 cm²
2 Multiple answers possible
3 **a** 42 m² **b** 22 cm² **c** 64 cm² **d** 17.5 mm²
4 **a** 5 cm **b** 12 m **c** 10 cm **d** 7.5 mm
5 **a** 12 cm² **b** 8 cm² **c** 15 cm² **d** 6 cm²
   e 26 cm² **f** 24 cm²
6 **a** 200 cm² **b** 100 cm²

2e Area of a parallelogram and a trapezium

Objectives	
• Derive and use the formulae for the area of a parallelogram and trapezium (L6)	

Key ideas	Resources
1 To learn and use the formula for the area of a parallelogram 2 To learn and use the formula for the area of a trapezium	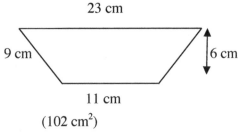 Area of a parallelogram (1108) Large cardboard triangles, parallelograms and trapeziums Pre-prepared tangrams Scissors, glue, squared paper

Simplification	Extension
The use of squared paper to count squares in an accurate drawing can be used to develop confidence in the application of the formulae. Finding the area of trapeziums using the formula is challenging – use isosceles trapeziums and allow students to break them into a rectangle and two equal right-angled triangles to find the area of each and total.	An accuracy challenge – give students two side lengths for a parallelogram, for example, 8 cm and 5 cm and an area of 12 cm² – can they construct this parallelogram (or draw it accurately on squared paper)?

Literacy	Links
Use the words parallelogram and quadrilateral to examine some word roots, asking students to think of other words that include parts of the words, i.e. para…; gram…; quad…; lateral… Students can then explore features that share the same connection to the word part. A resource that helps here is: http://www.thefreedictionary.com/quad	Sanders parallelogram is an optical illusion published in 1926 by the German psychologist Friedrich Sander. Sander's parallelogram can be found together with a selection of other optical illusions at http://www.wyrmcorp.com/galleries/illusions/geometry.shtml

Alternative approach
Materials from the Secondary National Strategy as referenced in **2d** may be used in extending exploration of area to parallelograms and further developed for trapeziums. Alternatively, divide the group into two with pairs of students in one half finding ways to getting the area of a parallelogram, and the other half the area of a trapezium. It will help to give specific details for each shape, including a good visual image. Students working on the same shape can share and compare different approaches before agreeing on an efficient approach. Groups of four with a pair from each shape can then share these approaches and apply them using exercise **2e**.

Checkpoint
1 Find the area of each of these shapes 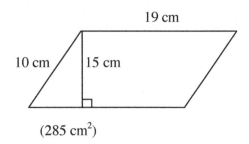

Starter – Calculating height

Give the area and base of triangles and ask students for the heights, for example,

Area = 18 cm^2 and base = 3 cm (12 cm)

Area = 24 cm^2 and base = 6 cm (8 cm)

Area = 25 cm^2 and base = 10 cm (5 cm)

This can be extended by using numbers that will generate decimal heights.

Teaching notes

As an introduction to the lesson, students could be shown and challenged to understand the formulae for area of parallelograms and trapeziums – clear explanations are provided in the student book.

Using large cardboard shapes allows the derivation of the formulae to be illustrated. For example, two identical triangles could be fitted together to make a parallelogram or a triangle cut off the end of a parallelogram and the pieces rearranged to make a rectangle. Likewise, two identical trapeziums could be fitted together to make a parallelogram, or a trapezium could be cut down the middle, parallel to the two parallel sides, and the pieces fitted together to make a long narrow parallelogram.

Once the formulae are understood, examples can be provided to show how they are applied and how the answers should be set out. For the parallelogram, emphasise that it is the perpendicular height and not the 'slope height' which is relevant for the area. For the trapezium, it may help students to think of the ½ $(a + b)$ term as the average length of the two parallel sides.

Plenary

Give students the area 10 cm². In pairs can they sketch out a rectangle, triangle, parallelogram, trapezium and square of this area (allow 3.1–3.2 cm for the side of the square). Compare answers. Are they unique? Only the square has just one solution, how can students find the exact measurements required for the square?

Exercise commentary

Question 1 – Similar to the first example; check that units are given.

Question 2 – Similar to the second example; check that students are correctly applying the formula.

Question 3 – 'Inverse' problems with parallelograms.

Question 4 – Students will need squared paper, scissors and possibly glue to stick solutions into their books. Emphasise the need for clear workings and explanations. This may be done as a paired activity.

Answers

1   a   171 cm^2 b   360 cm^2 c   34 m^2

2   a   63 cm^2 b   50 mm^2 c   10.5 m^2 d   64 cm^2

3   a   6 cm   b   12.5 m   c   30 mm

4   a   36 cm^2

    b   i   ii   iii

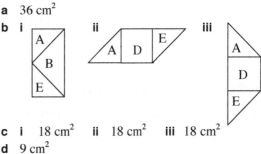

    c   i   18 cm^2 ii   18 cm^2 iii   18 cm^2

    d   9 cm^2

Key outcomes	Quick check
Use appropriate units to measure length, mass and capacity and convert between metric units. L5	Convert the following: **a** 4.5 m into cm (450) **b** 4300 ml into litres (4.3) **c** 0.23 kg into grams (230) **d** 1250 mm into metres (1.25)
Know rough metric equivalents to imperial units. L5	**a** Approximately how many inches are there in 75 cm? (25) **b** Approximately how many pounds are there in 11 kg? (24.2)
Read and interpret scales. L5	A scale on a ruler is marked in cm and mm. Write down, in cm and mm, the value of the mark which is seven marks after 8 cm (8.7 cm, 87 mm)
Calculate the perimeter and area of a rectangle. L5	A rectangle has dimensions 5 cm by 8 cm. **a** Find the area (40 cm^2) **b** Find the perimeter (26 cm)
Calculate the area of a triangle. L6	A triangle has base 8.2 cm and height 4 cm. Find its area. (16.4 cm^2)
Calculate the area of a parallelogram and a trapezium. L6	**a** A parallelogram has base 5 cm and perpendicular height 11 cm. Find its area. (55 cm^2) **b** A trapezium has parallel sides of length 8 m and 6 m. If the perpendicular distance between them is 5 m, find the area. (35 m^2)

⊞ MyMaths extra support

Lesson/online homework			Description
Units of length	1101	L4	Estimating and using standard units of length
Units of capacity	1104	L4	Estimating and using standard units of capacity
Units of mass	1105	L5	Estimating and using standard units of mass
Converting measures	1091	L5	Converting different units of mass, capacity and length
Measures	1232	L2	Everyday units of length, mass and volume. Reading scales

MyReview

Check out

You should now be able to ...

	Test it ➡ Questions
✓ Use appropriate units to measure length, mass and capacity and convert between metric units.	1, 2
✓ Know rough metric equivalents to imperial units.	3
✓ Read and interpret scales.	4
✓ Calculate the perimeter and area of a rectangle.	5–7
✓ Calculate the area of a triangle.	8
✓ Calculate the area of a parallelogram and a trapezium.	9, 10

Language	Meaning	Example
Length	How long something is	The length of a man's stride is about 1 m
Mass	How heavy something is	The mass of a bag of sugar is 1 kg
Capacity	How much something holds	The capacity of a drinks can is 330 ml
Perimeter	The distance around the edge of a shape	The perimeter of a square of side 5 cm is 20 cm
Area	The amount of space inside a 2D shape	The area of a square of side 5 cm is 25 cm²
Rectangle	A four-sided shape with four right-angles and two pairs of equal length sides	The shape of this book is a rectangle
Parallelogram	A four-sided shape with two pairs of parallel sides	
Trapezium	A four-sided shape with one pair of parallel sides	The cross-section of a trough is a trapezium

In the following questions you must state the units of your answer.

1 Write an appropriate metric unit for each measurement.
 a My sister is 0.9 .... tall.
 b The cross-country race was 5 .... long.
 c The ant is 3 .... long.
 d I weigh 45 ....

2 Convert
 a 27 km to cm   b 1250 g to kg
 c 550 cl to litres   d 5000 mm to km

3 Convert
 a 5 inches into cm
 b 10 pints into litres.

4 Write down the readings on this scale.

5 Calculate the area of this rectangle.

11 cm, 7 cm, 7 cm, 11 cm

6 The area of this rectangle is 45 m². What is its perimeter?   45 m²   9 m

7 Calculate the area of this shape which has been made using two rectangles.
 4 cm, 6 cm, 1 cm, 10 cm

8 Calculate the area of these triangles.
 a 5 cm 3 cm 5 cm 8 cm
 b 12 mm 5 mm 13 mm

9 A parallelogram has a base of length 8 cm and an area of 48 cm². Calculate the height of the parallelogram.

10 12 cm 8 cm 5 cm
 a What is this shape called?
 b Calculate the area of the shape.

What next?

Score		
	0 – 3	Your knowledge of this topic is still developing. To improve look at Formative test: 2B-2; MyMaths: 1061, 1084, 1108, 1110, 1129 and 1191
	4 – 8	You are gaining a secure knowledge of this topic. To improve look at InvisiPen: 312, 313, 314, 315, 332 and 333
	9 – 10	You have mastered this topic. Well done, you are ready to progress!

Question commentary

Question 1 – Students need to understand the meaning of the term 'metric'.

Questions 2 and **3** – Students need to learn the metric conversions and the approximate conversions between metric and imperial. Reference to a table of conversions may be required.

Question 4 – Make sure the students work out the value of the subdivisions first.

Questions 5 and **6** – Students must recall the difference between area and perimeter and link this with an understanding of the correct units to use.

Question 7 – Students need to decide which measurements to use in calculating the areas. Emphasise the area can be split up in more than one way.

Questions 8 and **9** – Students need to memorise the formulae here and apply them correctly. In question **9**, they are working backwards.

Question 10 – The formula for the area of a trapezium does not necessarily need to be memorised but students need to know how to apply it and be able to identify trapeziums.

Answers

1	a	m	b	km	c	mm	d	kg
2	a	27 00 000 cm			b	1.25 kg		
	c	0.55 litres			d	0.005 km		
3	a	12.5 cm			b	6 litres		
4	a	3 kg	b	20 kg	c	24 kg	d	36 kg
	e	48 kg						
5	77 cm²							
6	28 m							
7	34 cm²							
8	a	12 cm²			b	30 mm²		
9	6 cm							
10	a	(Right) trapezium			b	50 cm²		

Page 38

2a

1 Copy and complete each sentence, using the most appropriate metric unit of length.

a A banana weighs 150 ___.

b I can walk 1 ___ in 15 minutes.

c The weight of a football is just over 400 ___.

d A ruler is 30 ___ long.

e A small flask holds 300 ___ of liquid.

2 Convert these measurements to the units indicated in brackets.

a 380 mm (cm)   b 4.5 kg (g)   c 6.5 ℓ (cl)

d 3500 mm (m)   e 2500 kg (t)   f 500 ml (litre)

2b

3 Convert these measurements to the units indicated in brackets.

a 8 inches (cm)   b 132 lbs (kg)   c 40 km (miles)

d 5 pints (litre)   e 10 gallons (litre)   f 1 metre (inches)

4 Write down each reading on the scales.

2c

5 Copy and complete the table for the rectangles.

	Length	Width	Perimeter	Area
a	15 cm	10 cm		
b	25 cm	20 cm		
c	9 cm			63 cm²
d	4.5 cm			18 cm²
e	5.5 cm		20 cm	
f	7.5 cm		26 cm	
g			28 cm	48 cm²

Page 39

2c

6 Calculate the perimeter and area of these shapes made from rectangles.

a

6 cm
5 cm
4 cm
8 cm

b

12 cm
10 cm
5 cm
4 cm
4 cm
4 cm

c

3 cm
2 cm
6 cm

7 Calculate the area of the shaded region.

a

20 cm
10 cm
5 cm
12 cm

b

12 cm
9 cm

The shaded border is 2 cm wide.

2d

8 On square grid paper, draw

a two different rectangles, each with an area of 6 cm²

b two different right-angled triangles, each with an area of 6 cm²

c two different triangles, neither of them right-angled each with an area of 6 cm².

2e

9 Calculate the area of these parallelograms.

a

12 m
18 m

b

10 cm
6.5 cm

c

3.5 m
8 m

10 Calculate the area of these trapeziums.

a

14 cm
24 cm
14 cm

b

7.5 m
15 m
14.5 m

c

10 cm
5 cm
15 cm

Question commentary

Questions 1 and **2** – Students could work together on question **1** to identify the correct units to use. In question **2**, check students are multiplying or dividing correctly.

Question 3 – Reference to the table of approximate conversions may be needed.

Question 4 – Check that students know what the subdivisions stand for in each case.

Question 5 – Basic practice in table form.

Questions 6 and **7** – Students can split the shapes in different ways but they should all lead to the same answer.

Question 8 – Lots of answers here, students could be encouraged to show justification for their diagrams or ask a partner to check them.

Questions 9 and **10** – Basic practice questions. Ensure students set out the working clearly.

Answers

1 a g   b mile   c g
   d cm   e cl

2 a 38 cm   b 4500 g   c 650 cl
   d 3.5 m   e 2.5 tonnes   f 0.5 litres

3 a 20 cm   b 60 kg   c 25 miles
   d 3 litres   e 45 litres   f 39 inches

4 a 5 cm   b 25 cm   c 1.5 gallons
   d 3.5 gallons e 200 ml   f 800 ml

5 a 50 cm, 150 cm^2 b 90 cm, 500 cm^2
   c 7 cm, 32 cm   d 4 cm, 17 cm
   e 4.5 cm, 24.75 cm^2 f 5.5 cm, 41.25 cm^2
   g 8 cm, 6 cm

6 a 28 cm, 38 cm^2 b 54 cm, 100 cm^2
   c 34 cm, 60 cm^2

7 a 140 cm^2 b 68 cm^2

8 Multiple answers possible, for example
   a 1×6, 2×3, 6×1, 2.5×2.4
   b, c Base × perpendicular height must equal 12

9 a 216 m^2 b 65 cm^2 c 28 m^2

10 a 266 cm^2 b 165 m^2 c 100 cm^2

3 Expressions and formulae

Learning outcomes

A1 Use and interpret algebraic notation, including:
- ab in place of $a \times b$
- a^2 in place of $a \times a$, a^3 in place of $a \times a \times a$; a^2b in place of $a \times a \times b$
- a/b in place of $a \div b$
- $3y$ in place of $y + y + y$ and $3 \times y$
- coefficients written as fractions rather than as decimals
- brackets   (L5)

A2 Substitute numerical values into formulae and expressions, including scientific formulae   (L5)

A3 Understand and use the concepts and vocabulary of expressions, equations, inequalities, terms and factor   (L5)

A4 Simplify and manipulate algebraic expressions to maintain equivalence by:
- collecting like terms
- multiplying a single term over a bracket   (L5)

A6 Model situations or procedures by translating them into algebraic expressions or formulae and by using graphs   (L5)

Introduction

The chapter starts by revising algebraic notation and evaluating simple expressions. It introduces index notation (for positive integers) and the idea of simplifying products by adding indices. Collecting like terms and expanding a single bracket are covered followed by evaluating and creating simple formulae.

The introduction discusses the Voyager 1 space probe. Its primary goal was to investigate Jupiter and Saturn and their moons before heading into the outer solar system and beyond. It has been sending back information for over 36 years and is currently almost 20 billion kilometres away – the furthest any manmade object has ever been. It takes a signal over 19 hours to reach us at that distance. Should 'anyone' encounter the space probe they will find a gold record which contains, amongst other things, whale song, greetings in 50 languages and a recording of Chuck Berry's *Johnny B Goode*. Voyager 1 has a sister probe Voyager 2, actually launched 16 days earlier, which also visited Neptune and Uranus before heading into outer space.

Algebra is the language mathematicians use to write down general statements that can apply to one or more numbers. An equation for an unknown is a familiar example. Likewise, formulae tell you what one thing equals given the value of another arbitrary quantity. For example, the total cost as a function of the number of items sold. Learning how to write and manipulate algebraic expressions allows you to solve more complex problems – like successfully sending a satellite into outer space.

Prior knowledge

Students should already know how to...
- Use basic algebraic notation
- Carry out arithmetic operations in the correct order
- Extract information from a written description
- Calculate perimeters and areas of simple shapes

Starter problem

This is a problem which gives you the opportunity to demonstrate the use of algebra.

Students could be encouraged to use algebra to describe the particular staircase you are building, for example, S(10) = the tenth staircase.

You can use this shorthand to describe the number of blocks for a particular staircase for example S(10) = 55

Students should see that S(10) = 1 + 2 + 3 + 4 + 5 + 6 + 7 + 8 + 9 + 10 but the question is how do you work this out quickly... using algebra!

(You could tell the story of Carl Gauss adding up all the numbers from 1 to 100 by spotting that the addition = 50 × 101.)

Students could use the geometry of two identical staircases joined to make a rectangle and finally algebra to express it more succinctly as $n(n + 1)/2$ where n is the number of steps.

Emphasise that the algebra describes every possible staircase made to this pattern no matter what the size.

Students could investigate a tower built to some repeating pattern of their own choosing.

Resources

MyMaths

Indices 1	1033	Rules and formulae	1158	Simplifying 1	1179
Substitution 1	1187	Single brackets	1247		

Online assessment

InvisiPen solutions

Chapter test	2B–3	Using symbols	211	Collecting like terms	212
Formative test	2B–3	Expanding brackets	214	Laws of indices	221
Summative test	2B–3	Creating a formula	252	Substitution	254

Topic scheme

Teaching time = 6 lessons/2 weeks

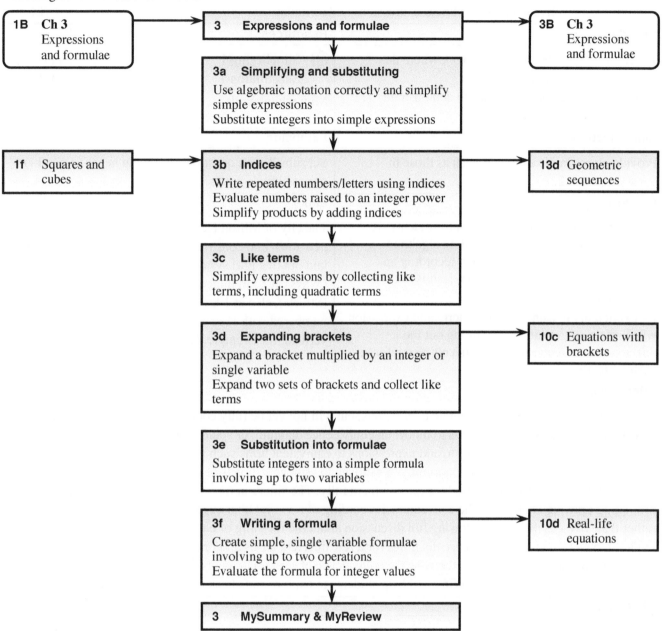

1B Ch 3
Expressions
and formulae

3 Expressions and formulae

3B Ch 3
Expressions
and formulae

3a Simplifying and substituting
Use algebraic notation correctly and simplify simple expressions
Substitute integers into simple expressions

1f Squares and cubes

3b Indices
Write repeated numbers/letters using indices
Evaluate numbers raised to an integer power
Simplify products by adding indices

13d Geometric sequences

3c Like terms
Simplify expressions by collecting like terms, including quadratic terms

3d Expanding brackets
Expand a bracket multiplied by an integer or single variable
Expand two sets of brackets and collect like terms

10c Equations with brackets

3e Substitution into formulae
Substitute integers into a simple formula involving up to two variables

3f Writing a formula
Create simple, single variable formulae involving up to two operations
Evaluate the formula for integer values

10d Real-life equations

3 MySummary & MyReview

Differentiation

Student book 2A   44 – 63

Using symbols
Substitution
Simplifying expressions
Expanding brackets
Simplifying harder expressions
Formulae
Writing a formula

Student book 2B   40 – 57

Simplifying and substituting
Indices
Like terms
Expanding brackets
Substitution into formulae
Writing a formula

Student book 2C   40 – 63

Indices in algebra
Index laws
Collecting like terms including powers
Expanding brackets
Factorising expressions
Formulae 1
Rearranging formulae
Writing expressions
Algebraic fractions

Objectives	
• Understand that algebraic operations follow the rules of arithmetic	(L5)
• Substitute positive integers into linear expressions and formulae	(L5)

Key ideas	Resources	
1 Know that algebra is number work where the 'number' is a variable	Simplifying 1	(1179)
	Substitution 1	(1187)
2 Be able to use specific values to demonstrate equivalence of expressions	Mini whiteboards	

Simplification	Extension
Provide more simple examples such as those in questions **1** and **2**.	Set substitution questions involving negative numbers or possibly decimals.

Literacy	Links
As given in the teaching notes, ensure students are aware of the conventions surrounding algebraic notation, while making it clear that recording an expression as, say × 3, is not wrong, but is not conventional. Be explicit about using the words term and expression when referring to examples, pointing out the differences and requesting that students also refer to such correctly.	The city of Milton Keynes in the UK was designed as a new town and construction began in 1967. The town is laid out in a grid system with ten horizontal roads (Ways) at 1 km intervals and eleven vertical roads (Streets), also at 1 km intervals. The roads are numbered with H or V numbers for horizontal or vertical, for example, H6 Childs Way.

Alternative approach

Students will be familiar with algebraic expressions, but will not yet be fully confident with using them in flexible ways. A good way to start is to model an equivalence diagram, or spider diagram with the term $5x$ in the centre. Request individual students to add expressions to equivalent arms such as $2x + 3x$, or $7x - 2x$, or $x + x + x + x + x$. This will provide a good opportunity to evaluate the students' levels of understanding and to begin to tackle some typical misconceptions by exposing them fully. The situation $6x - 1x$ may well occur for instance, prompting drawing attention to the conventional recording of $6x - x$. Other suggestions may include $10x \div 2x$ rather than $10x \div 2$, thus again allowing full discussion about the meaning of each. Pairs of students may be required to work on their equivalence diagrams for a few different terms and/or expressions. Extend by requesting that students justify or otherwise the equivalence of some statements such as $7x = 21x \div 3x$. Modelling such a justification by substitution first will help students to explore and check their own equivalence diagrams.

Checkpoint

1 Write the expression $5 + 2p$ in at least three different ways. (e.g. $p + p + 7 - 2$ and so on)

2 Show that $2n + 3 + 3n = 3 + 5n$

(Substituting a value into the left side then the right side should result in the same value.)

Starter – What is my number?

I am greater than 3^3 and...

I am less than 4^3 and...

I am a multiple of 7 and...

I have exactly 3 factors. (49)

This can be extended by asking students which clue could have been omitted and asking them to make up their own puzzles.

Teaching notes

As a precursor to constructing and substituting into formulae it is important to ensure that students are comfortable with the notation: x for $1x$, $2x$ rather than $x2$ for $x + x = 2 \times x = x \times 2$.

Questions **4** onwards involve generating expressions from a description. This is a skill that large numbers of students struggle with and it is well worth focusing here. Not specifying a letter to represent the variable helps students to quickly realise the nature of the variable. After providing an example, organise students into small groups and ask them to write their own sentences. Then, in turn, the first student reads out his or her sentence and challenges the second to supply the correct formula, the second then reads his or her sentence and challenges the third, *etc*. Not using the same specific variable should not hinder this task. Ensure all students agree on whether the answers are correct albeit not necessarily the same.

The second example involves substitution into a 'two operation' expression. This assumes that students understand the order of precedence. Using mini whiteboards, a few numerical BIDMAS examples should allow you to asses if this is the case. Further examples can be used to check that students understand how to substitute into formulae.

Plenary

Use the best two or three examples generated by the class in the activity outlined above to share as a whole class and, through this task, encourage students to collaborate with others to work towards common goals.

Exercise commentary

Question 1 – A point for discussion is the difference between $3 \times z = z \times 3$ and $3 \div z \neq z \div 3$. Compare with $y + 3 = 3 + y$ but $y - 3 \neq 3 - y$ (in general).

Question 2 – Substitution can be into either the simplified or un-simplified expressions.

Question 3 – A development of question **2**. Check students take care with negative numbers.

Questions 4 to **9** – Applications where students first form their own expression and then substitute into it. Some students may need to be reminded of the method for finding the perimeter.

Answers

1	a	$5x$	b	$3y$	c	$4z$			
	d	$3z$	e	$\frac{8}{x}$	f	$5y$			
	g	$\frac{x}{2}$	h	$\frac{y}{5}$	i	$\frac{z}{3}$	j	$4y$	
2	a	50	b	15	c	24			
	d	18	e	0.8	f	25			
	g	5	h	1	i	2	j	20	
3	a	8	b	-8	c	0			
4	a	$x + 4$	b	16					
5	a	$y - 10$	b	40					
6	a	$4n$	b	24					
7	a	$4y$ metres			b	48 metres			
8	a	$2r + 2s$ metres			b	170 metres			
9		$3x + 2y$ cm, 10 routes				32 cm			

3b Indices

Objectives

- Use index notation for small positive integer powers   (L5)

Key ideas	Resources
1 Understand the ways of recording and communicating constant multiplication	Indices 1 (1033) Mini whiteboard

Simplification	Extension
Supply more examples like those in questions **1** and **2**.	Introduce harder versions of question **4** that use a variable or combinations of numbers and variable(s).

Literacy	Links
Explicitly deal with the terms index and indices, together with the word power. Use the opportunity to ensure that sentencing is accurately recorded, with correct use of equals sign.	The traditional nursery rhyme below is a riddle that can be investigated using indices. As I was going to St. Ives (1) I met a man with 7 wives Each wife had 7 sacks Each sack had 7 cats Each cat had 7 kits Kits, cats, sacks, wives How many were going to St. Ives? $(1 + 1 + 7 + 7^2 + 7^3 + 7^4 = 2802)$ Of course the answer to the riddle is actually 1 as everyone else is on their way back!

Alternative approach

Students will be familiar with the key idea of this chapter, but not be necessarily confident. Follow a similar line as that given in the alternative 3^a approach using an equivalence spider diagram with the whole group. Use one numerical centre, say of 4^3, as a memory jogger, followed by a more challenging centre of, say, $3m^2$. Going around the group for individual equivalent leg additions will enable common misconceptions to be exposed. Suggestions might be given by whole group using mini whiteboards, allowing the teacher to select which to include on the diagram and which to offer for open discussion to enable corrections to occur. Commonly, $3m^2$ may be perceived as $(3m)^2$ and this can be easily corrected when other equivalent statements are used. Further equivalent statements can form the basis of paired work, which should make equal use of variables as well as specific numbers using the style of question **4** as centre statements. The choice of the centre statement affords an easy way to differentiate appropriately for the student pairs. From the equivalence work discussion about which term or expression is the simplest or most efficient recording can take place.

Checkpoint

1 Write a term that is equivalent to $2n^3 \times 3n^2$ $(6n^5)$

2 Is this statement true or false: $3x^2 + 2x^2 = 3x^2 \times 2x^2$? Explain your answer.
   (False – equivalent statements for each side of the equation may demonstrate reasoning here, e.g. LHS is $5x^2$, but RHS is $6x^4$; also using substitution is an appropriate reasoning strategy.)

Starter – MAX PROD of 12

The number 12 can be made up of a number of sums:

e.g. $6 + 6$, $11 + 1$. $2 + 3 + 7$, but which gives the largest product?

In the space of no more than 10 minutes, students should be able to establish that the maximum evolves to either 2^6 or 3^4, and will help highlight the difference between product and sum. It is worth establishing with the group that the best answer actually lies somewhere between these, and that this exploration can be followed up on a different occasion and extended to values other than 12.

Teaching notes

Ensure that students understand the notation and do not confuse, say, 2^3 and 2×3. This is a potentially persistent problem which should be tackled early. The meaning of the notation can be emphasised by providing examples of how expressions can be expanded out as a product or collected as a power.

Question **9** places an emphasis on numerical values. This gives an opportunity to demonstrate how quickly numbers become very big when using powers and how indices allow very large numbers to be written succinctly. This will lay the foundation for future work on standard form and can also be linked to units that arise in science.

Plenary

Revisit some of the more challenging questions using the mini whiteboards to assess understanding and clear up any confusion.

Exercise commentary

Questions 1 and **2** – Could be done as a whole class with mini whiteboards. Question **2** may require re-ordering of the individual terms.

Question 3 – In parts **e** and **h** check that 1^n is not interpreted as n.

Questions 4 and **5** – It may be helpful for students to rewrite the expressions in full.

Question 6 – It may help to write the RHS of each question as the product of (prime) factors.

Questions 7 and **8** – A chance to expand on how indices naturally arise when discussing real-life situations.

Question 9 – It is useful to encourage students to investigate big numbers as this will be solid groundwork when they move on to use standard form later on. This question would make a good homework task.

Answers

1. a 2^4　　b 7^5　　c 9^6
   d n^3　　e y^7　　f z^2
2. a $4^3 \times 5^4$　b $8^2 \times 6^5$　c $2^3 \times 3^4$
   d $5^3 \times 9^2$　e $6^4 \times 4^2$　f $3^4 \times n^2$
   g $r^2 \times s^5$　h $a^2 \times b^2 \times c^3$
3. a $2 \times 2 \times 2 \times 2 = 16$　　b $3 \times 3 \times 3 = 27$
   c $5 \times 5 = 25$　　d $2 \times 2 \times 2 \times 2 \times 2 = 32$
   e $1 \times 1 \times 1 \times 1 \times 1 \times 1 = 1$
   f $2 \times 2 \times 3 \times 3 = 36$
   g $2 \times 2 \times 2 \times 5 \times 5 = 200$
   h $1 \times 1 \times 1 \times 1 \times 6 \times 6 = 36$
   i $3 \times 3 \times 10 \times 10 \times 10 \times 10 = 90\,000$
   j $0 \times 0 \times 0 \times 0 \times 0 \times 7 \times 7 \times 7 = 0$
4. a 6^7　　b 8^6　　c 2^9　　d 3^9
   e 5^8　　f 7^{12}　g 10^9　h 3^9
   i 5^7　　j 6^8　　k 4^{10}　l 10^8
5. a $2^7 \times 3^7$　b $9^7 \times 7^5 \times 5^5$
6. a 3　　b 2　　c 3
   d 3　　e 3　　f 5
7. a 10^3 cm^3　b 1000
8. a x^2 cm^2, x^3 cm^3
   b Discuss students' answers.
9. Billion　　10^9 in USA,　　10^{12} in UK
   Trillion　　10^{12} in USA,　　10^{18} in UK
   Quadrillion　10^{15} in USA,　　10^{24} in UK
   The American definitions are increasingly common in Britain.
   Googol　　10^{100} introduced by US mathematician Edward Kasner (1878–1955), whose 9-year-old nephew invented it.
   Googolplex: $10^{10^{100}}$ is 10 to the power of a googol.

Objectives	
• Simplify or transform (linear) expressions by collecting like terms	(L5)

Key ideas	Resources	
1 Recognising the different ways in which terms and expressions can be expressed correctly 2 Recognising which response of many may be the best response to the instruction simplify	Simplifying 1 Coloured beads Mini whiteboards	(1179)

Simplification	Extension
Encourage students to rewrite the expressions with like terms placed together before collecting. Further examples that do not involve powers and follow the progression in the early questions may be helpful.	Encourage more able students to try to generate a puzzle of their own that uses their understanding of expressions, using the one at the end of the exercise as a model.

Literacy	Links
Continue to check the students correct use of the vocabulary term and expression, making clear and frequent reference to both yourself.	Beads have been found dating back 100 000 years and are the oldest form of jewellery ever found. There are pictures of ancient shell beads at http://www.nhm.ac.uk/about-us/news/2007/june/news_11808.html How long is a necklace made from 12 shells each 1 cm long, 6 shells each 1.5 cm long and 2 shells each 2 cm long?

Alternative approach
Model the use of an equivalence spider diagram with an expression such as $3a + 5b + 2a - b$ at the centre. Encourage students to suggest equivalent expressions using their mini whiteboards and select a variety to add to the diagram. Encourage students to offer longer and more creative expressions as well as shorter and succinct ones. A discussion about the most simple result can evolve, but it is important that students understand that all equivalent statements are equally valid. Further challenges can include the instruction 'simplify'. Using pyramid puzzles can provide further consolidation for the students. Use examples such as those found on NRICH (http://nrich.maths.org/488) involving variables.

Checkpoint	
1 Give three statements that are each equivalent to $7b + 4x - 2b + 3x$.	(Any that simplify to $5b + 7x$)
2 Write the expression $11m - 4m + 15m - 6p + 2p$ in simplest form.	($22m - 4p$)

Starter – Power products

Draw a 4 × 4 table on the board. Label the columns 3^2, 2^5, 2^3 and 3^4.

Label the rows 2^2, 2^4, 3^5 and 3^2.

Ask students to fill in the table with the products, for example, the top row in the table would read $2^2 \times 3^2$, 2^7, 2^5, $2^2 \times 3^4$.

This can be differentiated by the choice of powers.

Teaching notes

Start by challenging students to write definitions for the four keywords (Expression, Like terms, Simplify, Term); allow pairs of students to confer. Then share ideas as a class before agreeing on a best definition.

Sources of error are likely to include failing to take into account the ½ signs in front of terms or failing to distinguish between terms with different powers of the same variable. Carefully explained examples should help students know what to look for and how to proceed.

Plenary

Invite students to challenge each other by writing a 'complicated' expression for their friend to simplify and to swap examples. They must be sure to work out the answer to their own example first, of course!

Exercise commentary

Question 1 – An introductory example: check that students understand what $6x$ and $4x$ mean.

Question 2 – Develops question **1** by also involving subtraction.

Question 3 – Develops question **1** by introducing two variables.

Question 4 – This develops question **3** by also involving subtraction.

Questions 5 and **6** – Similar to the second example. The presence of different indices is likely to cause difficulty: suggest first re-writing the expression, collecting all the like terms together. Check that like terms are correctly identified and that signs are kept with individual terms.

Question 7 – Students may need reminding about area and perimeter and how they are calculated.

Question 8 – This could be done as a paired activity or a practical activity.

Answers

1	**a**	$10x$	**b**	$7y$	**c**	$7z$	
2	**a**	$6n$	**b**	$12m$	**c**	$5p$	**d** $3q$
	e	$12t$	**f**	$3r$	**g**	0	**h** x
	i	$2x$	**j**	$7y$	**k**	$2z$	**l** 0

3 a $6x + 2y$ cm **b** $4x + 6y$ cm

4 a $5x + 2y$ **b** $2x + 8y$ **c** $2x + 5y$

d $6s + 6t$ **e** $2u + 7v$ **f** $7r + 3s$

g $5x + 2y$ **h** $5a + 3b$ **i** $2a + 2b$

5 a $6x + 8x^2$ **b** $9y + 3y^2$ **c** $7z + 4z^2$

d $5u + 3u^2$ **e** $2v + 3v^2$ **f** $6x + 5x^2$

g $2z$ **h** $9h^3 + 2h$ **i** $2j^2 + j$

6 a $6a + 4b^2$ **b** $u^2 - u + 13v$ **c** $4x^2 - 3x + y^2$

d $-7s^2 - 2s + 5t^2$ **e** $4p^2 - 6q^2 + 4r$

f $4n^2 + 2m + 2n - 3m^2$

7 a $3x^2 + 3xy$ **b** $8x + 2y$

8 10

3d Expanding brackets

Objectives

- Multiply a single term over a bracket (L5)
- Use index notation for small positive integer powers (L5)

Key ideas	Resources
1 Expanding an expression with a single bracket	Single brackets (1247) Standards Unit: Mostly algebra – evaluating expressions http://www.nationalstemcentre.org.uk/elibrary/resource/2002/evaluating-algebraic-expressions-a4

Simplification	Extension
Offer further graduated examples similar to those in questions **1–4**. The word problems, questions **5** and **6**, can be completed as a paired activity with the starting point being to identify the key information.	Ensure that more able students have access to expanding brackets which include directed numbers. More able students could produce annotated PowerPoint presentations showing how to solve one of the questions that was generally found to be most challenging. This could be shown to the class and/or could be made available as a student led tutorial on the school website. Parents would also find this helpful to support their children with homework.

Literacy	Links
Reading an expression that includes a bracket in different ways will help to reinforce the concept behind the notation. For example $2(x + 5)$; rather than 'two brackets…' can be read as '2 lots of x and 5' or 'x add 5, doubled', and so on. Also address the convention of not including 1 when meaning 'one lot of…' when reading say $(2x + 3)$. The instruction 'expand' needs to be explicitly addressed in order to establish a clear understanding of the requirement.	Bring in some dictionaries for the class to use. The word *bracket* can have several meanings and can be used as a noun or a verb. What do the meanings have in common? (group or hold something together)

Alternative approach

Use a simple number problem asking students to identify the steps towards its solution such as 'The bus fare to school is £1.20, but one student only uses the bus for part of the journey on the way home, costing just 80p. What would be the weekly cost of travel for this student?' This is likely to result in two types of approaches within any group: either that of finding the daily cost first then multiplying by 5, or finding the cost of the five morning journeys, and adding this to the five evening journeys. Each method can be recorded: $5 \times £1.20 + 5 \times 80p$ or $5(£1.20 + 80p)$ thus demonstrating the equivalence of the two approaches and the resulting solution. Expanding brackets can then be drawn out from this work. Using card sorts with pairs of students linking expressions and their expansions helps to consolidate these concepts. A good source of card sorts here can be found in the Standards Unit: Improving the Learning of Mathematics, as referenced in the resource section.

Checkpoint

1 What is wrong with these statements:
   a $3(p - 7) = 3p - 10$ (should be $= 3p - 21$)
   b $4(x + 2) = 4x + 2$ (should be $= 4x + 8$)
   c $12 - (n - 3) = 12 - n - 3$?   (should be $= 12 - n + 3$ or $15 - n$)

Starter – Expressions

$a = 2, b = 3, c = 5$

Ask students for expressions that have a value of 24, for example, $3b + 3c$.

This can be extended by changing the target number or values of a, b and c.

Teaching notes

The visual prompt of the rectangle provided here will be very helpful to visual learners and also to students who find this work more difficult as it is a useful reminder strategy to fall back on.

The abstract nature of the work often leads to difficulty. The emphasis on beginning with a word problem from which to generate an expression places this topic in a context which many will find helpful. The process skill of analysing through using appropriate mathematical procedures is developed where students expand expressions.

Where x^2 is involved, some students will need support to recall their previous work on powers. Many make careless errors where there are subtraction signs.

Plenary

Display three examples similar to those in question **6**. Ask students to choose one and to write an annotated answer that they think would explain this work to a student who had been absent from the lesson. Pair students who have answered different examples and ask them to read through each other's work and identify two things they thought were particularly helpful and one thing they could improve. This supports students in inviting feedback and dealing positively with praise, setbacks and criticism.

Exercise commentary

Question 1 – Simple introductory examples.

Question 2 – Similar to the first example; remind students to take care with negative signs.

Question 3 – Similar to the first example but with algebraic terms outside the brackets.

Question 4 – Similar to the second example. Check the collection of like terms at the end and care with negatives.

Questions 5 and **6** – Word problems: a whole class discussion may be necessary to model how to extract the relevant information.

Question 7 – Requires an understanding of factors. This could be carried out as a paired activity to promote mathematical dialogue.

Answers

1 a $3x + 6$ b $2x + 8$ c $4x + 4$
   d $x^2 + 2x$
2 a $5x + 15$ b $10x + 10$ c $5x + 15$
   d $10x - 25$ e $18u + 12$ f $3v - 12$
   g $10a - 15$ h $12b - 4$ i $15 - 10c$
   j $12b - 18$
3 a $x^2 + 3x$ b $5x^2 + 3x$ c $2x^2 + 4x$
   d $3x^2 - 2x$ e $4x^2 - 5x$ f $2x^2 - 7x$
   g $4x - 5x^2$ h $2x + x^2$ i $7x + 3x^2$
   j $7x - 2x^2$
4 a $14x + 9$ b $27x + 4$ c $17x + 2$
   d $10x + 3$ e $16x - 9$ f $15x - 8$
   g $11x + 14$ h $40 - 17x$ i $3x + 66$
   j $10x - 16$
5 a $4(x + 8)$ kg   b $4x + 32$ kg
6 a $3(20y + 150)$ g   b $60y + 450$ g
7 Four ways using only integers: $3(4x + 8)$, $4(3x + 6)$, $6(2x + 4)$ and $12(x + 2)$

Objectives	
• Substitute integers into simple formulae	(L5)
• Use formulae from mathematics and other subjects	(L5)

Key ideas	Resources	
1 Recognise what the purpose of a formula is 2 Be able to apply a given formula to provide a correct solution	Substitution 1 Mini whiteboards	(1187)

Simplification	Extension
Students struggling with this unit will need to consolidate simple substitution, questions **1** and **2**, and build confidence through working on more of the simple formulae before working with brackets or using two values, questions **3** onwards.	Ask students to investigate a number of mobile phone tariffs to make a recommendation as to which represents best value and justify their decision.

Literacy	Links
Check that students can read the given formula using typical operational language rather than just reading the sentence. For example, $P = 17 + x$ as 'p equals 17 plus x' or 'perimeter is seventeen added to x'. Students frequently get confused with formulae by trying to include units with numeric values. Explicitly discuss this with students to help them handle substitution efficiently.	Anders Celsius was a Swedish astronomer who proposed the Celsius temperature scale in 1742. He chose 0° as the boiling point of water and 100° as the freezing point and named the scale the centigrade scale (from the Latin for a hundred steps). Carl Linnaeus, another Swedish scientist, reversed the scale in 1745 and the scale is now used across the World. There is more information about Anders Celsius at http://en.wikipedia.org/wiki/Anders_Celsius

Alternative approach
Reverse the themes of sections **3e** and **3f**, by encouraging students to construct formulae for themselves first, then follow by using common or given formulae. To introduce this session show students a rectangle with given dimensions and ask them to write down how they would find the perimeter. Compare all the variety of ways that students respond to this, emphasising the equivalence of all the correct versions. Now repeat for a rectangle with dimensions given as $x + 3$ and $2x + 4$. Compare the variety of correct responses and request that every student provides a simplified expression, thus evolving a formula for this case. Repeat for different shapes and/or dimensions. Further formulae may be generated by students exploring patterns made with matchsticks linking the total number of matches to shape dimensions, for example, n by n square grids. Exercise **3f** can provide further consolidation. Use checkpoint **3f** if taking this alternative approach.

Checkpoint	
1 When hiring a car the total cost, £T, is given by the formula $T = 12d + 50$, where d is the number of days hired. How much would it cost to hire a car for 3 days?	(£86)
2 The formula for distance covered, s, of an object travelling for time, t, if its initial speed is u and its final speed is v is given by $s = (u + v)t \div 2$. Find s if $u = 10 \text{ ms}^{-1}$ $v = 16 \text{ ms}^{-1}$ and $t = 40$ s.	(520 m)

Starter – Priceless!

If A costs 1p, B costs 2p, C costs 3p, etc. how much is your name worth?

Are you more expensive than the person beside you?

Which of your school subjects is worth the most?

How much does your favourite hobby cost?

Teaching notes

This spread develops process skills in algebra. The capacity of students to represent problems is developed through using formulae. Their evaluation skills are developed through communicating and reflecting on links to related problems or to different problems with a similar structure.

Students may need a brief recap of substitution and the first two worked examples could be used as a whole class discussion activity.

The use of brackets in formulae and the occasions where two values will be substituted will need greater clarification for some and again offer an opportunity to make connections with prior learning.

There is an opportunity here to make links to formulae specifically relevant to the students, such as mobile phone tariffs.

Plenary

Ask students to identify as many formulae as possible that they know or use in other areas of the curriculum or in real life – for example in science or when working out cooking times, etc.

Exercise commentary

The emphasis on using formulae in real-life contexts supports the embedding of functional skills in mathematics.

Questions 1 and **2** – Similar to the first example.

Question 3 – Similar to the second example.

Question 4 – Discuss whether it is better to work out the value inside the brackets first and then multiply, or expand the brackets first. Ask students to try both methods and then justify which method they think is easiest.

Question 5 – Despite the apparent complexity, this is numerically straightforward.

Question 6 – Is it realistic that boys eat more cakes at parties than girls?

Question 7 – This science-based activity lends itself to further investigation and findings could be presented back to the class next lesson. Students are encouraged to plan and carry out research.

Answers

1	**a**	50	**b**	80	**c**	170	
2	**a**	50 mph	**b**	35 mph	**c**	23 mph	
	d	320 mph	**e**	20 mph	**f**	170 mph	
3	**a**	34	**b**	88	**c**	60	**d** 70
4	**a**	50	**b**	30	**c**	50	
5	**a**	19	**b**	14	**c**	18	
6	**a**	32	**b**	24	**c**	30	

7   **a**   212 °F = 100 °C   Boiling point of water
         32 °F = 0 °C   Freezing point of water

     b   All five surnames are used for temperature scales.

3f Writing a formula

Objectives	
• Substitute integers into simple formulae, including examples that lead to an equation to solve	(L5)
• Derive simple formulae in different contexts	(L5)

Key ideas	Resources
1 Be able to interpret and use simple formula to solve a problem 2 Be able to give instructions as a formula in order to solve a simple problem	Rules and formulae (1158) SMILE spreadsheets: http://www.nationalstemcentre.org.uk/elibrary/resourc e/7376/smile-spreadsheets

Simplification	Extension
Where students struggle with this work, it will be necessary to identify whether it is the algebra work or the particular prior content knowledge that is the stumbling block to progress. Encourage paired work, as developing dialogue between students is supportive of overcoming difficulties.	More able students can be challenged to draw further upon their prior knowledge in geometry and measures to create their own questions, using the examples as a model. This supports the consolidation of understanding of constructing formulae and substitution and also helps to embed functional application of skills.

Literacy	Links
Check that students are exposed to the difference between and equation and a formula. An equation can arise from a specific or particular case of a formula, but each has a different mathematical purpose.	Albert Einstein's famous formula $E = mc^2$ says that mass can be converted into energy. The amount of energy contained in a piece of matter can be found by multiplying the mass m by the square of the speed of light, c. This means that, in theory, there is enough energy in a grain of sand to boil 10 million kettles.

Alternative approach
Reversing the themes of **3e** and **3f**. Begin this section on using formula by exploring the students' knowledge of any formula such as area of a triangle, some from science, as in Links or conversion ones such as current £ to euros. Take the opportunity to make the difference between a formula and an equation clear. It is possible to draw links here to computing where algorithms for calculations are needed. Use a selection of the formulae to provide practice with substitution either to find the 'subject' or to use inversely when given the value of the 'subject'. Use exercise **3e** for consolidation as well as checkpoint **3e**. As another approach set up a challenge that involves students setting up their own excel spreadsheets with appropriate simple formulae. Typical challenges here might include cafe or tuck shop tools or 'Rich Aunt' from SMILE spreadsheets at the link given in resources.

Checkpoint

1 Write down an equation in x using the information provided by the diagram. $(3x + 58 = 180)$

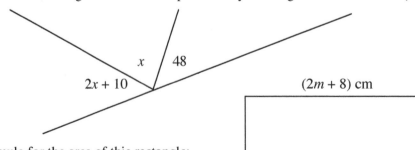

2 Write down the formula for the area of this rectangle:
 $(A = 6(2m + 8)$ or $A = 12m + 48)$

Write the following on the board and ask students which are always **T**rue, **S**ometimes true, always **F**alse:

$x^2 = (-x^2)$	**S**, $x = 0$
$2(x - 3) = 2x - 3$	**F**
$x - y = y - x$	**S**, $x = y$
$x^2 = (-x)^2$	**T**
$3(2x + 4) = 2(3x + 6)$	**T**

Ask students to justify their answers using substitution.

Teaching notes

This unit fully supports the development of links within mathematics, using geometry and measures as a foundation upon which to build skills in algebra. There is also a major emphasis throughout on using formulae in real-life functional situations.

A stumbling block for many students is known to be weak literacy skills and the main thrust of the work here is around word problems. Emphasise the need to focus on identifying key information, pairing weaker students as necessary.

Maximum benefit to learning will be gained through encouraging discussion of each of the worked examples, wherever possible asking students to explain both the question and their solution in their own words. Encourage students to think creatively and make connections of their own through asking questions to extend their thinking.

Plenary

Ask students to reflect on the work they have done on using and constructing formulae and on substitution and to list three key points that they think are the most important to remember. Take feedback and agree a whole class 'top three tips'.

Exercise commentary

This exercise strengthens students' capacity to approach word problems.

Question 1 – Students could check their answers to part **b** by replacing x by 4 in the diagrams and adding up the lengths directly.

Question 2 – The meaning of 'in terms of x' may need to be explained.

Question 3 – Similar to the first example.

Question 4 – Highlight the strategy of breaking a problem down into smaller parts.

Questions 5 and 6 – In principle, very similar to question **3** but its potential to cause confusion may require whole class discussion and agreement.

Question 7 – If the language proves troublesome, ask students to work in pairs to write a 'student friendly' version. Take feedback as a whole class.

Question 8 – The diagram clarifies this problem; to develop fuller understanding, challenge students to describe the question in words, imagining that the diagram was not there.

Answers

1 **a** **i** $P = 13 + x$ **ii** $P = 18 + x$ **iii** $P = 4x + 12$
   b **i** 17 cm **ii** 22 cm **iii** 28 cm
2 **a** $y = 180° - x$ **b** 120°
3 $3x + 10, 28$
4 **a** 48 cm^2, $3x$ cm^2 **b** $A = 48 + 3x$
   c 63 cm^2
5 **a** $4n + 4$ **b** $n^2 + 2n$ **c** $P = 24, A = 35$
   d $n = 4$
6 **a** $P = 10x + 10$ cm **b** $A = 6x^2 + 9x - 6$ cm^2
   c $P = 60, A = 189$ cm^2 **d** $x = 1$
7 **a** $C = 4p + 6$
   b **i** 126 **ii** 146
8 **a** $A = 80 - x^2$ cm^2 **b** 44 cm^2

Key outcomes		Quick check	
Simplify algebraic expressions.	L5	Simplify:	
		a $g + g + 2g$	$(4g)$
		b $4 \times x$	$(4x)$
Substitute into simple algebraic expressions.	L5	If $t = 3$, evaluate	
		a $4t$	(12)
		b $t + 7$	(10)
		c t^2	(9)
Use indices to simplify expressions and simplify by collecting like terms.	L5	**a** Simplify $7^2 \times 7^6$	(7^8)
		b Simplify $3x + 6z + 8x - 2z$	$(11x + 4z)$
Expand brackets.	L5	Expand	
		a $4(2a + 1)$	$(8a + 4)$
		b $3(x + 1) + 5(2x - 1)$	$(13x - 2)$
Substitute into formulae.	L5	A formula is given by $C = 3a + 2b$	
		Find C if $a = 4$ and $b = -2$	(8)
Construct a formula for different situations.	L5	A car hire company charges £50 plus £15 per day. Write down a formula for the the total cost C of hiring a car for d days.	$(C = 50 + 15d)$

MyMaths extra support

Lesson/online homework			Description
Simplifying 2	1178	L7	Multiplying and dividing simple algebraic expressions

MyReview

Check out

You should now be able to ...

Test it ➡
Questions

✓ Simplify algebraic expressions.	Ⓢ	1
✓ Substitute into simple algebraic expressions.	Ⓢ	2
✓ Use indices to simplify expressions and simplify by collecting like terms.	Ⓢ	3, 4
✓ Expand brackets.	Ⓢ	5, 6
✓ Substitute into formulae.	Ⓢ	7, 8
✓ Construct a formula for different situations.	Ⓢ	9, 10

Language	Meaning	Example
Expression	A series of letters and numbers in algebra	$2a$, $4a - 3b$ and $2x^2$ are all expressions
Substitute	To replace a letter in an algebraic expression with a number	Substituting $x = 2$ into $3x - 1$ gives $3 \times 2 - 1 = 5$
Index	Another name for a **power** such as 'squared' or 'to the power of 5' (plural: indices)	5 is the index in x^5
Like terms	Algebraic terms which have the same combination of letters in them	$3a$ and $4a$ are like terms but $5b$ and $2c$ are not
Simplify	Collect like terms in an algebraic expression	$2a + 6a = 8a$
Expand	To multiply out a bracket in algebra	$2(3a + 1) = 6a + 2$
Formula	An algebraic statement that connects things (plural: formulae)	$d = s \times t$, distance = speed × time

1 Simplify these expressions.
   a $b \times 5$ b $t + t + t$
   c $k \div 2$ d $2f + f$

2 If $s = 8$, evaluate these expressions.
   a $s + 4$ b $4 - s$
   c $s \div 2$ d $5s$

3 Use indices to simplify these expressions.
   a $3^5 \times 3^4$ b 5×5^6

4 Simplify these expressions.
   a $3n + 4m - n + 2m$
   b $6g - 8h + 5h - 8g$
   c $3y + 4y^2 + 5y + y^2$

5 Expand these brackets.
   a $9(p + q)$ b $3(2v - 4)$
   c $x(x + 1)$ d $x(3x - 4)$

6 Expand the brackets and collect like terms in these expressions.
   a $3(u + 4) + 2(2u - 1)$
   b $8(3v - 5) - 7(4v + 3)$

7 A number of tables, T, are arranged in such a way that the number of chairs required is given by C where

   $C = 4T + 2$.

   Calculate the number of chairs needed when there are five tables.

8 The number of sandwiches, s, needed for a primary school picnic is calculated using this formula:

   $s = 3a + 2c$

   where a = the number of adult and c = the number of children.

   How many sandwiches are needed if there are five adults and 30 children?

9 Find a formula for the perimeter, P, of each shape.
   Simplify your answers.
   a

   b
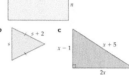
   c

10 A taxi costs £2.50 to hire plus 50p per mile for the journey. If your journey is x miles long
   a write a formula for the cost of the journey
   b find the cost of a 7 mile journey.

What next?

Score		
0 – 3		Your knowledge of this topic is still developing. To improve look at Formative test: 2B–3; MyMaths: 1033, 1158, 1179, 1187 and 1247
4 – 7		You are gaining a secure knowledge of this topic. To improve look at InvisiPen: 211, 212, 214, 221, 252 and 254
8 – 10		You have mastered this topic. Well done, you are ready to progress!

🌐 **MyMaths**.co.uk

Question commentary

Students need to understand the difference between an expression and a formula.

Question 1 – Letters must follow numbers, e.g. $5b$ not $b5$. For part **c** $\frac{1}{2}k$ or $0.5k$ are also permissible.

Question 2 – Should be basic practice.

Question 3 – Students should not calculate any of the numerical answers.

Question 4 – Check students are correctly subtracting terms where required.

Questions 5 and 6 – Students often neglect to multiply the second term inside the brackets by the term outside the brackets. Check negatives are being worked with correctly.

Questions 7 and 8 – These should be straightforward substitutions.

Questions 9 and 10 – Note that a formula is asked for as opposed to an expression.

Answers

1 a $5b$ b $3t$ c $\dfrac{k}{2}$ d $3f$

2 a 12 b -4 c 4 d 40

3 a 3^9 b 5^7

4 a $2n + 6m$ b $-2g + 3h$
  c $8y + 5y^2$

5 a $9p + 9q$ b $6v - 12$
  c $x^2 + x$ d $3x^2 - 4x$

6 a $7u + 10$ b $-4v - 61$

7 22

8 75

9 a $P = 26 + 2n$ b $P = 3s + 4$ c $P = 4x + 4$

10 a $C = 250 + 50x$ b $600p$ or £6

3 MyPractice

3a

1 Write these expressions in a simpler way.
  a $x + x + x$
  b $y + y + y + y$
  c $2 \times 3 \times z$

2 There are x biscuits in a packet. You buy five packets.
  a How many biscuits do you buy?
  b You open one of the packets and eat six biscuits. How many biscuits do you now have altogether?
  c If $x = 10$, how many biscuits are you left with?

3 If $p = 12$ and $q = 4$, find the values of
  a $p + 2q$
  b $2p - q$
  c $\dfrac{p}{q}$
  d $\dfrac{5q + 4}{p}$

3b

4 Find the values of
  a $3 \times 3 \times 3$
  b 2^4
  c 10^2
  d $5^2 \times 10^3$

5 Simplify each of these, using indices in your answers.
  a $a \times a \times a \times b \times b \times c \times c \times c \times c$
  b $3^4 \times 3^2$
  c $6^5 \times 6^3$

6 What values of n makes these statements true?
  a $2^n = 16$
  b $5^3 \times 5^n = 5^7$
  c $3^6 \times 3^n \times 3^2 = 3^{10}$

3c

7 A necklace is made from two kinds of beads of length x cm and y cm.
Write the total length of this necklace as simply as you can.
$3x + 2y + 2x + 3y = \square$

8 A patio with this pattern of paving slabs uses four identical hexagons and four identical triangles.

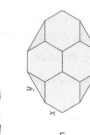

Write an expression for the perimeter of the shape in terms of x and y.

9 Simplify these expressions by collecting like terms.
  a $3p + 2p + 5q - 2q$
  b $4m + 2n + m - 3n$
  c $3x^2 + 4x + 6x^2 - 5x$
  d $z^2 + 5z + z^2 - 2z - 2z^2 - 3z$

3d

10 a Find the total area of rectangles A and B together.
   b Expand this bracket. $5(x + 2)$

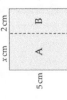

11 a Expand these brackets. i $4(x + 3)$ ii $3(5x + 4)$
   b Expand these brackets and simplify your answers by collecting like terms.
     i $2(y + 3) + 4(5y + 2)$ ii $3(2z + 4) + 2(z - 5)$

12 a A box weighing 20 grams contains 10 screws weighing x grams each. Write an expression for the total weight of the box and its contents.
   b Mr Sturman buys five of these boxes. Write an expression (using brackets) for the total weight of these five boxes and their contents.
   c Expand this bracket.

3e

13 The time T hours to cook a turkey weighing W pounds is given by $T = \dfrac{W}{3} + 1$.
Find T when
   a $W = 12$
   b $W = 18$
   c $W = 20$

14 The charge $£C$ for excess baggage when you fly depends on the weight W kg of your luggage where $C = 5(W - 20)$.
Find C when
   a $W = 32$
   b $W = 65$
   c $W = 20$

15 If $p = 4$, $q = 2$ and $r = 5$, find the values of
   a $2p + q$
   b $4r - 5p$
   c $3(p + 2q - r)$

3f

16 This trapezium has two sides of 8 cm and 5 cm and two equal unknown sides.
   a Write a formula for its perimeter P.
   b Find the value of P when $x = 4$ cm.

17 A triangle has three angles x, y and A.
   a Write a formula for angle A in terms of x and y.
   b Find the value of A when $x = 60°$ and $y = 45°$.

MyMaths.co.uk

Question commentary

Questions 1 to **3** – Simplification of and substitution into simple expressions.

Questions 4 to **6** – Evaluation is expected in question **4** but not question **5**. Students may find writing out the full expansions helpful.

Questions 7 to **9** – Contextualised along with more basic practice at collecting like terms.

Questions 10 to **12** – Contextualised along with more basic practice at expanding brackets. Check negatives in question **11** part **bii**.

Questions 13 to **15** – Substitution questions. Questions **13** and **14** are in context.

Questions 16 and **17** – Applied questions where students first form and then substitute into formulae.

Answers

1 a $3x$ **b** $4y$ **c** $6z$

2 a $5x$ **b** $5x - 6$ **c** 44

3 a 20 **b** 20 **c** 3 **d** 2

4 a 27 **b** 16 **c** 100 **d** $25\,000$

5 a $a^3b^2c^3$ **b** 3^6 **c** 6^8

6 a 4 **b** 4 **c** 2

7 $5x + 5y$

8 $6x + 4y$

9 a $5p + 3q$ **b** $5m + n$ **c** $9x^2 - x$ **d** 0

10 a $5x + 10$ cm^2 or $5(x + 2)$ cm^2

    b $5x + 10$

11 a **i** $4x + 12$ **ii** $15x + 12$

    b **i** $22y + 14$ **ii** $8z + 2$

12 a $20 + 10x$ grams

    b $5(20 + 10x)$ grams

    c $100 + 50x$

13 a 5 **b** 7 **c** $7\frac{2}{3}$

14 a 60 **b** 225 **c** 0

15 a 10 **b** 0 **c** 9

16 a $P = 2x + 13$ cm   **b** 21 cm

17 a $A = 180° - x - y$ **b** $75°$

Related lessons		Resources	
Mental multiplication and division problems	7f	Word problems	(1393)
Multiplication and division problems	11f	Multiply decimals by whole numbers	(1010)

Simplification	Extension
Most of the calculations required here are straightforward but some students might focus on two or three of the different items rather than considering the whole range. The numbers in tasks **2** and **3** could be simplified to aid the use of mental strategies.	All of the information given is about 'typical' costs and savings. Students could be asked to consider a *range* of savings and/or costs which will affect the time over which the savings/repayment costs are made. They could also investigate further the effects of the location of things like solar panels and wind generators in terms of their effectiveness at generating the required amounts of electricity.

Links

Most energy companies now offer government subsidised deals on things like new home insulation and solar panels. Private contractors also have access to these deals and students could look up the various offers on the internet and in both local and national newspapers. Can they find a range of suppliers that could provide all of the various installations free of charge?

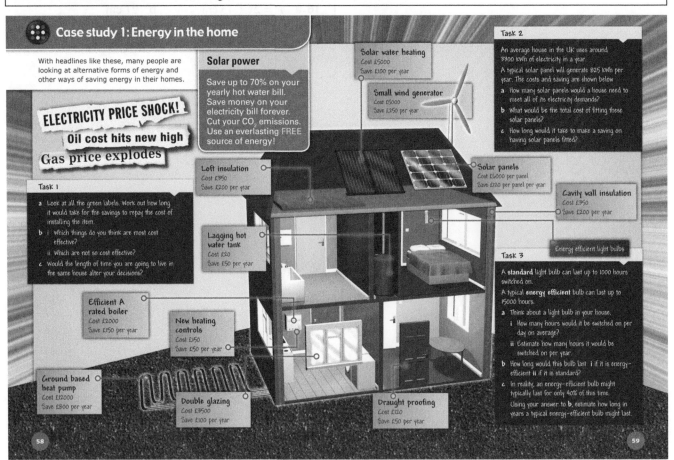

Teaching notes

With energy prices rising and environmental concerns about the climate, there is much interest in reducing energy use around the house and obtaining energy in a cheaper or cleaner way.

This case study looks at a number of things that can be done to a house to make it more energy efficient. It looks at them in terms of how much they could reduce the cost of energy used over a year at current costs and considers their cost effectiveness by working out how long it would take for the savings to pay back the cost of purchase and installation of the items.

Look at the case study and explain that the house shows ways of either saving energy or of providing the energy in a different way. Ask the students some general questions such as: which items would save energy and which are alternative sources of energy? Do you have any of these things in your house? Why do you think that there is so much interest in saving energy these days? Establish that rising energy costs and concerns for the environment can both drive people to think about the way they use energy.

Task 1

Look at the information about loft insulation. What do you notice about the information that is given? Roughly how long would it take for the savings in costs to repay the cost of installing the insulation? Discuss how figures for items such as this are often given as ranges, as the actual figure will vary from house to house depending on its size, type and construction. Do you think that is a reasonable time in which to recoup the cost? What will happen for every year after that? Now look at the information for the A rated boiler and ask similar questions. The payback time is considerably longer. Discuss whether this is cost effective by asking questions such as if you have a perfectly good working boiler at the moment, do you think that it would be worth paying to have it changed for a new one? If you needed to change your current boiler, would it be worth having an A rated boiler as the replacement?

Task 2

Work through the section about the solar panels. When discussing answers, ensure that students comment on the fact that the payback time might shorten due to the electricity costs of supplied electricity increasing over time thereby increasing the annual savings.

Task 3

Look at the information about the energy efficient light bulbs. The students are guided through the working for both types of bulb using a series of estimates. Is there another way to save money when considering lighting the home? (Turn off the lights!)

Answers

1. **a** Loft insulation: 1.75 years; Lagging hot water tank: 0.4 years; Boiler: 13.3 years; Controls: 3 years; Heat pump: 15 years; Double glazing: 35 years: Draught proofing: 2.4 years; Cavity wall insulation: 1.75 years; Solar panels: 50 years; Wind generator: 20 years; Solar heating: 50 years.

   b **i** Lagging hot water tank, loft insulation, cavity wall insulation.

   ii Double glazing, efficient boiler, heat pump.

   c More likely to buy expensive items like solar panels if you intend to stay longer. May not see the benefit, could increase the value of house.

2. **a** 4 panels

   b £24 000

   c 50 years

3. **a** **i** 4–5 hours/day   **ii** 1500 hours/year

   b **i** 10 years   **ii** 8 months

   c 4 years

   Students' estimates may vary.

4 Fractions, decimals and percentages

Learning outcomes

N2 Order positive and negative integers, decimals and fractions; use the number line as a model for ordering of the real numbers; use the symbols =, ≠, <, >, ≤, ≥ (L5)

N4 Use the 4 operations, including formal written methods, applied to integers, decimals, proper and improper fractions, and mixed numbers, all both positive and negative (L6)

N9 Work interchangeably with terminating decimals and their corresponding fractions (such as 3.5 and 7/2 or 0.375 and 3/8 (L5)

N10 Define percentage as 'number of parts per hundred', interpret percentages and percentage changes as a fraction or a decimal, interpret these multiplicatively, express one quantity as a percentage of another, compare two quantities using percentages, and work with percentages greater than 100% (L6)

Introduction

The chapter starts by looking at ordering decimals and sorting decimals into class intervals, including inequality notation. It covers conversions between (terminating) decimals, fractions and percentages using a variety of methods. Then calculating fractions and percentages of an amount and writing one amount as a fraction or percentage of another amount.

The introduction discusses places where fractions are used in everyday life. For example, one penny is one-hundredth of a pound and in telling the time one might say a quarter (of an hour) to four O'clock or half (an hour) past one O'clock. Up until 1984 halfpenny coins were legal tender and in pre-decimal currency a farthing – quarter penny – was used until 1960. Earlier coins included a half-farthing and a quarter-farthing.

It may be interesting to review the fractions that arise due to our units of time and money. A day is a seventh of a week, and hour a twenty-fourth of a day, a minute a sixtieth of an hour and a second a sixtieth of a minute. A shilling is a twentieth of a pound and a penny a fifth of a schilling. In pre-decimal currency a pound contained twenty shillings and a shilling contained 12 pence, so 240 pence in a pound.

The pupils should be able to think of lots of real-life examples of where you use fractions. You could begin to collect their responses and discuss which ones are numbers and which ones are expressions of proportion.

NCTEM have produced a booklet on fractions which you might find useful.

https://www.ncetm.org.uk/public/files/257666/fractions_boo klet.pdf

Prior knowledge

Students should already know how to...

- Interpret place notation for decimals
- Carry basic arithmetic including division

Starter problem

This is likely to be a challenging problem for students and introduces the concept of percentage increase. It can be approached in stages: reviewing fractions and percentages and how to calculate a percentage increase by finding the percentage and adding this to the amount (rather than use a single multiplier).

The interest is £1800, which is greater than the repayment so the debt grows. This is because 15% > 1200/12 000 = 1/10. Encourage students to investigate making larger repayments (or lowering the interest rate) so that Andy starts to pay off the capital. This could naturally be done using a spreadsheet. How much has Andy repaid after three years? How much is left to repay; what fraction of the original £12 000 is this? How long will it take to clear the debt?

There is scope to discuss financial management and the idea of a repayment scheme such as hire-purchase or a mortgage. What advice would the students give to Andy? How would they handle the situation? You could add complications by discussing what happens if he sells the car, which brings in the idea of depreciation.

Resources

MyMaths

Fractions, decimals and percentages 2	1015	Fractions to decimals	1016
Adding subtracting fractions	1017	Fractions of amounts	1018
Fractions, decimals and percentages 1	1029	Percentages of amounts 2	1031
Ordering decimals	1072		

Online assessment

Chapter test	2B–4
Formative test	2B–4
Summative test	2B–4

InvisiPen solutions

Place value	111	Fractions of amounts	142
Adding and subtracting fractions			145
Fractions and decimals			161
Percentages, fractions and decimals			162

Topic scheme

Teaching time = 6 lessons/2 weeks

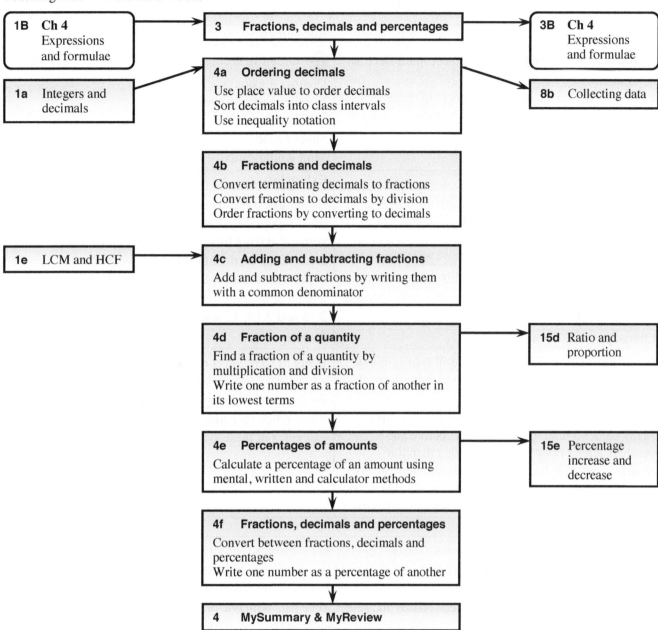

1B   Ch 4
Expressions and formulae

1a   Integers and decimals

3   **Fractions, decimals and percentages**

3B   Ch 4
Expressions and formulae

8b   Collecting data

4a   Ordering decimals
Use place value to order decimals
Sort decimals into class intervals
Use inequality notation

4b   Fractions and decimals
Convert terminating decimals to fractions
Convert fractions to decimals by division
Order fractions by converting to decimals

1e   LCM and HCF

4c   Adding and subtracting fractions
Add and subtract fractions by writing them with a common denominator

4d   Fraction of a quantity
Find a fraction of a quantity by multiplication and division
Write one number as a fraction of another in its lowest terms

15d Ratio and proportion

4e   Percentages of amounts
Calculate a percentage of an amount using mental, written and calculator methods

15e Percentage increase and decrease

4f   Fractions, decimals and percentages
Convert between fractions, decimals and percentages
Write one number as a percentage of another

4   MySummary & MyReview

Differentiation

Student book 2A 66 – 85	**Student book 2B** 60 – 77	**Student book 2C** 66 – 83
Fractions	Ordering decimals	Fractions and decimals
Fractions and decimals	Fractions and decimals	Adding and subtracting fractions
Adding and subtracting fractions	Adding and subtracting fractions	Multiplying and dividing fractions
Fraction of a quantity	Fraction of a quantity	Percentage change
Finding 10 percent	Percentages of amounts	Percentage problems
Percentages	Fractions, decimals and percentages	Fractions, decimals and percentages
Fractions, decimals and percentages		

Objectives

- Understand and use decimal notation and place value (L4)
- Order decimals (L4)

Key ideas	Resources
1 Know the fractional values of places in the decimal system 2 Confidently place decimal numbers in order	Ordering decimals (1072) Diennes apparatus Number partition cards Number lines Sheet music Mini whiteboards

Simplification	Extension
Some students will be challenged with the ordering task and may well need additional practice to consolidate place value in whole numbers – it will be helpful to use more examples such as asking how eleven units should be written. Visual images such as number lines, partitioning cards and Diennes apparatus will support these students.	Encourage more able students to spend additional time on grouping data that includes decimal values – perhaps making links to how this may be used in other areas of the curriculum, particularly in science experiments. Students could also be challenged to find a number halfway between two decimals: 6.7 and 6.8, 2.18 and 2.19, 3.7 and 3.76.

Literacy	Links
Make the notation clear and include all four symbols <, ≤ and >, ≥. Use the Links section to help secure the meanings. Make sure that students read number values correctly. Many students tend to read numbers before and numbers after a point separately rather than the complete number. For example, they should read 'five point two seven' and not 'five point twenty seven', as the word twenty refers to the place value of 2 in tens.	Bring in some sheet music for the class to use. The inequality signs are similar to the musical symbols *crescendo* (becoming louder) and *decrescendo* or *diminuendo* (becoming softer). Ask the class to find examples of these symbols on the music.

Alternative approach

Students should already be familiar with the concepts in this section, so activity here needs to expose and rehearse the students' prior knowledge as well as correct any misconceptions students may have. Begin with a simple ordering activity in pairs using mini whiteboards. For example, ask students to order these values: 2.7; 2.07, 2; 2.078, 2.27, 2.268. Check boards and select some lists with one or two errors to share with the group for discussion. Delve into one or two possible areas by widening the discussion if necessary, for example: which is bigger, 2.07 or 2.078, and why? Or which is bigger, 2.27 or 2.268 and why? Pairs of students should be encouraged to share and hone their explanations before then picking some key pairs for sharing with the group. Using number lines and/or Diennes apparatus may help to support the students' reasoning. Groups of 3 or 4 students can play The Nasty Game, where a grid with unit, tenths, hundredths and thousandths columns is completed in turn using the roll of dice to place numbers *anywhere*. Each row, however, is 'owned' by one of the students. The student who wins will be the student whose final number is, for example, the largest or the smallest or the closest to five, and so on. This game is easily differentiated for each ability group. A further class activity can be used where every student has to add 0.05 to the previous spoken number, speed and fluency being encouraged and perhaps supported with the use of a number line or counting stick.

Checkpoint

1 What does the value 7 represent in the number 3.478? (seven hundredths or 0.07)

2 How do you know that 3.05 is bigger than 3.048?

(Any appropriate explanation with or without apparatus/visual support.)

Starter – Decimal grid

Write 9 decimal numbers in a 3 × 3 grid. Ask students to find

- the sum of the top row
- the product of the top left number and bottom right number
- the difference between the middle left and middle right numbers, etc.

This can be differentiated by the number of decimal places in the chosen numbers.

Teaching notes

Use an initial classroom discussion to assess students' prior knowledge of place value in whole numbers. Then invite students to explain how to write 45 hundredths as a decimal. Emphasise that

$$\frac{45}{100} = \frac{40}{100} + \frac{5}{100} = \frac{4}{10} + \frac{5}{100}$$ and that the 4 goes in the tenths column and the 5 in the hundredths column: the diagram supplied should help to make this clear.

The comparison of decimals causes difficulty through KS3 and into KS4, so it is important that the basic understanding is secure. Using a diagram with columns labelled tenths (t), hundredths (h), thousandths (th), etc. will help students correctly order decimals. An *aide-memoire* for the inequality signs is 'the narrower end always points to the smaller number'. Ensure students have the opportunity to discuss the common misconception that a number with more digits is bigger, or a larger digit is always worth more than a smaller digit (0.10, 0.09) linking this to the use of columns.

The second example and question **6**, involving class intervals, can both be done as whole class activities and provide the opportunity to clear up any misconceptions and consolidate understanding in a real-life context.

Plenary

Invite students to challenge each other by asking them to generate a set of decimals to be either ordered or grouped (according to their ability) and to swap with a friend and check that they agree or debate where they disagree. This activity offers an opportunity for students to support their conclusions, using reasoned arguments.

Exercise commentary

The exercise allows opportunities for paired discussion to encourage the development of mathematical language and to open up debate where there are misconceptions.

Question 1 – Could be done as a whole class oral activity to promote dialogue and debate. The meaning of 'as a fraction where appropriate' may need clarifying.

Question 2 – Similar to example one. Students could work in pairs and be asked to explain how they know which answer is largest.

Question 3 – Suggest students check with and justify answers to a partner.

Question 4 – Ask students to explain why it is important to use consistent units.

Question 5 – Similar to example two. Ask students to explain why some numbers are harder to place than others.

Question 6 – Emphasise the link between students' maths and real-life scenarios. Students could be encouraged to suggest their own ideas for data collection.

Question 7 – A number line may help students visualise this question.

Question 8 – Check students read the inequality signs carefully. Again a number line may be useful.

Answers

1. a 700 b 7000 c 70 d 700 000
    e 700 000 f 7 g $\frac{7}{10}$ h $\frac{7}{1000}$
2. a < b > c <
    d > e > f <
3. a 3, 3.23, 3.3, 3.39, 3.4
    b 3.72, 3.74, 3.757, 3.8, 3.88
    c 0.03, 0.033, 0.035, 0.0351, 0.0362
4. a < b > c < d >
5.

Height h (metres)	Frequency
$1.3 \leq h < 1.4$	3
$1.4 \leq h < 1.5$	4
$1.5 \leq h < 1.6$	5
$1.6 \leq h < 1.7$	5
$1.7 \leq h < 1.8$	3

Numbers most difficult to place are those on the boundaries.

6. Group work, multiple answers are possible.
7. a $x = 5.8$ b $y = 0.45$
8. $5 \leq x \leq 7$

4b Fractions and decimals

Objectives	
• Convert terminating decimals to fractions	(L5)
• Use division to convert a fraction to a decimal	(L5)
• Order fractions by converting them to decimals	(L5)

Key ideas	Resources	
1 Know that, for example, 3/7 means $3 \div 7$ 2 To recognise the equivalence of fractions, decimals and percentages, and have strategies to move across these forms	Fractions to decimals Scientific calculators	(1016)

Simplification	Extension
Provide simple examples to support understanding of how to cancel down fractions and how to carry out short division, as used in converting fractions to decimals.	Give examples that include mixed numbers or that include the equivalence of percentages for comparison and ordering. Further exploration of fractions using Egyptian themes: http://nrich.maths.org/1173

Literacy	Links
All the language used here is that of proportional reasoning and it is very helpful for students to be encouraged to use equivalent statements as frequently as possible, and then to be able to state whether a value is a vulgar fraction, a decimal fraction or a percentage. Emphasise the division symbol in the fractional notation, and encourage students to read, say, 2/3 as 'two thirds' and also 'two divided by 3'.	The Ancient Egyptians represented all their fractions as Egyptian fractions. An Egyptian fraction is the sum of a number of unit fractions, where all the unit fractions are different. All positive rational numbers can be represented by Egyptian fractions. More information about Egyptian fractions, including a calculator to convert a fraction to an Egyptian fraction can be found at http://www.mcs.surrey.ac.uk/Personal/R.Knott/Fractions/egyptian.html

Alternative approach

Again, none of the concepts will be new to students in this section, so begin by asking students to complete some equivalent lists on their whiteboards such as $\frac{1}{2} = 0.5 = 50\%$. This will also help you to assess the general number knowledge of the students. Using four digits of their own choice, ask students to make up several fractions, for example 1, 2, 3 will produce 1/1, 1/2, 1/3, 2/1, 2/2, 2/3, 3/1, 3/2, 3/3. (How many will possible? Why?) Students should now group their results into three: those less than one, those equal to one and those greater than one. (Explore the vocabulary, how do we know which groups?) Finally ask students to place the 'less than one' group of fractions in order, discussing the variety of approaches that might be taken by students to do this. Give sufficient thinking time here before opening this discussion. Approaches may involve simple size reasoning, equivalence statements using known percentage or decimal links, using number lines, drawing denominator/numerator graphs and calculators.

Further exploration using the equivalent decimal/fraction fractions of the calculator are also good activities for students to undertake, introducing them to further possibilities of a calculator.

Checkpoint	
1 Write 2.35 as a value using fractions.	$(2\frac{7}{20})$
2 Write 7/8 as a decimal.	(0.875)

Starter – Sums and products

Challenge students to find two numbers

with a sum of 8.9 and a product of 7.2 (0.9, 8)

with a sum of 1.1 and a product of 0.24 (0.3, 0.8)

with a sum of 0.75 and a product of 0.035 (0.05, 0.7)

with a sum of 1.3 and a product of 0.42 (0.6, 0.7).

Teaching notes

Prepare students for this work by making links to their prior learning with a brief recapitulation of the associated vocabulary. Ensure students know and understand terms such as numerator, denominator and discuss terminating and recurring decimals.

In the first example, attention should be drawn to the need to cancel down fractions to their simplest form. Students could be invited to generate examples (for which they have an answer) that can be set as challenges for the class to simplify. When converting from fractions to decimals, students should be encouraged to discuss whether mental, written or calculator methods are most efficient (Key Process for number). They should be discouraged from saying 'calculator' as a default response.

The second example covers an important skill used throughout KS3 and KS4 and is a Key Indicator for level 6. A careful approach should be adopted as it brings together a number of skills. Rather than converting to decimals, an alternative approach is to rewrite the fractions with a common denominator.

Plenary

Provide an example for ordering that includes both fractions and decimals. Ask students to check the reasonableness of their answer by sketching a diagram of the number line.

Exercise commentary

Question 1 – The meaning of terminating and recurring may need to be reiterated.

Question 2 – Similar to the first example. The second step, simplifying the fraction, may need additional support.

Question 3 – Consider getting students to work in pairs to support one another and explain their working, perhaps working on alternate parts.

Question 4 – A question to focus on as it requires an important skill and combines several ideas from this section and **4a**.

Question 5 – Similar to the second example.

Question 6 and **7** – How to handle mixed numbers may need explanation/discussion.

Question 8 – This can be done in pairs or small groups. Emphasise the need for students to clearly explain their findings.

Answers

1 **a, d, e**

2 a $\frac{3}{10}$ b $\frac{3}{5}$ c $\frac{3}{4}$ d $\frac{7}{25}$

e $\frac{33}{50}$ f $\frac{1}{20}$ g $\frac{3}{8}$ h $\frac{37}{200}$

i $\frac{19}{200}$ j $\frac{1}{125}$

3 a 0.1 b 0.65 c 0.28 d 0.66

e 0.6 f 0.6 g 0.95 h 0.75

i 0.7 j 0.22

4 a > b > c > d >

e < f < g > h >

5 a $\frac{3}{7}, \frac{3}{4}, \frac{4}{5}, \frac{7}{8}$ b $\frac{4}{19}, \frac{2}{9}, \frac{3}{13}, \frac{1}{3}$

c $\frac{2}{5}, \frac{7}{16}, \frac{4}{9}, \frac{9}{20}$

6 a $1\frac{1}{2}$ b $2\frac{3}{4}$ c $3\frac{2}{5}$ d $1\frac{7}{20}$

e $1\frac{19}{40}$ f $2\frac{21}{40}$

7 a 1.7 b 1.75 c 1.35 d 2.3125

e 3.44 f 4.325

8 He is not correct, as denominators of 8, 16 will also give terminating decimals.

Objectives	
• Identify equivalent fractions	(L5)
• Add and subtract fractions by writing them with a common denominator	(L6)

Key ideas	Resources
1 Have a clear sense of the many ways that a fraction may be recorded 2 Apply addition and subtraction principals to fractions	Adding subtracting fractions (1017) Squared paper Mini whiteboards

Simplification	Extension
Provide examples showing how to find lowest common multiples and develop this into the addition of simple fractions requiring a common denominator. Encourage the use of diagrams such as in question **3** to support understanding of the method being used to add and subtract fractions.	Set questions involving addition and subtraction of mixed numbers or three fractions. Use The Greedy Algorithm activity found at: http://nrich.maths.org/6541

Literacy	Links
Reading problems out loud should be encouraged as this helps to avoid .some major misconceptions. For example, 1/5 + 3/5 should be read as 'one fifth add three fifths' and not 'one over five add...'.	In chemistry, a fraction is a mixture of liquids with similar boiling points. The fractions in crude oil have individual names, (for example, diesel, kerosene, petrol) and have different properties and uses. They are separated using a fractionating column. There is more information at http://www.bbc.co.uk/schools/gcsebitesize/science/edexcel/oneearth/fuelsrev2.shtml

Alternative approach
As a fraction of a quantity is an easier concept to grasp, an alternative approach would be to tackle section **4d** before section **4c** establishing some of the language and building confidence when handling fractions work. Begin by asking students to respond to simple oral questions using mini whiteboards, such as what is half of...? Use a variety of quantities with units and a variety of simple fractions, prompting students to also give the equivalent percentage or decimal. Go on to explore the recording of these types of problems, to establish clear links between the written requirements and outcomes. Apply 'amounts of' spider diagrams for consolidation, making sure to include decimals and percentage as well as 'fractions of' arms. Include using such a diagram for reversing the process as well, so that an arm for example gives a proportional amount of the centre, requiring the student to say what the proportion is, as a vulgar fraction, decimal fraction or a percentage. Use checkpoint **4d** if reversing the order.

Checkpoint

1 $1\frac{7}{8} - \frac{3}{4}$ $\hspace{3cm}$ ($1\frac{1}{8}$)

2 An answer to the question: $\frac{3}{5} + \frac{3}{8}$ is given as $\frac{6}{13}$. Explain why this is wrong.

(Any appropriate explanation showing that the answer does not make sense and pointing towards the use of equivalent fractions with a common denominator.)

Starter – Dice fractions

Ask students to draw six boxes representing the numerators and denominators of three fractions side by side.

Throw a dice six times. After each throw, ask students to place the score in one of their boxes.

Students score points if the first fraction is bigger than the second fraction which in turn is bigger than the third fraction.

Teaching notes

A precursor to being able to add/subtract fractions is the ability to find equivalent fractions and to identify a suitable (lowest) common denominator. Taking time to make sure students can multiply up/cancel down fractions and find lowest common denominators will allow them to focus on the essentials of adding two fractions.

To help understand the mechanics of adding fractions the visual approach used in the first example and question **3** is likely to be very valuable. Students should be encouraged to suggest their own examples using diagrams.

A common mistake is to add both numerator and denominator. Tackle this misconception with a simple example: clearly $\frac{1}{2} + \frac{1}{2} = 1$ but the 'wrong' method would give $\frac{1+1}{2+2} = \frac{2}{4} = \frac{1}{2}$ which leads to the absurdity $1 = \frac{1}{2}$. Another more careless mistake is to forget whether the calculation calls for an addition or a subtraction.

Plenary

Provide a word problem similar to the last question in the exercise and ask students to identify the key information and the mathematics required to answer it. The strengthening of literacy skills in this way is important for developing students' understanding and capacity to be functional in mathematics.

Exercise commentary

Question 1 – Links to work on cancelling down. Ask students to 'Explain how you did this'.

Question 2 – Similar to the first example. Check students add or subtract appropriately.

Question 3 – This approach provides both understanding and a good 'fall back' method.

Question 4 – Similar to the second example. Encourage students to discuss what the best denominator to use is.

Question 5 – An example of more functional maths. Literacy skills, rather than mathematical competency, may be an issue in this word problem. Suggest students work in pairs in order to help identify key information and the maths to use.

Question 6 – Focuses on a common misconception. Detailed explanations should be given and this could be discussed as a class or in pairs/small groups.

Answers

1	a	3	b	10	c	12	d	28
	e	72	f	48	g	21	h	80

2	a	$\frac{5}{7}$	b	$\frac{3}{4}$	c	$\frac{3}{5}$	d	$\frac{1}{4}$
	e	$\frac{8}{11}$	f	$\frac{3}{13}$	g	$\frac{4}{3}$ or $1\frac{1}{3}$	h	$\frac{4}{5}$
	i	1	j	$\frac{2}{3}$	k	$\frac{3}{5}$	l	$\frac{1}{2}$
	m	$\frac{2}{3}$	n	$\frac{1}{5}$	o	$\frac{3}{7}$	p	$\frac{1}{17}$

3	a	$\frac{7}{10}$	b	$\frac{11}{12}$	c	$\frac{11}{15}$		

4	a	$\frac{7}{12}$	b	$\frac{13}{15}$	c	$\frac{11}{30}$	d	$\frac{11}{15}$
	e	$\frac{23}{24}$	f	$\frac{19}{30}$	g	$\frac{13}{45}$	h	$\frac{5}{33}$

5 $\frac{7}{20}$

6 a She has just added the tops and the bottoms, and has not used a common denominator

 b Because $\frac{4}{7}$ is more than $\frac{1}{2}$

 c $\frac{50}{63}$

4d Fraction of a quantity

Objectives	
• Calculate fractions of quantities (fraction answers)	(L6)
• Multiply an integer by a fraction	(L6)
• Express a smaller whole number as a fraction of a larger one	(L5)

Key ideas	Resources	
1 To find fractions of a quantity	Fractions of amounts	(1018)
	Mini white boards	
	World atlas	

Simplification	Extension
Provide simple examples designed to develop and reinforce students' confidence in applying mental strategies, beginning with unit fractions.	More able students can be given a variety of examples and be asked to identify and then justify which calculation method they would use to find a solution.

Literacy	Links
Students can struggle here with the recorded problem while confidently able to give verbal responses to oral problems. For this reason it is important to address how to say or read these problems, prompting students to say or read out loud such questions for each other. Make sure that the 'of' word in such problems is linked to the operation of multiply, and also explicitly show equivalence of order, for example ¾ × £20 is the same as £20 × ¾.	Use an atlas to show Sierra Leone on the West Coast of Africa. The country has a lush tropical climate and is rich in diamonds but is still recovering from a bitter civil war which ended in 2002. During the war, over 2M people left their homes. If the population of Sierra Leone is around 6M, what fraction is this? There is more information about Sierra Leone at https://www.cia.gov/library/publications/the-world-factbook/geos/sl.html

Alternative approach
If the order **4c** and **4d** has been reversed, then tackling addition and subtraction can now take place, starting by requesting that students provide a diagram to illustrate a simple question such as ¾ + ½. The emphasis here is not on the solution, but the images that students use to help them tackle such problems. Share different responses and ask the students to explain where relevant. 'Pizza' or circle images are quite common, but are not necessarily a helpful image, so alternatives such as number lines, rectangles or 'chocolate' bars are worth sharing. Equivalent spider diagrams with any fraction in the centre will remind students. That any fraction can be written in a different way, including percentage and decimal equivalents. Use checkpoint 4c if reversing the order.

Checkpoint	
1 Find 4/7 of £749.	(£428)
2 What proportion of 250 kg is 50 kg?	(1/5 or 20% or 0.2)

Starter – Fraction sort

Write the following fractions on the board.

$$\frac{14}{49}, \frac{2}{12}, \frac{7}{42}, \frac{18}{30}, \frac{2}{7}, \frac{4}{24}, \frac{3}{5}, \frac{6}{21}, \frac{1}{6}, \frac{24}{40}, \frac{4}{14}, \frac{15}{25}$$

Ask students to sort the fractions into three sets of equivalent fractions. This can be extended by asking students to make up their own fraction sort puzzle.

Teaching notes

The spread places an emphasis on using mental calculation strategies. Using mini whiteboards challenge the class to write down the answer to simple 'fraction of an amount' problems, beginning with unit fractions. Ask successful students to share the methods they used to do the calculations until you have built up a battery of suitable tricks. For example, $\frac{1}{5} = 2 \times \frac{1}{10}$, $\frac{1}{4} = \frac{1}{2} \times \frac{1}{2}$, $\frac{1}{6} = \frac{1}{2} \times \frac{1}{3}$, etc. An alternative way to approach the same topic is to use a spider diagram with, say, 450 in the middle and various fractions of this number surrounding it.

As necessary, it may help to recapitulate how to convert improper fractions into mixed numbers, as in the first example, and how to cancel down a fraction, as in the second example. Students can also be reminded of the connection between fractions and division.

It may also help to give an example which can be done using mental, written and calculator methods. Ask students which is the best method in a given case and how the answers can be checked.

Plenary

Ask students to identify two things they can do now that they were unable to do at the start of the unit and one thing that they are still unclear about. Use this to inform further teaching. This activity also encourages students to review their own progress and act on the outcome.

Exercise commentary

Encourage students to use mental, written and calculator methods as part of their strategy for checking answers. Also emphasise the functional aspects of maths being used in the real life contexts.

Question 1 – Similar to the first example. In parts **e** and **f** beware of students still using unit fractions.

Questions 2 and **3** – Similar to the first example. A discussion of how to change an improper fraction to a mixed number and then simplifying may be helpful here.

Question 4 – Here students may need to revisit converting a fraction to a decimal and to discuss rounding to a given number of decimal places.

Question 5 – Students should be encouraged to pause to identify the important information and what they need to calculate.

Question 6 – Similar to the second example. Ask able students to generate their own real life questions with which to challenge a partner.

Question 7 – A question in context which combines the two key ideas.

Question 8 – This could be done as a paired activity. In part **b** check that students know to calculate 11/10 of the new height 66 ft (not 60 ft).

Answers

1	a	£5	b	5 MB	c	4 DVDs	
	d	5 pupils	e	20 shops	f	80 g	
2	a	$\frac{4}{9}$	b	$\frac{1}{2}$	c	$\frac{2}{3}$	d $1\frac{1}{3}$
	e	$1\frac{3}{4}$	f	$3\frac{1}{3}$			
3	a	$5\frac{1}{4}$ feet	b	$9\frac{1}{3}$ million	c	$18\frac{3}{4}$ km	
	d	120 kg	e	$17\frac{6}{7}$ m	f	$11\frac{1}{5}$ mm	
4	a	88.8 kg	b	£122.92	c	6.82 km	
	d	2.86 kg	e	88.89 litres	f	54°	
5	a	£9.07	b	$\frac{9}{14}$			
6	a	$\frac{2}{5}$	b	$\frac{11}{12}$	c	$\frac{2}{3}$	d $\frac{7}{31}$
7	a	i 28	ii	21			
	b	35	c	$\frac{5}{12}$			
8	a	66 feet	b	72.6 feet	c	6 years	

4e Percentages of amounts

Objectives

- Recognise the equivalence of percentages, fractions and decimals   (L5)
- Express one given number as a percentage of another   (L6)
- Calculate percentages   (L5)

Key ideas	Resources
1 Confidently use mental strategies to find simple percentages 2 Understand the proportional vocabulary and the equivalence of fractions, decimals and percentages	Percentages of amounts 2 (1031) Scientific calculators Fraction & percentage card game from: http://nrich.maths.org/2739

Simplification	Extension
Students who struggle with calculating percentages could be given more opportunity to develop mental methods. Mental strategies are essential for full understanding and are an excellent checking strategy for all abilities.	More able students could be challenged to find as many different ways of finding a mental solution to a given problem as possible (for example, how many different ways are there of finding 65%?) and could be offered further challenge by being asked to solve increasingly difficult word problems, always being required to explain their thinking. Encourage further flexible use of number properties by exploring for example 16% of £25 as equivalent to 25% of £16.

Literacy	Links
Make the link that the word 'of' relates to the operation of multiplication, reinforcing earlier work with this word involving fractions. Students will often overlook this verbal clue because 'parts of' are being found in these types of problems, which are often linked to divide rather than multiply.	Crisps are made from slices of potato fried in oil. The amount of fat absorbed during frying depends on the kind of oil used and the temperature. Manufacturers have lowered the amount of saturated fat in the crisps. by using different oils A typical 35 g bag of crisps still contains about 2.5 teaspoons of oil. How many teaspoons of oil will you consume if you eat one bag of crisps every day for a month?

Alternative approach

Students will already have some mental skills for finding simple percentages, so use this as a starting point by requesting that groups of three students work on an advice sheet for younger students on doing just this. Share the key strategies that arise with the whole group for discussion, and make links to the equivalent proportional terms of both vulgar and decimal fractions. Extend the challenge by asking students to find less common percentages such as 37%, and how this might be achieved efficiently with the help of a calculator. Ask pairs of students what does the % do? Share key points arising with the whole group. Pairs or three may go on to explore and develop advice about using a calculator. The use of a calculator provides a strong natural link of percentage with decimals.

The fraction and percentage card game from nrich provides further practice at finding proportional amounts.

Checkpoint

1 Find 35% of 60 km, without a calculator.   (21 km, for example, 15 km + 6 km, or 3 × 6 km + 3 km)

2 Calculate 72% of £238.   (£171.36)

3 A test result is 24 out of 40, what is this as a percentage?   (60%)

Starter – Half-way fractions

Ask students to find the fraction that is half-way between $\frac{1}{3}$ and $\frac{2}{3}$, $\frac{3}{5}$ and $\frac{7}{10}$, $\frac{3}{8}$ and $\frac{1}{2}$.

Answers: $\frac{1}{2}$, $\frac{13}{20}$, $\frac{7}{16}$

This can be extended by asking for other fractions in the given ranges.

Teaching notes

To assess and develop students' mental methods draw a spider diagram with centre labelled 100% and surrounding bubbles labelled 10%, 20%, 5%, 1%, etc. Supply a value for the central bubble, say 280, and invite students to find the values that should go in the surrounding bubbles (28, 56, 14, 2.8). The surrounding percentages can be made harder as students gain in confidence: 43%, 2.5%, 1.5%, 17.5%, etc. This will allow students to take responsibility, showing confidence in themselves and their contribution.

The examples given can be used to provide templates for how written solutions should be laid out.

All of these questions can be approached in different ways, based on fraction-decimal-percentage equivalences, and computed using mental, written and calculator methods. Students should be encouraged to try different approaches and once confidence is gained the efficiency of the various approaches discussed.

It may be necessary to devote time to discussing questions like questions **5** and **6** where language may be an issue and it is necessary to identify relevant information.

Plenary

Ask students to write a word problem that involves calculating a percentage in an everyday situation. Use question **5** from the exercise as a model. Take a few examples that students have generated and consider using them as starter activities next lesson.

Exercise commentary

Questions can be answered using a variety of methods: encourage students to compare methods and gain confidence in their ability to use a range of strategies.

Question 1 – Ask students to write a sentence explaining how they obtained their answers: for example '50% means half, so I divided by 2'.

Question 2 – Similar to the first example. Encourage pairs of students to compare their methods and invent new ones: 5% = 1/10 × 50% versus 1/2 × 10% or 5 × 1%, etc.

Question 3 – Similar to the second example. Written methods should be carefully laid out.

Question 4 – Students may need reminding how to round and why it is appropriate.

Question 5 – Students may need guidance extracting the relevant information and deciding what to calculate.

Question 6 – This could form the basis of a group-based project in which students investigate other foods and report their findings to the class via a presentation or display.

Answers

1	**a**	£35	**b**	4.5 kg	**c**	15 m	**d**	64 MB
	e	£10	**f**	10 cm	**g**	42 kg	**h**	19 m
2	**a**	£8	**b**	3 DVDs	**c**	3 MB	**d**	£30
	e	£420	**f**	27°	**g**	£605	**h**	75 N
	i	19.2 ml	**j**	£7000	**k**	286 yards	**l**	380 kJ
3	**a**	£7.20	**b**	4.97 kg	**c**	6.38 km		
	d	€13.6	**e**	2.25 mm	**f**	13.2 kB		
	g	5.22 litres	**h**	32.2 mph	**i**	21.16 m		
	j	44.1 MB	**k**	9.45 cm	**l**	69.3°		
4	**a**	£17.76	**b**	33.6 kg	**c**	266.24 MB		
	d	305.3 km	**e**	7.4 mm	**f**	231 ml		
	g	£20	**h**	434.75 g	**i**	6 N		
	j	£3280	**k**	613.2 kJ	**l**	5.5 million		
5	**a**	54	**b**	5.2 GB	**c**	9 g	**d**	27
6	**a**	Sugar 12 g, fat 0.48 g, protein 11.76 g, carbohydrates 31.2 g						
	b	184.56 g						

4f Fractions, decimals and percentages

Objectives	
• Recognise the equivalence of percentages, fractions and decimals	(L5)
• Express one given number as a percentage of another	(L5)

Key ideas	Resources	
1 Understand the proportional vocabulary and the equivalence of fractions, decimals and percentages 2 Recognise that an amount can be expressed as a percentage of another amount	Frac dec perc 2	(1015)
	Frac dec perc 1	(1029)
	Newspapers and magazines	
	Matching fractions, decimals and percentage game:	
	http://nrich.maths.org/1249	

Simplification	Extension
As a confidence building exercise ask students to complete a fraction-decimal-percentage table containing entries which involve straightforward conversions. They could also choose their own values.	More able students could create a PowerPoint presentation showing how to convert between fractions, decimals and percentages, which could be made available on the school website for students having difficulty with this topic.

Literacy	Links
Using the Links activity, perhaps even as homework, will emphasise how important a form of communication the ideas in this chapter are.	Bring in some newspapers or magazines. Ask students to find any article or advertisement where a decimal, percentage or fraction is used. Which format is used most frequently? Would the article or advertisement have the same effect if, for example, a decimal was used in place of a percentage, or a percentage in place of a fraction? Are there any examples where a conversion has been used?

Alternative approach
Take the opportunity to ensure that students are reasonably confident at finding and recognising amounts as a fraction or percentage of another amount. This can be done by preparing cards with a variety of '– out of –' values together with percentage values and fraction values. Ask students to group equivalent values together. If one card is included with no other group members, then students can be requested to seek the 'odd one out', which gives a quick check method for the whole group. A further challenge can both check and extend this chapter's concepts in the form of the question; 'Does it matter what order a % discount and an additional % tax is applied to, say, a bill for a meal?'

Checkpoint	
1 Give the decimal and percentage equivalent of 4/5.	(0.8, 80%)
2 If 30 out of 40 families have a pet, express this as a percentage.	(75%)

Starter – Percentage bingo

Ask students to draw a 3 × 3 grid and enter nine amounts from the following list:

£2 £3 £4 £5 £6 £7 £8 £9 £10 £11 £12 £13 £14 £15 £16 £17

Give questions, for example, 36% of £25, 68% of £25, 44% of £25.

The winner is the first student to cross out all nine amounts. (Hint: 36% of 25 = 25% of 36.)

See also the plenary spread **4e.**

Teaching notes

Students are required to synthesise a large amount of information on various methods and approaches.

Begin by giving a number of worked examples that illustrate the different techniques, their inter-connections, relative merits and how to check calculations. Then ask the class to supply 'helpful hints' on the important points they need to know. This could be developed as a homework activity to produce a poster showing a model worked example that is annotated with hints and explanations.

As the lesson progresses, it may be useful to collate a list of problematic questions and identify common mistakes. Classroom discussion could then be used to understand where the errors lie and to agree correct approaches.

Plenary

Invite students to refer back to the exercise and take a vote on what was found to be the hardest question (or part question). Model a solution to this and then set a similar challenge to 'try again'.

Exercise commentary

Question 1 – It may help students to understand what to do if the first two numbers are matched as a class.

Question 2 – Remind students to cancel. Parts **h**, **i** and **l** may require discussion of percentages ≥ 100%.

Question 3 – In parts **g** to **i** students may need to discuss 'fractional' percentages.

Questions 4 and **5** – Part **d** of question **4** and subsequent parts may require discussion of fractions > 1. Ask students how they might 'sensibly' round some answers.

Question 6 – Similar to the first example. Discuss rounding in part **i**.

Question 7 – Similar to the second example.

Question 8 – This exemplifies a practical and very relevant use of percentages.

Answers

1 **a** $35\% - \text{E}$ $0.8 - \text{C}$ $1\frac{1}{4} - \text{J}$ $60\% - \text{G}$
    $0.45 - \text{F}$ $0.1 - \text{A}$ $110\% - \text{I}$ $\frac{19}{20} - \text{D}$
    $\frac{3}{4} - \text{H}$ $\frac{1}{5} - \text{B}$

   b $\text{A} = 10\%, \frac{1}{10}, 0.1$ $\text{B} = 20\%, \frac{1}{5}, 0.2$

     $\text{C} = 80\%, \frac{4}{5}, 0.8$ $\text{D} = 95\%, \frac{19}{20}, 0.95$

     $\text{E} = 35\%, \frac{7}{20}, 0.35$ $\text{F} = 45\%, \frac{9}{20}, 0.45$

     $\text{G} = 60\%, \frac{3}{5}, 0.6$ $\text{H} = 75\%, \frac{3}{4}, 0.75$

     $\text{I} = 110\%, 1\frac{1}{10}, 1.1$ $\text{J} = 125\%, 1\frac{1}{4}, 1.25$

2 **a** $\frac{2}{5}$ **b** $\frac{3}{4}$ **c** $\frac{17}{20}$ **d** $\frac{9}{20}$

   e $\frac{8}{25}$ **f** $\frac{1}{20}$ **g** $\frac{1}{100}$ **h** $\frac{5}{4}$ or $1\frac{1}{4}$

   i $\frac{21}{20}$ or $1\frac{1}{20}$ **j** $\frac{1}{40}$ **k** $\frac{3}{20}$ **l** $\frac{7}{5}$ or $1\frac{2}{5}$

3 **a** 0.8   **b** 0.25   **c** 0.08   **d** 0.35

   e 0.99   **f** 1.3   **g** 0.235   **h** 0.072

   i 0.0475   **j** 1.45   **k** 1.5   **l** 1.75

4 **a** 30%   **b** 58%   **c** 56%   **d** 175%

   e 32.5%   **f** 160%   **g** 144%   **h** 115%

   i 117.5%   **j** 287.5%   **k** 320%   **l** 680%

5 **a** 56.3%   **b** 67.5%   **c** 68%   **d** 125%

   e 52%   **f** 87.5%   **g** 77.8%   **h** 135%

   i 83.3%   **j** 66.7%   **k** 11.1%   **l** 88.9%

6 **a** 58%   **b** 8%   **c** 80%   **d** 108%

   e 180%   **f** 3.5%   **g** 41.5%   **h** 105%

   i 155.5...%   **j** 99.9%   **k** 126%   **l** 302%

7 **a** 60%   **b** 60%

8 **a** Science as he got 77.5%

   b History as he got 68.6% (1 dp)

   c History, Geography, RE, English, French, Maths, Science

4 Fractions, decimals and percentages – MySummary

Key outcomes	Quick check
Understand, compare and order decimals. L4	Order these decimals, smallest to largest: $0.05, 0.005, 0.55, 0.055, 0.555$ $\qquad$ $(0.005, 0.05, 0.055, 0.55, 0.555)$
Convert between decimals, fractions and percentages. L5	Convert 0.55 to **a** a percentage (55%) **b** a fraction $(\frac{11}{20})$ Convert 24% to **a** a decimal (0.24) **b** a fraction $(\frac{6}{25})$
Order fractions. L5	Order these fractions, smallest to largest: $\frac{1}{2}, \frac{2}{3}, \frac{5}{7}, \frac{3}{8}$ $\qquad\qquad$ $(\frac{3}{8}, \frac{1}{2}, \frac{2}{3}, \frac{5}{7})$
Add and subtract fractions. L6	Calculate: **a** $\frac{1}{7} + \frac{2}{3}$ $(\frac{17}{21})$ $\qquad$ **b** $\frac{5}{8} - \frac{1}{3}$ $(\frac{7}{24})$
Find a fraction of a quantity. L6	What is $\frac{5}{6}$ of £132? $\qquad\qquad\qquad\qquad\qquad\qquad\qquad$ (£110)
Express one number as a fraction of another. L5	Express 40 as a fraction of 72. Give your answer in the simplest terms. $\qquad\qquad\qquad\qquad\qquad\qquad\qquad\qquad\qquad\qquad\qquad$ $(\frac{5}{9})$
Calculate percentages of amounts. L5	**a** Calculate 40% of 85 kg $\qquad\qquad\qquad\qquad\qquad\qquad$ (34 kg) **b** Calculate 36% of £821 $\qquad\qquad\qquad\qquad\qquad\qquad$ (£295.56)
Express one number as a percentage of another. L5	**a** What percentage of 120 is 54? $\qquad\qquad\qquad\qquad\qquad$ (45%) **b** What percentage of 25 is 16? $\qquad\qquad\qquad\qquad\qquad$ (64%)

⊕ MyMaths extra support

Lesson/online homework	Description
Percentages of amounts 1 1030 L4	Finding percentages of whole numbers including 10%, 25%, 75%
Finding fractions 1062 L5	Finding fractions of whole numbers
Simple equivalent fractions 1371 L4	Learning about equivalent fractions and decimals

4 MySummary

Check out
You should now be able to ...

Test it ➡
Questions

✓ Understand, compare and order decimals.	④	1, 11–13
✓ Convert between decimals, fractions and percentages.	⑤	2, 3
✓ Order fractions.	⑤	4
✓ Add and subtract fractions.	⑥	5
✓ Find a fraction of a quantity.	⑥	6, 7
✓ Express one number as a fraction of another.	⑤	8
✓ Calculate percentages of amounts.	⑤	9, 10
✓ Express one number as a percentage of another.	⑤	14

Language	Meaning	Example
Decimal	A number which has digits after the decimal point, representing tenths, hundredths, thousandths, etc	$1.27 = 1 + \frac{2}{10} + \frac{7}{100}$ is a decimal
Terminating decimal	A decimal which has a fixed number of decimal places	$0.125 = \frac{1}{8}$ has three decimal places
Recurring decimal	A decimal which goes on for ever and has a repeating pattern	$0.333... = \frac{1}{3}$ has the number 3 repeating forever
Fraction	A fraction is written as the *ratio* of the numerator and the denominator	$\frac{3}{4}$ is a fraction with numerator 3 and denominator 4
Equivalent fractions	Fractions which have the same value	$\frac{1}{3}, \frac{2}{6}, \frac{3}{9}$ and $\frac{10}{30}$ are all equivalent fractions
Percentages	A number which means 'out of 100'	85% means $\frac{85}{100}$

4 MyReview

1 Write these decimals in order starting with the smallest.
  a 2.5   2.57   2.45   2.56
  b 0.07   0.077   0.008   0.0078

2 Write these fractions as decimals without using a calculator.
  a $\frac{3}{10}$ **b** $\frac{4}{5}$ **c** $\frac{3}{20}$ **d** $\frac{7}{25}$

3 Write these decimals as fractions in their simplest form.
  a 0.7   **b** 0.02   **c** 0.008   **d** 1.75

4 Order these fractions from lowest to highest.
  $\frac{2}{5}$ $\frac{3}{10}$ $\frac{3}{8}$ $\frac{1}{4}$

5 Calculate each of these, giving your answer as a fraction in its simplest form.
  a $\frac{11}{12} - \frac{9}{12}$ **b** $\frac{2}{5} + \frac{4}{15}$
  c $\frac{8}{9} - \frac{1}{6}$ **d** $\frac{6}{7} + \frac{5}{8}$

6 Use a mental method to calculate
  a $\frac{1}{5}$ of £20   **b** $\frac{3}{8}$ of 32 students.

7 Calculate these using a suitable method.
  a $12 \times \frac{3}{4}$ **b** $\frac{3}{10} \times 15$

8 Give your answers to these questions in their simplest form.
  a What fraction of 72 is 48?
  b What fraction of a day is four hours?

9 Calculate these percentages using a mental method.
  a 5% of 50   **b** 40% of 140
  c 15% of 660   **d** 99% of 800

10 Calculate these percentages using a written or calculator method. Give your answers to two decimal places.
  a 37% of 44   **b** 112% of 320

11 Write these fractions and decimals as percentages without using a calculator.
  a $\frac{3}{5}$ **b** $\frac{8}{40}$ **c** 0.04   **d** 1.2

12 Write these percentages as decimals.
  a 73%   **b** 16.5%

13 Write these percentages as fractions in their simplest forms.
  a 65%   **b** 8%

14 a What percentage of 90 is 36?
  b A pet shop has 17 cats and 8 dogs. What percentage of the pets are dogs?

What next?

Score		
	0 – 4	Your knowledge of this topic is still developing. To improve look at Formative test: 2B-4; MyMaths: 1015, 1016, 1017, 1018, 1029, 1031 and 1072
	5 – 11	You are gaining a secure knowledge of this topic. To improve look at InvisiPen: 111, 142, 145, 161 and 162
	12 – 14	You have mastered this topic. Well done, you are ready to progress!

MyMaths.co.uk

Question commentary

Question 1 – It is useful to have a number line available for this question.

Question 2 – Students may know some of these by sight (such as 0.3) but if not suggest they find an equivalent decimal fraction.

Question 3 – Students will need to write each number as a decimal fraction first then simplify. Part **d** may cause issues. They can write as a mixed number $1\frac{3}{4}$ or an improper fraction.

Question 4 – A number of possible common misconceptions here such as thinking $\frac{3}{10}$ is bigger than $\frac{3}{8}$. A possible strategy is to write each fraction as a decimal first (0.25, 0.3, 0.375, 0.4).

Question 5 – Emphasise the need for the lowest common denominator. In part **d**, a mixed number is also acceptable $1\frac{27}{56}$.

Questions 6 and **7** – A common mistake in **7** would be to multiply the numerator and the denominator – discuss how this creates an equivalent fraction.

Questions 8 and **9** – Different methods are possible: good for class or group discussions.

Questions 10 to **14** – A combination of calculator skills, basic practice and simplification.

Answers

1 **a** 2.45, 2.5, 2.56, 2.57
  b 0.0078, 0.008, 0.07, 0.077

2 **a** 0.3   **b** 0.8   **c** 0.15   **d** 0.28

3 **a** $\frac{7}{10}$ **b** $\frac{1}{50}$ **c** $\frac{2}{250}$ **d** $\frac{7}{4}$

4 $\frac{1}{4}, \frac{3}{10}, \frac{3}{8}, \frac{2}{5}$

5 **a** $\frac{1}{6}$ **b** $\frac{2}{3}$ **c** $\frac{13}{18}$ **d** $\frac{83}{56}$

6 **a** £4   **b** 12 students

7 **a** 9   **b** $4\frac{1}{2}$

8 **a** $\frac{2}{3}$ **b** $\frac{1}{6}$

9 **a** 2.5   **b** 56   **c** 99   **d** 792

10 **a** 16.28   **b** 358.40

11 **a** 60%   **b** 20%   **c** 4%   **d** 120%

12 **a** 0.73   **b** 0.165

13 **a** $\frac{13}{20}$ **b** $\frac{2}{25}$

14 **a** 40%   **b** 32%

4 MyPractice

4a

1 Write these numbers in order starting with the smallest.

a 4.5   4.48   4.4   4.34   4

b 5.96   5.979   5.94   6   5.9

c 0.066   0.068   0.06   0.0695   0.0684

d 2.8   2.771   2.16   2.776   2.77

2 Copy these and place < or > between each pair of numbers to show which number is the larger.

a 0.46 ☐ 0.5   b 1.61 ☐ 1.6   c 4.375 ☐ 4.384   d 5.24 ☐ 5.2

e 7.13 ☐ 7.14   f 2.753 ☐ 2.76   g 8.0444 ☐ 8.044   h 6.999 ☐ 7.1

3 Rebecca measured the weight, in kilograms, of 20 people in her maths class. Make a copy of this table and help Rebecca by filling in the frequencies.

45.20, 39.75, 51.09, 46.49, 35.21, 33.00, 38.19, 42.83, 35.50, 53.61, 44.29, 46.38, 37.01, 32.76, 43.35, 49.81, 30.57, 41.72, 46.85, 41.29

Weight, W(kg)	Frequency
$30 \leqslant W < 35$	
$35 \leqslant W < 40$	
$40 \leqslant W < 45$	
$45 \leqslant W < 50$	
$50 \leqslant W < 55$	

4b

4 Change these fractions into decimals using division. Use an appropriate method.

a $\frac{7}{8}$ b $\frac{7}{16}$ c $\frac{7}{20}$ d $\frac{1}{6}$ e $\frac{5}{9}$ f $\frac{11}{40}$ g $\frac{7}{15}$

5 Put these fractions in order from lowest to highest.

a $\frac{2}{9}$ $\frac{1}{4}$ $\frac{3}{10}$

b $\frac{2}{3}$ $\frac{4}{13}$ $\frac{13}{18}$

c $\frac{3}{5}$ $\frac{9}{16}$ $\frac{13}{20}$

d $\frac{2}{7}$ $\frac{6}{25}$ $\frac{3}{10}$

6 Write these decimals as fractions in their simplest forms.

a 0.125   b 0.55   c 1.75   d 0.05   e $2.\dot{6}$ f 3.15

4c

7 Find the missing number in each of these pairs of equivalent fractions.

a $\frac{2}{3} = \frac{\square}{15}$ b $\frac{3}{7} = \frac{\square}{21}$ c $\frac{4}{9} = \frac{\square}{36}$ d $\frac{5}{7} = \frac{\square}{49}$

e $\frac{4}{11} = \frac{44}{\square}$ f $\frac{3}{13} = \frac{\square}{39}$ g $\frac{5}{12} = \frac{\square}{72}$ h $\frac{7}{16} = \frac{\square}{80}$

4c

8 Calculate each of these additions and subtractions, giving your answer as a fraction in its simplest form.

a $\frac{2}{5} + \frac{1}{4}$ b $\frac{3}{7} + \frac{1}{5}$ c $\frac{1}{3} + \frac{1}{5}$ d $\frac{3}{4} + \frac{1}{9}$

e $\frac{3}{15} + \frac{9}{20}$ f $\frac{5}{6} - \frac{4}{9}$ g $\frac{5}{8} + \frac{7}{12}$ h $\frac{6}{7} - \frac{2}{21}$

4d

9 Use an appropriate method to calculate these amounts. Where appropriate give your answer to 2 decimal places.

a $\frac{2}{7}$ of 236g   b $\frac{7}{16}$ of £500   c $\frac{4}{7}$ of 18km   d $\frac{8}{5}$ of 47 miles

e $\frac{5}{12}$ of 48 hours   f $\frac{3}{5}$ of $25   g $\frac{7}{9}$ of 25 tonnes   h $\frac{2}{5}$ of 360°

10 a In Karla's class there are 14 boys and 21 girls. What fraction of the class are boys?

b Spencer has 12 music CDs, 10 of which are classical music. What fraction of Spencer's CDs are not classical music?

4e

11 Calculate these using an appropriate method, giving your answers to 2 decimal places where appropriate.

a 7% of £50   b 12% of 45kg   c 31% of 18km

d 57% of 39 euros   e 29% of £87   f 41% of 63kg

12 A packet of sausages weighs 275g. The label says it contains 75% meat, 11% bread crumbs and 2% salt. What weight of meat, breadcrumbs and salt does the packet contain?

4f

13 Bethany's form teacher has been supplied with the following marks from her subject teachers.

a Convert all the marks into percentages and list Bethany's subjects in order from best to worst.

b Write a sentence to summarize her results.

Subject	Mark
Art	66/100
Maths	59%
PE	28/40
Science	17/50
History	18/25
English	51/70

MyMaths.co.uk

Question commentary

Questions 1 to **3** – Ordering and then grouping decimals to test basic understanding of the relative magnitude of decimals.

Question 4 – Students can set these out using short or long division (where necessary) or use an informal method. Some will require (sensible) rounding.

Question 5 – Working in decimals or using common denominators are both legitimate methods.

Question 6 – Students may be able to work some of these out by recall. Part **e** may cause some confusion.

Question 8 – Encourage students to use the lowest common denominator rather than just multiplying the two denominators together.

Questions 9 and **10** – Fractions of and amounts as fractions. Calculators can be used where appropriate and check rounding.

Questions 11 and **12** – Percentage calculations. Calculators can be used where appropriate.

Question 13 – An application of all the work covered in Chapter 4.

Answers

1 **a** 4, 4.34, 4.4, 4.48, 4.5
   b 5.9, 5.94, 5.96, 5.979, 6
   c 0.06, 0.066, 0.068, 0.0684, 0.0695
   d 2.16, 2.77, 2.771, 2.776, 2.8

2 **a** < **b** > **c** < **d** >
   e < **f** < **g** > **h** <

3 3, 5, 5, 5, 2

4 **a** 0.875 **b** 0.4375 **c** 0.35
   d $0.1\dot{6}$ **e** $0.\dot{5}$ **f** 0.275
   g $0.4\dot{6}$

5 **a** $\frac{2}{9}, \frac{1}{4}, \frac{3}{10}, \frac{4}{13}$ **b** $\frac{2}{3}, \frac{13}{18}, \frac{11}{15}, \frac{3}{4}$
   c $\frac{5}{9}, \frac{9}{16}, \frac{3}{5}, \frac{13}{20}$ **d** $\frac{6}{25}, \frac{3}{11}, \frac{2}{7}, \frac{3}{10}$

6 **a** $\frac{1}{8}$ **b** $\frac{11}{20}$ **c** $1\frac{3}{4}$ **d** $\frac{1}{20}$
   e $2\frac{2}{3}$ **f** $3\frac{3}{20}$

7 **a** 10 **b** 9 **c** 16 **d** 35
   e 121 **f** 9 **g** 30 **h** 35

8 **a** $\frac{13}{20}$ **b** $\frac{22}{55}$ **c** $\frac{8}{15}$ **d** $\frac{31}{36}$
   e $\frac{13}{20}$ **f** $\frac{7}{18}$ **g** $1\frac{5}{24}$ **h** $\frac{16}{21}$

9 **a** 67.43 g **b** £218.75 **c** 10.29 km
   d 75.2 miles **e** 20 hours **f** $15
   g 19.44 tonnes **h** 144°

10 **a** $\frac{2}{5}$ **b** $\frac{1}{6}$

11 **a** £3.50 **b** 5.4 kg **c** 5.58 km
   d 22.23 euros **e** £25.23 **f** 25.83 kg

12 206.25 g of meat, 30.25 g bread crumbs, 5.5 g salt

13 **a** English 73%, History 72%, PE 70%, Art 66%, Maths 59%, Science 34%
   b Students' own answers, e.g. Bethany passed all of her subjects apart from Science; Bethany's highest mark was for English and her worst mark was for Science.

MyAssessment 1

These questions will test you on your knowledge of the topics in chapters 1 to 4.
They give you practice in the types of questions that you may see in your GCSE exams.
There are 95 marks in total.

1 Calculate
a $-6 - -3$ b $-16 + -24$ c -9×-4
d $-35 \div -7$ e 7×-3 f $-42 \div 6$ (6 marks)

2 Place these decimals in order of size from largest to smallest.
0.014   -0.052   0.01   -1.099   1.109   -0.555   (2 marks)

3 Which one of these numbers does **not** have 9 as one of its factors?
189   801   739   486   639   2052   (2 marks)

4 Find the HCF and LCM of 81 and 36.   (3 marks)

5 Work out the value of
a 7^2 b $(-8)^3$ c 5^3 d $(-2.5)^2$ (4 marks)

6 a Find two consecutive numbers with a product of 3080.   (4 marks)
   b Briefly explain your method for solving this problem.   (1 mark)

7 Convert these measurements to the units in the brackets.
a 1750kg (tonnes)   b 560cl (litres)   c 24 litres (pints)
d 33lb (kg)   e 32km (miles)   f 8 gallons (litres)   (6 marks)

8 The flag of Denmark is being made.
a Calculate the area of the white material.   (3 marks)
b Calculate the area of the red material.   (3 marks)
c What is the total area of the flag?   (1 mark)

9 The flag of Eritrea is made from three triangles
a Calculate the area shaded green.   (2 marks)
b Calculate the area shaded red.   (3 marks)
c Work out the total area of the flag.   (2 marks)

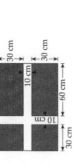

10 The parallelogram is split into two trapeziums.
a Find the area of the parallelogram.   (2 marks)
b Find the areas of the two trapeziums and show that one trapezium is $\frac{4}{9}$ ths of the area of the parallelogram.   (3 marks)

11 a Write these expressions in their simplest form.
   i $5 \times x$ ii $x+x+x$ iii $y \div 4$ iv $x \times y$ v $x+y+x+y+y$ (5 marks)
   b Find the value of these expressions if $x = 7$ and $y = 8$.   (5 marks)

12 Simplify these expressions.
a $5^3 \times 5^8$ b $10^6 \times 10^3 \times 10^8$ c $z^2 \times z^5 \times z^{12}$ d $s^6 \times t^3 \times u^8$ (4 marks)

13 Simplify these expressions by collecting like terms with the same indices.
a $4p + 8p - 2p - p$ b $12q - 4q + 16q - q$
c $3z + 2z^2 - 7z + 5z^2$ d $6t^2 - 6t^3 + 3t^2 - 6t$ (4 marks)

14 Expand these brackets.
a $5(2x + 5)$ (1 marks)   b $p(7p - 3)$ (1 marks)
c $3(2y - 1) + 2(3y + 1)$ (2 marks)   d $u(3u + 2) + 2u(u - 1)$ (2 marks)

15 a Find a formula for the perimeter, P, of this quadrilateral.   (2 marks)
b If $x = 4$ find the value of the perimeter.   (1 mark)
c Find an equation for the fourth angle, y, and solve this to find y.   (3 marks)

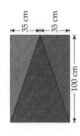

16 a Write the value of the digit 3 in words in each of these numbers.   (5 marks)
   i 0.437   ii 0.034   iii 0.374   iv 0.473   v 0.043
b Place these numbers in order from smallest to largest.   (2 marks)

17 A stamp is $2\frac{3}{5}$ cm high and $1\frac{2}{3}$ cm wide.
a Work out the perimeter of the stamp.   (2 marks)
b What is the difference between the height and width of the stamp?   (2 marks)

18 Using a calculator work out the following.   (4 marks)
a 56% of 450ml   b $\frac{5}{9}$ of 3.6km   c 0.65 of 800MB   d 2% of 5200g

19 In a recent test only seven students out of 42 gained a grade A.
a Write this as   i a fraction in its simplest terms
            ii a decimal to 2 decimal places
            iii a percentage to 1 decimal places.   (3 marks)
b Twelve students gained a B grade. What percentage of the students gained a grade A or B (give your answer to one decimal place)?   (2 marks)

 MyMaths.co.uk

Mark scheme

Questions 1 – 6 marks

a	1	-3	**b**	1	-40
c	1	36	**d**	1	5
e	1	-21	**f**	1	-7

Questions 2 – 2 marks

2    $-1.099. -0.555, -0.052, 0.01, 0.014, 1.109$

Questions 3 – 2 marks

2   739

Questions 4 – 3 marks

1   HCF: 9
2   LCM: 324

Questions 5 – 4 marks

a	1	49	**b**	1	-512
c	1	125	**d**	1	6.25

Questions 6 – 3 marks

a   2   55, 56
b   1   Take square root of 3080 and look for whole numbers above/below the answer.

Questions 7 – 6 marks

a	1	1.75 tonnes	**b**	1	5.6 litres
c	1	48 pints	**d**	1	16–17 kg
e	1	20 miles	**f**	1	32 litres

Questions 8 – 7 marks

a	3	1600 cm^2	**b**	3	5400 cm^2
c	1	7000 cm^2			

Questions 9 – 7 marks

a	2	1750 cm^2	**b**	3	3500 cm^2
c	2	7000 cm^2			

Questions 10 – 5 marks

a   2 54 cm^2
b   3 30 cm^2 and 24 cm^2 , $\frac{24}{54} = \frac{4}{9}$

Questions 11 – 10 marks

a i	1	$5x$	**b i**	1	35
ii	1	$3x$	**ii**	1	21
iii	1	$\frac{y}{4}$	**iii**	1	2
iv	1	xy	**iv**	1	56
v	1	$2x + 3y$	**v**	1	38

Questions 12 – 4 marks

a	1	5^{11}	**b**	1	10^{17}
c	1	z^{19}	**d**	1	$s^6 t^3 u^8$

Questions 13 – 4 marks

a	1	$9p$	**b**	1	$23q$
c	1	$7z^2 - 4z$	**d**	1	$-6t^3 + 9t^2 - 6t$

Questions 14 – 6 marks

a	1	$10x + 25$	**b**	1	$7p^2 - 3p$
c	2	$12y - 1$	**d**	2	$5u^2$

Questions 15 – 6 marks

a	2	$P = 12 + x$	**b**	1	$P = 16$ cm
c	3	$240° + y = 360°, y = 129°$			

Questions 16 – 7 marks

a i	1	One hundredth	**ii**	1	One hundredth
iii	1	One tenth	**iv**	1	One thousandth
v	1	One thousandth			

b   2 $0.034, 0.043, 0.374, 0437, 0.473$

Questions 17 – 4 marks

a   2 $8\frac{8}{15}$; need to see working
b   2 $\frac{14}{15}$; need to see working

Questions 18 – 4 marks

a	1	252 ml	**b**	1	2 km
c	1	520 MB	**d**	1	104 g

Questions 19 – 5 marks

a i	1	$\frac{1}{6}$	**ii**	1	0.17
iii	1	16.7%			

b   2   45.2%

5 Angles and shapes

Learning outcomes

G5 Describe, sketch and draw using conventional terms and notations: points, lines, parallel lines, perpendicular lines, right angles, regular polygons, and other polygons that are reflectively and rotationally symmetric (L6)

G7 Derive and illustrate properties of triangles, quadrilaterals, circles, and other plane figures (for example, equal lengths and angles) using appropriate language and technologies (L6)

G10 Apply the properties of angles at a point, angles at a point on a straight line, vertically opposite angles (L5)

G11 Understand and use the relationship between parallel lines and alternate and corresponding angles (L6)

G12 Derive and use the sum of angles in a triangle and use it to deduce the angle sum in any polygon, and to derive properties of regular polygons (L6)

Introduction

The chapter starts by a review of angles in a straight line, angles at a point and vertically opposite angles before moving on to angles in a triangle and angles in parallel lines. Properties of quadrilaterals and other polygons are then covered before an introduction to the concept of congruence.

The introduction discusses the use of basic geometrical shapes, principally triangles, in the creation of 3D images for computer games. This process, which significantly simplifies the creation of 3D graphics, is used in many other areas as well such as architecture and 3D product design (e.g. in the design of cars).

Vector graphics, as opposed to 'bitmap' graphics, defines the points, lines and planes using simple mathematical equations rather than single point definitions and it significantly reduces the amount of computer power and storage requirements and can therefore be a lot more efficient, saving time and computational complexity for the designers.

This website gives a brief description of some of the differences between vector and bitmap graphics: http://www.animationpost.co.uk/tech-notes/bitmaps-vs-vectors.htm

Prior knowledge

Students should already know how to…

- Do simple arithmetic using whole numbers
- Find missing angles in a variety of contexts, at a basic level
- Name and describe the basic properties of triangles and quadrilaterals

Starter problem

The starter problem is an investigation into quadrilaterals on a 9-pin geoboard. Students are invited to investigate how many different quadrilaterals they can find. Encourage them to think about quadrilaterals that look different, even when rotated and/or reflected. This can lead into a discussion of congruence (section **5.6**).

As an extension, students could be asked to find examples of other polygons on the geoboard, for example different triangles or pentagons. The discussion could develop into finding polygons that are concave as well as the more commonly identifiable convex versions. The geoboard could also be extended to 16-pin or even 25-pin if time and ability allows.

Resources

MyMaths

Angle reasoning	1080	Angle sums	1082	Interior exterior angles	1100
Angles in parallel lines	1109	Sum of angles in a polygon	1320		

Online assessment

Chapter test	2B–5
Formative test	2B–5
Summative test	2B–5

InvisiPen solutions

Congruent shapes	317	Angles on a straight line	342
Types of triangles and angles			343
Properties of quadrilaterals and angles			344
Opposite angles	345	Polygon angles	346

Topic scheme

Teaching time = 6 lessons/2 weeks

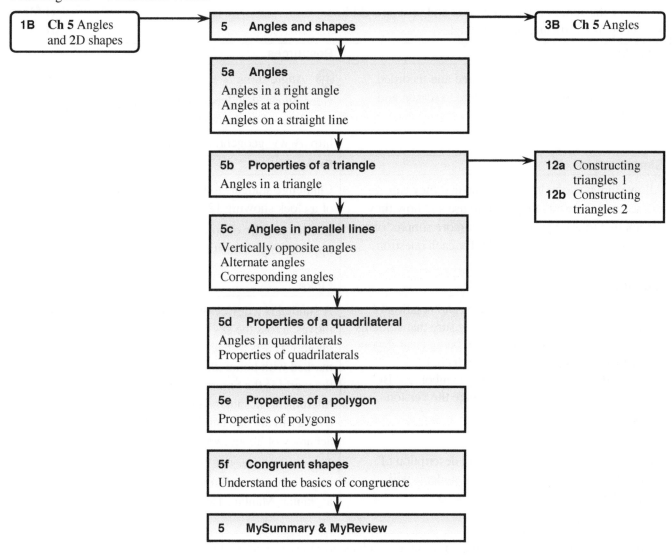

1B Ch 5 Angles and 2D shapes	

5 Angles and shapes

3B Ch 5 Angles

5a Angles
Angles in a right angle
Angles at a point
Angles on a straight line

5b Properties of a triangle
Angles in a triangle

12a Constructing triangles 1
12b Constructing triangles 2

5c Angles in parallel lines
Vertically opposite angles
Alternate angles
Corresponding angles

5d Properties of a quadrilateral
Angles in quadrilaterals
Properties of quadrilaterals

5e Properties of a polygon
Properties of polygons

5f Congruent shapes
Understand the basics of congruence

5 MySummary & MyReview

Differentiation

Student book 2A   88 – 105

Angles
Opposite angles
Properties of triangles
Angles in a triangle
Parallel lines
Properties of quadrilaterals

Student book 2B   80 – 97

Angles
Properties of a triangle
Angles in parallel lines
Properties of a quadrilateral
Properties of a polygon
Congruent shapes

Student book 2C   86 – 99

Angles and parallel lines
Properties of a triangle and a
      quadrilateral
Properties of a polygon
Congruent shapes

Objectives

- Use correctly the vocabulary, notation and labelling conventions for angles (L5)
- Know the sum of angles at a point and on a straight line (L5)
- Recognise vertically opposite angles (L5)

Key ideas	Resources
1 Understand how turn is measured and recorded 2 Begin to use basic angle measure to reason and explore shape properties	⊞ Angle sums (1082) Geometer's Sketch pad or Cabri or equivalent or - GeoGebra download: (free) http://www.geogebra.org/cms/download

Simplification	Extension
Allow students to work in pairs, so that they can discuss which results they need to use and how they are applied to each problem. Offer more simple 'one step' problems, like question **3a**, for each question type.	Challenge students to find the angle between the hands of a clock showing 12:15 or 10:20, etc. Challenge pairs of students to justify why vertically opposite angles must be equal.

Literacy	Links
Fully explore labelling conventions and notation of angle. Share angle symbols, making sure that students are aware of the variety in use, and being clear if your department has a policy about which are used consistently in your school. Likely symbol: ∠ABC meaning 'angle ABC', but also share the version ⌒ ABC Make sure that students use the full description of vertically opposite angles, as many students will simply describe them as 'opposite' only.	A sundial is a device that measures time. As the sun moves across the sky, a vertical pole or plate (the gnomon) casts a shadow which moves across a dial marked with hours like a clock. The largest sundial in the world is the Samrat Yantra (The Supreme Instrument) at Jantar Mantar in Jaipur in India. It is over 27 m tall and can be used to tell the time to an accuracy of about two seconds. There are pictures of the Samrat Yantra at http://commons.wikimedia.org/wiki/File:Samrat_Yantra,_Jantar_Mantar,_Delhi,_early_19th_century.jpg

Alternative approach

Pairs of students can be encouraged to recall as much as possible of their angle knowledge in order to help you establish the knowledge base and its security. Check students can recognise/label, measure and draw a range of angles by getting them to do a simple 'round robin' activity on a folded A4 sheet of paper – draw 8 different angles; label angle types; estimate size; measure; evaluate responses. Encourage students to practise naming and identifying angles correctly using the agreed conventions, by using appropriate geometry software, either as a modelled whole group activity, or for direct hands-on experience. This software can also be used to check and or explore basic measure facts such as 360 degrees in a whole turn; 180 degrees in a half turn or straight line, and so on. Vertically opposite angles can also be explored with the help of such software. The exercise can be carried out by pairs of students jointly, encouraging students to verbalise reasoning, and then to record this efficiently and effectively. Discuss with the whole group what efficient and effective recording might look like.

Checkpoint

1 A whole turn is made up of a reflex angle and an acute angle.
   If the reflex angle is 295° what is the size of the acute angle? (65°)

2 A full turn is made up of six equal angles. What is the size of one angle? (60°)

Starter – Angle estimation

Draw a mixture of acute, obtuse and reflex angles on the board.

Ask students to estimate the size of each angle in degrees then measure the angles.

Students score 6 points for an exact answer, 4 points for within 10 degrees and 2 points for within 15 degrees.

Teaching notes

Many students find it difficult to describe angles using three letters and it is important to emphasise the use of three letters when describing angles. It should also be realised that there are often two angles at angle ABC: the reflex and the acute or obtuse.

Draw a straight line and another line coming off it at a specified angle, say 45° or 120°, and ask students to work out the supplementary angle (135°, or 60°). Now extend the line and ask students if they can work out the size of the angle vertically opposite the original angle (45° or 120°) – again angles on a straight line. Draw out the general result and set students a problem similar to question **3b** and then a problem similar to the second example. Encourage students to tell you how to solve the problems and show them how to lay out their answers: giving reasons, 'angles on a straight line', etc., and showing their workings. Emphasise the need to set out their answers as a series of logical steps.

Plenary

Ask students to find the missing angles in this diagram. Ask them to tell you what arguments to use and how to apply them.

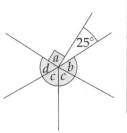

Exercise commentary

Question 1 – Ask students to give a third way of describing each angle, for example, C, r, BCD or DCB.

Question 2 – Similar to part **a** of the first example: uses the angle on a straight line.

Question 3 – Similar to the second example. Parts **b** and **c** use the angle on a straight line. Part **d** is similar to part **b** of the first example.

Question 4 – Similar to part **b** of the first example. As an extension for part **f**, ask students to also calculate the angles measured clockwise from North of the compass directions.

Question 5 – It will help if students work out the angles around the clock: 0°, 30°, 60°, 90°, etc. In part **c**, remind students that the hour hand also moves.

Answers

1	**a**	r	**b**	s	**c**	p		
	d	q	**e**	u	**f**	t		
2	**a**	42°	**b**	58°	**c**	38°	**d**	45°

3 **a** 64°   **b** $c = 95°$, $b = d = 85°$
   c $c = 28°$, $d = 81°$, $e = f = 71°$ **d** 72°

4	**a**	30°	**b**	43°	**c**	120°
	d	144°	**e**	119°	**f**	45°
	g	30°	**h**	60°		
5	**a**	90°	**b**	30°	**c**	105°

Objectives

- Solve geometric problems using side and angle properties of equilateral, isosceles and right-angled triangles and special quadrilaterals, explaining reasoning with diagrams and text   (L5)
- Understand a proof that the exterior angle of a triangle is equal to the sum of the two interior opposite angles   (L6)

Key ideas	Resources
1 Recognition and identification of the 4 types of triangle 2 Knowing and using angle facts related to triangles	Angle reasoning (1080) Interior exterior angles (1100) Paper Ruler Scissors Dictionaries A dynamic geometry software pack

Simplification	Extension
Get students to work in pairs, so that they can discuss which results they need to use and how they are applied in each problem. Offer more simple 'one step' problems similar to question **1a**, for each question type.	Challenge students to find the sum of the angles in a quadrilateral; hint at drawing in a diagonal and looking at the two triangles formed. Can they generalise this to other polygons?

Literacy	Links
Introduce/use the notation for 'triangle ABC' as △ABC. Examine also the conventions that indicate sides of equal length and equal-sized angles. Use the triangle vocabulary to emphasise the properties and to examine the spelling, using the Links example, and perhaps extending to other word routes.	Bring in some dictionaries for the class to use. The word *isosceles* derives from the Greek *isos* meaning 'equal', and *skelos* meaning 'leg'. Ask the class to find other words beginning with *iso* that are related to the word equal. For example, *isobar* – a line on a map linking points with the same atmospheric pressure, *isometric* – having equal dimensions.

Alternative approach

Put students into groups of four and allocate one type of triangle to each group, differentiating as appropriate. Small coloured bits of paper may be used for each group member, each triangle type sharing the same colour. Each group then develops and explores as much information as possible about 'their' triangle, including symmetries, area, etc. These groups should then be changed and 'rainbowed', so that the new groups of four contain an 'expert' on every one of the four types (every colour represented in the group). The new groups build information about every triangle, and also about each special one. Use a dynamic software with the whole group to explore the exterior angle relationship. Use the exercise for consolidation purposes.

Checkpoint

1 a If a triangle has two angles each equal to 47°, calculate the third angle.   (86°)

   b What else can you say about the triangle?   (Isosceles, one line of symmetry)

2 Can a triangle have two or more obtuse angles? Explain your answer.

                                            (Not possible as two obtuse angles > 180°, or equivalent)

Starter – Straight line pairs

Write the following list of angles on the board:

73°, 156°, 116°, 13°, 107°, 104°, 35°, 64°, 145°, 49°, 89°, 151°, 131°, 55°, 24°, 76°, 29°, 167°, 125°, 91°.

Challenge students to match up the pairs (that add up to 180°) in the shortest possible time.

This can be extended by using pairs that add up to 360°.

Teaching notes

Question **6** could be done as a whole class. This would then serve as motivation (but not proof) for stating that the sum of the angles in a triangle equals the angle on a straight line. If the alternative approach of tearing off the corners is used, make sure that the students first label the angles A, B, and C, so that they can easily identify which vertices to place together on a line.

In geometric arguments, it is important that students learn to state the results that they are using as well as writing down an equation, so that their logic is clear. Model this approach with a suitable example, taking the opportunity to remind students how to lay out the algebra.

Give students a problem to work on and then ask them to swap books with a partner. Go through the answer on the board assigning marks for stating the results used, layout of workings, checking the answers and 1 mark for the numerical answer. Ask students to assign a score and to write two sentences one saying what was good about the answer and one saying how it could be improved.

Plenary

Ask students to define acute, right, obtuse and reflex angles. Then challenge them to say what types of angles can be in a triangle (A-A-A or A-A-Ri, A-A-O). Why can't you have two obtuse angles? What are the allowed ranges of values of the angles in an isosceles triangle?

Exercise commentary

Question 1 – Make sure that students state the result they are using and show their working.

Question 2 – Encourage students to sketch triangles with the given angles to make the problem less abstract.

Questions 3 and **4** – Similar to the example.

Question 5 – Students could approach these problems using the result that an exterior angle of a triangle is equal to the sum of the other two interior angles or using the results for the sum of the angles on a straight line and in a triangle. Both are correct.

Question 6 – To find a starting point, students may need reminding that they know the corner angles of the rectangle are right angles.

Question 7 – Students will need to be fairly accurate when finding the midpoint and folding the paper: it may help to place the edge of a ruler along the fold line.

Answers

1   **a**   55°   **b**   53°   **c**   107°   **d**   71°

2   **a**   60° equilateral   **b**   71° isosceles
    c   90° right-angled   **d**   78° scalene
    e   42° isosceles   **f**   51° isosceles

3   **a**   96°   **b**   14°   **c**   150°   **d**   90°

4   **a** $a = 37°$ **b** $b = 48°, c = 84°$
    c $d = 66°, e = 57°$ **d** $f = 72°$

5   **a**   115°   **b**   69°   **c**   42°   **d**   127°

6   $a = b = c = d = 45°, e = 90°$

7   Check students' explanations

5c Angles in parallel lines

Objectives	
• Identify parallel and perpendicular lines	(L5)
• Identify alternate and corresponding angles	(L6)
• Solve problems using properties of angles, of parallel and intersecting lines, and of triangles, justifying inferences and explaining reasoning with diagrams and text	(L6)

Key ideas	Resources	
1 To learn about angles in parallel lines	⊞ Angles in parallel lines	(1109)
2 To calculate angles in parallel lines	Mini whiteboards	
	Ruler, protractor, coloured pencils	

Simplification	Extension
Students may find it difficult to identify alternate and corresponding angles given the many choices available, especially in a complex case such as question **5**. Suggest that students work in pairs to agree which angles go together. Ask them to copy the diagrams and, with a coloured pencil, mark on a Z or an F to help match angles.	Put students in pairs and ask them to make up their own question like those in question **5**, together with a mark scheme for their answer. Then get pairs to swap questions and then mark one another's answers giving one good feature of the answer and one area for improvement. Using question **5** as a hint, ask pairs of students to prove that the angle sum of a triangle is 180°.

Literacy	Links
Check the vocabulary vertical and horizontal. These are often confused with the word perpendicular, so it is worth including and using them together to help establish the concepts of each and expose any misconceptions. Check the notation for indicating parallel lines, including if there are two sets of different parallels. Be aware that students tend to latch on to part of the angle concepts here rather than the whole, so take time to explicitly address this by making sure that it is because, for example, alternate angles are described by parallel lines that they are equal. Alternate angles are not equal if the lines are not parallel. Further, it is the correct language that is required – not the 'Z' or 'F' shape upon which to nail the knowledge.	Parallel lines are used in road markings. Yellow lines laid parallel to the kerb indicate that vehicles must not park at certain times. Double yellow lines mean no waiting is permitted at any time. Red lines prevent all stopping, parking and loading. Double white lines down the centre of the road are used to prevent overtaking and reduce speeds.

Alternative approach

It is worth using a visualisation as a starter with the whole group. For instance, start by asking students to see in their mind's eye a horizontal line, then a vertical line intersecting the horizontal – how many angles, what size are they? Now tell them that the vertical line is now going to turn about the intersection point – no longer being vertical – when it stops – what happens to those angles; which are equal, why? Now add another horizontal line to the 'picture' – imagine the two horizontal lines moving closer then further apart – how many angles now; which are equal, what happens to them as the lines move? In this way parallel lines can be discussed, alternate angles and corresponding angles introduced as well as vertically opposite angles rehearsed. Make use of mini whiteboards to check student knowledge and recognition.

Checkpoint

1 On a mini white board draw a shape indicating two equal alternate angles.

   Also... two equal corresponding angles; vertically opposite angles (appropriate diagrams)

Starter – Triangle bingo

Ask students to draw a 3 × 3 grid and enter nine angles from the following list:

30°, 35°, 40°, 45°, 50°, 55°, 60°, 65°, 70°, 75°, 80°, 85°, 90°, 95°, 100°, 105°, 110°, 115°, 120°, 125°.

Give two angles of a triangle, for example, 83° and 42°.

If students have the third angle in their grid (55°) they cross it out. The winner is the first student to cross out all nine angles.

Teaching notes

It is important for all students to realise that, when there are parallel lines, many angles are the same and, where possible, this should be easy to identify by inspection. The introduction to the lesson should show alternate (**Z**) and corresponding (**F**) angles. Students should be reminded to write these reasons in brackets whenever they use them to solve a problem.

Measuring angles, question **1**, can often lead to problems and it is useful go through the procedure for doing this. First, estimate the angle (is it acute, obtuse or reflex?). Using a protractor, place the cross at the vertex, the base line along one edge and read off from the scale starting at zero. Finally, check the measurement agrees with the initial estimate. If the diagram has short lines, place a ruler over the top of the protractor to see exactly where the line will cross the scale.

Question **5** offers the opportunity to develop one of the standard proofs that the sum of the angles in a triangle is 180°.

Plenary

Put up a multifaceted question, like **5**, and go round the class asking students how to solve it and what to write at each stage. It would be useful to introduce some deliberate mistakes or omissions to keep students focused. Emphasise the need to always consider whether the solution makes sense. It is likely that some students will want to solve the problem in a different sequence; it will be instructive to follow this trhough and demonstrate that the same answers are obtained.

Exercise commentary

Question 1 – Ensure that students' diagrams are big enough to enable easy measurement of the angles.

Questions 2 and **3** – These could be completed as a class using mini whiteboards. Check that parallel lines are correctly marked.

Question 4 – Similar to the first example.

Question 5 – This question brings together material from sections **5a**, **5b** and **5c**. Let students work in pairs to decide which results to apply to find each angle before writing out carefully argued solutions.

Question 6 – Students should be able to give examples from everyday life (including road markings).

Answers

1   **a**   Students' own diagram measurements.
    b   Corresponding

2   **a** 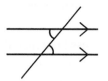   **b**

    c 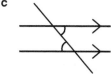   **d**

3   **a**    **b**

    c   **d**

4   **a**   115° (alternate)   **b**   108° (corresponding)
    c   135° (alternate)   **d**   61° (vertically opposite)

5   **a** $a = 35°, b = 15°, c = 130°$
    b $b = 45, c = 135°, d = e = 55°, f = 125°$

6   Students' answers. Possible examples include: railway tracks, line markings on roads, windows, picture frames, parallel bars in gymnastics.

Objectives

- Classify quadrilaterals by their geometrical properties (L6)
- Understand a proof that the angle sum of a triangle is 180° and of a quadrilateral is 360° (L6)

Key ideas	Resources
1 Be able to group and classify quadrilaterals 2 Know and use the angle sum fact of quadrilaterals	Protractor Ruler Scissors Glue

Simplification	Extension
For question **2**, provide students with a sheet showing the five quadrilaterals, without names. After identifying the shapes students can draw in the diagonals and make measurements. Likewise, have available pre-prepared sheets for questions **3** and **5**.	In the final activity ask students to use two equilateral triangles, then three, then four, etc. How many different shapes they can make joining these along a common side?

Literacy	Links
The vocabulary on shape is crucial here, and needs to be tackled in terms of sorting and classifying to avoid common misconceptions about properties associated with the vocabulary. Some vocabulary to add and discuss here includes that connected to the arrowhead – sometimes referred to as convex kite; also can be named a delta.	The Trapezium cluster is a bright cluster of stars in the constellation of Orion discovered by Galileo in 1617. The four brightest stars form the shape of a trapezium. There is more information about the Trapezium cluster at http://en.wikipedia.org/wiki/Trapezium_cluster and at http://www.astropix.com/HTML/B_WINTER/TRAPEZ.HTM

Alternative approach

Students will be familiar with quadrilaterals, but will not be confident about the properties of each. Begin by asking students to name as many different quadrilaterals as possible. Small groups of students can then be allocated a particular quadrilateral in order to explore that shape fully, preparing a poster in order to present or show to the rest of the group. Use some cardboard or plastic examples of each shape with the appropriate group to help the work. Parallelogram, rhombus and/or trapeziums may be represented with connected lengths or rods that help students to examine the effect on diagonals as angles/lengths change. Do allow time for each group to share their results. Raise questions with the whole group following these activities, such as which of the quadrilaterals are rectangles; which are parallelograms; and so on drawing together features that are common and/or unique to a particular shape. Demonstrating 360° in any quadrilateral can be achieved in a number of ways, but it helps also to explore the exterior angle sum by using a pencil or ruler to mark the edges in order and watching the amount of rotation; draw/mark out large quadrilaterals on the floor and get students to walk the shapes to 'feel' and see the amount of rotation in a complete tracing.

Checkpoint

1 I am a four-sided shape whose diagonals meet at right angles but are not equal – what am I?   (Kite)

2 Can a rectangle also be a square? Explain.

(It might be, but not necessarily, though every square is a rectangle)

3 Is a rectangle a parallelogram? Explain.   (Yes, because opposite sides are parallel)

4 Give the fourth angle of a quadrilateral if the other three angles are 48°, 112°, 115°.   (85°)

Starter – One hundred and eighty!

Ask students to write down the 180 times table. Extend by asking students questions, for example,

How many 360s in 1080? (3)

What is the angle sum of 8 triangles? (1440°)

How many triangles will give an angle sum of 900°? (5)

How many 180s are there in 4500? (25).

Teaching notes

To introduce the topic, ask students to name and describe different quadrilaterals. These could be drawn by the students on the board and all characteristics marked in as a whole-class activity. Alternatively, students could work in pairs to draw the named quadrilateral marking in appropriate characteristics.

Having shown the students how to establish the sum of the angles inside a quadrilateral, challenge them to repeat the proof for a concave quadrilateral.

Plenary

Use some large quadrilaterals cut from paper or card – include a parallelogram, kite, square, rectangle, rhombus and trapezium. In turn, hold each shape behind a piece of card and gradually reveal it so that students can make educated guesses about the shape you are holding. For example, as you reveal the rectangle it may look like a square (or a kite) if you reveal one corner first.

Exercise commentary

Questions 1 and **2**– Allow students to work in pairs on finding the missing angles and naming the quadrilaterals. It may help to draw the shapes.

Question 3 – Ask students to make accurate drawings of the various quadrilaterals so that they can draw in the diagonals and make measurements in order to complete the table.

Question 4 – It will be nice to have multiple copies of the pentagonal diagrams available so that students can mark on the various quadrilaterals.

Question 5 – Have a sheet available showing a number of circles with six equal markings on the circumference to help students make regular hexagons. This should provide sufficient triangles to make all the target shapes which could be put on a poster with space for students to write the required explanations.

Answers

1 a 88°   **b** 55°   **c** 90°   **d** 100°

2 a 90° rectangle or square

  b 60° rhombus, parallelogram or isosceles trapezium

  c 70° trapezium or kite

  d 30° arrowhead

  e 100° quadrilateral (no parallel sides or equal angles)

  f 100° rhombus, parallelogram or isosceles trapezium

  g 100° quadrilateral (no parallel sides or equal angles)

  h 250° arrowhead

3

	Equal in length	Bisect each other	Perpendicular
Parallelogram	No	Yes	No
Kite	No	No	Yes
Rhombus	No	Yes	Yes
Square	Yes	Yes	Yes
Rectangle	Yes	Yes	No

4 Isosceles trapezium, rhombus

5 Check students' work

Properties of a quadrilateral   **89**

5e Properties of a polygon

Objectives	
• Explain why inscribed regular polygons can be constructed by equal divisions of a circle	(L6)

Key ideas	Resources
1 Recognise and name simple polygons 2 Understand that 'regular' polygons have BOTH equal sides AND equal angles	Interior exterior angles (1100) Sum of angles in a polygon (1320) A4 paper; squared paper Protractor Ruler Scissors Paper magic: folding polygons: http://www.nationalstemcentre.org.uk/elibrary/resource/9105/paper-magic-folding-polygons

Simplification	Extension
Accurate drawing and construction can take a long time: for those students where support is needed allow extra time or ask them to complete only one tessellation pattern accurately. Do not complete the drawings for them.	In question **3,** can students find an easy way of working out the interior angle of a nonagon? (180 – 40)° How can they find the angle sum of other regular polygons? Paper folding – how do you know that the angle of a shape must be, say, 60°?

Literacy	Links
The key here is for students to recognise that the names such as hexagon or octagon do not refer *only* to regular shapes. Asking students to find, say, hexagons from a number of different polygons, then to further find the regular hexagons will help to dispel those common misconceptions. Further vocabulary references can be made about the arrowhead: sometimes referred to as a convex kite, sometimes also known as a delta. The reasoning behind this language can be explored.	The Giant's Causeway is a formation of thousands of columns of basalt which jut into the sea. It resulted from a volcanic eruption 60 million years ago. According to local legend, the Causeway was a bridge for two giants who wanted to cross the sea to do battle.

Alternative approach
Recalling polygon names from previous experiences provides a simple starting point, which can then be extended to linking names to a variety of displayed, drawn or flat plastic polygons, ideally a mix of regular and irregular. Using square or isometric dotty grids to draw polygons quickly helps. Folding a variety of polygons from A4 paper is also useful, and results in students having good examples of their own – use the Paper magic resource as referenced. Dynamic geometry packages may also be used by students to draw and explore a variety of polygons, and to help them determine exactly what a regular polygon is. The exterior angles of any polygon can be traced out, as with quadrilaterals, and students led to realise no matter how many sides, a polygon's exterior angle sum will always be 360°. Extending from here, interior angles can also be discussed, and the sum of interior angles explored.

Checkpoint	
1 Three angles of a quadrilateral are 65°, 80° and 78°. What is the fourth angle?	(137°)
2 What is the size of an interior angle in	
a an equilateral triangle	(60°)
b a regular hexagon?	(120°)

Starter – SHP!

Write words on the board missing out the vowels, for example, SHP. Ask students for the original words: shape. Possible 'words':

NGL, PRLLL, RHMBS, LTRNT, RCTNGL, DGNL, SSCLS, KT, PRPNDCLR, QLTRL

(angle, parallel, rhombus, alternate, rectangle, diagonal, isosceles, kite, perpendicular, equilateral).

This can be extended by asking students to make up their own examples.

Teaching notes

It is appropriate for all students to have a copy of the table showing the names of polygons from three to ten sides. In pairs, ask students to draw a blank table for number of sides and name of polygon (do not use the student book!) Now give them two minutes to complete the table writing in the names of polygons that they know. Many will write square for quadrilateral, a discussion point, and most will need help with heptagon and nonagon.

If students have drawn a regular hexagon previously through the equal divisions of a circle method then they will easily be able to draw a regular pentagon as in the example, otherwise some guidance will be needed.

Plenary

Consider tessellations of triangles, squares and hexagons: how many of each meet at a point to form a tessellation (6 at 60°, 4 at 90° and 3 at 120°). Why can't other polygons tessellate?

Exercise commentary

In the constructions, emphasise the importance of accuracy.

Question 1 – It may help to draw the shapes.

Question 2 – Part **c** uses the sum of angles on a straight line.

Question 3 – Similar to the first example. It may help to draw a circle the same radius as the protractor. Ask students to check that their answers to parts **b** and **c** are consistent.

Question 4 – Similar to the second example. There are multiple ways to tessellate the shapes in parts **a** and **d**.

Question 5 – Ask students if they can see why a regular octagon alone cannot tessellate. The question can be extended to other regular polygons.

Question 6 – If completed accurately, the students should have six identical isosceles and six identical equilateral triangles. Check that students do not confuse themselves by drawing in the diameters. The small central hexagon can be used as a base on which to build the other hexagons.

Question 7 – Having prepared shapes (possibly made from card) will help students investigate the possible tessellations.

Answers

1. **a** Equilateral triangle **b** Square
2. **a** 57° **b** 104°
    c $c = 125°, d = 70°, e = 55°, f = 55°$
3. **b** 140° **c** 1260°
4. Check students' answers
5. 135°
6. Check students' work
7. Check students' work

Objectives	
• Know that if two 2D shapes are congruent, corresponding sides and angles are equal (L6)	

Key ideas	Resources
1 Understand the difference between shapes that are similar and shapes that are congruent 2 Mentally turn congruent shapes in order to identify matching attributes	Squared paper Tracing paper Scissors Coloured pencils Cat Faces – Y9 proportional reasoning resource from: http://www.emaths.co.uk/index.php/4-teachers/other-resources/professional-development-materials/item/interacting-with-mathematics-in-key-stage-3

Simplification	Extension
It may help students to trace a copy of one shape so that they can test whether it fits on top of another shape (is congruent) and to help in identifying the corresponding angles and sides.	Part c of question 5 is already challenging. Students could also be asked to count how many of each shape can be found within the diagram or how many triangles there are in the diagram.

Literacy	Links
Include the word similar to help students acquire a firm concept of the meanings. It can help to link congruent to 'identical'. Compare the common usage of the word similar to the mathematical one, drawing out the idea of same shape but different size. Ask them what is the same and what is different between congruent and similar shapes once students have been introduced to the definitions.	Patchwork is a form of needlework in which pieces of different fabric are cut into shapes and then joined together to form a larger design. Congruent shapes are often used and tessellated to form decorative quilts. There are examples of quilt patterns using congruent shapes at http://quilting.about.com/od/picturesofquilts/ig/Scrap-Quilts-Photo-Gallery/

Alternative approach
Congruent is not an easily remembered or understood word for students, so it helps to link it with the word similar, thus giving them concrete attributes to compare and decide between. Use a sheet of a variety of shapes, such as Cat faces from the Y9 proportional reasoning pack as referenced in resources, and ask students to identify which are similar and which are congruent. Identification between the congruent and similar establishes conceptual links that can be more readily developed later with work on enlargement and similarity. Folding and tearing A4 sheets into squares and rectangles allows students to group similar shapes and congruent ones together, and will provide further practice in identification.

Checkpoint	
1 A triangle ABC has side lengths equal to 4 cm, 5 cm and 6 cm. Triangle DEF is congruent to ABC. Write down the side lengths of DEF.	(4 cm, 5 cm, 6 cm)

Starter – Guess the polygons

I have exactly four lines of symmetry. (Square)

Each of my angles is exactly 120°. (Regular hexagon)

I have one pair of parallel lines and my angle sum is half of 720°. (Trapezium)

I have one angle of 90°. All my other angles are less than this. (Right-angled triangle)

My angle sum is 540°. (Pentagon)

This can be extended with students' own clues.

Teaching notes

Explain to students that congruent means exactly the same size and shape. Challenge then to think of pairs of letters that can be congruent:

b—d—p—q, W—M—E, i—l, H—I, u—n—c

Identifying corresponding sides and angles can be a little tricky. Display two congruent triangles, with sides and angles labelled, and ask the class how they should match up corresponding pairs. Agree on a correct way to do this and test understanding with another example, perhaps with triangles in a new set of orientations.

Work through a question similar to the second example to illustrate how congruence can be used to gain information.

Plenary

Draw an isosceles triangle and join the mid-point of the base to the opposite vertex. Ask students what they can say about the two sub-triangles: agree there are three pairs of equal length sides. Explain that this is enough to conclude that the triangles are congruent; what can they say about the angles? The two base angles must be equal. The two angles formed by the base and the line to the vertex must be equal, and, since they add up to a straight line, must both be right angles: the line is a perpendicular bisector.

Exercise commentary

Question 1 – Students could simply give the 'number' of the shape that is not congruent.

Questions 2 and **3** – Similar to the second example.

Question 4 – The shapes could be reproduced on squared paper so that students can cut them out and match them.

Question 5 – The diagram will be easier to copy on 1 cm^2 grid paper. It may help to identify congruent shapes if students cut up copies of the diagram. For part **c**, students will need to work systematically.

Question 6 – Students can use their imagination in this question. How do they *know* the shapes are congruent?

Question 7 – Emphasise the importance of giving carefully explained reasons in each part.

Answers

1. **a** The double-headed arrow, shape 4
   b The larger circle, shape 4
   c The square, shape 3
   d The small triangle, shape 2
   e The asymmetric L shape, shape 5
2. $A = B = 68°$, $C = D = 112°$
3. **a** 5 cm   **b** 12 cm   **c** 13 cm
4. Congruent sets are {A, C, G}, {B, F} and {E, D}
5. **a** Check students' work
   b Check students' work
   c Five
6. Students' answers. Possible examples include: paving slabs, textbooks, protractors.
7. **a** **i** Corresponding sides are equal
      ii Corresponding angles are equal
      iii Corresponding sides are equal
      iv Corresponding angles are equal and on AC must sum to 180°
   b Isosceles

Key outcomes	Quick check
Work with angles at a point and on a line. (L5)	**a** Four angles meet at a point. If three of them are 63°, 81° and 124°, what is the fourth angle? (92°) **b** Three angles meet on a straight line. If two of the angles are 72° and 15°, what is the third angle? (93°)
Work with angles in a triangle. (L5)	Two of the three angles in a triangle are 54° and 72°. Find the third angle and state the type of triangle. (54°, isosceles)
Work with angles on parallel and intersecting lines. (L6)	Complete the following sentences: **a** Alternate angles are… (Equal) **b** Corresponding angles are… (Equal)
Recognise quadrilaterals and know their properties. (L6)	Three angles in a quadrilateral are 54°, 126° and 54°. Calculate the fourth angle. What quadrilaterals could the shape be? (126°; parallelogram, rhombus, isosceles trapezium)
Know and use some properties of polygons. (L6)	**a** Calculate the size of the interior angle of a regular hexagon. (120°) **b** Explain why congruent equilateral triangles will always tessellate. (Six triangles fit round a point since 6 × 60° = 360°)
Recognise congruent shapes. (L6)	Triangle ABC is congruent to triangle DEF. **a** If AB = 6 cm, state the length of DE. (6 cm) **b** If angle ACB is 72°, write down the corresponding 72° angle in triangle DEF. (DFE)

MyMaths extra support

Lesson/online homework			Description
Lines and quadrilaterals	1102	L4	Parallel and perpendicular lines, properties of quadrilaterals
Properties of triangles	1130	L4	Classifying triangles and solving problems
Positioning and turning	1231	L2	Turning, giving directions and points of a compass

MyReview

Check out
You should now be able to ...

Test it ➡
Questions

✓ Work with angles at a point and on a line.	(5)	1
✓ Work with angles in a triangle.	(5)	2
✓ Work with angles on parallel and intersecting lines.	(5)	3
✓ Recognise quadrilaterals and know their properties.	(5)	4
✓ Know and use some properties of polygons.	(5)	5, 6
✓ Recognise congruent shapes.	(5)	7

Language	Meaning	Example
Angle	A measure of turn, given in degrees	90° is a quarter turn or right angle
Triangle	A 2D shape with three straight sides and three angles	Equilateral, isosceles, scalene and right-angled are special types of triangle
Perpendicular	Lines which meet at right angles	Horizontal and vertical lines are perpendicular
Parallel	Lines which are always the same distance apart	Railway tracks are parallel
Quadrilateral	A 2D shape with four straight sides and four angles	Squares, rectangles, kites and parallelograms are special types of quadrilateral
Polygon	A 2D shape with three or more straight sides	Pentagons, hexagons and octagons are examples
Tessellation	A tiling pattern with no gaps	A chess board shows tessellated squares
Congruent	Identical to	Shapes are congruent if their *corresponding* sides and angles are equal

1 Calculate the value of the letters in these diagrams.

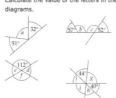

2 Calculate the value of the letters in these triangles.

3 Calculate the angles marked by the letters in these diagrams. Give reasons for your answers.

4 Which quadrilateral has
a 4 equal sides, 2 pairs of equal angles and 2 sets of parallel sides
b 2 sets of equal sides, 1 pair of equal angles and no parallel sides
c exactly 1 set of parallel sides?

5 Draw a regular octagon.

6 Calculate the value of the letters in this diagram.

7 The two triangles below are congruent. State
a the length of AB
b the length of AC
c the size of angle A.

What next?

Score		
0 – 3	Your knowledge of this topic is still developing. To improve look at Formative test: 2B-5; MyMaths: 1080, 1082, 1100, 1109 and 1320
4 – 6	You are gaining a secure knowledge of this topic. To improve look at InvisiPen: 317, 342, 343, 344, 345 and 346
7	You have mastered this topic. Well done, you are ready to progress!

● MyMaths.co.uk

Question commentary

Students should be aware that diagrams will not, in general, be accurately drawn. They should be calculating angles not measuring them.

Question 1 – Use of basic angle rules. Emphasise that the angles on a straight line *meeting at a single point* add up to 180°.

Question 2 – Students need to be able to identify which two angles are the same in isosceles triangles. For part **d**, they could work out the third angle in the triangle first.

Question 3 – The important thing here is the reason for each answer – the angles are easy to guess.

Question 4 – Students might answer a square here for part **a** so discuss the difference between '2 pairs of equal angles' and 'all angles equal'. It could be argued that a square also meets the definition given.

Question 5 – Students will need ruler, protractor, pair of compasses and a sharp pencil.

Question 6 – Students will need to recognise the pair of parallel lines.

Question 7 – It may be helpful to label the original diagram A, B, C.

Answers

1	$a = 97°$	$b = 113°$	$c = 128°$	$d = 68°$
	$e = 68°$	$f = 112°$	$g = 96°$	$h = 44°$
	$i = 96°$	$j = 40°$	$k = 147°$	$l = 270°$
2	$a = 51°$	$b = 76°$	$c = 70°$	$d = 85°$

3 $a = 125°$ Alternate angles
 $b = 85°$ Corresponding angles

4 a Rhombus   b Kite
 c Trapezium

5 Check interior angles are all 135° (allow ±2°) and all sides are the same length.

6 $a = 75°$ $b = 75°$ $c = 15°$

7 a 7 cm   b 15 cm   c 25°

5 MyPractice

5a

1 Calculate the value of the unknown angles.

a

87° 45°

b

53°

c

108°
c d
e

2 Arrange these six angle values so they fit on a straight line and at a point.

14°   22°   24°   124°   142°   214°

5b

3 Two angles in a triangle are given.
Calculate the third angle and state the type of triangle.
a 30°, 75°   **b** 43°, 47°
d 35°, 64°   **e** 45°, 90°
c 36°, 108°

4 One angle in an isosceles triangle is 70°.
What is the size of the other two angles?

> There are two possible answers to this question.

5c

5 Calculate the unknown angles.
Give a reason in each case.

a

115°
b

b

43°
b c
d

c

e
f 55°

6 Calculate the unknown angles.

a

a b
80° c
d e
25°

b

a b
50°
c d
e f

---

7 Calculate the unknown angles in these quadrilaterals.

a

95°
d

Kite

b

115°
c
d
b

Rhombus

c

15°
b

Arrowhead

5d

8 State which shapes are the same in this regular hexagon and give the mathematical name of each shape.

A B
C D E
F G H I
J K

5e

9 The diagram shows five regular pentagons and a rhombus.
One angle in the rhombus is 36°.

Calculate the values of a and b.

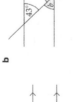

a 36
b

5f

10 Identify the triangles that are congruent to the green triangle.

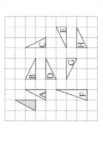

A B C
D E
F G H

Question commentary

Questions 1 and **2** – Recall of two angle rules is necessary. In question **2**, students could work together with a set of angles made up to experiment with.

Questions 3 and **4** – Sketching the triangles may help here.

Questions 5 and **6** – Recall of the angle rules for parallel lines is required here.

Question 7 – Recall of the symmetry properties of quadrilaterals is required. This is not a test of their knowledge of the angle sum of a quadrilateral.

Question 8 – Use the word congruent as appropriate.

Question 9 – Students will need to draw on the range of angle rules they have been introduced to in the chapter to solve this complex problem.

Question 10 – A copy of the diagram to cut out will help students who struggle to visualise the congruent triangles.

Answers

1 **a** 138° **b** 37° **c** $c = 108°, d = e = 72°$

2 14°, 24°, 142°
   214°, 22°, 124°

3 **a** 75° isosceles **b** 90° right-angled
   c 36° isosceles **d** 81° scalene
   e 45° right-angled isosceles

4 70°, 40° or 55°, 55°

5 **a** $a = 115°, b = c = 65°$
   b $b = c = 43°, d = 137°$
   c $c = d = 55°, e = f = 125°$

6 **a** $a = c = 100°, b = d = 55°, e = 125°$
   b $a = b = d = e = 65°, c = f = 115°$

7 **a** 95° **b** $b = 115°, c = d = 65°$ **c** 15°

8 A, F, K, H   Equilateral triangle
   B, J   Isosceles trapezium
   C, I   Equilateral triangle
   D, E, G   Rhombus

9 $a = 108°$ $b = 144°$

10 A, B, C, D, E, G, H

Learning outcomes

A6 Model situations or procedures by translating them into algebraic expressions or formulae and by using graphs   (L6)

A9 Recognise, sketch and produce graphs of linear and quadratic functions of one variable with appropriate scaling, using equations in x and y and the Cartesian plane   (L6)

A11 Reduce a given linear equation in two variables to the standard form $y = mx + c$; calculate and interpret gradients and intercepts of graphs of such linear equations numerically, graphically and algebraically   (L6)

Introduction

The chapter starts by looking at plotting straight-line graphs using a table of values before exploring the equation of a straight-line graph in a more general sense. Various real-life graphs are then looked at before the final section which covers time series graphs.

The introduction discusses how meteorologists use mathematical formulae and graphs to predict future weather patterns. By plotting historical data onto time series graphs, the meteorologists can look for patterns in the data and use this to predict long-term trends. They can then model this going forward in time, in order to predict the future patterns that we might experience. Meteorology is far more than the weather man on the evening news and is an extremely complex scientific pursuit. The work of the United Kingdom 'Met Office', along with examples of meteorological data, can be seen at: http://www.metoffice.gov.uk/

A specific example of a time series graph plotting weather patterns can be seen at: http://www.metoffice.gov.uk/climate/uk/summaries/actualmonthly

Prior knowledge

Students should already know how to…

- Substitute whole numbers into simple formulae
- Plot coordinates of a standard Cartesian grid

Starter problem

The starter problem is a game of 'four-in-a-line' where players use a coordinate grid to place counters and try and gain a winning line of four counters. The counters must all lie in a straight line and this can be used to introduce a discussion of the relationship between the coordinates that make up a straight-line graph. In a more general sense, players can be asked to investigate winning lines, rather than just playing the game and seeing what happens.

Winning lines that are not straight up or down, or at 45°, might be harder for the players to spot so they could be encouraged to aim for winning lines that are 'unusual'. More able students might be invited to describe winning lines with specific gradients and/or intersections with the x- or y-axes.

Resources

MyMaths

Conversion graphs	1059	$y = mx + c$	1153	Drawing graphs	1168
Real life graphs	1184				

Online assessment

Chapter test	2B–6
Formative test	2B–6
Summative test	2B–6

InvisiPen solutions

Plotting straight lines from tables	262
Equation of a straight line	265
Real-life graphs	275

Topic scheme

Teaching time = 5 lessons/2 weeks

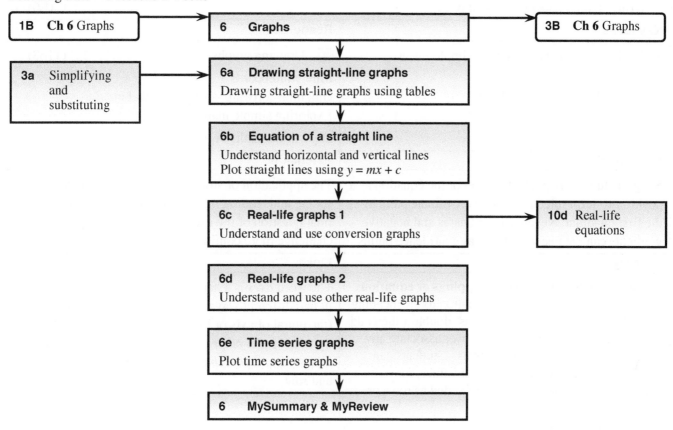

| 1B   Ch 6 Graphs | | 6   Graphs | | 3B   Ch 6 Graphs |

3a   Simplifying and substituting

6a   Drawing straight-line graphs
Drawing straight-line graphs using tables

6b   Equation of a straight line
Understand horizontal and vertical lines
Plot straight lines using $y = mx + c$

6c   Real-life graphs 1
Understand and use conversion graphs

10d   Real-life equations

6d   Real-life graphs 2
Understand and use other real-life graphs

6e   Time series graphs
Plot time series graphs

6   MySummary & MyReview

Differentiation

Student book 2A   106 – 125
Coordinates in four quadrants
Coordinates and straight lines
Drawing graphs
Horizontal and vertical graphs
Real-life graphs
Conversion graphs
Graphs and formulae

Student book 2B   98 – 113
Drawing straight-line graphs
Equation of a straight line
Real-life graphs 1
Real-life graphs 2
Time series graphs

Student book 2C   100 – 119
Graphs of linear functions
Equation of a straight line
Curved graphs
Midpoints of coordinate pairs
Graphs of implicit functions
Real-life graphs
Time series

Objectives

- Generate points in all four quadrants and plot graphs of linear functions, where y is given explicitly in terms of x, on paper (and using ICT)　　　　　　　　　　　　　　　(L6)

Key ideas	Resources
1　Find number pairs that satisfy simple linear functions 2　Plot and represent on a graph	⊞　Drawing graphs　　　　　　(1168) Mini whiteboards Graphing software such as GeoGebra Exploring simple mapping: http://nrich.maths.org/6951

Simplification	Extension
Suggest students begin by thinking of the equation as a position-to-term rule, to generate coordinate pairs in the first quadrant. Negative coordinates and negative gradients can then be introduced as confidence builds.	The application of straight-line graphs in a real-life setting and reading information from graphs as in the final question of the exercise can be developed to challenge more confident students.

Literacy	Links
Reading aloud the **functions**, **mappings** or **equations** should be encouraged, paying attention to the meaning of each, for example, $2x + 1$ read as 'double x then add 1'. Take care that students do not over associate any procedural points with key concepts – students can become fixated by drawing table of values, for example, and whether these are recorded as rows or columns.	The word *axes* is a heteronym as it can be pronounced in two different ways, each with a different meaning (the plural of axis or the plural of axe). Ask the class to try to list some other heteronyms. Some examples are *minute, lead, wind, buffet, refuse, tear, wind, wound* and *sow*.

Alternative approach

Begin by asking students to find pairs of numbers that 'work' or satisfy a simple equation such as $y = x + 4$, having modelled one example. Students can offer their results on mini whiteboards. Select several pairs as appropriate, discussing and checking for accuracy with the whole group. Students should already be familiar and comfortable with plotting coordinates, but will benefit from the modelling of plotting some of pairs onto a displayed graph, using appropriate display software. It is worth discussing where values 'in between' the plotted points might be, as well as considering what happens beyond the drawn/plotted areas. Encourage students to find a set of coordinates that were not offered originally to check if they 'work' with the equation. Further practice can take place using Exploring simple mapping found on the NRICH site, as referenced.

Checkpoint

1　Plot pairs of coordinates that satisfy the equation $y = 2x - 3$.

　　(Table of values:

x	-1	0	1	2	3	4
y	-5	-3	-1	1	3	5

　　Appropriate graph is drawn with a line representing the mapping)

Starter – ABC

If $A = 3$, $B = 5$, $C = 7$, ask students to form as many equations as they can in four minutes. Score 1 point for each different operation or pair of brackets used, for example, $2(C - B) = 4$ uses multiplication, brackets and subtraction and scores 3.

Teaching notes

The exercises focus on the first quadrant, but it will be useful revision to ensure students are confident plotting points in all four quadrants. Ask students to supply ways to remember which is the x- and y-axis: 'along the corridor and up the stairs', 'X a cross, and Y to the sky', etc.

A physical way to cement understanding of vertical and horizontal lines is as follows.

Stand students in a position defined as $x = 0$ then instruct them to move left or right to represent, for example, $x = 5$ or $x = -3$. Similarly, they can hold out their arms to represent $y = 0$ and then bend or stretch to represent, for example, $y = 4$ or $y = -2$.

When drawing tables of values, encourage students to look for a pattern in the numbers or a lack of one that would suggest an error. This is likely to be particularly useful when they start to use negative numbers.

Plenary

Ask students to draw a flow diagram that shows a step by step strategy for drawing a graph from an equation.

Exercise commentary

Question 1 – It may be helpful to discuss how to choose sensible scales for the axes. Check for errors: axes labelled '-2, -1, 1, 2' or points plotted (y, x).

Question 2 – Encourage students to look for the pattern in the numbers in their table so that they check for errors independently. Parts **e** and **f** involve negative gradients and may cause difficulty for some students.

Question 3 – Students may need reminding how to handle an implicit equation.

Questions 4 and **5** – For students who might struggle with the contexts here, suggest they call the cost £y. In question **5**, the time could also be given as x hours.

Question 6 – This activity provides a valuable opportunity to link terms used in mathematics with the use of language elsewhere.

Answers

1 a

x	0	1	2	3	4	5
y	4	5	6	7	8	9

b Students' own diagram
c Check students' graph

---

2 Check students' graphs for all sub parts **ii** and **iii**

a i

x	0	1	2	3	4	5
y	2	3	4	5	6	7

b i

x	0	1	2	3	4	5
y	-1	0	1	2	3	4

c i

x	0	1	2	3	4	5
y	1	3	5	7	9	11

d i

x	0	1	2	3	4	5
y	-3	-1	1	3	5	7

e i

x	0	1	2	3	4	5
y	10	9	8	7	6	5

f i

x	0	1	2	3	4	5
y	5	4	3	2	1	0

3 Check points plotted from each table of values below

a

x	0	2	4	6	8	10
y	10	8	6	4	2	0

b

x	0	2	4	6	8	10
y	6	4	2	0	-2	-4

c

x	0	2	4	6	8	10
y	8	6	4	2	0	-2

d

x	0	2	4	6	8	10
y	9	7	5	3	1	-1

4 a

x	1	2	3	4	5
C	6	10	14	18	22

b Check students' graph
c 2. 5 metres

5 a The following points plotted:

t	0	1	2	3	4	5	6
C	10	15	20	25	30	35	40

b i 3 hours   **ii** 4.5 hours

6 Students' answers. For example, function can mean:
1 An activity or purpose that something is designed for (*The function of a car is to carry passengers.*)
2 A public occasion or social gathering (*The hotel has a function room where you can have a wedding reception.*)
3 A factor that is dependent on other factors. (*The price of petrol is a function of supply and demand.*)
4 To work or operate in a particular way. (*Without batteries, the bell doesn't function.*)

In mathematics, a function is a relationship where every member of one set maps onto just one member of another set.

The Latin word *functio* means 'to perform'.

Objectives

- Recognise, sketch and produce graphs of linear functions of one variable with appropriate scaling, using equations in *x* and *y* and the Cartesian plane   (L6)

Key ideas	Resources
1 Being able to identify which functions are linear from the equation 2 Plot the graphs of linear functions	$y = mx + c$ (1153) Prepared grids

Simplification	Extension
Allow students to create tables of values and draw graphs for all the questions. Use the graphs to emphasise the important points to look for in the corresponding equations. Again, drawing axes particularly in real situations where labelling is not likely to be consecutive can be problematic, so pre-prepare grids as appropriate.	Challenge students to plot the graph corresponding to $y = 2x^2 + 1$. This could first be done by constructing a table for positive *x* values and then extending to negative *x* values. Explain that this is a general method that will work for any equations.

Literacy	Links
Re-examine the vocabulary of function, mapping and equation. An area that might arise in this work is that linking *x* values to 'input' or **independent** variable and *y* values to 'output' or **dependent** variable. Link and check with consistency of terminology here with other curricular groups, especially science.	René Descartes is considered the 'inventor' of the standard coordinate system we use today (Cartesian coordinates) and students could do some internet research to find out more about him. They could also investigate more of his mathematical (and philosophical) discoveries.

Alternative approach

Ask students to identify which functions are likely to be linear from a variety of functions, written using *x* and *y*, and include other variables. Explore what the students are picking up to enable them to identify accurately, and share this with the whole group. Extend to real situations. Simple £–Euro or other currency conversion graphs are worth discussing with students, pointing out these rates, or multipliers, or gradient; change constantly, whereas metres–yards, kilometres–miles don't change.

Checkpoint

1 Which of the following functions are horizontal? Which are vertical?

   $y = 3x - 6$; $y = 3 - 4x$; $y = 6$; $x = 17$; $y = 7x + 4$; $y = 2$

   (Horizontal: $y = 6$, $y = 2$; Vertical: $x = 17$)

Starter – Odd-one-out

Which numbers are the odd ones out in these sequences and why?

$1, 3, 5, 6, 7, 9$ (6: not odd)

$1, 4, 9, 16, 24, 36$ (24: not square)

The example sequences can be simplified or extended as required to suit the class.

Teaching notes

The most obvious way that students get confused is with thinking that $y =$ equations are vertical (parallel to the y-axis) and that $x =$ equations are horizontal (parallel to the x-axis). Encourage them to think about the coordinates on the line, rather than the definition: All coordinates on the line $y = 2$, for example, have a y-coordinate of 2.

Prepared axes can also help students who might be a bit slow at getting started.

Plenary

Ask students to draw a flow diagram that shows a step by step strategy for drawing a graph from a given equation.

Exercise commentary

Question 1 – A recognition question; ensure the students are classifying the horizontal and vertical lines correctly.

Question 2 – Again, ensure they are getting the horizontal and vertical lines the right way round.

Question 3 – Students must plot their own vertical and horizontal lines here so again, check they are getting them the right way round.

Questions 4 and **5** – Basic practice at drawing sloping straight line graphs.

Question 6 – Students may need to write out lists (or tables) of coordinate pairs to identify the two sloping lines.

Question 7 – A real-life scenario and good practice following on from questions **4** and **5**. Note the line should slope downwards.

Answers

1 a A   b B   c C   d C
    e B   f C   g A   h C

2 a $x = 2$ b $x = 3$ c $x = 5$
    d $y = 3$ e $y = 1$

3 Check students' drawings
    Area = 8 units^2

4 a

x	0	1	2	3
y	3	5	7	9

    b Check students' graph

5 a

x	0	1	2	3
y	-2	1	4	7

    b Check students' graph

6 a B   b D   c C   d A
    e Odd one out

7

x	20	30	40	50	60
y	60	50	40	30	20

Check students' graph

Objectives	
• Plot and interpret graphs of simple linear functions arising from real-life situations (for example, conversion graphs) (L6)	

Key ideas	Resources
1 Plot conversion graphs	Conversion graphs (1059)
2 Use conversion graphs to convert units	Prepared axes and/or tables
3 Interpret other real-life graphs	Mini whiteboards

Simplification	Extension
The conversion graphs used here are simple proportional conversions and therefore should not pose too many problems for the students. However, slower workers may benefit from prepared tables and/or axes so the emphasis can be on using them rather than copying out the tables, etc.	Conversion graphs that include a 'fixed' cost such as energy tariffs or possibly mobile phone tariffs can be looked at. For example, can the students draw a conversion graph for $C = 2x + 20$?

Literacy	Links
Conversion The idea of converting currencies links into financial literacy and also the development of students' understanding of different currencies and countries.	Students could be asked to find out (or recall) other common conversions (such as inches to cm ($\times 2.5$) and draw a conversion graph of this. Alternatively, they could look up some actual currency conversions ($ to £, for example) and have a go at working with these.

Alternative approach	
The approach in question **2** could be used first of all to get the students to think about the conversions numerically before using a graph at all. The graph for pounds to dollars in question **1** can be *derived* rather than simply given, and the students could then practice at reading off the graph once it has been drawn.	
For the work on distance–time graphs (question **3**), students could be asked to describe the journey, rather than just answering the comprehension questions.	

Checkpoint	
1 The exchange rate from pounds to euros is £1 = €1.20.	
a Draw a conversion graph for £0 to £10.	(Students' graphs)
b How many euros would I get for £5.50?	(€6.60)
c How many pounds would I get for €7.20?	(£6)

Starter – Pigeons and rabbits

Gareth was watching some pigeons and rabbits.

He counted the number of heads and feet. There were 19 heads and 52 feet. Ask students how many pigeons and how many rabbits there were.

(12 pigeons, 7 rabbits)

This can be extended by asking students to make up their own bird and animal puzzles.

Teaching notes

The key processes in algebra are developed here with the focus on interpretation and evaluation, as students interpret the shape and other features of graphs. The skills required for students to become functional in mathematics are highlighted and students are required to transfer their skills to new or different situations.

There is an emphasis on real-life graphs and on the use of graphs in other curriculum areas, especially science. Encourage students to identify other information that is shown in the graphs beyond that which is specifically asked for in the question. Discuss other real-life situations that could be represented with straight-line graphs.

Plenary

Ask students to draw a travel graph and swap with a friend. The friend should then describe, in words, his or her interpretation of the depicted journey.

Exercise commentary

Question 1 – Ensure students are reading from the correct axis. In part **g**, ask them what the conversion actually is: the 'exchange rate'.

Question 2 – The coordinate points don't quite match up with the scaling on the suggested graph axes so ensure students are plotting the points carefully within the intervals.

Question 3 – Students could come up with their own interpretation for this (and other) graphs.

Question 4 – Emphasise the need to explain the reasoning behind the answer.

Question 5 – A good opportunity for a research-based homework.

Answers

1 **a** £5   **b** £4   **c** £2.50   **d** $6
   e $7   **f** $5   **g** $\frac{1}{2}$

2 | **Kilometres** | 8 | 16 | 24 | 40 | 44 | 48 |
   | **Miles** | | 5 | 10 | 15 | 25 | 27.5 | 30 |

   Graph will be a straight line through $(0, 0)$ and $(40, 25)$
   a almost 19 miles $\left(18\frac{3}{4}\right)$ **b** 32 km

3 **a** 200 metres
   b 5 minutes
   c 10 minutes
   d 2 minutes
   e To eat when the food is as hot as possible

4 Discuss students' results

5 Discuss students' findings

Objectives	
• Discuss and interpret graphs arising from real situations	(L6)

Key ideas	Resources
1 Gaining a sense of a story behind any graph 2 Using such a graph to estimate values	Real life graphs (1184) Matching graphs and scenarios: http://www.nationalstemcentre.org.uk/elibrary/resourc e/6658/matching-graphs-and-scenarios

Simplification	Extension
To support students who are having difficulty with this work, provide some true and some false statements from the interpretation of a given graph. Ask students to work in pairs to sort the statements into those that are true and those that are false. Ask how do you know?	Ask more able students to research real-life graphs in the media, such as those depicting currency fluctuations or the rise and fall of profits in the retail industry.

Literacy	Links
What variable each axis represents is important when interpreting any graph. Ask students frequently, to check their understanding, and request suggestions for units as well. The important feature here is that the axes represent continuous data, so emphasise this by probing students' understanding of values anywhere in a graph, including, for example, possible times of the day when labelling just includes days of the week.	Human beings grow fastest before they are born – the fastest growth rate is at about the fourth month of pregnancy. There is a chart showing the average weight and height of an unborn baby during pregnancy at http://www.babycentre.co.uk/pregnancy/fetaldevelopm ent/chart/ Ask students to plot the graph of weight against age. Is the graph steeper or less steep than the graph in question 1?

Alternative approach
Begin with a simple distance–time graph displayed (or some other type of real-life graph) and request pairs of students to write the story behind the graph. Share some of the results, and discuss fully any exposed misconceptions as well probing understanding of possible units, etc., and how they might change for different scenarios. Use may be made of the resource and activity sheets and/or slideshow from Nuffield Mathematics, as referenced in resources. The card matching activity is best worked with pairs or three students in order to generate valuable discussion to consolidate the learning. Question 5 also offers another approach, perhaps in liaison with PE, where pupils explore their own pulse rates over a range of simple exercises, recovery and resting.

Checkpoint
1 Give students a scenario and ask them to produce a sketch of the scenario. This could be a description of a journey, or other scenario.   (Students' graphs, perhaps checked by comparison with others)

Starter – Containers

Ask students to imagine two unmarked containers. One holds exactly three litres; the other holds exactly five litres. Jamie says he can use these containers to get exactly four litres. Ask students to work out how this can be done.

What if the capacities are 5 litres and 7 litres?

Teaching notes

Again, the emphasis on real-life situations in this spread works towards developing functional mathematics and students' ability to interpret and sketch graphs.

Students will learn most effectively by collaborating on tasks and discussing their interpretations. Through this, they will develop the ability to support conclusions using reasoned arguments and evidence.

Whole-class discussion of the worked examples can lead to asking students to write a 'storyline' of their own, perhaps about their own school day or to describe a journey they have made. Students can then challenge each other to sketch a graph to depict this.

Alternatively, give students a graph on unlabelled axes and be asked to write a possible 'storyline' for the graph.

Plenary

Ask students to draw a sketch graph of how they felt during the course of this maths lesson. Ask them to write a written description to accompany this.

Exercise commentary

The questions in this exercise make explicit links with real-life situations and other areas of the curriculum. Encourage students to think of their own examples.

Questions 1 to **3** – These are similar to the first example. Students should be encouraged to share interpretations and compare ideas.

Question 4 – This is similar to the second example. Emphasise that a sketch graph is not entirely accurate but 'representative'.

Question 5 – This heart rate graph activity could be carried out as a genuine real-life example – make links with sport. There is not a unique answer to this task.

Answers

1   a   The baby loses weight slightly over the first 4 weeks and then starts to gain, reaching her original birth weight after 8 weeks.

    b   Her weight increases gradually over the first 13 to 14 years, with a sudden increase through puberty until the late teens.

    c   Discuss students' drawings

2   Jim started off quickly and then gradually slowed over the next 2 hours. He then had an hour's rest, before riding for another 2 hours, but this time he slowed down much more.

3   a P   b Q

   P blinks on and off at regular time intervals hence it is **a**, the car indicator.

4   Students' graph should have time on horizontal axis and distance on vertical axis. Graph should initially be a fairly steep slope, but less steep as Maria tires; horizontal line when stationary; remainder of journey less steep, a constant slope.

5   Compare and discuss students' answers.

Objectives	
• Construct simple line graphs for time series	(L6)

Key ideas	Resources	
1 Construct time series graphs 2 Read from and interpret time series graphs	Real life graphs Squared paper Mini whiteboards	(1184)

Simplification	Extension
For question **1**, provide partly-labelled, pre-prepared pair of axes so that students can concentrate on plotting and interpreting the data. In question **2** students may need support in choosing the scales for the axes for the time series graph.	Students could be asked to work out some simple moving averages for one of the time series and plot the points on a copy of the graph. This exercise will emphasise the 'trend' and how we can use the trend to make predictions.

Literacy	Links
The language 'over time' should be familiar to students but there is an emphasis throughout this exercise on comprehension and interpretation. Students could link this work to other curriculum areas and spot similar terminology.	The Consumer Price Index (CPI) is an official measure of the average price of goods and services including travel costs, food, heating and household goods. The index number is calculated each month by finding the price of a sample of goods that a typical household might buy, and comparing the price to a reference value. The percentage change in the CPI from the same month in the previous year is a measure of inflation. The latest figures for the CPI can be found at http://www.statistics.gov.uk/cci/nugget.asp?ID=19

Alternative approach
Reverse the order of the two key ideas. By focusing on the comprehension elements of the time series graphs (questions **3** and **4**) it links more obviously back to the previous two sections on interpreting real-life graphs. Once the time series have been analysed, then students can have a go at drawing some of their own time series by completing questions **1** and **2**.

Checkpoint
1 Describe a variable changing over time and ask students to sketch a time series graph for the variable. (Students' answers, could be checked using mini whiteboards or by comparison with others in the group)

Starter – Temperatures

Write a list of times and temperatures on the board:

6 am, 9°; 9 am, 16.5°; 12 noon, 21°; 3 pm, 23.5°; 6 pm, 17°; 9 pm, 14°.

Give students quick-fire questions, for example:

What is the biggest temperature difference?

By how much did the temperature change between 9 am and 12 noon?

Can be differentiated by the choice/amount of temperatures.

Teaching notes

Most students will have seen time series graphs before and may have drawn them (or used them) in science and in geography. As an introduction, give students data for the amount of sunshine per day for two weeks in June, for example:

Sun 6.5 hrs; Mon 8.2 hrs; Tues 2.7 hrs; Wed 3.4 hrs; Thurs 3 hrs; Fri 5.8 hrs; Sat 7.5 hrs; Sun 4.8 hrs; Mon 5.5 hrs; Tues 6.4 hrs; Wed 7.2 hrs; Thurs 7.8 hrs; Fri 8.4 hrs; Sat 9.5 hrs

Ask them to show this information on a graph. Allow them five minutes to do this in pairs. Remind students that they need to label their graphs correctly.

Now compare the graphs that students have drawn. Most will have drawn bar charts but if there are some who have drawn a time series graph, use these as an example. If not, then suggest that for this type of information a quicker way of showing the data is by drawing a time series graph.

Show them a time series graph discussing the solid line between the two data points. Explain that it shows a trend rather than an 'in between' value.

Plenary

Ask students to think about the homework they do during a school week. Can they draw a time series graph to show the amount of homework that is set each day (students could work together here to agree on what is the usual amount). On the same graph (with Saturday and Sunday!) can they show how much homework they actually do each day? Comment on the differences.

Exercise commentary

Question 1 – Similar to the first example. Ask students to explain any patterns that they see. Can they give a possible reason?

Question 2 – Students may need help to decide on suitable scales to use.

Question 3 – Ensure the students are reading the scales correctly. For part **b**, the 2.5 m points are conveniently marked on the graph already, so reading off should be easier.

Question 4 – This question could be used as the basis for further exploration of the CPI (see the **Links** section).

Answers

1 Check students' graph
2 Check students' graph
3 **a** Low tide is 0.8 m at just after 14:30. The depth of water then increases steadily to high tide of 7.8 m just before 20:30. The depth of water then decreases steadily to 1 m (low tide) at 03 00
   b 16:15 ; 00:25
4 Prices rose fairly steadily during the first 70 years of the 20th century. Prices were doubling roughly over each 20 year period during that time, apart from a period of stability between 1920 and 1940. Since 1970, inflation has been rampant with prices nearly quadrupling between 1970 and 1980, and almost doubling between 1980 and 1990, before inflation slowed down again between 1990 and 2000.

Key outcomes	Quick check
Draw a straight-line graph of a function. L6	Draw the following graphs: **a** $y = 3$ (horizontal line through 3 on the y-axis) **b** $x = -1$ (vertical line through -1 on the x-axis) **c** $y = 2x - 1$ (line with gradient 2 through (0, -1))
Recognise the equations of sloping lines and lines parallel to the axes. L6	Are the following equations vertical, horizontal or sloping? **a** $y = -2$ (horizontal) **b** $y = 4 - x$ (sloping (downwards)) **c** $y = 2x + 3$ (sloping (upwards)) **d** $x = 4$ (vertical)
Interpret and draw real-life graphs. L6	Draw the graph of the following journey: Alex walks 5 km in 1 hour, rests for 30 minutes and then walks back in 1 hour 30 minutes. (Students' graphs – should start from (0, 0), go up to (1, 5), across to (1.5, 5) and then down to (3, 0))
Construct and interpret simple line graphs for time series. L6	Draw a time series graph for the following daily rainfall: Mon: 5 mm, Tues: 7 mm, Wed: 8 mm, Thurs: 4 mm, Fri: 6 mm, Sat: 8 mm, Sun: 2 mm. (Check students' graphs – can be compared with other students)

⊕ MyMaths extra support

Lesson/online homework		Description
Coordinates 2	1093 L5	Coordinates in the four quadrants and midpoint of a line

MyReview

Check out

You should now be able to ...

Test it ➡
Questions

✓ Draw a straight-line graph of a function.	1
✓ Recognise the equations of sloping lines and lines parallel to the axes.	2, 4
✓ Interpret and draw real life graphs.	3, 5
✓ Construct and interpret simple line graphs for time series.	6

Language	Meaning	Example
Function	A rule that gives a unique output for a given input. The rule is usually written as an equation	$y = 2x + 1$ gives an output value y for an input value x. If $x = 2$ then $y = 5$
Equation	A function involving x and y which can be plotted on a graph using a table of values	$y = 7 - 3x$ and $y = 10x^2$ are both equations
Horizontal line	A line on a graph parallel to the x-axis	$y = 1$ or -3 or any constant
Vertical line	A line on a graph parallel to the y-axis	$x = 2$ or -1.5 or any constant
Straight line graph	A graph with an equation that can be written in the form $y = mx + c$	$y = 2x + 5$, $y = 5x$, $y = -6$ and $2x + 3y = 5$ are all straight lines
Real life graph	A graph which can be used to illustrate a real life situation	A graph of distance versus time for your journey to school
Time series graph	A graph which can be used to show how something changes over time or to show trends	A graph of your weekly pocket money versus the year

1 For the equation $y = 3x + 1$
   a copy and complete the table

x	0	1	2	3	4
y					

   b draw axes with x from 0 to 4 and y from 0 to 14 then draw the graph.

2 Write the equations of lines A, B, C and D.

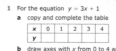

3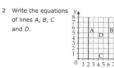

   This graph converts Celsius (°C) to Fahrenheit (°F).
   a What is 77 °F in degrees Celsius?
   b At what temperature in Fahrenheit does water freeze?

4 $y = -2$ $x = 5$ $y = 3x^2$
  $y = 4x$ $y + x = 8$
  Which of the equations above are
  a a horizontal   b a vertical
  c a sloping straight line
  d not a straight line?

5 Max drives to the shops and back, this graph shows his journey.

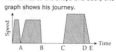

   a At what time, A, B, C, D or E, does he
     i leave the shop
     ii stop at traffic lights
     iii arrive home?
   b Does Max drive more quickly to the shop or home from the shop?

6 The number of children in an infant school is recorded over nine years.

Year	Children
2006	90
2007	95
2008	110
2009	145
2010	175
2011	180
2012	150
2013	120

   Draw a time series graph for this set of data.

What next?

Score		
0 – 3	▮	Your knowledge of this topic is still developing. To improve look at Formative test: 2B-6; MyMaths: 1153, 1168 and 1184
4 – 5	▮	You are gaining a secure knowledge of this topic. To improve look at InvisiPen: 262, 265 and 275
6	▮	You have mastered this topic. Well done, you are ready to progress!

Question commentary

Students should be using a ruler and sharp pencil for all graphs, ensure all axes are appropriately numbered and labelled.

Question 1 – Axes can be provided for students who struggle drawing them.

Question 2 – Students sometimes confuse x and y, get them to write down coordinates from the line to see that, e.g. for $x = 2$, the x-coordinate is always 2.

Question 3 – For **b** allow ±2°. Students should hopefully know that water freezes at 0°C.

Question 4 – Let students know that there are two answers for one of the questions but don't tell them which. If they are stuck they can plot points, but they should learn to recognise them.

Question 5 – Students sometime confuse speed–time graphs with distance–time graphs so they may think Max is at the shop when in fact he is travelling at a constant speed to or from the shop.

Question 6 – Sensible increments for the y-axis would be 5 or 10 children per square. Students do not necessarily need to start their y-axis from 0, but you could discuss how the graph has the potential to mislead if you don't.

Answers

1 a

x	0	1	2	3	4
y	1	4	7	10	13

   b Check students' graph

2 A $x = 2$ B $x = 6$ C $y = 0$ D $y = 4$

3 a 25 °C   b 32 °F

4 a $y = -2$ b $x = 5$
  c $y = 4x$, $y + x = 8$ d $y = 3x^2$

5 a i C   ii A   iii E
  b Home

6 Check students' graphs

6 MyPractice

1 a Copy and complete this table for the equation $y = x + 5$.
Plot points on axes labelled as shown here.
Draw the graph of the equation $y = x + 5$.

x	-1	0	1	2	3	4
y						

b Repeat for the equations
  i $y = x + 2$
  ii $y = 2x - 1$
  iii $x + y = 9$

2 For each of these equations, copy and complete this table.
Plot points for each equation on axes, both labelled from -2 to 8.
Draw the graph of each equation and label it.

a $y = x + 1$ **b** $y = x - 1$ **c** $y = 2x - 1$ **d** $y = 8 - x$

x	0	1	2	3	4
y					

3 Label both axes from 0 to 10. Draw the graphs of these lines
a $x = 6$ **b** $y = 5$ **c** $y = x + 1$ **d** $y = 2x$

4 a You can convert euros € into pounds £ with this formula: $£ = \dfrac{3 \times €}{4}$.
Copy and complete this table using the formula.

€	0	8	12	20
£				

b Draw a graph to convert euros to pounds, with both axes labelled from 0 to 20.
  i How many pounds will you get for €16?
  ii How many euros will you get for £3?

5 Khaleda walks the 500m to the shop in five minutes.
She spends three minutes in the shop and then returns home the same way in two minutes.
a Draw a graph to show her visit to the shop on axes as shown here.
b Was Khaleda faster going to the shop or coming back?

6 Sam heats some soup in the microwave for two minutes.
He takes it out and finds it is not warm enough.
He immediately reheats it for another minute and then leaves it for a further minute before starting to eat it.
Sketch a graph of the temperature of the soup during this time.

7 The graph shows the number of people getting on trains at a busy railway station.
a Describe the main features of the graph.
b Explain the shape of the graph.

8 In an experiment, Jackie heated up a beaker of water, and then left it to cool. She recorded the temperature every minute (in degrees Celsius). Here are her results.
95, 79, 67, 57, 49, 43, 38, 34, 31, 28, 26, 25, 23, 22
Draw a time series graph for this set of data.

9 A department store has five floors: ground, 1, 2, 3 and 4.
There are up and down escalators between each floor.
Each escalator takes one minute to go up or down one floor, and it takes 30 seconds to walk between escalators on each floor.
Monica starts on the ground floor, and travels up to the top floor as quickly as possible.
Draw a time series graph for her journey.

MyMaths.co.uk

Question commentary

Question 1 – This is basic practice at plotting straight-line graphs. The table and pre-drawn axes provide suitable scaffolding. The graphs could all be drawn on the same set of axes.

Questions 2 and **3** – These are also basic practice at plotting straight-line graphs. The table provides suitable scaffolding but now the students have to create their own axes. The graphs could all be drawn on the same set of axes.

Questions 4 and **5** – Students will need to create their own scales for question **4**. In question **5**, refer to the steepness of the lines when discussing speed.

Question 6 – Emphasise that sketches still have to be correct relative to each element.

Question 7 – Explain that descriptions should be clear and unambiguous. Evidence in the form of times or relative numbers should be used.

Question 8 – Students may need assistance choosing scales.

Question 9 – There are no units of distance so students should ensure that their graph is correct relative to each part of the journey.

Answers

1 a

x	-1	0	1	2	3	4
y	4	5	6	7	8	9

Straight line through (0, 5) and (4, 9)

b i

x	-1	0	1	2	3	4
y	1	2	3	4	5	6

Straight line through (0, 2) and (4, 6)

ii

x	-1	0	1	2	3	4
y	-3	-1	1	3	5	7

Straight line through (0, -1) and (4, 7)

iii

x	-1	0	1	2	3	4
y	10	9	8	7	6	5

Straight line through (0, 9) and (4, 5)

2 a

x	0	1	2	3	4
y	1	2	3	4	5

Straight line through (0, 1) and (4, 5)

b

x	0	1	2	3	4
y	-1	0	1	2	3

Straight line through (1, 0) and (4, 3)

c

x	0	1	2	3	4
y	-1	1	3	5	7

Straight line through (1, 1) and (4, 7)

d

x	0	1	2	3	4
y	8	7	6	5	4

Straight line through (0, 8) and (4, 4)

3 a Vertical line through (6, 0)

b Horizontal line through (0, 5)

c Straight line through (0, 1) and (9, 10)

d Straight line through (0, 0) and (5, 10)

4 a

€	0	8	12	20
£	0	6	9	15

b Straight line through the origin and (12,9)

i £12   **ii** €4

5 a Check students' graph

b Faster coming back

6 Check students' graph

7 a Most people get on trains between 5 and 6 pm. There is another peak between 7 and 8 am. During the day demand is low, and is constant from 12 to 4:30 pm. There are some sudden increases in demand at 10 am, 7 pm and 10:30 pm.

b People are trying to get to work at 7 am and home at 5 pm as many people work from 9–5.

8 Check students' graph

9 Check students' graph

Related lessons		Resources	
Properties of a quadrilateral	5d	Interior exterior angles	(1100)
Properties of a polygon	5e	Sum of angles in a polygon	(1320)
Symmetry	9c	Lines of symmetry	(1114)
		Rotation symmetry	(1116)
		Examples of patchwork	
		Isometric paper	

Simplification	Extension
Task **2** parts **b** and **c** could be scaffolded or omitted. Students could work on squared or isometric paper for task **3** to aid their designing. Patterns based on shapes other than the square could be omitted.	Ask students to find the internal angles in regular polygons, from equilateral triangle to dodecagon. (60°, 90°, 108°, 120°, $128\frac{4}{7}$°, 135°, 140°, 144°, $147\frac{3}{11}$°, 150°) Using knowledge of these angles ask students to see how many polygons of one type they can fit exactly around a point. (6 equilateral triangles; 4 squares; 3 hexagons). If you can use two polygons how many possibilities are there now? (2 squares and 3 equilateral triangles (two ways); 1 or 2 hexagons and 4 or 2 equilateral triangles; 2 octagons and 1 square; 2 dodecagons and 1 equilateral triangle) Can you use this knowledge to create six semi-regular tessellations? Can you find the other two semi-regular tessellations? (Based on 1 equilateral triangle, 2 squares and 1 hexagon or 1 square, 1 hexagon and 1 dodecagon)

Links
Students could research the work of the Dutch artist M C Esher and identify any of his work that they think is based on tessellation. Alternatively, they can look at tessellations they meet in everyday life or the Islamic art of the Alhambra Palace in Spain. http://www.alhambra-patronato.es/

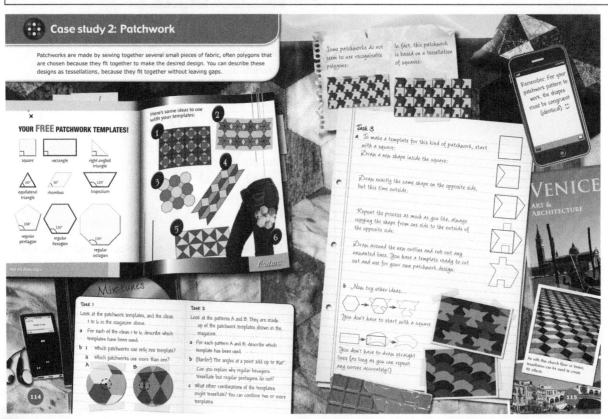

Teaching notes

Patchworks are mainly done as hobbies these days. In times of hardship, patchworks have been used as a way of recycling old clothes to make blankets and such like. Patchworks are often quite geometric in design. A person making the patchwork needs to consider how shapes fit together and often uses a template to make pieces of consistent size and shape. Similar considerations apply to designs using paving stones. This case study uses this geometric nature of patchworks to look at a shapes' internal angles and consider how these determine if a given shape will tessellate.

Introduce the idea of patchworks and remind students about tessellation. Look at the shapes that are used in typical patchworks and discuss what makes the shapes suitable for this purpose.

Look at the case study, focusing initially on the magazine and its free templates. What do you notice about the sizes of the templates? Agree that their dimensions are such that any shape will fit exactly with another.

How long do you think the rectangle is compared with its width? Establish that it is twice as long as it is wide so that it can be used alongside two squares or other shapes. How do you think the lengths of the sides of the trapezium relate to each other? The longer side is twice as long as the shorter sides, which are all the same length as each other. Why do you think the rhombus and the trapezium have both been made with an angle of 60°? Establish that the equilateral triangle has to have an angle of 60° and that if the rhombus and trapezium are going to fit with the triangle, they too have to have an angle of 60°.

Task 1

Now look at the example patchworks and ask students to think about which templates have been used in each patchwork. Give the students a few minutes to note their answers to this before discussing answers. Some students might have considered the lighter spaces in patchworks 2 and 3 as gaps while others might have included them as shapes and named their templates.

Task 2

Use the questions to initiate thinking about the angles in shapes and how these determine whether the shape will tessellate. Ask questions such as why will some shapes tessellate and others not? Is it just to do with the length of their sides or is it also to do with their angles? What is it about the angles of shapes that allow them to be used on their own?

Task 3

To make a template based on a square follow the instructions. Make sure that students understand how the method requires a new shape to be drawn **inside** the shape on one side and **outside** the shape on the other, and that the two shapes are aligned with each other. Look at the two tessellation examples at the end of the instructions to see how the original shape doesn't have to be a square. What shapes could you start with? Establish that the initial shape needs to be one that tessellates.

Answers

1. **a**
   1. Square, right-angled triangle
   2. Isosceles trapezium and rhombus
   3. Regular octagon and square
   4. Square and isosceles trapezium
   5. Right-angled triangle
   6. Regular hexagon
   b **i** 5, 6 **ii** 1, 2, 3, 4

2. **a** **A** Hexagon **B** Rhombus
   b To tessellate, a shape's interior angle must divide evenly into 360, since there are 360° at a point.
   Hexagon: $\frac{360}{120} = 3$, therefore hexagons tessellate;
   Pentagon: $\frac{360}{108} = 3.333...$, therefore pentagons do not tessellate.
   c Lots of possible answers

3. Students' own answers

Learning outcomes		
N4	Use the four operations, including formal written methods, applied to integers, decimals, proper and improper fractions, and mixed numbers, all both positive and negative	(L5)
N5	Use conventional notation for the priority of operations, including brackets, powers, roots and reciprocals	(L5)
N13	Round numbers and measures to an appropriate degree of accuracy (for example, to a number of decimal places or significant figures)	(L5)

Introduction

The chapter starts by looking at rounding numbers before considering mental techniques for adding and subtracting numbers. Multiplying and dividing by powers of 10 are then covered before moving on to mental methods for multiplication and division. The use of these methods in a problem-solving context is then covered in the final two sections.

The introduction discusses the historical background of calculation and gives a brief history of mechanical calculation devices, including the first mechanical calculator invented by Blaise Pascal in 1642. The development of machines to help perform complex calculations has been a major part of the history of calculation over the last 300 years, and eventually led to the development of the high-powered calculators and computers that we use today. Mathematicians such as Ada Lovelace (181 –1852), Charles Babbage (1791–1871) and Alan Turing (1912–1954) are all credited with significant contributions to the development of mechanical calculators and the eventual development of computers as we know them today. Biographies of these eminent mathematicians can be found at:

http://www-history.mcs.st-and.ac.uk/Biographies/Lovelace.html

http://www-history.mcs.st-andrews.ac.uk/Biographies/Babbage.html

http://www-history.mcs.st-andrews.ac.uk/Biographies/Turing.html

Prior knowledge

Students should already know how to…

- Add, subtract, multiply and divide whole numbers
- Use place value

Starter problem

The starter problem is a classic example of a 'Route inspection' problem, often called 'The Chinese Postman' problem (so-called not because of a Chinese postman, but because it was originally studied by a Chinese mathematician, Kwan Mei-Ko, in 1962).

The development of efficient algorithms to solve this kind of problem forms part of a branch of mathematics called 'discrete mathematics'.

Beginning and ending at A, the postman must cover all of the streets at least once. It can be shown that he will not be able to cover each street once only, but that he must walk along some streets more than once. If he repeats streets DE and HF, he can complete the route in the shortest distance. This is equal to the total length of all the streets, plus 0.9 km (DE again) and 1.5 km (HF again). The total distance is therefore 16.7 km.

A possible route would be: AHFHGFEGABCDEDA, but there are many others.

More able students could be asked to work out a route which visits each vertex once (the 'Travelling Salesman' problem) or be given more complex examples of these kinds of problems.

Resources

⊕ MyMaths

Rounding decimals	1004	Multiple decimals by whole numbers	1010
Multiply decimals by 10 and 100	1013	Mixed sums all numbers	1345
Word problems	1393		

Online assessment		InvisiPen solutions	
Chapter test	2B–7	Rounding	112
Formative test	2B–7	Multiplying and dividing by powers of 10	114
Summative test	2B–7	Mental methods of addition and subtraction	121
		Mental multiplication	122
		Mental division	123

Topic scheme

Teaching time = 6 lessons/2 weeks

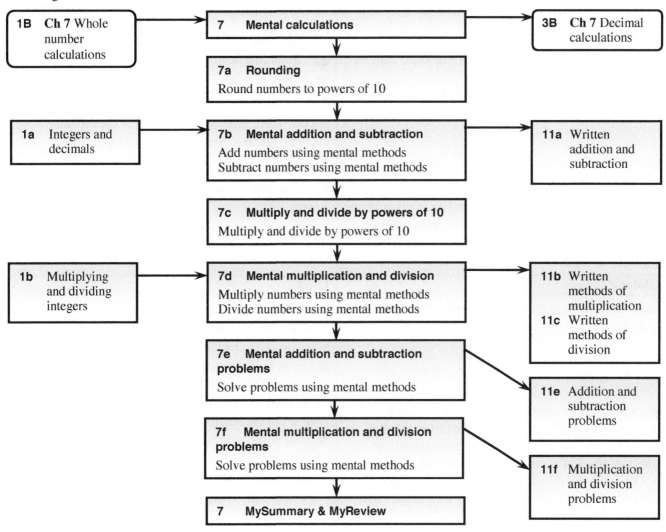

1B Ch 7 Whole number calculations

7 Mental calculations

3B Ch 7 Decimal calculations

7a Rounding
Round numbers to powers of 10

1a Integers and decimals

7b Mental addition and subtraction
Add numbers using mental methods
Subtract numbers using mental methods

11a Written addition and subtraction

7c Multiply and divide by powers of 10
Multiply and divide by powers of 10

1b Multiplying and dividing integers

7d Mental multiplication and division
Multiply numbers using mental methods
Divide numbers using mental methods

11b Written methods of multiplication
11c Written methods of division

7e Mental addition and subtraction problems
Solve problems using mental methods

11e Addition and subtraction problems

7f Mental multiplication and division problems
Solve problems using mental methods

11f Multiplication and division problems

7 MySummary & MyReview

Differentiation

Student book 2A   128 – 143

Order of operations
Mental addition and subtraction
Mental multiplication and division
Addition and subtraction problems
Multiplication and division
    problems

Student book 2B   116 – 133

Rounding
Mental addition and subtraction
Multiply and divide by powers
    of 10
Mental multiplication and division
Mental addition and subtraction
    problems
Mental multiplication and division
    problems

Student book 2C   122 – 135

Arithmetic with negative integers
Powers of 10
Mental addition and subtraction
Mental multiplication and division

Objectives

- Round positive numbers to any given power of 10   (L4)
- Round decimals to the nearest whole number or to one or two decimal places   (L5)

Key ideas	Resources
1 Understanding the continuum of 'measure' and its scale 2 Recognise the purpose and principles of rounding	⊕ Rounding decimals (1004) Mini whiteboards Number lines Soccer Math: http://www.math-play.com/rounding-decimals-game-1/rounding-decimals-game.html

Simplification	Extension
For students who have difficulty with this activity, encourage them to use a diagram and/or an appropriate number line to help them make a decision as in the worked example. The visual support will often move students forward.	For more able students, consider discussing significant figures.

Literacy	Links
Remind students of the notation used for approximate values ≈ and also ≙, or ≃. Address the important point that when rounding answers are usually given with the equality symbol, =. Go on to discuss the fact that the number itself can imply its level of accuracy, but that this level should not be assumed, thus 3.4 is *likely* to mean a value between 3.35 and 3.45.	In parliamentary elections in Germany in 1992, a rounding error caused the wrong results to be announced. Under German law, a party cannot have any seats in Parliament unless it has 5.0% or more of the vote. The Green Party appeared to have exactly 5.0%, until it was discovered that the computer that printed out the results only used one place after the decimal point and had rounded the vote up to 5.0%. The Green Party only had 4.97% of the vote and the results had to be changed.

Alternative approach

Following a modelling and discussion of the principles of rounding, pairs of students can be given a list of results, say from the last Olympics, or of current sporting records, (times, distances and weights) which they then record as values correct to the nearest integer, one decimal place and/or two decimal places. Make sure that the aspect of correctness is addressed by comparing what happens if a previously rounded up value is further approximated.

Checkpoint

1   A distance is 13.67 km.
    a   What would you record this value as to the nearest integer?   (14 km)
    b   What would it be recorded as correct to 1 decimal place?   (13.7 km)
2   If a weight is given as 4.8 kg, give a possible weight that it might be.   (Any between 4.75 kg and 4.85 kg)

Starter – What is my number?

I am even but not square.

I am a multiple of 3.

I am greater than the number of days in November.

I am less than the product of 8 × 9.

I have 8 factors. (54)

This can be extended by asking students to make up their own puzzles.

Teaching notes

An emphasis in this unit is on rounding to a 'sensible degree of accuracy' and it is helpful to discuss this, thereby making explicit links to the use of mathematics in a functional context.

Spend time talking through the procedure for rounding numbers and ensure that students understand that rounding down means keeping the last digit the same, not taking something away, as this is a common error .

Draw attention to the visual representation of the reading on the weighing scale as this clearly shows how a value is closer to one unit than another.

The spread supports learning through the process skill of communicating and reflecting, focusing on the effects of rounding.

Plenary

Ask students to think of a real-life example (for example, measurement, money, etc.) where it is appropriate to round to the nearest 1000, 10, whole number, 2 decimal places and take feedback. Produce a whole-class 'best three examples' in each category.

Exercise commentary

There are a number of opportunities in this exercise to link to the strengthening of literacy skills.

Questions 1 and **2** – Similar to the example. These questions could be completed as an oral whole-class activity or using mini whiteboards for assessment of understanding.

Question 3 – Insist on properly written explanations.

Question 4 – As this question involves other skills it may benefit from being completed as a whole-class exercise. Agree what is an appropriate degree of accuracy.

Question 5 – This provides an excellent opportunity to link mathematics with improving students' skills in writing.

Answers

1.
		i		ii		iii
a	i	4000	ii	4100	iii	4070
b	i	7000	ii	7200	iii	7190
c	i	4000	ii	3700	iii	3650
d	i	8000	ii	7500	iii	7530
e	i	6000	ii	5600	iii	5590
f	i	7000	ii	6600	iii	6570
g	i	5000	ii	4900	iii	4940
h	i	13 000	ii	13 400	iii	13 390
i	i	28 000	ii	27 600	iii	27 590
j	i	32 000	ii	31 700	iii	31 690
k	i	66 000	ii	66 000	iii	65 960
l	i	75 000	ii	75 000	iii	75 000

2.
		i		ii		iii
a	i	4	ii	3.7	iii	3.74
b	i	4	ii	4.2	iii	4.22
c	i	7	ii	7.3	iii	7.29
d	i	9	ii	9.3	iii	9.35
e	i	14	ii	13.9	iii	13.86
f	i	13	ii	13.0	iii	13.04
g	i	4	ii	4.3	iii	4.31
h	i	8	ii	7.9	iii	7.94
i	i	2	ii	2.0	iii	2.04
j	i	3	ii	2.6	iii	2.64
k	i	1	ii	1.3	iii	1.32
l	i	4	ii	3.6	iii	3.58

3. Yes, 17.999 is nearer to 18 than to 17. Also 17.999 is nearer to 18 than to 17.9. A better way of showing the answer to the nearest tenth would have been to write $17.999 \approx 18.0$.

4. a £3.25   b £2.29 (nearest penny)
   c £10.93   d 16p (nearest penny)

5. Check students' newspaper articles.
   Appropriate approximations would be
   6 hours 43 min $\approx 6\frac{3}{4}$ hours
   115.0779 mph $\approx$ 115 mph
   86.3085 mph $\approx$ 86 mph
   63 min $\approx$ 1 hour
   14 983 000 trees $\approx$ 15 million trees.

Objectives		
• Strengthen and extend mental methods of calculation, working with decimals		(L5)
• Solve problems mentally		(L5)

Key ideas	Resources	
1 To be flexible with the use of a variety of strategies enabling mental addition and subtraction	Mixed sums all numbers Mini whiteboards	(1345)

Simplification	Extension
To build confidence, encourage the use of a number line and show how to use this to break down the calculation as in the unit illustrations. Working with addition of consecutive whole numbers simplifies but strengthens skills of weaker students.	More able students will be familiar and confident with most of the strategies explored here and will gain most from discussion about the relative efficiency of various methods and when their use is most likely to be appropriate. Make sure that questions tackled by these students involve more than two numbers, and/or more than one step.

Literacy	Links
While the vocabulary can help here, it is not essential that students know this level of detail. However, understanding the commutativity of addition strengthens flexibility and use of strategies, so do emphasise this. For example, students will be familiar from earlier years to choose the largest value as the starting number when adding. They should also be ready to alter orders of numbers so that they can mentally pair compliments of ten.	There is an educational game about Viking Raiders at http://www.bbc.co.uk/history/ancient/vikings/launch_gms_viking_quest.shtml

Alternative approach
Group challenges can be set up for some problems here, encouraging team speed. Students can work in twos or threes to fully discuss their strategies, challenge and defend others. Mini whiteboards can encourage and strengthen mental images by being used for jottings when and as necessary. Card games to use can include pairing decimal numbers to make whole numbers or finding a maximum or minimum total involving two or three cards. Rapid addition or subtraction of a constant value such as 0.35 around the class out loud can be repeated aiming for faster completion times. Using time tables can also provide further practice, reminding students that there are 60 minutes in an hour, and not to confuse, say, 11:45 with 11.45.

Checkpoint	
1 Solve these mentally:	
a 38 + 69	(107)
b 2.4 + 3.9 + 7.6	(13.9)
c 405 − 399	(6)
d 5.7 − 3.9	(1.8)

Starter – NMBR!

Write words on the board missing out the vowels, for example, NMBR.

Ask students for the original words (number). Possible 'words':

CHNC, DCML, HNDRDTH, PRBBLTY, LVN, FRCTN, MLLN, TNTH, PRCNTG, NT

(Chance, decimal, hundredth, probability, eleven, fraction, million, tenth, percentage, unit)

This can be extended by asking students to make up their own examples.

Teaching notes

The process skill of communicating and reflecting is central to the work in this spread as students are involved throughout in discussing and reflecting on different approaches to solving a numerical problem and comparing the efficiency of calculation procedures.

When working through the examples, stress the point that there is no one correct method of working and that even if a favoured method is less efficient than another, that does not mean it is wrong to use it. The aim here should be to highlight a full range of strategies to ensure that students understand them and again to suggest that a different method could always be used as a mechanism for checking.

The worked examples offer two key points that need to be highlighted for students. First, the importance of approximating as a checking mechanism and second, to practise the skill of analysing text to identify key information.

Plenary

Ask students to work in small groups to design a poster explaining a variety of mental methods that might be used to solve a word problem along similar lines to the worked example.

Exercise commentary

Questions 1 and **2** – Ask students to discuss and compare the methods they use.

Question 3 – Ask students why using a written approach here would be inefficient.

Question 4 – This question could be used for whole class feedback to consider how many different options for calculation students can suggest and to discuss their suitability and efficiency.

Question 5 – Ask students to identify the operation and method they will use to solve each part. Beware of treating times as decimals, not minutes and seconds.

Question 6 – For part **c**, remind students that there is no year 0, so students will need to add on one. Possibly link this to some historical research and ask students to find out how many soldiers were involved in each battle, round the numbers to a sensible degree of accuracy.

Answers

1 a 15.1   b 20.6   c 7.8   d 25.4

2 a   b

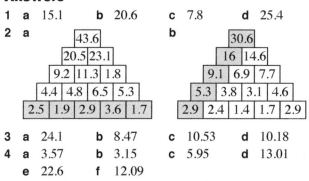

3 a 24.1   b 8.47   c 10.53   d 10.18

4 a 3.57   b 3.15   c 5.95   d 13.01
   e 22.6   f 12.09

5 a 47 seconds
   b 0.75 MB
   c 12 min 47 seconds
   d No. Total storage needed is 12.03 MB.

6 a Depends on year when question is attempted
   b 2476, 2327, 2228, 1954, 1900, 1727
   c 3905, 4054, 4153, 4427, 4481, 4654

Objectives

- Multiply and divide integers and decimals by 10, 100, 1000, and explain the effect (L5)
- Multiply and divide integers and decimals by 0.1 and 0.01 (L7)

Key ideas	Resources
1 Strengthening concepts of place value 2 Making the connections between multiply and divide – as inverse of each other	Multiply decimals by 10 and 100 (1013) Number charts of multiples of 10 Mini whiteboards

Simplification	Extension
If students struggle, discuss with them for any given calculation whether they expect the answer to be bigger or smaller after the operation. Discussion of this type exposes misconceptions about multiplying and dividing by numbers less than 1. Using multiples of 10 charts can help weaker students to remember the links to place value.	Provide work for more able students to 'mark' using examples such as those in the exercise that have been answered with some errors. This will offer consolidation in a more engaging format.

Literacy	Links
Encourage students to read questions out loud, making appropriate adjustments to give any question meaning. For example 567×0.1 might become 'find a tenth of 567'.	Number 10 Downing Street in London is the official residence of the First Lord of the Treasury, who is usually also the prime minister of Great Britain. The first prime minister to live at Number 10 was Robert Walpole in the early 1700s and most prime ministers have lived there since. The house is mainly comprised of offices and the Prime Minister's apartment is at the top of the building. Originally the apartment rooms were used by servants. There is more information about Number 10 at http://www.number10.gov.uk/history-and-tour

Alternative approach

A starting point might be to offer students a challenging statement: 'multiplying always makes values larger'. Ask them to discuss this in pairs and decide if it true or not. Be prepared to inject the idea of, say, $\times 0.5$ if necessary. This can be extended to simple responses of 'larger' or 'smaller' for any given operands of powers of 10. Include $\times 1$ and $\div 1$ with such questions. Students can respond either using mini whiteboards or using thumbs up or down. Students can be carefully led to realise the equivalence of, for instance, $\times 0.1$ and $\div 10$.

Checkpoint

1 Start with 7.8 then $\times 0.1$, $\times 10$, $\times 100$, $\div 0.1$, $\times 0.001$. What is the result? (7.8)

2 If you take any value then $\times 100$, then $\div 10$, then $\times 0.01$, then divide by 10, what is the result?

(Divide by 100 or $\times 0.01$)

Starter – Pocket money

Anwar received £10 pocket money each week.

Bryony's pocket money started at £5 and increased by 50p each week: £5 in week 1, £5.50 in week 2, etc.

Charlie said he would be happy if his pocket money started with 1p and it doubled each week: 1p, 2p, 4p, etc.

Ask students who would have accumulated the most money after 10 weeks. (Anwar)

How about 20 weeks? (Charlie)

Teaching notes

Make links with students' prior learning here, possibly using some of the earlier questions in the exercise as a whole-class mini whiteboard activity to facilitate assessment. Use the response to these questions to decide where to focus discussion when looking at the worked examples.

The most likely area requiring consolidation will be multiplication and division by tenths and hundredths. Support learning through the process skill of analysing – use mathematical reasoning about connections between number operations, for example, dividing by a number is the same as multiplying by its reciprocal.

One way to help students see the connection between dividing by, say 0.01, and multiplying by 100 is to pose questions involving units. 'How many centimetres are there in 3 m?' versus 'How many 0.01 m long items will fit into 3 m?' compared with, 'What is $3 \div 0.01$?'

Plenary

Extend the activity in question **7** of the exercise with additional examples asking students to identify which number will make the calculation correct. Convert this into a mini whiteboard activity to identify whether any problems in understanding persist here.

Exercise commentary

Question 1 – Similar to the first two examples.

Question 2 – Make links here with fractions and division.

Question 3 – This question helps to re-emphasise that division by 0·1 is the same as multiplication by 10, etc.

Question 4 – Similar to the last two examples.

Question 5 – Develops question **4** to use larger numbers.

Question 6 – Develops question **4** to use decimals.

Question 7 – An application of this work which links back to **2a**.

Question 8 – Reviews the material from a slightly different perspective.

Question 9 – Multiple step questions as an extension opportunity so make sure students are working from left to right and showing intermediate steps in working.

Answers

1	a	70	b	4	c	490	d	0.78
	e	300	f	0.47	g	0.94	h	0.0593
2	a	£30	b	4.5 kg	c	$40	d	3.85 km
3	a	30	b	200				
4	a	0.3	b	0.5	c	0.09	d	0.07
	e	60	f	90	g	500	h	300
5	a	2.5	b	0.29	c	360	d	4500
	e	29	f	3.7	g	4100	h	20 000
6	a	3.9	b	2470	c	0.29	d	41
	e	1740	f	93	g	3.45	h	0.027
	i	0.548	j	0.037	k	2700	l	0.8
7	a	1.56 litres	b	36 000 m	c	0.281 kg	d	572.6 cm
	e	53 600 ml	f	192 30 g				
8	a	10	b	100	c	10	d	10
	e	0.1	f	0.01	g	0.1	h	10
9	a	5700	b	1120	c	570	d	0.26

Objectives	
• Strengthen and extend mental methods of calculation, working with decimals (L5)	

Key ideas	Resources
1 Practice and extend related fact knowledge of number 2 Being flexible recognising clues within a problem	Multiply decimals by whole numbers (1010)

Simplification	Extension
Where students experience difficulty, allow them to decide which mental method they are most comfortable with and support them with this rather than placing too much emphasis on other strategies. Confidence building will be beneficial.	More able students could consolidate their understanding by putting together a PowerPoint presentation illustrating how to use a variety of mental methods. This could be shown to the class and made available on the school system for additional 'tutorial style' support for weaker students.

Literacy	Links
Being aware that it is possible to change order appropriately in these operations will help students to see problems in different ways, and select the most efficient methods for themselves. Another area to focus on with the students is the vocabulary of 'calculation'. When asked to calculate, some students assume that this means with a calculator, or will have a perception that a particular method is attached to the instruction. Take the opportunity to look at a variety of alternative equivalent instructions and assure students that methods are always a personal choice.	Question **4** refers to chocolate bars. Chocolate is made from the beans of the tropical cacao tree and was prized as a drink by the Aztecs. The first eating chocolate was produced by Joseph Fry in Bristol in 1848. On average, each person in the United Kingdom eats 10 kg of chocolate each year. The population of The United Kingdom is approximately 60 million. How many tonnes (= 1000 kg) of chocolate are eaten in the UK each year? (600 000 tonnes).

Alternative approach

Pick two or three 'rich' problems for students to discuss in pairs, aiming to find as many different ways of seeing the problems and hence of solving them. Share the results with the whole group and widen discussion into which prove to be the most efficient (quick) as well as the most effective (right) ways. Students should be encouraged to argue for themselves and it should be explicitly recognised that each of us have own favourites or quick ways of seeing any problem. Factors – especially doubling and halving – is a particularly useful strategy to share and model with students for both multiplying and dividing, but students need to be secure with the concepts of multiply and divide. For example $44 \times 0.4 = 88 \times 0.2 = 176 \times 0.1 = 17.6$. Division, however: $225 \div 15 = ((5 \times 45) \div (5 \times 3)) = 45 \div 3 = 15$ where recognition of a common factor here reduces the problem.

It is helpful to encourage students to use their own choices of strategies, so rather than working through Exercise **7d** using suggested strategies, mix the examples and request that students compare as well as check each other's approaches.

Checkpoint

1 Mentally calculate:
   a $175 \div 25$ (7)
   b 4.2×20 (84)
   c $175 \div 2.5$ (70)
Discuss the different strategies used by students.

Starter – 105

Ask students to make 105 by

the product of 2 odd numbers $(3 \times 35, 5 \times 21, 7 \times 15)$

the product of 3 odd numbers $(3 \times 5 \times 7)$

the product of 4 odd numbers $(1 \times 3 \times 5 \times 7)$

the sum of a square number and a prime number $(4 + 101, 16 + 89, 64 + 41, 100 + 5)$

the difference between 2 square numbers $(361 (19^2) - 256 (16^2), 169 - 64, 121 - 4)$.

Can any be done in more than one way?

Teaching notes

Whilst all the methods employed in this topic are mental methods, it greatly helps understanding to see examples that are supported by written workings. These examples will also serve as model solutions.

As a preliminary to using the method based on factors, check that students can explain what they are and are able to quickly identify useful factors.

For the method of partitioning and compensation, it may help to remind students how to multiply out a single term over a bracket.

In all cases, students should be encouraged to estimate the answer first using an approximate sum before calculating the exact result.

When discussing the examples, where appropriate, invite students to say whether the strategy illustrated would be the one they would have chosen. This not only emphasises the validity of alternative approaches but helps to build student confidence in taking responsibility for their own learning and in making and justifying decisions themselves.

Plenary

Ask students to work in pairs, give three example questions and ask them to explain how they would calculate the answer mentally in two different ways for each question.

Exercise commentary

All of questions 1 to 3 can be done using any of the methods and you could leave the choice up to the students rather than insisting on specified methods.

Question 1 – Similar to the first example.

Question 2 – Similar to the second example. Ask students if partitioning would have been their first choice.

Question 3 – Similar to the third example.

Question 4 – Ask students to identify and justify their chosen strategy.

Question 5 – A good way to illustrate that there is no one right or best method.

Answers

1	**a** 240	**b** 200	**c** 1800	**d** 3500
	e 500	**f** 510	**g** 600	**h** 6600
	i 4.8	**j** 0.15	**k** 9	**l** 0.6
	m 9.6	**n** 3.06	**o** 17.6	**p** 0.52
	q 26	**r** 35	**s** 22	**t** 24
	u 27	**v** 7	**w** 9	**x** 9
	y 27	**z** 56		
2	**a** 40.8	**b** 31.5	**c** 18.2	**d** 56
	e 30.8	**f** 64.5	**g** 46.8	**h** 86.8
	i 21 r 3	**j** 23 r 6	**k** 18 r 4	**l** 21 r 7
	m 22 r 2	**n** 25 r 10	**o** 25 r 10	**p** 21 r 18
3	**a** 60.9	**b** 83.6	**c** 170.1	**d** 111.6
	e 66.5	**f** 121.8	**g** 36.1	**h** 123.9
	i 72.2	**j** 52.8	**k** 28.8	**l** 122.5
	m 308.1	**n** 37.12	**o** 399	**p** 2449
	q 2496	**r** 4836	**s** 134.9	**t** 151.8
4	**a** 94.5 g	**b** 71.3 litres		

5 Each student will come up with different methods – check they are correct by checking answers obtained, that is 152, 147, 195, 39, 304, 408, 186, 12 r 6, 270, 165

Objectives	
• Strengthen and extend mental methods of calculation	(L5)
• Make and justify estimates and approximations of calculations	(L5)

Key ideas	Resources
1 Gain the sense of the estimate–calculate–check cycle of problem solving 2 Consolidate and extend mental calculation strategies	Mixed sums all numbers (1345) Mini whiteboards Digit cards Dog walking (AQA): http://filestore.aqa.org.uk/subjects/AQA-4367-4368-L1-W-TRB-DWT.PDF Paris (AQA) http://filestore.aqa.org.uk/subjects/AQA-4367-4368-L1-L2-W-TRB-PT.PDF

Simplification	Extension
Give students simple addition and subtraction questions to solve mentally. Then, in pairs, ask them to explain to one another how they did the calculations; if they disagree on the answer, ask them to work out what mistake was made. They can then attempt the exercises, working in pairs to identify what calculations to carry out.	Give students a train or coach timetable. Set questions on finding the times taken to travel between various places and the total time spent in stations. Remind students that there are 60 minutes in an hour.

Literacy	Links
Reading and communication should be fully promoted here strengthening students' literacy and mathematics skills through speaking and listening.	The world record for adding 100 single digit numbers randomly generated by a computer is 19.23 seconds and is held by Alberto Coto from Spain. Details of other mental calculation world records can be found at http://www.recordholders.org/en/list/memory.html#adding10digits

Alternative approach
Start with an emphasis on estimation and approximation, using some quick-fire activities such as estimating height/length of room or by playing a rounding game in pairs, using a set of digit cards. Students make three 2-digit numbers by drawing from the cards and take it in turns to estimate the sum of the three to the nearest ten, while the other checks with the exact sum. Continue with a focus on real-life problems, such as the task Dog Walking and/or Paris from AQA as referenced in Resources. These problems can be tackled in pairs, and each pair should aim to provide accurate, clear and well-presented solutions.

Checkpoint	
1 Ask students why the estimate–calculate–check cycle is useful when problem solving.	
2 Joseph has a £20 note and buys a calculator costing £5.99 and a pack of pens costing £4.95. How much change does he receive?	(£9.06)

Starter – Estimate

Ask students

to estimate the number of seconds in July

to calculate the number of seconds in July (2 678 400)

How close were their estimates?

Can be extended by comparing the accuracy of boys versus girls or students with names beginning A to M versus names beginning N to Z.

Teaching notes

Students will have a lot of ideas on how to solve mental maths problems. Give them six quick questions to answer and then ask students to explain how they did the calculations. Collect a selection of these methods on the board and then ask the students who offered explanations to set a question that can be calculated using their method.

Give students another six questions, with too many digits to do mentally, and challenge them to provide estimated answers as fast as they can. Again, ask students to explain how they approximated to simplify the calculation. Once the methods have been shared, check understanding with a few more questions.

Finally, pose a more complex word problem and work through it with the class. Ask students how they identify the important information and decide what to calculate: ask them to write down this calculation. How should they estimate the answer and perform the exact calculation? Does the estimate agree with the exact answer?

Plenary

Show students a map with a number of routes between towns and their lengths. Ask students quick-fire questions on estimating or mentally calculating the distances between destinations. Ask students to say which methods they prefer to use to do the calculations and explain why.

Exercise commentary

Insist that students show some workings for each answer.

Question 1 – Similar to the example but given in linear form rather than a table. Students could be encouraged to tabulate the distances as in the example for further practice.

Question 2 – Encourage students to first find an approximate answer and use this to check their calculation.

Question 3 – Remind students to add an extra 0 to help do the calculations, for example, 14.60 – 14.37. In part **b**, finding approximate differences will eliminate several possibilities.

Question 4 – It may help to use a number line to organise the information in the question.

Answers

1. **a** 36.16 km
   b Further from Preston to Accrington (26.14 km as opposed to 22.71 km)
   c 252.5 km (only travels Mon – Fri)
2. **a** £12.09; £7.91 change   **b** £43.55; £6.45 change
   c £20.83; £4.17 change
   d Valerie spends £13.84. Natasha spends £14.40 so Natasha spends more by £0.56
3. **a** 0.7 seconds   **b** Brett and Cris
4. **a** Stephanie 1.7 m   **b** 0.4 m   **c** 0.05 m

Objectives	
• Strengthen and extend mental methods of calculation	(L5)
• Make and justify estimates and approximations of calculations	(L5)

Key ideas	Resources
1 Gain the sense of the estimate–calculate–check cycle of problem solving 2 Consolidate and extend mental calculation strategies	Word problems (1393) Functional skills problem solving (OCR): http://www.ocr.org.uk/Images/73734-smp-problem-solving-tasks-for-functional-skills-maths.pdf

Simplification	Extension
Weaker students find it difficult to know when and how to approximate when working towards a solution. Development of these skills will require particular support.	More able students could spend additional time discussing the methods they have used with a friend. As they follow the logic of someone else's calculation, this will further develop the process skill of interpreting and evaluation, particularly the effects of rounding.

Literacy	Links
As in the last section, reading and communication can be promoted here strengthening students' literacy and mathematics skills through speaking and listening. In small group work, individual students may be given a role such as reader, checker, connector, or questioner. This helps to raise the quality of the final solution produced.	There is a suggestion that the total number of heart beats that an animal has over a lifetime is a fixed number. Information on heart rates and lifetimes for various animals can be found at http://www.sjsu.edu/faculty/watkins/longevity.htm Ask students to work out the total number of heart beats for an animal or, using the heart rate, estimate a lifetime. Do they think fitter people live longer?

Alternative approach
Begin by using the functional skills resource Reality Check as referenced in Resources. This can be done by pairs of students, and timing challenges may be added. As in the last section, it is best to maintain further questioning from real situations, which can be sourced from past functional skills papers, or from the OCR document, activities 1, 3 & 4, for example. Choose two or three problems for small group solution which can then be presented by the group to others. The choice of problem helps with differentiation and the follow-up sharing with discussion will help raise heighten the importance of evaluating different approaches.

Checkpoint
1 Given the three digits 3, 4, 6, where would you place them so that ▣ ▣ × ▣ results in a number as close to 140 as possible? (46×3)
2 Given the four digits 6, 7, 8, 9, where would you place them so that ▣ ▣ × ▣ ▣ results in a number as close to 6000 as possible? (67×89)

Starter – Sums and products

Ask students for

Three numbers where the sum is the same as the product. $(1 + 2 + 3 = 1 \times 2 \times 3)$

Four numbers where the sum is the same as the product. $(1 + 1 + 2 + 4 = 1 \times 1 \times 2 \times 4)$

Five numbers where the sum is the same as the product. $(1 + 1 + 2 + 2 + 2 = 1 \times 1 \times 2 \times 2 \times 2)$

Hint: the same number may be used more than once.

Teaching notes

In this spread, all problems are word-based and involve real-life scenarios. The focus is on students becoming functional mathematicians and using their mental skills to not only solve problems but, equally importantly, to be able to estimate sensibly to know whether they are going to be right.

Question **3** illustrates how to answer a question without actually doing the mathematics and this is very important for students to understand. The task is about seeing the bigger picture of the question and not getting drowned in the detail. For many students, this is a difficult concept to grasp.

Again, the value of the use of approximation as a checking mechanism cannot be over-estimated.

Plenary

Ask students to choose one of the examples from the exercise, or something similar, and turn this into an annotated example as if they were writing a revision guide. Use the worked examples as a model.

Exercise commentary

Question 1 – Remind students that $21 = 20 + 1$ and $19 = 20 - 1$. The explanation and justification element is very important.

Question 2 – Similar to the example. This can serve as a model for how to break the calculation down into smaller steps. This helps develop the process skill of representing.

Question 3 – Insist that students write down the calculation that they need to do and also the approximation/rounding before doing any mental calculations.

Question 4 – Encourage students to write down the calculations that they need to perform before calculating them mentally. Ask students also to supply an approximate calculation that they can use to check their calculation.

Answers

1 When she cycles (1764 beats as opposed to 1748 beats)
2 36 pages
3 a Yes, as cost will be less than £9 × 5 + £4 × 4 = £61
   b No. To the nearest penny, cost will be £12 × 12 + £11 × 7 = £221. But this is so close that we need to do the actual calculation, which gives £216.73
   c Yes, as cost will be less than £2 × 9 + £3 × 4 + £5 × 12 = £90
   d No, as cost will be greater than £8 × 6 + £3 × 6 + £6 × 6 + £11 × 6 = £168
4 a $6\frac{2}{3}$ b 4.2 litres, 5 cartons

Key outcomes	Quick check
Round numbers. (L5)	Round the following numbers: **a** 34.67 (1 dp) (34.7) **b** 23 071 (nearest hundred) (23 100) **c** 0.135 (2 dp) (0.14) **d** 18 903 451 (nearest thousand) (18 903 000)
Use a range of mental strategies for addition and subtraction. (L5)	Work out: **a** 4.5 + 3.6 (8.1) **b** 9.9 – 4.1 (5.8) **c** 18.2 – 15.05 (3.15)
Multiply and divide by 10, 100 and 1000, and 0.1 and 0.01. (L6)	Work out: **a** 35 × 100 (3500) **b** 42 × 0.1 (4.2) **c** 0.6 ÷ 0.01 (60)
Use a range of mental strategies for multiplication and division. (L5)	Work out: **a** 5.1 × 4 (20.4) **b** 37.5 ÷ 2.5 (15) **c** 81 × 9 (729)
Solve problems using mental strategies by breaking the problems down into smaller steps. (L5)	**a** Ella has a £10 note and pays for a drink costing £1.10 and a sandwich costing £2.40. How much change does she receive? (£6.50) **b** Phil has 9 music tracks each 3.2 minutes long. How long is this in total? (28.8 minutes)

⊕ MyMaths extra support

Lesson/online homework			Description
Doubling and halving	1023	L4	Doubling and halving whole numbers and money
Order of operations	1167	L5	Carrying out arithmetic in the correct order, dealing with brackets
Introducing money	1226	L3	Counting money and giving change
Best buys and value for money	1243	L5	Finding the best value when prices are given for different amounts
Mixed tables 2 to 12	1367	L4	Knowing and using all times tables up to 12
Money problems	1377	L4	Solving problems with money

MyReview

Check out
You should now be able to ...

Test it ➡
Questions

✓ Round numbers.	Ⓢ 1, 2
✓ Use a range of mental strategies for addition and subtraction.	Ⓢ 3
✓ Multiply and divide by 10, 100 and 1000, and 0.1 and 0.01.	Ⓢ 4, 5
✓ Use a range of mental strategies for multiplication and division.	Ⓢ 6–8
✓ Solve problems using mental strategies by breaking the problems down into smaller steps.	Ⓢ 9–11

Language	Meaning	Example
Round	To write a number as a near approximation	153 = 150 to the nearest 10 and = 200 to the nearest 100
Factors	Writing a number as a product of smaller numbers to make multiplication and division easier	$17 \times 0.3 = 17 \times 3 \times 0.1$ $= 51 \times 0.1$ $= 5.1$ $171 \div 9 = 171 \div 3 \div 3$ $= 57 \div 3$ $= 19$
Partitioning	To split a number into easier parts to make adding, subtracting or multiplying easier to do in your head	$27 + 18 = 27 + 10 + 8$ $= 37 + 8$ $= 45$
Compensation	A mental strategy that involves rounding one of the numbers and then adjusting the final answer to your sum	$27 + 18 = 27 + 20 - 2$ $= 47 - 2$ $= 45$
Inverse operation	A second operation that undoes the effect of a first operation	-5 is the inverse of $+5$ $+4$ is the inverse of $\times 4$

1 Round 29.507 to the nearest
  a whole number
  b tenth (1dp)
  c hundredth (2dp).

2 Work out these using a calculator and give your answers to an appropriate degree of accuracy.
  a 22.5% of £45 b $\frac{2}{3}$ of £25

3 Calculate these using a mental method.
  a 24.7 + 8.2 b 35.7 − 14.8
  c 27.8 − 9.9 d 5.34 + 7.82
  e 4.7 + 5.82 f 12 − 8.45
  g 6.23 − 5.81 h 14.45 + 9.67

4 Calculate
  a 56 × 10 b 103 ÷ 100
  c 7 × 0.1 d 4 × 0.01
  e 25 × 0.001 f 0.4 ÷ 0.01
  g 99 × 0.001 h 350 × 0.01
  i 87 ÷ 0.1 j 0.9 × 0.01

5 Calculate
  a $\frac{1}{10}$ of £650 b $\frac{1}{100}$ of 29 kg

6 Calculate these using factors.
  a 35 × 0.2 b 61 × 15
  c 468 ÷ 6 d 585 ÷ 50

7 Calculate these using the method of partitioning.
  a 5.4 × 15 b 18 × 5.2
  c 176 ÷ 16 d 492 ÷ 12

8 Calculate these using the method of compensation.
  a 12 × 19 b 32 × 31
  c 5.6 × 39 d 18 × 1.9

9 At the newsagents, fizzy drinks cost 89p each and magazines cost £3.99. Jamie buys two fizzy drinks and a magazine. Use mental methods to calculate how much change he gets from a £10 note.

10 Milk costs 78p per litre.
  a Suzy buys 19 litres. How much does it cost?
  Suzy fills 200 ml cups with the milk.
  b How many cups can she fill with her 19 litres?
  c What is the cost of a 200 ml cup of milk?

11 Richard buys a 3 kg jar of sweets for £22. He plans to divide the sweets into 125 g packets and sell them for 99p each.
  a How many packets can he make?
  b How much profit will Richard make?

What next?

Score		
	0 – 4	Your knowledge of this topic is still developing. To improve look at Formative test: 2B-7; MyMaths: 1004, 1013, 1345
	5 – 8	You are gaining a secure knowledge of this topic. To improve look at InvisiPen: 112, 114, 121, 122 and 123
	10 – 11	You have mastered this topic. Well done, you are ready to progress!

Question commentary

Calculators must not be used in this exercise (except on question **2**), and students should be able to explain their methods.

Question 1 – Some students may find it helpful to have a number line to refer to, particularly in part **a**.

Question 2 – Check that students round appropriately. The questions could be discussed as a class.

Question 3 – The partitioning method is the best to use for these questions.

Questions 4 and **5** – Remind students that multiplying by 0.1 is the same as dividing by 10, etc. Some may find ÷ 0.1, 0.01, etc. particularly confusing, it may be helpful to think of them as fractions.

Question 6 – Possible methods are:

a $35 \times 2 \times 0.1$　　　b $61 \times 3 \times 5$
c $468 \div 2 \div 3$　　　d $585 \div 10 \div 5$

Question 7 – Possible methods are:

a $(5.4 \times 10) + (5.4 \times 5)$　b $(18 \times 5) + (18 \times 0.2)$
c $(160 \div 16) + (16 \div 16)$

Question 8 – Possible methods are:

a $(12 \times 20) - (12 \times 1)$　　b $(32 \times 30) + (32 \times 1)$
c $(5.6 \times 40) - (5.6 \times 1)$

Questions 9–11 – Encourage students to show all working and estimate the answers beforehand.

Answers

1	a	30	b	29.5	c	29.51	
2	a	£10.13	b	£16.67			
3	a	32.9	b	20.9	c	17.9	d 13.16
	e	10.52	f	3.55	g	0.42	h 24.12
4	a	5.6	b	1.03	c	0.7	d 0.04
	e	0.025	f	40	g	99000	h 3.5
	i	870	j	0.009			
5	a	£6.50	b	0.29 kg			
6	a	7	b	915	c	78	d 11.7
7	a	81	b	93.6	c	11	d 41
8	a	228	b	992	c	218.4	d 34.2
9	£4.23						
10	a	£14.82	b	95 cups	c	15.6p	
11	a	24	b	£1.76			

7 MyPractice

1 Round each of these numbers to the nearest
  i 1000 ii 100 iii 10

| a 3182 | b 6273 | c 4765 | d 8632 | e 6713 | f 7682 |
| g 5049 | h 24505 | i 38 604 | j 42783 | k 76060 | l 39494 |

2 Round each of these numbers to the nearest
  i whole number ii tenth (1 dp) iii hundredth (2dp).

| a 4.847 | b 3.107 | c 8.3967 | d 8.238 | e 24.969 | f 22.623 |
| g 3.4172 | h 8.0495 | i 3.1405 | j 3.0078 | k 2.429 57 | l 4.54545 |

7a

3 Calculate these using a mental method.

a 492 − 187	b 799 − 203	c 2615 − 616	d 3639 − 1009
e 2215 − 1797	f 3011 − 1688	g 4383 − 3985	h 7473 − 4749
i 5629 − 730	j 1057 − 862	k 9087 − 8123	l 2536 − 1985

4 Calculate these using a mental method.

a 11.8 + 7.4	b 2.68 + 8.9	c 4.8 + 5.92	d 3.07 + 2.98
e 13.7 − 8.88	f 6.99 − 3.49	g 8.71 − 4.8	h 9.67 − 3.85
i 0.867 − 0.577	j 1.006 − 0.756	k 8.349 − 2.022	l 19.73 − 7.605

7b

5 Calculate

a 3 × 10	b 6 × 100	c 90 ÷ 10	d 400 ÷ 100
e 38 × 10	f 1.7 × 10	g 67 ÷ 100	h 497 ÷ 10
i 0.075 × 10	j 6.1 ÷ 100	k 48.2 ÷ 1000	l 0.0032 × 100

6 Calculate

a 4 × 0.1	b 6 × 0.1	c 7 × 0.01	d 2 × 0.01
e 34 × 0.1	f 65 × 0.1	g 30 × 0.01	h 58 × 0.01
i 85.4 × 0.01	j 0.73 × 0.1	k 68 ÷ 0.01	l 0.03 ÷ 0.1

7c

7 Calculate these using a mental method.

a 7.3 × 11	b 6.4 × 9	c 14 × 5.2	d 13 × 31
e 4.7 × 21	f 406 ÷ 7	g 3.4 × 13	h 300 ÷ 9
i 235 ÷ 4	j 16 × 1.9	k 576 ÷ 8	l 3.7 × 15

7d

8 Ali, Mary, Ben and Jules are planning a picnic. The prices of various item are shown below. For each possible order find
  i the cost ii the change that would be given.
  a Ali buys some fruit and lemonade, paid for with £10
  b Mary buys a salad pack and cheese, paid for with £20
  c Ben buys a small loaf and cheese, paid for with £5
  d Jules buys a cake and a bottle of lemonade, paid for with £10
  e How much would the most expensive three items cost?
  f How much more expensive is the lemonade than the loaf?

Fruit, 99p Loaf, £1.55 Salad, £2.05

Lemonade, £2.37 Cake, £3.95 Cheese, £1.67

7e

9 Estimate these.
  a The number of seconds in a week
  b i The number of hours you sleep in a year
    ii The equivalent number of days
    iii The equivalent number of weeks
  c The weight of a man in kilograms who weighs 12 stones (1kg is roughly 2.2 pounds, and there are 14 pounds in a stone)
  d The number of adults that would weigh as much as 170 tonne blue whale

10 The cost of hiring a car for a week was £235. This was made up of a £140 fixed charge and a 20p per mile mileage charge for distances over 200 miles. How far did the car travel in the week?

7f

MyMaths.co.uk

Question commentary

Questions 1 and **2** – Lots of basic practice questions that could be done orally or using mini whiteboards.

Questions 3 and **4** – Emphasise that the method the students choose should suit their preference rather than insisting on a specific approach.

Questions 4 and **6** – Again, lots of basic practice questions which could be done as a whole-class oral activity or using mini whiteboards.

Question 7 – Encourage students to vary their methods since some of the questions may be better approached in different ways.

Questions 8 and **9** – Students should show the steps in their working and also provide approximations to first estimate and then check the magnitude of their final answers.

Answers

1 a i 3000 ii 3200 iii 3180
   b i 6000 ii 6300 iii 6270
   c i 5000 ii 4800 iii 4770
   d i 9000 ii 8600 iii 8630
   e i 7000 ii 6700 iii 6710
   f i 8000 ii 7700 iii 7680
   g i 5000 ii 5000 iii 5050
   h i 25 000 ii 24 500 iii 24 510
   i i 39 000 ii 38 600 iii 38 600
   j i 43 000 ii 42 800 iii 42 780
   k i 76 000 ii 76 100 iii 76 060
   l i 39 000 ii 39 500 iii 39 490

2 a i 5 ii 4.8 iii 4.85
   b i 3 ii 3.1 iii 3.11
   c i 8 ii 8.4 iii 8.40
   d i 8 ii 8.2 iii 8.24
   e i 25 ii 25.0 iii 24.97
   f i 23 ii 22.6 iii 22.62
   g i 3 ii 3.4 iii 3.42
   h i 8 ii 8.0 iii 8.05
   i i 3 ii 3.1 iii 3.14
   j i 3 ii 3.0 iii 3.01
   k i 2 ii 2.4 iii 2.43
   l i 5 ii 4.5 iii 4.55

3 a 305 b 596 c 1999 d 2630
   e 418 f 1323 g 398 h 2724
   i 4899 j 195 k 964 l 551

4 a 19.2 b 11.58 c 10.72 d 6.05
   e 4.82 f 3.5 g 3.91 h 5.82
   i 0.29 j 0.25 k 6.327 l 12.125

5 a 30 b 600 c 9 d 4
   e 380 f 17 g 0.67 h 49.7
   i 0.75 j 0.061 k 0.0482 l 0.32

6 a 0.4 b 0.6 c 0.07 d 0.02
   e 3.4 f 6.5 g 0.3 h 0.58
   i 0.854 j 0.073 k 6800 l 0.3

7 a 80.3 b 57.6 c 72.8 d 403
   e 98.7 f 58 g 44.2
   h $33\frac{1}{2}$ or 33 r 1 i 58.75
   j 30.4 k 72 l 55.5

8 a i £3.36 ii £6.64
   b i £3.72 ii £16.28
   c i £3.22 ii £1.78
   d i £6.32 ii £3.68
   e £8.37
   f 82p

9 a $50 \times 50 \times 25 \times 10 = 625\,000$ hours (604 800)
   b i $10 \times 400 = 4000$ hours
      ii $4000 \div 25 = 160$ days
      iii $160 \div 10 = 16$ weeks
   c $10 \times 15 \div 2 = 75$ kg (76.20357…)
   d $200\,000 \div 100 = 2000$

10 $200 + (235 - 140) \div 0.2 = 675$ miles

Learning outcomes

S1 Describe, interpret and compare observed distributions of a single variable through: appropriate graphical representation involving discrete, continuous and grouped data; and appropriate measures of central tendency (mean, mode, median) and spread (range, consideration of outliers) (L5/6)

S2 Construct and interpret appropriate tables, charts, and diagrams, including frequency tables, bar charts, pie charts, and pictograms for categorical data, and vertical line (or bar) charts for ungrouped and grouped numerical data (L6)

S3 Describe simple mathematical relationships between two variables (bivariate data) in observational and experimental contexts and illustrate using scatter graphs (L6)

Introduction

The chapter starts by looking at primary and secondary data, discrete and continuous data and the methods of data collection we might employ. Pie charts and bar charts are then covered before looking at basic averages. Finding averages from grouped data is covered before scatter diagrams and stem-and-leaf diagrams.

The introduction discusses the principle of a census. This is where everyone living and working in the country is asked a number of questions about their lifestyles, etc. in order to build up a complete picture of the population of the country. This is as opposed to a sample where only a selection of people is asked. Censuses are useful for governments since they have to make important decisions that affect all of our lives. Understanding attitudes, behaviours and the needs of the population help them to make the correct decisions.

Censuses in the UK take place every ten years and the last UK census took place in 2011. Details can be found at: http://www.ons.gov.uk/ons/guide-method/census/2011/index.html

Prior knowledge

Students should already know how to…

- Add, subtract, multiply and divide whole numbers
- Draw simple diagrams representing discrete data

Starter problem

The starter problem poses four statistical questions for students to consider. In all cases, these questions could be answers (partially at least) from surveying the students in the class. This also provides a good opportunity to discuss how representative such a survey is. How might it be improved? How could we collect a more representative sample from the school year, or the whole school, or the local area?

The idea of a hypothesis, rather than a question, could also be discussed. This is where a statement is made about what you expect to find. For example, the first question could be converted into a hypothesis by saying that you believe 'most students travel to school by bus.' The third question could likewise be converted into a hypothesis such as 'boys take less time to get to school than girls.'

The methods of analysis available once the data is collected could also be discussed. Completion of the data cycle could be completed by using this analysis to reach a conclusion.

Resources

MyMaths

Mean and mode	1200	Median and range	1203
Reading pie charts	1206	Scatter graphs	1213
Stem-and-leaf	1215	Mean from frequency tables	1254

Online assessment

Chapter test	2B–8
Formative test	2B–8
Summative test	2B–8

InvisiPen solutions

Organising data in tables	411	Planning an enquiry	414
Bar charts	422	Pie charts	423
Scatter graphs	427	Stem-and-leaf diagrams	431
Mean of a list	441	Frequency table averages	442

Topic scheme

Teaching time = 8 lessons/3 weeks

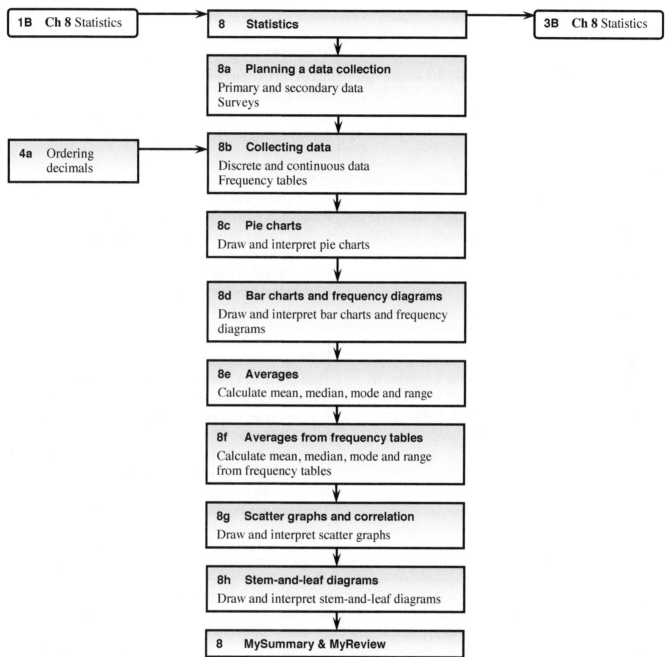

| 1B Ch 8 Statistics | → | 8 Statistics | → | 3B Ch 8 Statistics |

8a Planning a data collection
Primary and secondary data
Surveys

| 4a Ordering decimals | → | **8b Collecting data**
Discrete and continuous data
Frequency tables |

8c Pie charts
Draw and interpret pie charts

8d Bar charts and frequency diagrams
Draw and interpret bar charts and frequency diagrams

8e Averages
Calculate mean, median, mode and range

8f Averages from frequency tables
Calculate mean, median, mode and range from frequency tables

8g Scatter graphs and correlation
Draw and interpret scatter graphs

8h Stem-and-leaf diagrams
Draw and interpret stem-and-leaf diagrams

8 MySummary & MyReview

Differentiation

Student book 2A   144 – 169

Planning a survey
Collecting data
Frequency tables
Bar charts
Pie charts
Mode, median and range
The mean
Averages from frequency tables
Comparing data sets
Statistical reports

Student book 2B   134 – 155

Planning a data collection
Collecting data
Pie charts
Bar charts and frequency diagrams
Averages
Averages from frequency tables
Scatter graphs and correlation
Stem-and-leaf diagrams

Student book 2C   136 – 159

Planning a statistical
        investigation
Collecting data
Frequency tables
Constructing diagrams
Averages 1
Averages 2
Interpreting statistical diagrams
Scatter diagrams and correlation
Comparing distributions

Objectives

- Decide which data to collect to answer a question, and the degree of accuracy needed   (L5)
- Identify possible sources   (L5)
- Consider appropriate sample size   (L6)

Key ideas	Resources
1 Recognising that the quality of results relies on the initial planning 2 Beginning to consider possible problems or bias that might arise from choices made about collecting data	Access to the Internet M1 of Unit Library: Five Hypotheses http://www.nationalstemcentre.org.uk/elibrary/resource/4980/year-eight-handling-data-mini-pack

Simplification	Extension
To help make the difference between primary and secondary data more concrete and allow students to get a 'feel' for data, use real data for question **1** and allow students to discuss what it shows. In question **2** supply more specific statements, for example, 'men live longer in Scotland than in Japan'. Students would benefit from whole-class discussion of the answers to this exercise.	Use question **2** as the basis for an investigation. First, formulate a statement, for example in part **b**, 'most football games have three goals scored in them' or 'more goals are scored in the second half than the first'. Then plan what and how much data they would need and how they would get it.

Literacy	Links
Ask students to explore what they think is meant by the terms primary and secondary, and how this might relate to data. Allow them to explore all the various contexts that these words are used.	The Internet is a worldwide system of computer networks that allows the user to access information from any other computer (with permission). It was developed by the US government in 1969 to allow researchers to access information on computers at other universities and was first known as the Advanced Research Projects Agency Network or ARPANET. There is a timeline showing the development of the Internet at http://www.webopedia.com/quick_ref/timeline.asp

Alternative approach

Use one of the hypotheses, with data, from M1 of the resource referenced, in order to stimulate discussion between pairs of students about whether the data given is sufficient or appropriate for the question. Share and widen the discussion to consider what appropriate data might be for the question and how it might be collected. Also request that students consider possible problems or barriers as a result of the data collected. The approach offered by the unit plan given in the mini pack of this resource may also be used for this section.

Checkpoint

1 Give an example of secondary data.   (Any appropriate response that points to relevant sources.)

2 Explain why a small set of data might be a problem.   (Any response which indicates possible limitations.)

3 Explain why a large set of data might be a problem.
    (Any response which indicates the difficulties/expense of managing a large amount of data.)

Starter – Today's number is ...72

Ask questions based on 'Today's number', for example

What is double 72 and add 3? (147)

What are the factors of 72? ($2^3 \times 3^2$: 1, 2, 3, 4, 6, 8, 9, 12, 18, 24, 36, 72)

How many of the factors are square numbers? (4)

What is 10% of 72? (7.2)

The square root of 72 lies between which two whole numbers? (8, 9)

Teaching notes

As an introduction to the lesson, discuss the differences between primary and secondary data. In pairs, ask students to consider a statement such as, 'Year 8 girls are taller than Year 8 boys'. How could they show whether or not this was true? What data should they use? If they only use data collected from school, it will give information about Year 8 heights in that school but not more generally. Therefore there is a need to use both primary and secondary data.

A useful way to approach issues surrounding the collection of data is from a consideration of the possible sources of bias. If students can first identify ways in which data collection might be biased, then they can try to think of ways to avoid this.

Plenary

Give students two sets of data, the weight of ten Y7 school bags and ten Y10 school bags. In pairs, ask students to agree what they could do with the data to support investigating 'Y7 school bags are heavier than Y10 school bags'. Allow them a further two minutes to make comments about the data, for example, insufficient, gender, did Y10 have PE or maths (big thick books or...) Discuss the problem in general.

Exercise commentary

Question 1 – Pair students and ask them to agree on answers. This could be developed by asking them to think of projects they have completed, one using primary data and another using secondary data – they should explain each project and why primary or secondary data was used.

Question 2 – Ask students to think of ways in which the data they collect might be biased.

Questions 3 and **4** – Pair students and ask them to list two or three reasons why the statements may not be correct and to come up with two or three example questions that would require a different approach.

Question 5 – Set the challenge for students to plan for this. First they need to agree the statement they are going to investigate, for example, Y7 school bags are heavier than Y10 school bags, and then they need to plan how they would investigate this statement.

Question 6 – Students could actually carry out this project by collecting the data from their classmates or by doing a more widespread survey through the school.

Answers

1. **a** Secondary   **b** Primary
   c Primary   **d** Secondary
   e Primary   **f** Secondary

2. **a** Secondary: search the Internet
   b Primary: ask a sample of students in Year 8
   c Secondary: search the Internet
   d Secondary: look at the scores across a sample of leagues on a random Saturday
   e Primary: ask a sample of teenagers how many hours TV they watch per evening

3. For example, if you are looking for information about students in your school, you are unlikely to find it on the Internet (e.g. are students in favour of school uniform in the sixth form).

4. Many organisations (e.g. the Office of National Statistics) take great care in selecting samples that are representative of the whole population and they have the resources available to ensure they take a cross-section of all areas of the country, social classes and ages.
   Krysia would not be able to collect her own data to get an accurate measure of infant mortality rates in the UK, for example.

5. She needs to define light and heavy.
   She needs to weigh the bags.
   She needs to take a random sample of students, not just her friends or her class.

6. Q1 'Sometimes' could be changed to a set of more specific options: for example, once a week, twice a week, etc.
   Q2 Getting to school will not always take the same time. You could say 'on average' or provide intervals.
   Q3 The diagram needs a scale or landmarks, plus tick boxes for A, B or C.

Objectives

- Plan how to collect the data   (L5)
- Construct frequency tables with equal class intervals for gathering discrete and continuous data and two way tables for recording discrete data   (L6)

Key ideas	Resources
1 Understanding the need to plan or think ahead about the purpose required of the data 2 Consideration of efficiency when collecting data	School data from Census at school: http://www.censusatschool.org.uk/

Simplification	Extension
To support students in completing the frequency tables, reduce the amount of data to just one line. When this has been put into the table, provide the second and then third line of data.	We use tables to show information more clearly. Ask students to look at the tables they have made in questions **2** and **3**. In each case ask them to make four comments about what the table is showing and share the ideas with other students. Then, using twenty words, can they explain why information in a table is more helpful than a list.

Literacy	Links
Explore the terms discrete and continuous data and the differences between them. Relate this to the variety of graphs that might represent data, to emphasise how important this awareness is. Students often tackle completing tally charts by taking the chart to dominate search of data rather than to take the data, in order consistently. Expose this tactic, demonstrating that it is more accurate and efficient to go through a set of data just once, systematically. Make sure that students also discuss the usual notation used for grouped continuous data, with the appropriate symbols.	http://fishermansview.com/fishing_world_records.htm lists the world records by weight for many different types of fish caught on rod and line. What are the largest and smallest fish on the list? (Grass Pickerel 1 lb and Great White Shark 2664 lb). What is the range of the weights? (2663 lb) What is the range in kg? (about 1200 kg)

Alternative approach

Having established the terms discrete and continuous, request that students draw up a short list of examples of each category. Share and discuss the results. Model the transfer of data to a frequency chart, in order to emphasise the most efficient and accurate approaches. Data collected directly from the students can be used for consolidation purposes in this section. The data might include: height, shoe size, foot length (cm), hand span. The data might be collected prior to this session and presented in its raw form so that students can group, organise and sort it for themselves. Typical data like this can also be found at the Census at school website referenced in Resources. More able students may be encouraged to decide upon grouping for themselves, and to examine what might be a sensible amount of groups to aim for with particular sets of data.

Checkpoint

1 A set of grouped data has the following groups noted: 0–10; 10–20; 20–30; 30–40.
   Comment on possible problems that might occur with these headings.
                  (Any response which notes that a value such as 30 might be allocated to two of the groups.)

2 How can you check that you have included every piece of data in your tally chart?
                                                                (Totals of each are compared and agree.)

3 Are the following discrete or continuous data
   a number of eggs in a nest   (Discrete)
   b weight of each egg?   (Continuous)

Starter – Numbered cubes

Ask students to imagine a bag containing ten cubes numbered 1, 2 or 5.

Cubes are drawn out of the bag and replaced each time.

Write numbers on the board, for example, 5, 1, 5, 5, 2, 2, 2, 5, 2, 5, 2, 2, 2, 2, 5, 2, 2, 2, 5, 2

Ask students to estimate how many of each number there are in the bag. (For example, 1×1, 6×2, 3×5)

What is the mean of the numbers pulled out? (3)

Teaching notes

As an introduction to the lesson students should be made aware of different types of data – many find it difficult to determine the difference between continuous and discrete data. At this level it is very useful to highlight that continuous data tends to occur where you cannot get the exact data, for example, in height you may be 1.57 m or 5 feet 2 inches but you are always 'and a bit' or 'nearly'. Discrete data tends to occur where you are counting (often whole numbers).

Transferring data from a list into a table, as in questions **2** and **3**, is prone to silly mistakes (losing your place, double counting, missing out a category, etc.) and it will be instructive to work through an example where this is done systematically. Possible strategies to minimise the risk of errors include:

- Choose small groups of data to tally each time, for example, work through each column, where there are only 2 or 3 pieces of data.
- Tick off data values as they are entered (though not in books!).
- Check the number of entries in the table and in the list is the same.

Plenary

Statements such as $9.0 \leq x < 10.0$ are confusing. Give (groups of) students a number of similar mathematical and worded statements. Ask them to match statements (where possible) and supply any missing statements. For example,

$x < 10$, $9 < x \leq 10$, $9 \leq x \leq 10$, $9 < x < 10$

'x is smaller than 10', 'x is larger than 9 but less than or equal to 10', 'x is larger than or equal to 9 and smaller than or equal to 10'; 'x is less than 10 but larger than 9'

Exercise commentary

Question 1 – It may help students to list some possible data values for each part before deciding on the type of data. Whole-class discussion could be used to clarify the distinctions.

Question 2 – A discrete data version of the second example.

Question 3 – Similar to the second example. Check that students are correctly interpreting the intervals.

Question 4 – Students will need to select their own (sensible) intervals. A productive discussion could be had as to whether the data is discrete or continuous.

Question 5 – Constructing a two-way table like that in the first example.

Question 6 – A practical project that can be carried out in the class. There is lots of scope for discussion of the various stages in the project.

Answers

1   **a**   Discrete   **b**   Continuous
    c   Continuous   **d**   Discrete
    e   Discrete

2   Check students' tables. Correct tallies give frequencies of 21, 13, 9, 7; for occupants 1, 2, 3, 4

3   Check students' tables. Correct tallies give frequencies of 1, 6, 15, 7, 1; for length intervals from shortest to tallest groups.

4   Check students' tables. For example, five class intervals $30 \leq h < 40$, $40 \leq h < 50$, $50 \leq h < 60$, $60 \leq h < 70$, $70 \leq h < 80$. Correct tallies give frequencies of 6, 8, 10, 9, 7.

5   Check students' two-way tables. Correct frequencies are:
Large plates: 3 blue, 1 green, 4 orange
Small plates: 2 blue, 7 green, 1 orange

6   **a**   Check students' work
    b   Check students' work
    c   Frequency diagram as the data is continuous, no gaps between the bars
    d   Compare students' answers in group discussion (multiple answers possible)

Objectives

- Construct pie charts for categorical data   (L6)

Key ideas	Resources
1 Understanding the proportional nature of pie chart representation 2 Using proportional strategies in order to find the appropriate angle for sectors of the chart	Reading pie charts (1206) Calculator Compasses Protractor M3.2 from Y8 Handling Data unit library: http://www.nationalstemcentre.org.uk/elibrary/resource/4980/year-eight-handling-data-mini-pack

Simplification	Extension
Where students are unable to draw pie charts effectively at first give them two or three pie charts and ask them to explain what they show. Then give them a simple set of data with 36 items in three categories and the angles already worked out. Ask them to draw this as a pie chart and develop from here.	The pie chart in the second example shows colours of eyes in a group – ask students to survey their class, draw a similar pie chart and write a short commentary on similarities and differences.

Literacy	Links
The interpretation of data represented by two (pie) charts provides good opportunities for students to demonstrate understanding and communicate it effectively.	Eye colour is an inherited characteristic. Only one of the pair of genes that control eye colour is passed from each parent to a child. The combination of inherited genes determines the child's eye colour. There is an eye colour calculator at http://museum.thetech.org/ugenetics/eyeCalc/eyecalculator.html

Alternative approach

As a starter, use two pie charts to compare data, in order to draw out the idea that while pie charts effectively illustrate proportion of data; actual numerical data is not conveyed. A good source for this can be found at M3.2 from the referenced resource. Students can find drawing pie charts challenging and it is important to take students back to the basic principles using proportion of the circle. Weaker students more readily identify with this when the amounts result in common simple fractions. Many of the examples in this section fall into this category so encouraging the students to use their mental skills together with visualisation will help to establish correct approaches. Note that the calculator's fraction button may also be employed effectively with students for construction.

Checkpoint

1 Give an example of data that might be represented well by a pie chart.
              (Any appropriate comparative proportional data such as population breakdowns.)

2 Work out the angles to be drawn in a pie chart for this data set:
Brown hair (14), Blonde hair (12), Black hair (4)   (168°, 144°, 48°)

Starter – Student survey

Draw a Venn diagram on the board with three different attributes, for example: brown eyes, cereal for breakfast, plays football.

Enter possible numbers or enter students' own data and ask questions, for example, how many students have brown eyes, did not have cereal for breakfast and play football?

Teaching notes

Show students a simple pie chart with three shaded areas ($\frac{1}{4}, \frac{1}{3}$, and the remainder) and supply a simple scenario: it represents 24 pupils, the smallest proportion have had one mobile phone, the slightly larger proportion ($\frac{1}{3}$) have had two mobile phones, the largest proportion represents students who have had more than two different mobile phones. Take feedback on what the pie chart tells them. How can they be more accurate? (Measure angles)

Students should be taken through an example of how to calculate the angles in a pie chart, either as in the second example $\left(\frac{6}{17} \times 360\right)$ or by first calculating the angle associated with one entry $\left(6 \times \frac{360}{17}\right)$. As a check of the calculation the sum of the angles should be $360°$. Students may need to be reminded how to use a protractor and could be asked to explain the procedure to be followed: centre the cross, align the base, measure from zero, etc. Again, as a check of the drawing, the angle in the final sector should equal that calculated. This calculation can be related to earlier work on ratio and proportion.

Pie charts also arise in other subjects, for example geography, and it may be helpful to ask students how they are used and constructed in those subjects. Other variants of pie charts may also be available for comparison from the media.

Plenary

Give pairs of students either a frequency table (for 24 or 36 pieces of data) with three of four categories, or a pie chart for a similar amount of data in three or four categories. Students have to draw a pie chart from the data or construct the frequency table from the pie chart. Discuss which was easier to do.

Exercise commentary

Questions 1 and **2** – These form a pair. Ask students to compare their sketches and resolve any (significant) differences, identifying where they went wrong, before proceeding. Question **2** is similar to the second example; only part **a** involves 'nice' numbers. Weaker students could work together on calculating the angles before drawing and labelling their own pie charts.

Question 3 – Students should be able to give more than one reason why the pie chart is incorrect. One entry is 10°.

Question 4 – Emphasise that while the exact percentages for each film are debatable, the total must add up to 100.

Question 5 – You may need to remind students that the two towns may have very different populations.

Answers

1. **a** Sketch should have 3 sectors all roughly equal (120°)
   b Sketch should show approximate sectors Japan 180°, Spain 90°, Cuba and USA 45°
   c Sketch should show approximate sectors Fire, Police, Ambulance 110° and Coast Guard 30°

2. **a** Angles are: Dogs 120°, Cats 110°, Birds 130°
   Check pie chart sectors are labelled, and check sector angles are correctly measured.
   b Angles are: Spain 84.4°, Cuba 44.4°, USA 48.9° and Japan 182.3°
   Check pie chart sectors are labelled with countries and angles are correctly measured.
   c Angles are: Fire 117.6°, Police 102.9°, Ambulance 110.2° and Coast Guard 29.3°
   Check pie chart sectors are labelled with services and angles are correctly measured.

3. **a** Because the sectors are the wrong sizes. The sector for Reference looks larger than that for History when it should be the other way around.
   b Pie chart drawn should have these angles: Fiction 80°, History 120°, Reference 90°, Biography 70°

4. A 25%   B 30%   C 25%   D 20%

5. Students' own answers. Discuss with students.

Objectives	
• Construct bar charts and frequency diagrams for discrete and continuous data	(L5)

Key ideas	Resources
1 Understanding that scale indicates continuity 2 Categorical or discrete data require gaps between the categories	Charts and data from media sources

Simplification	Extension
Provide blank tables for questions **1** and **2**. Alternatively, if time (or a teaching assistant) is available, work with the weaker students to fill in the table, and discuss how best to do this systematically. See also spread **8b**.	Bar charts are one of the most useful diagrammatic representations because it is easy to understand the results of the diagram and they are also one of the easiest to draw. To challenge students, supply two sets of data (for example, weights of males and weights of females) and ask them to draw a single bar chart to highlight this information – they should draw dual bar charts similar to those in the discussion activity.

Literacy	Links
The difference between discrete and continuous data can be revisited in this section reminding the students about the use of graphs appropriate for the nature of the data. Students will commonly not include gaps in bar charts, so this is an opportunity to expose and correct this. Further, the students may be used to turn detective and look for common examples of misuse in media and/or other school texts. The term histogram might be introduced as another term the frequency diagram in the given example, especially for the more able students.	The Scottish wildcat is the only native member of the cat family in the British Isles and has been extinct in England and Wales since 1862. It is now found only in the Highlands of Scotland, where it is thought that about 500 remain. The Scottish wildcat is larger than a domestic cat and preys mainly on rodents and small mammals. There is more information about the Scottish wildcat at http://www.scottishwildcats.co.uk/

Alternative approach
If data has been collected directly from the students as suggested earlier in this chapter, that data – raw or organised – can be used for the constructions. Alternatively, a number of charts – bar/frequency – can be gathered from other curricular sources or media sources. Pairs of students can then be asked to evaluate critically the representations, looking for errors and/or improvements with justification.

Checkpoint
1 Give three key features that you would check for in a bar chart or frequency diagram. (Title; labelled axes; clear and appropriate scale; gaps/no gaps; and so on)

Starter – Favourite crisps

A pie chart represents the favourite crisps of 60 students. The flavours and angles are: onion, chicken, plain, prawn, salt and vinegar; 30°, 36°, 60°, 90° and 144°.

25% of students preferred prawn. Twice as many preferred salt & vinegar to chicken. $\frac{1}{10}$ preferred plain.

Ask students to match angles with flavours.

How many students prefer each flavour?

(Onion = 24, chicken = 5, plain = 6, prawn = 15, salt and vinegar = 10)

Teaching notes

Students are well aware of 'bar charts' but they rarely appreciate the difference between categorical data, numerical data that is discrete and continuous data and how this affects the type of 'bar chart' that is drawn. As an introduction to the lesson highlight the examples given in the textbook. Show that the bars for categorical and numerical discrete data have gaps between them. For continuous data we draw a frequency diagram where there are no gaps between the bars; this shows that the measures are continuous.

To complete questions such as **2** and **3** students will need to be shown how to design a table and systematically fill in the 30 entries, *cf*, lesson **11b**. In question **1**, the colour order for the bars does not matter, although this is often best done alphabetically. However, in question **2**, draw bars from smallest to largest shoe size and make sure that there is a gap between each bar.

Plenary

Project a bar chart with errors, for example:

- it is not named
- the vertical axis is not marked – bars have numbers at the top that don't relate to their height
- there are no spaces between the bars (which are colours) or there are spaces and the data is continuous
- some of the bars are not in the correct order
- the bars are of different widths

In pairs, students have to find the mistakes and then redraw the bar chart accurately.

Exercise commentary

In each question ask students to write one or two sentences describing what the bar charts show.

Question 1 – Categorical data as in part **b** of the first example. Suggest that the categories are listed alphabetically.

Question 2 – Discrete numerical data as in part **a** of the first example. Check that the shoe sizes are in ascending order.

Question 3 – Continuous numerical data as in the second example. Check that the bars now touch and that students are using a continuous *x*-axis scale, not labelling the bars.

Question 4 – This is a comprehension question. Make sure students are carefully reading the scale on the frequency axis.

Question 5 – Challenge pairs of students to find two advantages and two disadvantages for each graph. Pairs of pairs could then agree which are the two best and two worst features of each graph before presenting them to the whole class.

Answers

1

Colour	Tally	Frequency
Green	IIII	4
Grey	HHH HHH I	11
Yellow	II	2
Red	HHH	5
Black	III	3
Blue	III	3
White	II	2

Bar chart correctly drawn to frequencies given in above frequency table. Appropriate scale, correctly labelled.

2

Size	Tally	Frequency
3	I	1
4	III	3
5	HHH	5
6	HHH III	8
7	HHH	5
8	HHH	5
9	II	2
10	I	1

Bar chart correctly drawn to frequencies given in above frequency table. Appropriate scale, correctly labelled.

3 **a** $60 \leq w < 70$, the missing frequency is **3**

   b Check students' frequency diagrams. Bars drawn to correct frequencies with no gaps between bars. Labelled.

4 **a** 1   **b** 50   **c** 70   **d** 1.4

5 The first diagram is far better for comparing the number of wildcats in each region as the bars are side by side. However, the second diagram is better for seeing how the total number of wildcats has grown over the years.

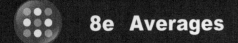
Objectives	
• Recognise when it is appropriate to use the range, mean, median and mode (L5)	

Key ideas	Resources
1 Understand the meaning of each average in terms of the context of the data 2 Begin to sense the impact different range has on knowing an average value	Mean and mode (1200) Median and range (1203) Mini white boards Y8 Data handling mini pack Unit M3.4 in Unit library: http://www.nationalstemcentre.org.uk/elibrary/resource/4980/year-eight-handling-data-mini-pack

Simplification	Extension
Give students the numbers or amounts written on cards, for example, a set of five cards with £3, £4, £4, £6 and £8. Ask, what are the mean (5), mode (4) and median? (4) Using only the last four cards, ask, what is the largest? (8) Smallest? (4) Mean? (5.5) Median? (5) Can they write questions of their own?	Following the discussion activity, ask students to make up a question of their own similar to this activity, together with its answer. Then exchange questions with another in the group.

Literacy	Links
The word average is commonly used when referring to the mean. This is worth discussing with the students, perhaps even sharing examples of misuses. Range is frequently understood, but commonly interpreted by students as an expression rather than a value. For example. '5 to 28'; rather than 23 (28 − 5). Explicitly address this to ensure accurate communication.	The word *average* comes from the French word *averie* which means 'damage sustained at sea'. Costs of losses at sea were shared between the ship owners and the cargo owners and the calculations used to assess the individual contributions gave rise to the modern sense of the word *average*.

Alternative approach
Students will already be familiar with all the terms in this section, but are less likely to be able to evaluate which is best used, and what the real differences are among the three averages. Begin by rehearsing the basic knowledge by using questions such as find the mean/median/mode of any three or four numbers, with students responding on mini whiteboards. Change the order of this questioning, for example by asking for 3 values whose mean/median/mode is, say, 5. Extend this, requesting an obvious set of three values, a different set, then a difficult or obscure set. Further exploration into the real implications of each average can be stimulated with the use of photos or visual diagrams such as those found in the resource referenced in Resources. Types of questions to pose are also suggested in this resource. Widen the discussion thus prompted to consider range of data displayed in a photo. Compare ranges of two similar groups, for example, a football team's weights and the sumo wrestler weights. Ask students to consider how the size of range impacts on the knowledge of an average value.

Checkpoint
1 Work out the mode, median, mean and range of this data set: 5, 7, 3, 2, 6, 8, 9, 3, 5, 3 (3, 5, 5.1, 7)

Starter – Today's number is ...111

Ask questions based on today's number', for example,

What is 50% of 111? (55.5)

What is the closest square number to 111? (121)

What is 400 subtract 111? (289)

111 is a multiple of 3. True or false? (T)

What are the factors of 111? (1, 3, 37, 111).

Teaching notes

A difficulty is remembering which average is which, ask students how they remember:

Mean: is the hardest one to calculate.

Med**I**an: is the m**I**ddle term.

M**O**de: is the m**O**st common term.

Work through an example, showing how the statistics are calculated. Emphasise the need to order the data; essential to calculate the median and useful for the mode, mean and range. (A table may help with ordering for a large data set.) How to treat no or multiple modes and finding the median for an even number of data values will need special attention.

It will be helpful to discuss when it is appropriate to use the various averages. The mean is useful for continuous data, for example, students' heights. The mode is the only one that is defined for categorical data, for example, students' eye colours. The median is useful when the data has long tails, for example, the typical (average) salary in the UK. (The mean can be distorted by the super-rich.)

Plenary

Pair up students and give them 30 seconds to agree an answer to each question.

I have four amounts of money:

- the mode is £6   What could the amounts be?
  $(n, 6, 6, m)$ Let all groups agree a possible solution.
- the mean is £5   What could they be now?
  $(n, 6, 6, 8 - n)$
- the median is £6   What could they be now?
  $(n = 0, 1, 2)$ Do all groups agree?

You could repeat this with another similar challenge.

Exercise commentary

Students could be asked to collect their own data to investigate, similar to that in questions **1** and **2**.

Question 1 – The case of multiple modes (Jen) and no mode (Jo) may merit discussion.

Question 2 – Students may need to be reminded how to handle an even number of data points and to order the data first. Ask if it makes a difference if the ordered list is ascending or descending.

Question 3 – For Sandra and Lizzie, ask if students can 'see' the answer without doing a calculation – how?

Question 4 – Units should be given for part **d**.

Question 5 – Ask students to work in pairs, with one pair's solution being checked by another pair. Further constraints can be introduced such as 'there are only four data values'. What is minimum number of data values needed to satisfy each constraint?

Answers

1	**a**	Amy 7	Jen 6	Selma 12	Jo 6
	b	Amy 5	Jen 9	Selma 6	
		Jo No mode			
2	**a**	James			
	b	Kalid 5	Emily 4	Dan $6\frac{1}{2}$	
		Steph 6	James 8		
3	**a**	Sandra 4	Abbie 5	Lizzie 4	Jill 6
		Maya 4			
	b	Sandra 5	Abbie 8	Lizzie 4.5	Jill 9.5
		Maya 5			
	c	6.74			
4	**a** 8	**b** 6	**c** 9	**d** 4.2
5	Compare students' answers in group discussion (multiple answers possible)

Objectives

- Calculate statistics for sets of discrete and continuous data   (L6)

Key ideas	Resources
1 To maintain a sense of the context with these calculations **2** Begin to consider the units of the average found	Mean from frequency tables (1254) Mini white boards

Simplification	Extension
To help understand the meaning of the frequency table, it may be useful to write out in full the list of values. For example in question **1**: 0, 0, 0, 0, 0, 0, 0, 0, 0, 0, 1, 1, 1, 1, 1, 1, 1, 1, 1, 1, 1, 2, 2, 2, 2, 2, 2, 2, 3, 3. It is also easier (but less efficient) to calculate a mean using the numbers in this format.	Give students the following data and ask them to calculate the mean (101.4). 102, 101, 101, 100, 103, 104, 102, 104, 99, 98 Is there an easier way to do the calculation? $\frac{1014}{10}$ Will this method work in other cases? More able students can also be encouraged to work with grouped data, and consider why the mean found can only be an estimate.

Literacy	Links
Students commonly allow procedure to overtake meaning when finding averages with frequency tables, so it is important to encourage students to describe the data in its real context, and ask what the 'units' of the average will be.	Bring in some newspaper/web articles on supposed superfoods. Do students think these are better than the usual five portions of fruit and vegetables that they eat a day? What do they think about nutraceuticals, like bread with added folic acid (vitamin B_9)? In the UK any health claim on a food label must be true and not misleading. How would students decide if a particular food was beneficial?

Alternative approach

Use the example and model the thought processes, including the early approaches to the frequency table, reading the values in context and considering the likely values of each average; i.e. estimating. When working through Exercise **8f**, encourage students to work in twos or threes, reading and checking the reasoning behind the calculations. The data in Exercise **8f** can be used without the structured questioning but with the request to find each of the three averages. The group then supports each other in the steps required towards the solutions. Encourage estimation of the results by the groups before solving. Make sure that each group checks any results with the initial estimations, asking does this value make sense? Make sure that student group records the averages fully; i.e. '4 pieces of fruit per day' rather than '4'.

Checkpoint

1 a When requested to find the mean number of pets per person from the following data, one person offers the answer of 8. Explaining your answer, do you think this is likely to be correct?

(No – any appropriate response)

Number of pets	Frequency
0	12
1	8
2	4

b Work out the modal and mean number of pets per person. (0; 2/3 or 0.67)

c Work out the range.   (2)

d Work out the median.   (0.5)

Starter – DVDs

Ask students to calculate the mean, median and range of the playing times of the following DVDs:

Harry Potter and the Chamber of Secrets	2 hours 34 minutes
Toy Story 2	1 hour 29 minutes
Spiderman	2hours 1 minute
Billy Elliot	1 hour 46 minutes
Batman Begins	2 hours 20 minutes

(Mean = 2hr 2min, median = 2 hr 1min, range = 1hr 5min)

Teaching notes

When using frequency tables, students often get confused over their meaning. To make things more concrete work through an example, simultaneously showing the data in an ordered list and in a table so that they can connect the two. When finding the total number of entries in the table, encourage students to note down their partial sums, as this will help them identify in which class(es) the 'median value(s)' lie.

When you have a large amount of data, a useful way to find the middle value is to calculate $\frac{n+1}{2}$; in the first example $\frac{27+1}{2} = 14$. For an even number of data values this gives a fractional value, say $3\frac{1}{2}$, which reminds you to take $\frac{1}{2}$(3rd +4th) values. When calculating the mean, emphasise the efficiency of performing a single multiplication in the table compared with many repeated additions in the ordered list.

It may help to show a bar chart of the data in the frequency table: the mode is the highest column, the median is the value for which there are as many values to the left as the right and the mean coincides with the centre of gravity or 'balance point'.

Plenary

Show the class a number of bar charts for discrete numerical data; include a symmetric distribution and one with a long tail or outlier. Ask them to give the mode and estimate the median and mean for each data set. For each data set, ask which is the best average to quote for a typical value and why.

Exercise commentary

Again students could be asked to collect their own data and carry out a statistical analysis using the questions as a guide.

Question 1 – Students could also be asked to find the median number of pets (16th data value, 1).

Question 2 – Students may need help with part **c**. Encourage them to note down the cumulative/running total frequencies $1, 3, 8, 12, 21, 27, 31, 32$, so that it is easy to identify the 16th and 17th data values.

Question 3 – Students need to be methodical and should follow the layout in the example. Check that students do not divide by 9, the number of classes.

Question 4 – Ask students if there are circumstances where it is easy to calculate the median and mean (symmetric distributions).

Answers

1	a	31	b	1	c	3
2	a	32	b	4	c	4
3	a	30	b, c	Total 66	d	2.2
4	a	$150 \le h < 160$			

    b You can't find mean, median or range easily because you don't know exact values, only ranges of data

Objectives

- Construct simple scatter graphs (L6)
- Construct and identify key features present in the data for scatter graphs to develop further understanding of correlation (L6)

Key ideas	Resources
1 Begin to use graphs to explore possible links between two variables **2** Recognising if correlation is possible and whether it is positive or negative from a graph	Scatter graphs (1213) Ruler Pencil Squared paper

Simplification	Extension
Provide assistance in drawing the axes and particularly the scale used. It would be possible to have grids available for students' use, but they need also to be able to draw these sensibly themselves. Extra help may be required.	With questions **1** and **2** the results are quite predictable, but do students agree with question **3**? How would students check that these results were reasonable? Challenge students in small groups to plan a survey that would give accurate information. What are the issues? (Can number of messages be counted accurately, should age and/or gender be taken into account?) If there is time before the next lesson (over a day!) then they should carry this out.

Literacy	Links
Encourage students to go beyond stating whether a correlation is positive or negative by adding the appropriate contextual descriptions, for example, as a car ages so its price is likely to drop. Be aware that students will have met lines of best fit which are not necessarily straight lines. Ensure that you are proactive about this, linking this work to graphs of functions. (Linear functions have *straight* lines.)	Bring in some advertisements for the class to use from local car dealers showing prices for second hand cars. Alternatively prices can be found at http://www.autotrader.co.uk/ or http://www.exchangeandmart.co.uk/iad Choose a particular brand of car and find prices for models of different ages. Is there any correlation between the age of the car and the price? What other factors affect the price of the car? (Mileage, model, condition)

Alternative approach

It is worth liaising with science and sharing some appropriate data that can be discussed in each curriculum area, and to check consistency of vocabulary. Students readily grasp the idea of correlation, but perhaps too readily want to add a line of best fit, perhaps because this is what is often required in science. Begin by asking students to give pairs of data that they think are connected or influence each other, for example height and weight. Extend to include unrelated sets of data. Then explore the nature of positive and negative correlation using real/contextual data, to encourage students to discuss the relationships in context. Do not rush to encourage students to add lines of best fit – it is not always appropriate. Ask students to consider when a line of best fit would assist their work if it is not requested.

Checkpoint

1 Is there likely to be a correlation between the cost of living and the year? Explain fully.

(Yes – likely to be positive as the cost of living rises over time)

Starter – Range bingo

Ask students to draw a 3 × 3 grid and enter nine numbers between 15 and 35 inclusive.

Give pairs of numbers, for example, 17 and 41 and ask students find the range.

Winner is the first student to cross out all their numbers.

Teaching notes

Encourage students to think about the use of appropriate scales before starting to draw a scatter graph. These should start and stop so as to avoid large areas of wasted white space. For example, in question **2**, it would not be appropriate to start the scales from 0.

Students usually find it easy to differentiate between negative, no and positive correlations but often confuse the strength of a correlation with the steepness of the 'line of best fit'. Emphasise that the strength, or weakness, is a measure of how tightly the data cluster about a sloping line. Encourage students to describe correlations in two ways. There is a positive correlation between maths and science test scores. Students who get high (low) scores in maths tests tend to also get high (low) scores in science tests.

Plenary

Working in pairs, students draw 6–10 pairs of axes as grids. Give them these axis headings –

- The size of car engine (litres)
- The size of the boot (cubic metres)
- The top speed (mph)
- The price of the car (£)
- The fuel economy rate (miles per litre)
- The age of the car

Label the vertical axis 'size of the engine' and use the other headings on the horizontal axes for different grids. The task is to estimate a scatter graph for each and describe the correlation. This is a discussion topic but, with time, this will allow some students to consider other pairings, for example, top speed against economy rate.

Exercise commentary

Question 1 – There is a strong (positive) correlation that suggests a line of best fit. Ask, if someone scored 14 in their maths test could you predict their science score?

Question 2 – Ensure that students use an appropriate scale, 130–170 for both axes, and that data is plotted at the correct points. The correlation is similar to question **1**.

Question 3 – Again check that students use appropriate scales and plot the data points correctly.

Question 4 – This question can be used to help reinforce the need for carefully drawn axes and scales. It could be completed before questions **1** to **3**.

Question 5 – This hints at the key idea of a correlation being evidence for (but not a proof of) a causal link.

Answers

1 a Check students' diagrams are accurately drawn. The plots should roughly form a straight line with positive slope.

   b Maths and science scores show positive correlation; a student who gets a good score in one test also tends to get a good score in the other test.

2 a Check students' diagrams are accurately drawn. The plots should roughly form a straight line with positive slope.

   b Arm span and height are positively correlated.

3 a Check students' diagrams are accurately drawn. The plots should be scattered randomly without forming a straight line.

   b There is no correlation between emails and texts.

4 a Simon used inconsistent scales with the same intervals representing different amounts. He did not even label his scales in numerical order.

   b Check students' diagrams are accurately drawn with consistent scales. Correctly labelled. Diagrams should show negative correlation.

5 No. There is a direct relationship between the two variables but it is not causal.

Objectives	
• Construct stem-and-leaf diagrams	(L6)

Key ideas	Resources
1 Understanding how stem-and-leaf diagrams display data	Stem and leaf (1215)
2 Being able to read data from a stem-and-leaf diagram	Squared paper SAT questions: http://www.sats-papers.co.uk/sats-papers-ks3.php

Simplification	Extension
Making sense of data is a challenge; many students will need additional stem-and-leaf diagrams that they have to describe rather than spending much time drawing the diagrams.	The stems on all the stem-and-leaf diagrams seen have gone up in tens. Challenge students to draw a stem-and-leaf diagram to represent small or large numbers so that the scale is a challenge (involving decimals or thousands).

Literacy	Links
Point out the links to the stem, as of a plant, and the leaves branching outwards. Note that it is usual to draw this as a single line column.	The tallest man ever in the world was Robert Pershing Wadlow from the USA who was 2.72 m tall and died in 1940. The world's shortest man is Pingping from China who is 73 cm tall. Add these two pieces of data to the boys' heights in the example. What is the new range? There are pictures of Robert Wadlow and Pingping at http://en.wikipedia.org/wiki/Image:Robert_Wadlow.jpg

Alternative approach
It is possible to model a stem-and-leaf diagram using heights of students in the class physically by arranging the students in height order as a complete line, then arrange them in groups of 10 cm from this line. It is worth noting that the diagrams in this section all show the largest values in the top row, but that this is not a requirement and working from smallest in the top row is acceptable. Both versions can be modelled physically, then students can construct their own class height stem-and-leaf diagrams. Having constructed one or two such diagrams, engage the students in exploring where the averages are on one of their diagrams, before widening to the given discussion point with pairs of students trying to identify key advantages and disadvantages of the diagrams. Share these results fully with the whole group.

Checkpoint
1 Use the stem-and-leaf diagram in data question 16 from 2008 SATs paper 1 (level 5-7). Orally ask the questions (a), (b), (c) for response via mini whiteboards.   ((a) 4; (b) 2.8; (c) 15.3)

Starter – More jumble

Write a list of anagrams on the board and ask students to unscramble them. Possible anagrams are

AGRAVEE, CQUEENFRY, GAREN, TRAINCOROLE, CASTISITT, EDAMIN, MISTIREESE (2 words), ACIPERTH (2 words)

(Average, frequency, range, correlation, statistic, median, time series, pie chart)

Can be extended by asking students to make a data handling word search.

Teaching notes

When drawing a stem-and-leaf diagram it is necessary to follow a process that will not allow data to be missed. After drawing the stem students should plot each result as a leaf (one per square) but not ordered for each ten. They then re-draw the stem-and-leaf diagram but now with the results ordered from smallest to largest along each leaf.

Finding the median can cause problems and a foolproof way (if a little slow) is a tactile method. Starting with the largest and smallest results and count in (and out) one each time until you meet. If you finish on two adjacent results (an even number of data) then the median is the value half-way between them.

Plenary

Give half the class a set of data as a table of numbers, for example, 30 numbers between 0 and 50 mixed in order (the results of a maths test). Give the other half of the class the same numbers but as a stem-and-leaf diagram. Give each student two minutes to bullet point a description of the numbers. Then ask students to compare their descriptions. Those with the diagram should have been able to give far more detail than the groups with the list of numbers.

Exercise commentary

Question 1 – Ask students when they should use mode and modal class.

Question 2 – Check that students are putting the numbers on the leaves directly below the one above and spacing them out evenly. Question **1** and the first example provide good models.

Question 3 – A good model for the back-to-back stem-and-leaf diagram is in the second example. What numbers should go in the stem? (1 to 5)

Question 4 – Suggest that students work in two stages: first produce an unordered stem-and-leaf diagram and then produce an ordered one.

Question 5 – Allow students to work in small groups to make a table listing advantages and disadvantages for each type of representation. As a class decide what are the best 'pro' and 'con' points. Ask if there are types of data for which one representation is clearly the best.

Answers

1 a 225   **b** 250–259 **c** 56

2

100	1
110	3 9
120	1 4 4 6
130	0 1 4 7 8
140	0 5 5 7
150	0 5 6
160	2
170	1

3 a

Test 1		Test 2
	10	8
7 4 4 1	20	4 5 5 6 9
9 7 6 5 5 4 3 2 1 0	30	0 2 5 6 8 8
8 8 6 4 2	40	1 1 3 4 8 9
	50	0 0 0

4 | 30 | 1 means

34 test 1

31 test 2

b The scores in Test 2 tended to be higher with a median of 38 compared with a median of 34.5 for Test 1. The scores in Test 1 are more spread out then Test 2 with a range of 30 compared to 26.

4 a

30	4 6 7
40	0 1 2 4 5 8
50	1 2 2 3 5 7 7 8 9
60	0 3 3 4 5 8
70	2 4
80	1

40 | 5 means 45 kg

b 55 kg

5 With a stem-and-leaf diagram you can see the actual data (rather than a grouping).
However, the bar chart or pie chart is clearer at showing the relative sizes of the various categories, because it is pictorial and drawn to scale.

Key outcomes		Quick check
Identify and collect data.	L6	Is the following data discrete or continuous?
		a Number of cars in a household (discrete) **b** Time taken to run 50 metres (continuous)
Construct pie charts.	L6	Work out the angles for this pie chart:
		Blue eyes (17), Brown eyes (6), Green eyes (1) (255°, 90°, 15°)
Construct bar charts and frequency diagrams.	L6	Write down one key difference between a bar chart and a frequency diagram.
		(Bars do not touch in a bar chart, they do touch in a frequency diagram)
Calculate statistics for sets of discrete and continuous data.	L6	Work out the mean, median, mode and range for this set of data:
		4, 5, 6, 7, 4, 5, 6, 8, 2, 5, 6, 5 (5.17, 5, 5, 6)
		Work out an estimate of the mean for this data:

Number of TVs	1	2	3
Frequency	4	6	3

(1.92)

What is the modal number of TVs? (2)

Construct scatter diagrams and understand correlation.	L6	Describe the possible correlation:
		a The age of a car and its value (negative)
		b The number of people on the beach and the temperature (positive)
Draw and interpret stem-and-leaf diagrams.	L6	Draw a stem-and-leaf diagram for this data:
		12, 13, 15, 17, 18, 21, 22, 22, 25, 26, 29, 30, 31, 33, 33, 34
		(Check students' answers – stems should be 1, 2, 3, check a key is included)

MyMaths extra support

Lesson/online homework		Description
All averages 1192	L5	Using the three types of average to compare two data sets
Frequency tables and bar charts 1193	L3	Planning and drawing bar charts and frequency diagrams; reading information from charts
Median, mode from freq tables 1202	L7	Working out the mode and median from a frequency table
Pictograms and bar charts 1205	L3	Planning and drawing pictograms and bar charts
Drawing pie charts 1207	L6	Calculating the angles for a pie chart; how to draw a good chart
Introducing data 1235	L3	Sorting data into groups using Venn diagrams and tally charts
Types of data 1248	L7	Types of data; advantages and disadvantages of primary and secondary data

MyReview

Check out

You should now be able to ...

		Test it ➡ Questions
✓	Identify and collect data.	1
✓	Construct pie charts.	2
✓	Construct bar charts and frequency diagrams.	3
✓	Calculate statistics for sets of discrete and continuous data.	4, 5
✓	Construct scatter diagrams and understand correlation.	6
✓	Draw and interpret stem-and-leaf diagrams.	7

Language	Meaning	Example
Primary data	Data which you collect yourself	The results of a survey or experiment that you carried out
Secondary data	Data which you did not collect yourself	Information from a book or the internet
Discrete data	Data which is obtained by counting	The number of pets or brothers and sisters that you have
Continuous data	Data which is obtained by measuring	Your height, weight or age
Categorical data	Data which is obtained by describing	The colour of your eyes
Bar chart	Used to represent categorical or discrete data	Examples of bar charts are on page 142.
Frequency diagram	Used to show continuous data	There is a frequency diagram on page 142.
Average	A measure of the 'typical value' of data	The mode, median and mean are averages
Range	A measure of the spread of data	The range of -5, -1, 2, 4 and 9 is 9 − (-5) = 14
Scatter diagram	A graph which allows you to see patterns in pairs of data	A graph of height versus weight for students in your class
Stem-and-leaf diagram	A diagram which allows you to see the shape of the distribution of data while retaining the actual numerical values of the data	See page 150

152 **Statistics** Collecting and representing data

1 Explain whether the data below is
i primary or secondary
ii discrete or continuous.
a Lengths you measure in a science class.
b Days spent in hospital taken from patient records.
c Number of house points won at your school's sports day.

2 Draw a pie chart to show peoples' favourite type of film.

Action	10	Comedy	7
Romance	5	Musical	2
Horror	4	Other	2

3 The table shows the weights of 12 mice (g).

Weight (g)	Frequency
$15 \leq w < 20$	1
$20 \leq w < 25$	4
$25 \leq w < 30$	4
$30 \leq w < 35$	2
$35 \leq w < 40$	1

Draw a frequency diagram for this data.

4 Here are the shoe sizes of 12 women.
5, 7, 6, 4, 3, 3, 5, 6, 5, 7, 6, 4
Find
a the mode   b the mean (1dp)
c the median   d the range.

5 The table shows how many packets of crisps students ate in one week.

Packs of crisps	0	1	2	3	4	5	6	7
Frequency	6	4	9	10	5	3	2	1

a Find the modal number of packs eaten.
b Calculate the mean number of packs of crisps per student.

6 The number of hot drinks and of fizzy drinks sold at a cafe on seven different days is shown in the table.

Hot	65	40	50	30	20	15	60
Fizzy	25	35	30	40	50	45	25

a Draw a scatter diagram for this data.
b Describe the correlation.

7 The stem-and-leaf diagram shows the age of the first 20 people to arrive at a theme park.

```
0 | 5  9
1 | 0  0  1  3  5  6
2 | 1  6  8  9
3 | 5  7  8
4 | 3  5  5
5 | 8
6 | 1            3 | 5 = 35 years old
```

Find a the range   b the median.

What next?

	Score	
	0 – 2	Your knowledge of this topic is still developing. To improve look at Formative test: 2B-8; MyMaths: 1200, 1203, 1206, 1213, 1215 and 1254
	3 – 6	You are gaining a secure knowledge of this topic. To improve look at InvisiPen: 411, 414, 422, 423, 242, 427, 431, 441 and 442
	7	You have mastered this topic. Well done, you are ready to progress!

MyMaths.co.uk

153

Question commentary

Question 1 – For part **c**, if you collect the data or arrange for it to be collected it would be primary. Remind students that discrete data is be counted but continuous data must be measured.

Question 2 – Students will need to use a sharp pencil, ruler and protractor, they will also need a pair of compasses or something circular to draw around. The sections of the pie chart should either be labelled or coloured in and a key provided. Allow 2° tolerance on angles.

Question 3 – You could suggest suitable scales for the axes if necessary; axes must be labelled and the bars much touch.

Question 4 – It will help to write the numbers in size order first. The total is 61.

Question 5 – An answer of 13.25 for **c** would indicate student has divided by 8 not the total frequency (40).

Question 6 – Check that students are choosing appropriate scales and labelling the axes correctly.

Question 7 – The range is 61 − 5, the median is the average of 26 and 28.

Answers

1 a i Primary   ii Continuous
   b i Secondary   ii Discrete
   c i Secondary   ii Discrete
   c Discrete

2 Angles are
   Action = 120°   Romance = 60°   Horror = 48°
   Comedy = 84°
   Musical = Other = 24°

3 Check students' diagrams. Bars drawn to correct frequencies. No gaps between bars.

4 a 5 and 6   b 5.1   c 5   d 4
5 a 3   b 2.65
6 a Check points correct: $(65, 25), (40, 35), (50, 30)$, $(30, 40), (20, 50), (15, 45), (60, 25)$
   b Negative
7 a 56   b 27

8a
1 Give some examples of primary and secondary data that you could use to investigate these topics.
   a Recycling
   b Mobile phone use
   c Exercise and sport

8b
2 Tom asked 30 people in his class how many books they currently had out on loan from the school library. Here are his results.

```
3 2 2 2 1 0 3 0 1 4
4 3 1 0 0 1 2 3 3 4
1 3 2 2 2 3 3 4 0 1
```

Organise this data into a frequency table.

8c
3 Sara recorded the size and colour of crayons in a box.
There are three colours of crayon – red, blue and green.
There are two sizes of crayon – large and small.
Sara used upper and lower case letters to represent the crayons.
She used G for a large green, and b for a small blue, and so on.

```
R r G r b B r G g
B B g g r R r r b b
g g g R B R G r G B
```

Draw a two-way table for this set of data.

8c
4 Here are one season's results for two football teams.

United	Wanderers
Won 14	Won 10
Drew 8	Drew 6
Lost 8	Lost 14

Draw a pie chart for each team's results.

8d
5 This set of data shows the number of phone calls received by a shop each day for 20 days.

```
4 5 5 3 0 2 7 4 6 5
4 4 1 0 3 2 1 5 5 4
```

Draw a bar chart to show the data.

8e
6 This set of data shows the length (in minutes and seconds) of 20 phone calls received by a shop.

```
0:35  1:22  2:47  1:26  3:55  2:50  0:15  1:03  3:35  4:09
3:10  0:59  3:09  2:26  3:11  3:28  2:05  3:54  2:12  1:08
```

Draw a frequency diagram to show the data.

8f
7 Find the mean, median and range of each of these sets of numbers.
   a 4, 8, 16, 19, 25
   b 34, 67, 92, 108
   c 3.5, 9.2, 7.3, 8.3, 4.1
   d 106.3, 88.9, 71.4, 58.7, 91.9

8f
8 The students in a class were asked how many people live in their house. The table shows the result.

Number of occupants	2	3	4	5	6	7	8
Frequency	3	5	11	6	4	0	1

For this set of data, find
   a the mode   b the median   c the mean   d the range.

8g
9 John recorded the length and weight of 10 earthworms.

Length (cm):	7	8	7	9	11	6	10	5	6	5
Weight (g):	22	24	21	28	30	16	28	17	18	16

Draw a scatter diagram for this set of data.

8h
10 The ages (in years) of 20 customers in a shop were

```
15  61  42  33  38  29  53  17  44  32
39  45  41  26  22  44  43  49  55  60
```

Draw a stem-and-leaf diagram for this set of data.

Question commentary

Question 1 – Students can be encouraged to be inventive and to discuss their answers with others.

Questions 2 and **3** – Students should understand that different ways of organising data are appropriate for different situations. Model grids could be given out.

Question 4 – Check that calculated angles add to 360° before proceeding and also that students have sharp pencils and protractors. Allow ± 2° for each sector.

Questions 5 and **6** – Check that students are clearly demonstrating the difference between the two types of diagram and that they are scaling and labelling their axes correctly in both cases.

Question 7 – Check students are ordering the lists for median and range calculations.

Question 8 – Check students do not divide by 7 for the mean. Adding an extra row to the table might help them work out the total number of people for each class.

Question 9 – Check students are using a continuous scale on both axes and labelling them correctly.

Question 10 – Students may be advised to produce and unordered stem-and-leaf diagram first of all. Check they include a key. Stems should be 1 to 6.

Answers

1 Discuss students' ideas

2 Check students' frequency tables. Correct tallies give frequencies of 5, 6, 7, 8, 4 for books on loan 0, 1, 2, 3, 4

3

		Colour		
		Red	Blue	Green
Size	Large	4	5	5
	Small	8	3	5

4 United: Won 168°, Drew 96°, Lost 96°
Wanderers: Won 120°, Drew 72°, Lost 168°

5 Check students' bar charts. Correct tallies give frequencies of 2, 2, 2, 2, 5, 5, 1, 1, for number of phone calls: 0, 1, 2, 3, 4, 5, 6, 7.

6 This answer will depend on the intervals chosen by the students. Check diagrams correctly drawn to correct frequencies. No gaps between bars.

7 | | Mean | Median | Range |
|---|---|---|---|
| **a** | 14.4 | 16 | 21 |
| **b** | 75.25 | 79.5 | 74 |
| **c** | 6.48 | 7.3 | 5.7 |
| **d** | 83.44 | 88.9 | 47.6 |

8 **a** 4   **b** 4   **c** 4.2   **d** 6

9 Check points correctly plotted: (7, 22), (8, 24), (7, 21), (9, 28), (11, 30), (6, 16), (10, 28), (5, 17), (6, 18), (5, 16)

10 Check students' diagrams. Correctly labelled with appropriate scale.

MyAssessment 2

These questions will test you on your knowledge of the topics in chapters 5 to 8.
They give you practice in the types of questions that you may eventually be given in your GCSE exams. There are 75 marks in total.

1 a Calculate the unknown angles a, b, c and d. (3 marks)

b Show that the angle $(b + c)$ is identical to angle d. (1 mark)

c What name do we give to these types of angles? (1 mark)

d What is the mathematical name for the triangle enclosed between the parallel lines? (1 mark)

2 What is the name given to quadrilaterals that have the following properties?

a One set of equal sides, two pairs of equal angles and one set of parallel sides. (1 mark)

b Four equal sides, two pairs of equal angles and two sets of parallel sides. (1 mark)

3 a Calculate the interior angle of a regular pentagon. (1 mark)

b Use this knowledge to determine the missing angles a, b and c. (3 marks)

c What is the name given to this triangle? (1 mark)

d Use a protractor and a ruler to accurately construct a regular pentagon with side length 5cm. (3 marks)

4 a State whether any two of these triangles are congruent. (1 marks)

b Give your reasons. (3 marks)

5 a Draw x and y-axes from -5 to +5. (2 marks)

b Copy and complete the table for the equation $y = x - 2$. (2 marks)

x	-2	-1	0	1	2	3	4
y							

c Plot these points on the graph and draw a straight line connecting them. (3 marks)

d Draw on the same graph the lines $x = -2$ and $y = 1$. (2 marks)

e Give the coordinates of the points where all of these lines cross. (3 marks)

6 This graph shows the potential difference (volts) versus current (amps) for a resistor.

a What is the potential difference when the current is 3.0 amps? (1 mark)

b What is the potential difference when the current is 2.0 amps? (2 marks)

7 Round each of these numbers to the accuracy stated.

a 2859 (nearest 10) b 7.392 (1 dp)

c 25.9855 (to 2 dp) d 37798 (nearest 10) (4 marks)

8 Calculate

a 54×0.01 b $0.56 \div 0.1$

c $621 \div 0.01$ d 12.5×0.1 (4 marks)

9 Calculate these either mentally using factors or by the methods of partitioning or compensation.

a 43×20 b $276 \div 12$

c 8.3×12 d 7.2×19 (4 marks)

10 An 8-person expedition camps for one night at a camp site. The costs are £6.50 per tent plus an additional cost per person per night. If the total cost was £49.50, and three tents were used, find the cost per person per night. (3 marks)

11 The temperature in °C is recorded in twenty cities and major towns in one day across the UK.

24 18 23 19 20 20 24 23 22 8
17 18 19 23 21 19 22 9 20 18

a Draw a stem-and-leaf diagram for this data. (3 marks)

b Find the median temperature. (2 marks)

c Find the range of temperatures and the mode. (2 marks)

d Find the mean temperature across all twenty cities and towns. (2 marks)

12 In a science experiment one end of a metal rod was heated and the temperatures, at equal distances along the rod, were recorded.

Position (cm)	1	2	3	4	5	6	7	8	9
Temperature (°C)	14.5	18.2	29.6	38.4	47.9	60.2	71.2	82.3	94.8

a Draw a scatter graph to show this data using the x-axis from 0 to 10cm to represent position and the y-axis from 0 to 100°C to represent temperature. (4 marks)

b Draw the line of best fit. (1 mark)

c Comment on the correlation shown. (2 marks)

13 A packet of breakfast cereal showed its nutritional information per 100g amount as

Protein 18g, Carbohydrate 64g, Fat 4g, Fibre 14g.

a If 360° represents 100g of cereal, what angle represents 1g? (2 marks)

b Calculate the angles of the sectors for each ingredient. (4 marks)

c Draw a pie chart to show this information. (3 marks)

 MyMaths.co.uk

Mark scheme

Questions 1 – 6 marks

a 3 $a = 41°$, $b = 19°$, $c = 120°$, $d = 139°$

b 1 $b + c = 19° + 120° = 139° = d$

c 1   alternate; accept corresponding

d 1   scalene

Questions 2 – 2 marks

a 1   isosceles trapezium; not trapezium

b 1   rhombus

Questions 3 – 8 marks

a 1   108°

b 3 $a = 72°$, $b = 72°$, $c = 36°$

c 1   isosceles triangle

d 3   Check students' drawings. Angles and side length correct

Questions 4 – 4 marks

a 1   A and B are congruent

b 3   Students answers. Two pairs of equal angles, corresponding sides are equal, not congruent to C, C has an obtuse angle; any three

Questions 5 – 12 marks

a 2   Correct x- and y-axes drawn and labelled

b 2   Correct values in table; -4, -3, -2, -1, 0, 1, 2

c 3   Check students' drawings. All points correctly plotted; ruled straight line through points; -1 each error

d 2   Correct vertical and horizontal lines drawn

e 3   (-2, 1) (3, 1) and (-2, -4)

Questions 6 – 3 marks

a 1   20 volts

b 2   from graph ~ 13.5 ± 0.2 volts or 1A = 20/3 volts then 2A = 40/3 = 13.3 volts; accept both methods

Questions 7 – 4 marks

a 1   2860

b 1   7.4

c 1   25.99

d 1   37 800

Questions 8 – 4 marks

a 1   0.54

b 1   5.6

c 1   62 100

d 1   1.25

Questions 9 – 4 marks

a 1   860

b 1   23

c 1   99.6

d 1   136.8

Questions 10 – 3 marks

3   £3.75; 1 mark if £19.50 seen; 1 mark if £30 seen.

Questions 11 – 9 marks

a 3   Correct stem and leaf

0| 8 9

1| 7 8 8 8 9 9 9

2| 0 0 0 1 2 2 3 3 3 4 4

b 2   20 °C; between 10th and 11th

c 2   Range 16 °C, mode 18 °C, 19 °C, 20 °C and 23 °C; all modal temperatures needed

d 2   19.4 °C (1 dp); accept 19.4 °C

Questions 12 – 7 marks

a 4   Check students' graphs. Correct x- and y-axes drawn; correct labelling; correct points plotted

b 1   Check students' drawings. Rule best line fitted; no freehand lines

c 2   Strong positive correlation; shows strong relationship between position and temperature

Questions 13 – 9 marks

a 2   100 g = 360°, 1 g = 360/100 = 3.6°

b 4   protein = 65°, carbohydrate = 230°, fat = 14°, fibre = 50°

c 3   Check students' drawings. Correct pie chart drawn, correct angles; labelled.

9 Transformations and symmetry

Learning outcomes

G5 Describe, sketch and draw using conventional terms and notations: points, lines, parallel lines, perpendicular lines, right angles, regular polygons, and other polygons that are reflectively and rotationally symmetric (L5)

G8 Identify properties of, and describe the results of, translations, rotations and reflections applied to given figures (L5)

G9 Identify and construct congruent triangles, and construct similar shapes by enlargement, with and without coordinate grids (L6)

Introduction

The chapter starts by looking at rotations, reflections and translations before moving on to look at combining these transformations. Rotational and reflective symmetry is then covered before the concept of an enlargement is introduced. Enlargements from a given centre are covered in the final section.

The introduction discusses the idea of symmetry in art. Buddhist sand mandalas are the main focus but it also mentions Islamic and Hindu art as well as more contemporary artists such as M C Escher. Symmetry in the natural world is also considered. There are many great examples of traditional and contemporary art that uses extensive symmetry to create what is referred to as 'formal' art, designed to affect the viewer through the appreciation of the patterns, rather than the emotions that the art stirs.

The following websites provide a wealth of examples that could be used to illustrate these art forms:

http://patterninislamicart.com/

http://www.mysticalartsoftibet.org/mandala.htm

http://en.wikipedia.org/wiki/Rangoli

http://www.mcescher.com/

Prior knowledge

Students should already know how to…

- Perform simple transformations
- Recognise the symmetry properties of simple shapes

Starter problem

The starter problem gives the students a simple rectangle reflection in the line $y = x$ and asks them to consider how the coordinates are transformed under the reflection. Students should quickly be able to identify that the x- coordinate and the y-coordinate are interchanged.

Students could be directed to test this hypothesis by carrying out their own reflection in the line $y = x$ for another shape.

The second part of the starter activity asks students to consider the effect of a reflection in the line $y = -x$. Here, not only are the coordinates interchanged, but the signs of the coordinates are also changed. Positive y-coordinates become negative x-coordinates, for example. Again, students could be directed to try out their hypothesis on other shapes reflected in the line $y = -x$.

Resources

MyMaths

Enlarging shapes	1099	Reflecting shapes	1113	Lines of symmetry	1114
Rotating shapes	1115	Rotation symmetry	1116	All transformations	1125
Translating shapes	1127				

Online assessment

Chapter test	2B–9
Formative test	2B–9
Summative test	2B–9

InvisiPen solutions

Reflection and rotation symmetry			361
Reflection	362	Translation	363
Rotation	364	Enlargements	366
Combined transformation not enlargement			368

Topic scheme

Teaching time = 5 lessons/2 weeks

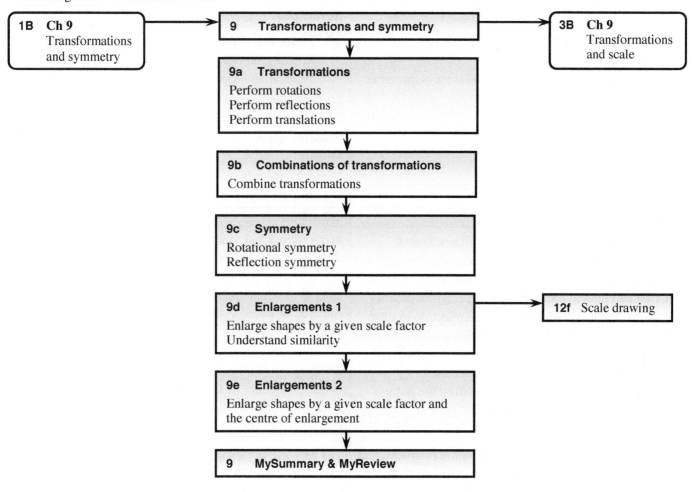

1B Ch 9 Transformations and symmetry	

9 Transformations and symmetry

3B Ch 9 Transformations and scale

9a Transformations
Perform rotations
Perform reflections
Perform translations

9b Combinations of transformations
Combine transformations

9c Symmetry
Rotational symmetry
Reflection symmetry

9d Enlargements 1
Enlarge shapes by a given scale factor
Understand similarity

12f Scale drawing

9e Enlargements 2
Enlarge shapes by a given scale factor and the centre of enlargement

9 MySummary & MyReview

Differentiation

Student book 2A 172 – 189	**Student book 2B** 158 – 173	**Student book 2C** 162 – 177
Reflection	Transformations	Transformations
Reflection symmetry	Combinations of transformations	Combinations of transformations
Rotation	Symmetry	Symmetry
Rotational symmetry	Enlargements 1	Enlargements 1
Translation	Enlargements 2	Enlargements 2
Tessellation		

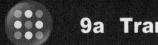

Objectives

- Transform 2D shapes by rotation, reflection and translation, on paper (and using ICT) (L5)

Key ideas	Resources
1 Recognise and identify each of the three transformations 2 Understand what changes and what stays the same with each transformation	Reflecting shapes (1113) Rotating shapes (1115) Translating shapes (1127) Large squared paper Tracing paper Isometric paper Mirrors Mini whiteboards Dynamic geometry software

Simplification	Extension
Copying the diagrams accurately will need most support in this exercise. It will be helpful to provide a prepared grid for question 3. Ask students to plot shape A first and then to translate that shape before plotting shape B. Weaker students may find reflection in lines other than vertical or horizontal challenging. Adjust the challenge as required and support extending skills by encouraging students to move or rotate their grids/exercise books. They may also find the jump from grids to sets of axes challenging.	In question 3, ask students to use the mathematical short hand to describe the translation, for example, 6 units to the right and 0 units up becomes $\binom{6}{0}$. Students can then be asked to design their own translation problem using this notation.

Literacy	Links
Take the opportunity to revisit the word congruent, and encourage students to use it when examining resulting shapes. While students will be familiar with the vocabulary here, they may not readily be able to give the full detail required in order to communicate fully. Prompting students and encouraging them to challenge each other to give full detail will be helpful.	The painting shown in the 'Did you know?' is the Mona Lisa, also known as La Gioconda. It was painted by Leonardo Da Vinci in the 16th century and now hangs in The Louvre in Paris. There is an optical illusion based on a transformation of part of the Mona Lisa's face at http://www.exploratorium.edu/exhibits/mona/mona.html

Alternative approach

Begin by asking students to watch a folding and cutting exercise, in order to predict the outcomes be sketching on mini whiteboards. Fold either once or twice, and cut a sheet of A4 paper clearly for all students to observe carefully. Before unfolding the paper, ask students what the result might look like. They can indicate the fold lines or axes with either one or two lines on their boards. Now explore what the students remember about these transformations. Use can be made of any dynamic geometry software to perform transformations, so can be effective in asking students to predict what will happen, allow them time to discuss and sketch in pairs before running a demonstration.

Checkpoint

1 What information is required in order to perform a rotation accurately?

(Centre of rotation, amount of turn/rotation, direction)

2 What information is required in order to perform a translation accurately?

(How many steps across and up/down)

Starter – Palindromic dates

1st November 2010 is palindromic if written using two digits for the day, month and year: 01.11.10

Ask students to find other palindromic dates occurring between 2010 and 2060. (11.11.11, 21.11.12, 02.11.20, 12.11.21, etc.)

Teaching notes

Students should have previous knowledge of basic translations; this can be reviewed in a class discussion.

Taking reflections, rotations and translations in turn, ask students to supply the facts needed to define the transformation and also to explain how to carry out the transformation. The emphasis can be placed on their practical know how and on their tips for avoiding any mistakes. Working together through examples on the board should consolidate the ideas.

If a large sheet of tracing paper is available, fixing a centre of rotation with your finger should allow you to demonstrate on the board how to use it to help rotate a shape.

Plenary

As a literacy challenge, ask students to work in pairs and give them 4–5 minutes to write definitions (in less than 10 words) for each of the following: regular shape; translation; rhombus; centre of rotation; congruent. Ask pairs to share their answers and agree the best definitions.

Exercise commentary

If you usually use small squared paper (0.5 mm or 0.7 mm), it is advisable to use larger squares for this work.

Question 1 – Emphasise the need to draw all shapes accurately and ensure that distances from the mirror line are equal.

Question 2 – Have available small pieces of tracing paper.

Question 3 – Students may need to be reminded of the order in which to plot coordinates. To avoid confusion, join up one set of points before moving on to the next. After drawing each translation students should name the new shape A′ or B′, etc.

Question 4 – It may help to complete the first few parts collectively. The mirror line should be dashed.

Answers

1 **a** (3, 1)   **b** (-3, -1)   **c** (-1, -2)
2 **a** D   **b** C   **c** B   **d** A

Exercise 9a

1 Check students' drawings
   a Square, regular   **b** Hexagon, irregular
   c Square, regular   **d** Rectangle, irregular
2 **a** Check students' drawings
   b All angles and all sides equal
   c Square
3 **a** Check students' drawings, correct points plotted
   b A, B, E, F are rectangles
        C is a scalene triangle
        D is an isosceles trapezium
   c The new coordinates are
        A′ (9, 7), (10, 8), (8, 10), (7, 9) and (9, 7)
        B′ (10, 8), (11, 7), (13, 9), (12, 10) and (10, 8)
        C′ (11, 9), (10, 10), (9, 6) and (11, 9)
        D′ (12, 3), (11, 5), (9, 5), (8, 3) and (12, 3)
        E′ (8, 4), (10, 6), (9, 7), (7, 5) and (8, 4)
        F′ (12, 4), (13, 5), (11, 7), (10,6) and (12, 4)

4 **a–g** Check students' drawings

Objectives	
• Try out mathematical representations of simple combinations of these transformations (L5)	

Key ideas	Resources
1 Investigating and testing effects of combinations of transformations 2 Investigating links of transformations, including commutativity	All transformations (1125) Squared paper Tracing paper Scissors Dynamic geometry software Examples Islamic art, M C Escher pictures

Simplification	Extension
To simplify tessellation problems, let students cut out a template of the basic shape, transform it and then draw around the template.	Any quadrilateral will tessellate – or will it? Challenge students to construct any quadrilateral and try to develop a tessellation. Remember angles at a point add up to 360° and all four angles of a quadrilateral add to 360° so there will need to be one of each of the quadrilateral angles at the meeting point! It can be done!

Literacy	Links
Students will already be aware that order can matter in both literacy and mathematics. Remind them that 6 × 4 = 4 × 6, but that 30 ÷ 3 ≠ 3 ÷ 30. This simple but powerful idea helps to build logical thought, so is useful to address with students.	Islamic art does not use images of living things, but instead uses geometric patterns and tessellations. The Alhambra palace in Granada, Spain is richly decorated with Islamic art. For more information about the Palace see http://en.wikipedia.org/wiki/Alhambra

Alternative approach
If students have access to dynamic geometry software then they may be encouraged to investigate combinations of transformations for themselves. Suggest that they explore the effects of two transformations, firstly where both are similar, for example, both reflections, but not necessarily in the same line; then of two different transformations. Pose the questions: Can a combination be replaced by one transformation? Does order of transformation matter? Can the resulting one transformation be predicted from the individual ones? Encourage the students to work in pairs in order to generate valuable discussion. Pair to pair sharing can be encouraged after each main question. Encourage students to predict and test any hypothesis generated.

Checkpoint
1 A shape is reflected in a line then rotated. Will the result be the same if the shape was rotated first then reflected? (Yes)
2 A shape is translated 5 units to the right and 3 units up. This new shape is then translated 2 units to the left and 4 units down. Describe the translation that maps the original shape to this final shape. (3 units right, 1 unit down)

Starter – Moving triangles

Ask students to plot (or imagine) a triangle with vertices at $(1, 1), (2, 1), (1, 5)$. Then ask students to imagine the x-coordinates are multiplied by -1, that is, $(-1, 1) (-2, 1) (-1, 5)$. What will the triangle look like? What transformation has taken place? (Reflection in y-axis)

What if the y-coordinates are multiplied by -1? (Reflection in x-axis)

What if the x- and y-coordinates are reversed, that is, $(1, 1), (1, 2), (5, 1)$? (Reflection in line $y = x$)

Teaching notes

Students will have seen tessellations before and will be familiar with the idea of a repeating shape filling the plane. They will be less familiar with knowing which transformations to use to achieve tessellations. A good way into the topic would be to show examples of tessellations – paving, M C Escher, Islamic art, etc. – and invite students to explain how to create the pattern starting with a single shape. Move descriptions on from 'turn it upside down and move it over' to specifying rotations (centre-angle-direction) etc. with increasing mathematical precision.

A collective activity is to ask groups of students to produce sets of identical shapes – accurate drawing will be very important here – and put them together to create tessellations. This may form the basis of posters for the classroom, which can be annotated with details of the transformations involved.

Plenary

Ask students to look at their answer to question **4** – it should be 1 unit right and 4 units down. Can they explain how they reached the answer one right and four down? The target is to show this as an arrow (vector) diagram.

$$\begin{pmatrix} 2 \\ -1 \end{pmatrix} + \begin{pmatrix} -1 \\ -3 \end{pmatrix} = \begin{pmatrix} 1 \\ -4 \end{pmatrix}$$

Exercise commentary

This exercise requires neat and accurate sketching, a major challenge for many students. Encourage students to be proud of their efforts.

Question 1 – The same tessellation could be achieved with translations.

Question 2 – To help students get started, demonstrate one of the rotations about a mid-point. Tracing paper is useful here.

Question 3 – The dots show the centres of rotation. It may help to cut out a template to manipulate/draw around or use tracing paper.

Question 4 – Ensure that students do not apply both translations to the original hexagon.

Question 5 – Tracing paper may be needed for this question.

Question 6 – It may help if students cut out the resulting shape and then tessellate it by drawing around it.

Question 7 – This could form part of a homework task and/or a research-based task.

Answers

1		Check students' drawings
2	a, b	Check students' drawings
3	a, b	Check students' drawings
4	a, b	Check students' drawings
	c	Translation 1 unit right and 4 units down
5	a, b	Check students' drawings
	c	Rotation of 90° anticlockwise about the black dot
6	Check students' work.	
7	Check students' work.	

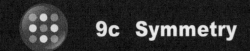

Objectives

- Identify all the symmetries of 2D shapes (L5)

Key ideas	Resources	
1 Recognise and identify line symmetry 2 Recognise and identify rotational symmetry	Lines of symmetry	(1114)
	Rotation symmetry	(1116)
	Squared paper	
	Tracing paper	
	Mirrors	
	Cardboard shapes	
	Reflecting Squarely: http://nrich.maths.org/1840	
	Attractive Rotations: http://nrich.maths.org/6987	

Simplification	Extension
The use of mirrors to highlight lines of symmetry and the ability to fold shapes to show lines of symmetry (or not!) is always helpful to overcome areas of doubt.	Give students three squares as a rectangle. By placing a mirror what different shapes can be made? Develop this so that the three squares form a small L shape and set the same problem.

Literacy	Links
Order of symmetry can be problematic for students so examining symmetry of 'order 1' can help to show that any and every shape must be of at least order 1.	The flag of the United Kingdom has rotational symmetry of order 2. Ask students to identify other flags with rotational symmetry.

Alternative approach

Students will be familiar with the basics of symmetry and will be bringing previous experiences of it with them. Using games which involve challenges in symmetry can help to consolidate and extend confidence. Reflecting Squarely from NRICH is one such referenced in Resources. Further challenges might include students working in pairs, allocating themselves a particular quadrilateral or other shape, and describing themselves using only symmetry statements. Can their partner guess which shape they are? Attractive Rotations, also from NRICH, provides stimulus for exploring rotations.

Checkpoint

1   a   Sketch a quadrilateral that has two lines of symmetry.   (Any rhombus or rectangle)
    b   What order of rotational symmetry will it have?   (Order 2)

Starter – Hexominoes

Ask students to draw hexominoes that will fold up to form a cube.

How many can they find? (11 possible nets)

Which ones are symmetrical?

Teaching notes

Symmetry is all around us and students have a fair knowledge of reflection symmetry. As an introduction to the topic ask pairs of students to think about the school and surrounding environment. Can they draw four objects with reflection or rotation symmetry or both? Remind students to show mirror lines as dashed lines. If these are drawn neatly on paper, a class poster could be made.

Two common misconceptions should be addressed. First, explain that an object with rotation symmetry of order one is defined to have no rotation symmetry. Second, stress that a parallelogram has no lines of symmetry. This can be convincingly demonstrated by folding a paper cut-out.

Supply pairs of students with sets of small cardboard shapes (a square, rectangle, rhombus, parallelogram, isosceles trapezium, etc.). Ask them to identify each shape and to explain its defining features. Ask questions such as, which shape(s) have two lines of symmetry? (Rhombus, rectangle); which shapes have rotational symmetry of order two? (Rectangle, rhombus, parallelogram); which shape has no lines of symmetry? (Parallelogram), etc.

Plenary

Challenge students to draw a shape which satisfies various conditions: two lines of symmetry and order of rotation symmetry 2 (rectangle); a shape with order of rotation symmetry three (equilateral triangle) – does the shape have to have lines of symmetry? (No) etc.

Exercise commentary

Insist that student diagrams are accurate, so that any symmetries are clear.

Question 1 – Similar to the example.

Question 2 – Mirror lines should be marked as dotted lines as in the example given with the question.

Question 3 – Students will need to use symmetry properties and the sum of the angles in a triangle.

Question 4 – It may help students to identify symmetries if they physically rotate the page.

Question 5 – Small mirrors could be provided if you have them. Pairs of students could compare answers.

Question 6 – Encourage students to find more than one solution and try to identify what they have in common.

Answers

1   Check students' drawings
   a   order 1   **b**   order 1   **c**   order 2
   d   order 1   **e**   order 1   **f**   order 5
2   **a**   2 lines of symmetry
      Rotation symmetry of order 2
   b   4 lines of symmetry
      Rotation symmetry of order 4
   c   4 lines of symmetry
      Rotation symmetry of order 2
   d   1 line of symmetry
      No rotation symmetry
3   $100°, 80°, 100°, 80°$
4   Check students' drawings
   a   Square, 4 lines of symmetry, order 4
   b   Rectangle, 2 lines of symmetry, order 2
   c   Rhombus, 4 lines of symmetry, order 2
   d   Parallelogram, no lines of symmetry, order 2
   e   Isosceles trapezium, 1 line of symmetry, order 1
   f   Kite, 1 line of symmetry, order 1
   g   Arrowhead, 1 line of symmetry, order 1
   h   Trapezium, no lines of symmetry, order 1
   i   Irregular (quadrilateral), no lines of symmetry, order 1
5   **a**   Check students' drawings
   b   They all have at least one line of symmetry.
6   Check students' drawings. Discuss ideas with class.

Objectives

- Understand and use the language and notation associated with enlargement   (L6)

Key ideas	Resources
1 Understanding that an enlargement alters the size of a shape 2 Using a scale factor in order to create an enlargement	Enlarging shapes (1099) Squared paper Protractor and ruler A3 coloured paper

Simplification	Extension
As a preliminary to question **3**, give students three or four pairs of diagrams where there is a mistake in each enlargement. Ask them to identify this mistake and then correct the enlargement drawing.	Can scale factor enlargement give a smaller shape? Introduce a scale factor half enlargement for question **3** parts **a**, **b**, **d**, **f** and **g**. Can students draw these?

Literacy	Links
Revisit the words congruent and similar, establishing that similar shapes are in fact enlargements.	Magnifying glasses and microscopes are used to make an object appear larger. The magnification value is the scale factor. There are microscope images at different magnification values at http://micro.magnet.fsu.edu/primer/java/scienceopticsu /virtual/magnifying/index.html

Alternative approach

Use different coloured A3 paper. Model, with students following and repeating, tearing an A3 sheet of paper – firstly to create the largest square, then half the square to result in 2 rectangles; half one of the rectangles to produce 2 squares, and so on. Students may swap pieces with each other in order to have a range of different coloured shapes. Again working in pairs, students can then identify congruent shapes and similar shapes, not forgetting the first rectangle from the A3 sheet which will be unique. The similar shapes can then be explored in terms of their relationship with each other, thus exploring the scale factor, and what it means. Scale factor 1 being congruent can also be discussed. Scale factors which are linked such as double and half, can also be discussed. There is also potential to enquire about what feature of the shape is doubled/halved, thus establishing connection to length.

Checkpoint

1 When a shape is enlarged, what changes and what stays the same?

(Lengths change – by the same proportion; angles remain the same)

Starter – Order 4

Ask students to draw

shapes that have rotation symmetry of order four but no reflection symmetry

shapes that have rotation symmetry of order four and do have reflection symmetry.

Ask students how many lines of symmetry these shapes have.

Can be extended using different orders of symmetry.

Teaching notes

Draw an object and its enlarged image. Ask students to describe what they have in common: corresponding angles are equal. What is different and how? Encourage students to check that all corresponding lengths (not just edges) are increased by the same 'scale factor'. Ask if the shapes are congruent and introduce the term 'similar'.

Demonstrate and explain the enlargement of a right-angled triangle. Emphasise the need to enlarge every side, not just some. Also clarify that, scale factor 2 means multiply by 2, not add 2: avoid using a shape with side 2 and scale factor 2 as $2 \times 2 = 2 + 2$. Once the diagram is complete, demonstrate the use of a protractor to measure all the angles. The use of squared paper will help greatly with the accuracy of the drawings.

Plenary

Consider any rectangle, with clearly marked dimensions, under a scale factor 2 enlargement. What is the factor of enlargement for the area? Allow students to consider five or six different rectangles under the same enlargement. Can they see a pattern in the scale factor for the enlargement of the area? What if it was a scale factor 3 enlargement?

Exercise commentary

Question 1 – Students need to check that corresponding angles are equal and that corresponding sides are in the same ratio. Ask students to write down their reasons and then compare them with a partner. Each pair should agree a best explanation and then compare this with another pair's best explanation. Which is best now?

Question 2 – Similar to the first example.

Question 3 – Similar to the second example. Encourage students to mark one another's work, giving neatly worded explanations when a question is marked incorrect.

Question 4 – An introduction to using a centre of enlargement. It may help to follow the instructions if students work in pairs (but on individual diagrams), or by demonstrating the procedure for, say, a rectangle.

Answers

1. **a** No   **b** Yes   **c** Yes
   Only **b** and **c** show enlargements
2. **a** 3   **b** 3   **c** 2
3. Check the enlargements are as follows:
   a An L-shape with short sides 2 and long sides 4.
   b A 4 × 4 square.
   c A trapezium with base 6 and vertical sides 3 and 6.
   d A T-shape with top 6 and all other sides 2.
   e A rectangle with base 3 and height 6.
   f A downward arrow with top width 4, widest part 8 and depth 4.
   g An isosceles triangle with vertical side 4 and width 4.
   h A rhombus with diagonals 6.
   i A 9 × 9 square with a 3 × 3 square hollowed out inside.
   j Check drawing has been enlarged by scale factor of 2
4. **a–f** Check students' drawings
   g The triangles are similar. The scale factor is 2
   h Students' investigations

Objectives	
• Enlarge 2D shapes, given a centre of enlargement and a positive integer scale factor (L6)	

Key ideas	Resources
1 Recognising the importance of a centre of enlargement 2 Using the centre in order to create an enlargement	Enlarging shapes (1099) Squared paper 30 cm rulers

Simplification	Extension
Students will find copying the drawings from the exercise difficult: provide the initial diagrams on a printed sheet. For weaker students a practical approach really helps to establish the concepts.	For those students who have completed question **4**, look at question **2** parts **a**, **c**, **d** and **f** again and ask them to draw an enlargement of scale factor 1/2.

Literacy	Links
The concept of a centre of enlargement is one that is a challenge for many students. While students will recognise one when given as an example, many will struggle to interpret and use the link. Emphasise its nature through the use of rays or lines, relating to examples such as the pin hole camera.	Pictures can be copied and enlarged or reduced using a device called a pantograph. A pantograph consists of several hinged rods joined together in a parallelogram shape with extended sides. One end is traced over the image and a pencil attached to the other end reproduces the image to the desired scale. Pantographs are often sold as toys. There is more information about pantographs at http://en.wikipedia.org/wiki/Pantograph

Alternative approach
If the paper tearing exercise was used in the last section, reuse them here in order to establish the idea of a centre of enlargement. The different coloured similar shapes can be grouped and displayed by pairs of students. Model one or two such arrangements to generate the activity. Begin with the set of squares all sharing one common vertex. 30 cm rulers or lengths of string can help students to line up the shapes, extend and connect vertices, thus exploring whether each student pair can find examples of centres which: lie on a side, lie inside, or lie outside a shape.

Checkpoint
1 Given a shape and its enlargement, how would you find
a the scale factor   (Find the multiplicative factor)
b the centre of enlargement?   (Connect and extend the corresponding vertices with straight lines)

Starter – Jumbled up

Write a list of anagrams on the board and ask students to unscramble them.

Possible anagrams are

ATTORNIO, SATTINNAROL, AGEMI, GRONNTUCE, INFLECETOR, JOTBEC, TRYSMYME, DERRO

(rotation, translation, image, congruent, reflection, object, symmetry, order)

Can be extended by asking students to make a transformation word search.

Teaching notes

This develops the previous spread by introducing a centre of enlargement. Completing a worked example together will demonstrate the basic method. Discuss how a centre of enlargement fixes both the position and orientation of the image, unlike in the previous spread. Also emphasise that all the lines joining corresponding points on object and image pass through the centre of enlargement, as this is needed for question **1**.

The examples emphasise that distances should be measured from the centre of enlargement. Students should also confirm that the ratio of corresponding lengths between object and image are in the ratio 1 : scale factor.

Plenary

Show a diagram with an object and an enlarged image. Students work in pairs to write a bullet point explanation of how to find the centre of enlargement. They develop this so that their explanation is twenty words or less. After a few minutes, each pair shares their explanation with another pair. Which is the best and most concise explanation?

Exercise commentary

Question 1 – A general method for finding a centre of enlargement. The diagram must be drawn accurately otherwise the extended lines will not cross at a unique point. Pairing students may help them to follow the instructions.

Question 2 – Similar to the first example. Check that students place their diagrams in such a way that the image will fit on the page.

Question 3 – Challenge students to find the centre of enlargement, using logic rather than guess work. As in question **1**, the centre will lie on the line joining the two bottom-left vertices and the distances from any centre should be in the ratio 1 : 3.

Question 4 – An introduction to an enlargement with a fractional scale factor, giving a reduced-size image. Discuss the confusing language and the relationship between inverse transformations.

Answers

1 **a, b** Check students' drawings
   c $BC = 1$, $B_1C_1 = 2$ $AC = 2$, $A_1C_1 = 4$
   d 2
2 **a–f** Check students' enlargements
3 $(6, 0), (6, 9)$
4 Open ended

Key outcomes	Quick check
Reflect, rotate and translate 2D shapes. L5	A triangle has coordinates A(1, 1), B(3, 1) and C(3, 4). Write down the coordinates of the image triangle after: **a** A reflection in the *x*-axis (A(1, -1), B(3, -1) and C(3, -4)) **b** A rotation of 180° about (0, 0) (A(-1, -1), B(-3, -1) and C(-3, -4)) **c** A translation right 3, up 1 (A(4, 2), B(6, 2) and C(6, 5))
Transform 2D shapes using combinations of transformations. L5	Describe the single transformation equivalent to reflecting a shape in the *x*-axis and then in the *y*-axis. (Rotation of 180° about (0, 0))
Recognise reflection and rotation symmetry. L5	State the order of rotational symmetry and the number of lines of symmetry in the following shapes: **a** Equilateral triangle (3, 3) **b** Parallelogram (2, 0) **c** Square (4, 4)
Enlarge a 2D shape. L6	The triangle above is enlarged by scale factor 2 using (0, 0) as the centre of enlargement. Find the coordinates of the image. (A(2, 2), B(6, 2) and C(6, 8))

MyMaths extra support

Lesson/online homework	Description
Symmetry 1230 L3	Symmetrical shapes; simple reflection in a mirror line

MyReview

Check out
You should now be able to ...

Questions

✓ Reflect, rotate and translate 2D shapes.	⑤	1–2
✓ Transform 2D shapes using combinations of transformations.	⑤	3
✓ Recognise reflection and rotation symmetry.	⑤	4
✓ Enlarge a 2D shape.	⑥	5–7

Language	Meaning	Example
Transformation	A procedure for changing the position, orientation or shape of an object	Rotations, reflections, translations and enlargements are all transformations
Rotation	A transformation that turns an object through a given angle about a given centre of rotation	Turning this book through 90° clockwise about its bottom right corner is a rotation
Reflection	A transformation which flips an object over a mirror line	Looking at this book in a mirror is a reflection
Translation	A transformation which slides an object	Sliding this book across your desk is a translation
Enlargement	A transformation which changes the size of an object	If you enlarged this book by a scale factor of two about its centre its lengths would grow to twice their size
Scale factor	The multiplier in an enlargement	
Reflective symmetry	Shapes have reflective symmetry if they have a mirror line of symmetry	A rectangle has reflective symmetry in both the horizontal and vertical lines through its centre
Rotational symmetry	A shape has rotational symmetry if it fits exactly over its original position more than once in a full turn	A rectangle has rotational symmetry of order 2 about its centre

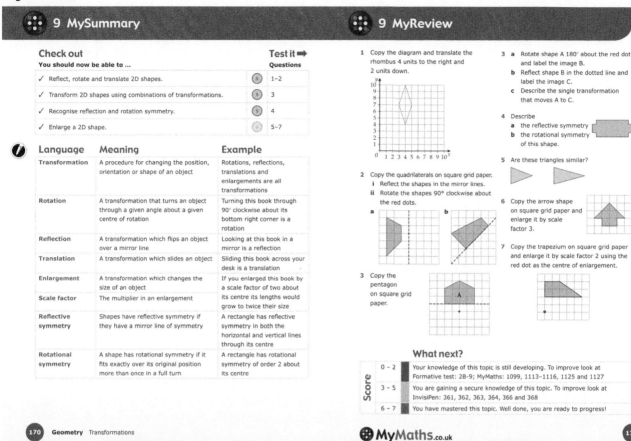

1 Copy the diagram and translate the rhombus 4 units to the right and 2 units down.

2 Copy the quadrilaterals on square grid paper.
  i Reflect the shapes in the mirror lines.
  ii Rotate the shapes 90° clockwise about the red dots.
  a b

3 Copy the pentagon on square grid paper.

3 a Rotate shape A 180° about the red dot and label the image B.
  b Reflect shape B in the dotted line and label the image C.
  c Describe the single transformation that moves A to C.

4 Describe
  a the reflective symmetry
  b the rotational symmetry of this shape.

5 Are these triangles similar?

6 Copy the arrow shape on square grid paper and enlarge it by scale factor 3.

7 Copy the trapezium on square grid paper and enlarge it by scale factor 2 using the red dot as the centre of enlargement.

What next?

Score		
0 – 2	Your knowledge of this topic is still developing. To improve look at Formative test: 2B-9; MyMaths: 1099, 1113–1116, 1125 and 1127
3 – 5	You are gaining a secure knowledge of this topic. To improve look at InvisiPen: 361, 362, 363, 364, 366 and 368
6 – 7	You have mastered this topic. Well done, you are ready to progress!

MyMaths.co.uk

Question commentary

Students should be using a sharp pencil, ruler and squared paper.

Question 1 – Student sometimes confuse the term 'translation' with 'transformation'.

Question 2 – Students can use a mirror to check their answers if they are unsure. Students need to know which direction is clockwise and they can use tracing paper to do the rotation if necessary.

Question 3 – Students should read carefully which shape they are being asked to transform.

Question 4 – Encourage use of proper terminology: 'rotational symmetry order...', '...lines of reflective symmetry'.

Question 5 – Students need to be aware of precise mathematical definition of the term 'similar'. Although these triangles are both isosceles they are not similar: the angles are different.

Questions 7 and 8 – Question 7 is more straightforward as no centre of enlargement is involved. In question 8, encourage student to find where one point transforms to (the bottom left corner of the trapezium is a good choice) then enlarge the rest of the shape by the scale factor from this point.

Answers

1 Rhombus with vertices at $(8, 2), (7, 5), (8, 8), (9, 5)$

2 **a, b** Check students' reflections and rotations

3 **a, b** Check students' rotation and reflection
  c Translation of 2 units up

4 **a** 2 lines of symmetry **b** Order 2

5 No

6 Check students' enlargement

7 Check students' enlargement, correct centre of enlargement

9a

1 Copy the diagram on square grid paper.

a Reflect the blue hexagon using the x-axis as the mirror line.
Label the shape A and give the coordinates of the vertices.

b Rotate the blue hexagon through 180° about the point (0, 0).
Label the shape B and give the coordinates of the vertices.

c Translate the blue hexagon by 4 units to the left.
Label the shape C and give the coordinates of the vertices.

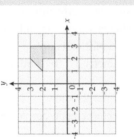

9b

2 a Tessellate a parallelogram using repeated translations.

b Colour the equal angles in your tessellation.

3 Copy the diagram on square grid paper.

a Reflect the green triangle in the mirror line M_1.
Call the image I_1.

b Reflect I_1 in the mirror line M_2.
Call the image I_2.

c Describe the single transformation that moves the green triangle to I_2.

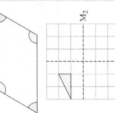

9c

4 Draw these symbols from Steph's calculator.
Draw any lines of reflection symmetry and state the order of rotation symmetry for each symbol.

a   b   c   d   e

5 a Draw a polygon with three lines of symmetry and rotational symmetry of order 3.

b Give the mathematical name of this shape.

9d

6

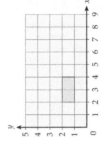

Object   Image

Part of an enlargement of the face is shown.

a Calculate the scale factor of the enlargement.

b Copy and complete the table of measurements.

	Object	Image
Length of the forehead	1 cm	
Slanting length of the nose		
Slanting length of the top of the head		
Thickness of the neck		
Width of the mouth		

c Draw the completed image on square grid paper.

9e

7 a Draw the rectangle on a coordinate grid.

b Enlarge the rectangle by scale factor 2 using (0, 0) as the centre of enlargement.

c Write down the coordinates of the vertices of the object and the image.

d Explain the relationship between these coordinates.

8 Chelsea began to enlarge the pink shape to give the green shape but she was distracted.

a Find the coordinates of the centre of enlargement and the scale factor.

b Complete the green shape.

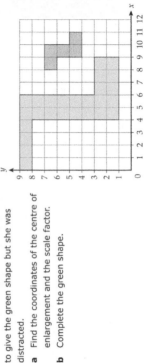

MyMaths.co.uk

Question commentary

Question 1– Tracing paper can be used for the rotation in part **b**. Note it is the original shape being transformed in each part.

Questions 2 and **3** – Copies of the shape and the grid could be given to the students to help them here.

Questions 4 and **5** – Encourage students to use precise mathematical language. Mirror lines should be drawn dotted and tracing paper can be used to check rotations.

Question 6 – Students should see that all visible lengths are enlarged by the same scale factor, making the table easy to complete. The final image will need to be placed carefully on their page to ensure it fits on.

Questions 7 and **8** – Encourage students to use 'ray' lines in both questions. Prepared grids might be useful for some.

Answers

1 Check students' drawings
   a (1, -2), (2, -2), (2, -1), (3, -1), (3, -3), (2, -3)
   b (-2, -1), (-3, -1), (-3, -3), (-2, -3), (-1, -2), (-3, -2)
   c (-2, 1), (-2, 2), (-3, 2), (-2, 3), (-1, 3), (-1, -1)

2 Check students' tessellations

3 **a, b** Check students' drawings
   c Rotation of 180° about the origin (i.e. the intersection of M_1 and M_2).

4 Check students' drawings
   a 2 lines of symmetry, order 2
   b 4 lines of symmetry, order 4
   c No reflection symmetry, order 1
   d 2 lines of symmetry, order 2
   e 2 lines of symmetry, order 2

5 **a** Check students' drawings
   b An equilateral triangle

6 **a** 2
   b

	Object	Image
Forehead	1 cm	2 cm
Nose	2.2 cm	4.4 cm
Top of head	3.2 cm	6.4 cm
Neck	3 cm	6 cm
Mouth	1 cm	2 cm

   c Check face has vertical depth 8 cm, i. e. diagram is extended 3 squares down from that given.

7 **a, b** Check students' drawings
   c (2, 1), (4, 1), (4, 2), (2, 2) Object
         (4, 2), (8, 2), (8, 4), (4, 4) Image
   d The image coordinates are double the object coordinates

8 **a** (12, 5.5) SF = 2.5
   b Check students' drawings

Case study 3: Food crops

Related lessons		Resources	
Time series graphs	6e	Add and subtract decimals	(1007)
Bar charts and frequency diagrams	8d	Real life graphs	(1184)
Addition and subtraction problems	11e	Examples of graphs from newspapers	

Simplification	Extension
Students may need structured guidance working through the table in task **1**.	Students could be asked to look at the percentage changes of wheat production, consumption and stocks and the percentage change of the price of wheat and the production of biodiesel. Further research could also be carried out into misleading graphs that appear in the press or online.

Links

Students should be encouraged to look in more detail at the range of crops that are being used for various purposes and research the effects this is having worldwide on food prices and levels of availability. There is much useful data on the internet, for example www.hgca.com or www.ukagriculture.com/crops/crops.cfm.

Students could be organised to research different aspects to bring together as a class.

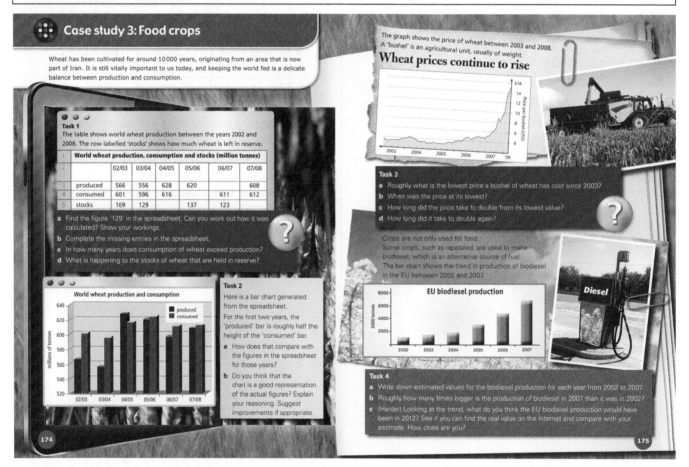

Teaching notes

Many students will be aware of the rising use of biofuels through hearing about cars that run on chip fat and other oils. Some may have experienced it or know adults who use biofuels. Running cars in this way is often portrayed as being 'alternative' and 'green'. Students might also be aware that prices for wheat and other crops have recently been rising quite rapidly, and know that there is a shortage of food crops in some parts of the world.

This case study focuses on production figures for wheat and biodiesel to raise the possibility that there could be a partial link between the increasing use of biodiesel and the increasing price and shortage of wheat.

Task 1

Introduce the case study and look at the spreadsheet shown at the top left. Discuss what is meant by 'produced', 'consumed' and 'stocks' and look at the first two columns to see how the figures relate to each other. Discuss how you have to find the surplus or deficit of production compared with consumption and then adjust the stocks level accordingly. Give the students a few minutes to work out the missing values on the spreadsheet and answer the related questions.

Task 2

When the students have considered the questions relating to this bar chart, discuss their opinions about the reasonableness or otherwise of the vertical scale. For example, the differences would be very hard to determine if the vertical axis started at zero. However, starting the axis at 520 million tonnes means that the shortfall between wheat production and consumption appears exaggerated. In the first two columns the production appears to provide only about half the amount of wheat that is needed.

Task 3

Look at the graph showing wheat prices for the past few years. What do you notice about the graph? The most obvious thing is that the prices rise very rapidly in the last two years shown on the graph. Students should then work through the questions about the graph.

Task 4

Look at the final graph on the spread that shows figures for biodiesel production in Europe. Do you notice anything familiar about this graph? Elicit that the shape is very similar to the shape of the wheat price graph, increasing only slowly for a while and then increasing much more rapidly. Conclude by considering whether the production of biofuels could be having an influence on the cost of wheat and other crops.

Answers

1 a $169 - (596 - 556)$

b

	02/03	03/04	04/05	05/06	06/07	07/08
Produced	566	556	628	620	597	608
Consumed	601	596	616	624	611	612
Stocks	169	129	141	137	123	119

c 5 years

d Decreasing trend

2 a Appears to be half the height but should be 95% of the height.

b Students' answers. The suppressed zero makes the size of the difference misleading, but allows it to be seen.

3 a Just over $3

b May, 2004

c $2\frac{1}{2}$ years

d $\frac{1}{2}$ year

4 a 1300, 1800, 2000, 3200, 4800, 6600

b 5

c Students' own answers

Learning outcomes	
A3 Understand and use the concepts and vocabulary of expressions, equations, inequalities, terms and factors	(L5)
A4 Simplify and manipulate algebraic expressions to maintain equivalence by: collecting like terms, multiplying a single term over a bracket, taking out common factors, expanding products of 2 or more binomials	(L5/6)
A7 use algebraic methods to solve linear equations in 1 variable (including all forms that require rearrangement)	(L5/6)

Introduction

The chapter starts by looking at one-step equations and then moves on to solving multi-step equations using the balance method. Equations with brackets are then introduced before the final section which looks at equations which might appear in real life.

The introduction discusses how biologists use equations to model things like population growth among species of animal. This concept uses a form of equation known as an exponential equation where the growth (or decline) in a population is related to the population present at the time (among other factors). There are many other things that behave according to these kinds of rule. Bacteria growth can be modelled using exponential equations, for example. Radioactive substances which 'decay' over time can also be modelled using the concept of exponential decay. Each radioactive substance has what is called a 'half-life': the length of time it takes for the radioactivity to halve. Carbon-15 has a half-life of 2.449 seconds so its rate of decay is very fast, whereas titanium-44 has a half-life of close to 63 years. The longest half-life known is that of the isotope tellurium-128 which has a half-life of 2.2×10^{24} years – over 100,000,000,000,000 times longer than the universe has been in existence!

Prior knowledge

Students should already know how to...

- Perform simple arithmetic operations on positive and negative whole numbers
- Collect like terms and expand single brackets

Starter problem

The starter problem is a spider diagram showing s simple equation which has been modified in six different ways. Students are invited to describe the six changes and continue each one a further step.

In order, clockwise from top left:

- 1 has been subtracted from both sides
- both sides have been doubled
- 1 has been added to both sides
- x has been added to both sides
- both sides have been halved
- x has been subtracted from both sides

Students are then directed to invent some changes of their own. These could be further examples of changes to the original equation given, or they could be invited to make up their own equation and complete a similar exercise to this one.

Resources

MyMaths

Simple equations	1154	Rules and formulae	1158	Solving equations	1182
Single brackets	1247				

Online assessment

Chapter test	2B–10
Formative test	2B–10
Summative test	2B–10

InvisiPen solutions

Balancing equations	233	One-step equations	234
Two-step equations	235	Equations with brackets	236
Unknowns on both sides	237		

Topic scheme

Teaching time = 4 lessons/2 weeks

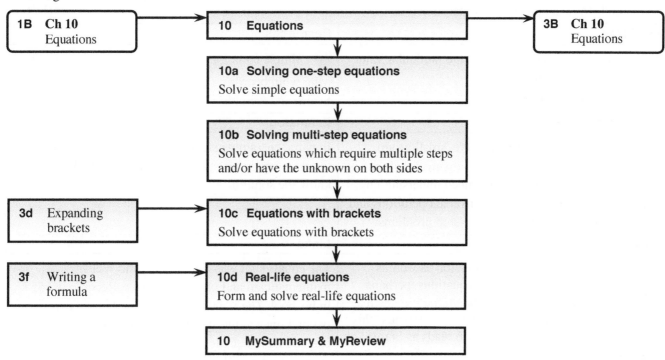

1B Ch 10 Equations	→ **10 Equations**	→ **3B Ch 10** Equations

10 Equations

↓

10a Solving one-step equations
Solve simple equations

↓

10b Solving multi-step equations
Solve equations which require multiple steps and/or have the unknown on both sides

↓

3d Expanding brackets → **10c Equations with brackets**
Solve equations with brackets

↓

3f Writing a formula → **10d Real-life equations**
Form and solve real-life equations

↓

10 MySummary & MyReview

Differentiation

Student book 2A   192 – 205

One-step equations
Equation puzzles
Two-step equations
Making equations

Student book 2B   176 – 189

Solving one-step equations
Solving multi-step equations
Equations with brackets
Real-life equations

Student book 2C   180 – 195

Linear equations 1
Linear equations 2
Equations with fractions
Trial and improvement 2
Real-life equations

10a Solving one-step equations

Objectives

- Solve simple linear equations with integer coefficients (unknown on one side) using an appropriate method (for example, inverse operations)   (L5)

Key ideas	Resources
1 Recognition of the need to find the particular value of a variable for an equation 2 Using the concept of inverse	Simple equations (1154) Mini whiteboards Scales and weights

Simplification	Extension
For those students who struggle here, small group work and the development of mathematical dialogue is crucial to build confidence and embed understanding. Ensure that students understand inverse operations and offer additional examples of single-step problems.	In pairs, encourage students to challenge another with two-step equations, as in question **4,** to which they know the solution.

Literacy	Links
Remind students of the term expression as well as equation, and encourage reading equations, perhaps replacing the variable's letter with alternatives such as 'this number' or 'this value', thus $x + 5 = 9$ reads 'this number added to 5 is 9' and $x/3 = 6$ reads as 'a third of this number is 6'	The equals sign was first used by the Welsh mathematician and physician Robert Recorde in 1557 in his book *The Whetstone of Witte*. He used two parallel lines in the symbol because 'noe 2, thynges, can be moare equalle' However, other symbols for 'is equal to' were still used until the 1700s including the Latin abbreviation *ae* or *oe* (for *aequalis* or 'equal') There is more information about Robert Recorde at http://en.wikipedia.org/wiki/Robert_Recorde

Alternative approach

As an alternative to balances for visual prompts here, the number line is useful. For example

$$x \quad + \quad 5$$

Representing $x + 5 = 9$

$$? \qquad 5 \quad = 9$$

This style of representation has limitations when the variable's particular value is a negative, but otherwise it works well as an introduction.

Checkpoint

1 Solve these equations:

   a $x + 7 = 22$ $(x = 15)$

   b $5x = 35$ $(x = 7)$

Starter – Algebra scores 24

Each consonant scores 2 and each vowel scores 1. Multiply the total consonant score by the total vowel score to get the word score. Write down mathematical words and find their scores. Bonus points for scores that equal 24 (algebra, brackets, decimal, formulae, straight).

Can be differentiated by the score allocated to a consonant or vowel.

Teaching notes

Make links with students' prior knowledge of this topic through the use of the first questions in the exercise. This can be completed as a whole-class mini whiteboard activity to ensure all students are involved and to identify any problems early on.

Exploration of the balancing method to explain inverse operations provides a solid foundation for many students to progress in this topic, as this approach helps students to develop a more concrete understanding. Using an actual pair of scales with mystery weights may consolidate understanding further. It is worth highlighting the meaning of inverse when discussing the example.

Use the later questions in the exercise as small group work to encourage student collaboration and develop dialogue early on, as many students lack confidence when solving equations. This approach also fosters the ability to reach agreements, managing discussions to achieve results.

Plenary

Write three examples of the type of equation in question **4** involving more than one step – offer a range of difficulty levels – and invite students to choose one and write an annotated solution. They should then swap and compare, discussing any disagreements.

Exercise commentary

Question 1 – This should be relatively familiar and mini whiteboards could be used to assess students' prior learning.

Question 2 – Similar to the examples. Using mini whiteboards would ensure that all students have the opportunity to contribute and to help identify any difficulties early on. Ask students to also say what the inverse was that was needed.

Question 3 – Consider grouping students into threes and asking each group member to answer every third question and then to explain their examples to the other two. This will develop mathematical discussion and consolidate understanding.

Question 4 – The balance approach of question **1** applied to two-step equations.

Question 5 – Encourage students to write down each equation using formal mathematical notation and explain why they have chosen that particular equation.

Answers

1	**a**	5	**b**	5	**c**	2		**d**	3
2	**a** i	2	ii	9	iii	1		iv	2
	v	4	vi	9	vii	1		viii	2
	b i	9	ii	9	iii	7	iv	10	
	v	14	vi	$3\frac{1}{2}$	vii	11	viii	14	
	c i	5	ii	4	iii	2	iv	9	
	v	4	vi	2	vii	11	viii	5	
	d i	10	ii	12	iii	8	iv	18	
	v	14	vi	20	vii	60	viii	18	
3	**a**	1	**b**	15	**c**	4		**d**	6
	e	10	**f**	4	**g**	18		**h**	18
	i	11	**j**	6	**k**	60		**l**	5
4	**a**	$x = 3$	**b**	$x = 4$	**c**	$x = 5$			
5	**a**	$z + 12 = 40$ $z = 28$			**b**	$y - 7 = 25$ $y = 32$			
	c	$4x = 28$ $x = 7$			**d**	$w \div 2 = 21$ $w = 42$			
	e	$3v + 3 = 39$ $v = 12$			**f**	$(u \div 4) - 2 = 2, u = 16$			

10b Solving multi-step equations

Objectives

- Construct and solve linear equations with integer coefficients (unknown on either or both sides) using appropriate methods (for example, inverse operations, transforming both sides in the same way)   (L6)

Key ideas	Resources
1 Recognition of the need to find the particular value of a variable for an equation 2 Using the concept of inverse	Solving equations (1182) A3 sheets

Simplification	Extension
Students who struggle with this work may benefit from additional consolidation of solving equations with unknowns on one side only. Using number lines to represent each side of an equation will assist them in making progress.	For more able students, offer additional examples of word problems that can be used to generate equations to be solved. This can be challenging for even the most able. Students who grasp this work easily could try to design a puzzle of their own using question **6** as a model. This embeds awareness of the opportunity for skill application and strengthens skill transferability.

Literacy	Links
Encourage students to read the equations out loud with meaning. Share the convention that a variable is represented by any lower case letter with the students. Try to use a variety of lower case letters, not just x, with the students. Check that examples involve working with unknowns either on left or right side so that students are as comfortable with statements such as $4 = x$ as they are with $x = 4$. This avoids adding an unnecessary procedural step, though where students already have this perception, do not discourage this equivalent representation.	In Africa, India and the Far East, seeds were traditionally used as standard weights in balance pans to weigh small amounts. Carob seeds were often used because of their uniform size. A typical carob seed weighs 200 mg. The carat is the unit used to weigh gold and diamonds today and originates from the weight of a carob seed. The weight of one carat is precisely 200 mg, or 0.2 g.

Alternative approach

Where two or more stages are involved request students to examine equivalent expressions for each side of the equation. Use equivalent spider diagrams for this with students working in pairs on A3 sheets. Encourage students to be creative and consider many possibilities before examining most useful versions. Examples for the given example might be $x + x + 5 = 10 + 7$; $5x - 3x = 12 + 5$. A useful version would be $2x + 5 = 12 + 5$ which can then reduce to $2x = 12$, and so on. Consider also using number lines when the variable has a positive value to visually represent an equation to help with both equivalent statements and inverse concepts.. For example:

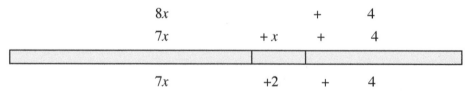

Checkpoint

1 Solve $3m + 4 = 5m - 6$.   ($5 = m$ or equivalent)

2 Does $p = 7$ if $6 = 2p - 8$? Explain how you can check this.

   (Yes – either demonstrate that using $p = 7$ in the RHS produces a consistent result or solve the equation)

Starter – Algebraic products

Draw a 4 × 4 table on the board. Label the columns a, b, a^2, 7 and the rows a, $2a$, b, c.

Fill in the table with the products, for example, the top row in the table would read a^2, ab, a^3, $7a$.

Can be differentiated by the choice of terms.

Teaching notes

This spread emphasises the use of substitution to check answers. It merits particular attention as self-check is empowering for students, enabling them to become increasingly independent rather than waiting for teacher input. Also it supports them in using errors positively.

A further focus in the worked examples is the issue of on which side of the equation the letters will be organised. Again this challenges a large number of students and misunderstandings are very common. Time spent discussing approaches here will benefit all abilities.

The work in this spread supports the process skill of analysing through using appropriate mathematical procedures, where students work towards solving equations and strengthens skills in interpreting and evaluating, where students consider different approaches, for example where another student has used a different method of finding a solution.

Plenary

Give students three examples of solutions to equations where two out of three are answered incorrectly. Ask them to identify the errors and to provide written feedback that they think would help the student who had made the errors.

Exercise commentary

Question 1 – Similar to the first example.

Question 2 – An elaboration of question **1** with unknowns on both sides. Encourage students to check their solutions using back substitution as a way to promote independence and confidence.

Question 3 – Parts **i** (with fractions) and **l** (with more xs on the RHS) may cause difficulty.

Questions 4 and **5** – Elaborations of question **3**, some involving negative numbers (answers positive).

Question 6 – Consider allowing time for students to work on this in pairs before taking feedback and working towards a whole-class solution.

Answers

1	a	3	b	5	c	4	d	2
	e	4	f	5	g	6	h	$4\frac{1}{2}$
	i	4	j	3	k	4	l	$3\frac{1}{2}$
2	a	5	b	5	c	3		
3	a	3	b	2	c	4	d	9
	e	3	f	2	g	1	h	$2\frac{1}{2}$
	i	2	j	4	k	2	l	3
4	a	6	b	6	c	3	d	4
	e	4	f	2	g	2	h	3
	i	2	j	2	k	7	l	2
5	a	4	b	7	c	4	d	2
	e	3	f	7	g	2	h	0
	i	4	j	6	k	3	l	3
6	a	$7n + 4 = 5n + 28$	b	$n = 12$				

Objectives	
• Use formulae from mathematics and other subjects	(L5)
• Construct and solve linear equations with integer coefficients (unknown on either or both sides, without and with brackets) using appropriate methods (e.g. inverse operations, transforming both sides in the same way)	(L6)

Key ideas	Resources	
1 Solve linear equations which include brackets 2 Begin to consider efficient approaches to solving equations.	Single brackets Books, magazines	(1247)

Simplification	Extension
Encourage weaker students to refer to the visual representation using number lines or scales and to adapt this to support the solution of examples causing difficulty. Recap expanding brackets where this is a stumbling block. Use this exercise to develop students' capacity to explain and justify their thinking.	Students can be challenged with additional word problems from which they will need to generate an equation as in question **6**. Encourage paired working to develop student dialogue and to develop skills in justification. More involved equations leading to negative or fractional solutions may also be set.

Literacy	Links
Encourage reading equations out loud with meaning, including those with brackets to help establish priority of operation and therefore the inverses required.	Bring in some written text, for example, books and magazines. Ask the students to find examples of the use of brackets. Round brackets (*parentheses*) are often used for explanations or to add to the information already given. They can also be used for translations and abbreviations. Why are the brackets used in the examples?

Alternative approach
The example given in the introduction is worth discussing with all students after presenting them with the challenge to solve it for themselves individually, followed by sharing with a partner. Expanding brackets can be discussed, but also point out that in this case it is not necessary, as if 2 lots of $(x + 4)$ is 18 then $x + 4$ must be 9. Ask students to evaluate which approach is most efficient and request comments for sharing. Equivalent expressions strategies can still be applied effectively, and can be particularly helpful when a variable's value is negative. For example $2x + 9 = 3$ $$2x \quad = 3 - 9 \qquad \text{and so on.}$$

Checkpoint	
1 Solve $3(c - 7) = 12$.	$(c = 11)$
2 A rectangle has a perimeter of 24 cm. Its length is three times its width. What is the width?	(3 cm)

Starter – Budgies and hamsters

Luxmi had some budgies and hamsters. In total she counted 18 heads and 56 feet.

How many budgies and how many hamsters were there? (8 budgies, 10 hamsters)

Can be extended by asking students to make up their own bird and animal puzzles.

Teaching notes

The mathematics in this spread supports students' capacity to generate ideas and explore possibilities and to ask questions to extend their thinking.

The spread brings together several aspects of prior learning: expanding brackets and collecting like terms, rearranging and solving equations using inverse operations and negative numbers. Be prepared to practise these skills separately before bringing them together in the examples. Carefully showing the necessary workings will provide students with a model for setting out their solutions and checking answers by back substitution.

Many skills developed here involve making links with other learning and the activities promote the process skill of communicating and reflecting, particularly making links to related problems or problems with a similar structure

The initial discussion using scales will help the more visual learners grasp what the use of brackets in an equation represents. Where difficulties are experienced, encourage the use of this method of representation to solve problems.

Plenary

Ask students to vote on the example from the lesson that has generated most challenge and agree a whole class model answer on the board. Indicate that a similar example may be used as a starter activity for next lesson.

Exercise commentary

Question 1 – Encourage self-checking through substitution.

Questions 2, 3, 4 and **5** – Students could be organised into small groups, sharing out the questions and explaining and justifying their solutions to each other.

Students may need reassurance that the negative and fractional solutions are valid.

Question 6 – Similar to the second example. It provides an opportunity to promote mathematical discussion by asking students how to tackle the problem. Check that any solution works both now and in ten years' time.

Question 7 – Here, students make links with previous work on formulae and use an equation in a real-life context. There is also a link with work that will have been met in geography.

Answers

1	a	5	b	2	c	2	d	3
	e	4	f	$4\frac{1}{2}$	g	$4\frac{1}{2}$	h	2
2	a	2	b	5	c	2	d	7
	e	$6\frac{1}{2}$	f	11	g	9	h	10
	i	3						
3	a	1	b	3	c	4	d	1
	e	2	f	0	g	5	h	1
	i	$\frac{1}{2}$	j	1	k	2	l	2
4	a	0	b	-1	c	-3	d	-6
	e	-2	f	-3	g	-1	h	-2
	i	-2	j	0	k	-2	l	-2
	m	5	n	0	o	-1	p	2
5	a	$3\frac{1}{2}$	b	$2\frac{1}{2}$	c	$1\frac{1}{4}$	d	$3\frac{1}{8}$
	e	$4\frac{1}{2}$	f	$4\frac{1}{4}$	g	$2\frac{1}{2}$	h	$1\frac{1}{8}$
	i	$\frac{3}{4}$	j	$\frac{3}{4}$				
6	10							
7	-40°							

Somewhere very cold, e.g. Siberia

Objectives

• Construct and solve linear equations with integer coefficients	(L6)
• Use formulae from mathematics and other subjects	(L6)

Key ideas	Resources
1 Students are able to generalise linear relationships 2 Students are able to apply and solve formulae	Rules and formulae (1158) Solving equations (1182) Mini white boards Constructing Linear Equations (DCSF): http://www.nationalstemcentre.org.uk/elibrary/resourc e/4633/constructing-and-solving-linear-equations

Simplification	Extension
Weaker students may benefit from working mainly with number wall or pyramid puzzles. Have number wall grids available for recording.	Students could extend the work of question **4** by researching other currency conversions at present-day rates. Consider also where students may meet conversions in everyday contexts.

Literacy	Links
When examining formulae from other curricula sources it is worth noting with students that a few do use upper case letters, for example V for volumes, or when linked to the name of a scientist such as Celsius. However, continue to stress that the usual convention is to use lower case letters for a variable.	Diophantus was referred to as 'the father of algebra' though this has been disputed. One of his famous problems is known as his 'epitaph' as the poem translates to an equation whose solution is his age at death. Students may wish to construct and solve it for themselves. http://en.wikipedia.org/wiki/Diophantus

Alternative approach

Introduce the idea of students responding to questions of the format Give me an example of...., now a peculiar example of, now a general example of.... Ask for examples of an even number; odd number; multiple of 5; a fraction. Share and discuss the results fully using mini whiteboards, addressing any misconceptions which are exposed. Using algebraic pyramid puzzles or number walls is a good way to rehearse construction strategies. Suggestions for variations of these can be found in the Y8 booklet on Constructing Linear Equations (DCSF). Finding expressions for the perimeters of shapes is useful to assist students creating their own equations. Investigations such as matchstick shapes can also generate valuable practice in generalisation. Compile a list of some common formulae, including conversion ones such as $p = 22k/10$ (kilograms to pounds). Which are familiar to the students? What others have they found in other subjects? Use some for rehearsing substitution skills in order to find a particular value.

Checkpoint

1 A metre length of string has to be cut into two pieces so that one piece is four times longer than the other piece.

   a What are the lengths?   (80 cm and 20 cm)

   b Write this problem as an equation with the letter, l, representing the length, in centimetres, of the shorter piece. $(100 = l + 4l)$

Starter – Placeholder

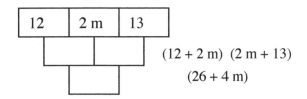

| 12 | 2 m | 13 |

$(12 + 2\,m)$ $(2\,m + 13)$

$(26 + 4\,m)$

Ask students to complete the number pyramid on mini whiteboards. Check grid entries with a neighbour. Now tell students that the final box is actually 52, so what particular value is m? ($m = 6.5$)

Teaching notes

There is lots of scope for mini whiteboard work at the start of the lesson with problems such as 'I think of a number...' and substitutions into simple formulae. Dice can be used to generate 'random' numbers.

The topic naturally splits into two key areas: using given equations to find missing values and writing down equations from a context.

The first part of this can be done again using quick-fire question and answer before allowing students to complete further examples of their own from the textbook. Encourage them to substitute first and then solve when working backwards.

The second aspect of the lesson can be modelled using examples similar to those in the textbook. Provide a scenario for the students and show how this translates into an equation which can then be solved.

Plenary

Further quick-fire examples can be provided for the students to complete 'against the clock' or in a race with a partner. Points can be awarded for correct answers to ensure that the students focus on getting the question right rather than racing through the questions making careless mistakes.

Exercise commentary

Question 1 – Further questions that use the formula given in the first example.

Questions 2 and **3** – Check that students have correctly written out their own equations before substituting in for question **3**.

Question 4 – Students will need a calculator for this question. Ensure they are correctly dividing when working backwards.

Question 5 – A practical application linking to something the students may have experience of. Alternative tariffs could also be included or students could be asked to research currently available tariffs as part of a homework task.

Answers

1 a 212 °F   b -40 °F   c 60 °C   d −17.8 °C
2 a $T = 0.25m + 3$ b $T = 0.35m + 2.5$
   c $T = 0.4m + 2$ d $T = 0.48m$
3 a i £6   ii 12 miles
   b i £6.70   ii 10 miles
   c i £6.8   ii 10 miles
   d i £5.76   ii 12.5 miles
4 a $153.20   b $383   c $1256.24   d £489.56
   e £1000   f £6853.79
5 a i $y = 5 + 0.15x$ ii $y = 10 + 0.1x$
   b i CheapTalk   ii CheapTalk
      iii BargainPhone
   c i $5 + 0.15x = 10 + 0.1x$ ii $x = 100$
   d Consider $y = 5 + 0.15x$ and $z = 10 + 0.1x$ where x is the expected number of minutes. If $y > z$ pick BargainPhone, otherwise pick CheapTalk.

Key outcomes	Quick check
Solve simple one-step equations. L5	Solve **a** $3 + x = 8$ (5) **b** $2x = 5$ (2.5) **c** $x/3 = 8$ (24)
Solve multi-step equations including with the unknown on both sides. L6	Solve **a** $2x - 3 = 17$ (10) **b** $3x - 1 = x + 7$ (4)
Solve equations including with brackets. L6	Solve **a** $3(x - 4) = 18$ (10) **b** $2(x + 3) = 3(2x - 1)$ (2.25)
Solve real-life equations. L6	An equation for converting miles (m) to kilometres (k) is $k = 8m/5$ **a** How many kilometres are in 50 miles? (80) **b** How many miles are there in 120 km? (75)

10 MySummary

Check out
You should now be able to ...

	Test it ➡ Questions
✓ Solve simple, one-step equations.	1
✓ Solve multi-step equations including with the unknown on both sides.	2
✓ Solve equations including with brackets.	3–5
✓ Solve real life equations.	6–8

Language	Meaning	Example
Equation	A mathematical statement, written in algebra and including an equal sign, which is true for one or more values of the unknown	$2x + 1 = 7$ is an equation
Solution	The value(s) of the unknown that the equation is true for	$x = 3$ is the only solution of the equation above
Inverse	A second operation that undoes the effect of a first operation	The inverse of -6 is $+6$ and the inverse of $\times 2$ is $\div 2$
Expand	To multiply out all brackets and then collect like terms	Expanding $2(3x + 5) - 7 + 4x$ gives $10x + 3$
Substitution	A method for checking if your solution to an equation is correct by replacing the unknown with the solution	Substituting $x = 3$ into $2x + 1$ gives $2 \times 3 + 1 = 6 + 1 = 7$

10 MyReview

1 Solve these equations.
a $x - 9 = 24$ b $x - 7 = 14$
c $6 + x = 35$ d $x + 12 = 20$
e $5x = 55$ f $3x = 27$
g $\frac{x}{3} = 12$ h $\frac{x}{4} = 4$

2 Solve these multi-step equations.
a $2x + 5 = 23$
b $3x + 7 = 25$
c $4x - 8 = 60$
d $5x - 2 = 43$
e $2x - 14 = x - 8$
f $6x - 17 = 4x + 1$
g $5x - 9 = 3x + 15$
h $4x + 3 = x + 18$

3 Solve these equations.
a $3(4x - 5) = 33$
b $2(6x - 8) = 5(x + 8)$
c $3(x + 7) - 4(2x + 1) = 12$
d $5(2x - 3) - 4(x - 2) = 71$

4 Solve these equations.
a $x + 8 = 5$
b $x - 7 = -5$
c $3x + 11 = 8$
d $2(x + 4) = 0$
e $5x + 7 = 7$
f $6x - 9 = -33$

5 Solve these equations, using fractions in your answers.
a $4x + 10 = 12$
b $5(6x - 7) = 10$
c $6x + 3 = 2x + 8$
d $2(4x - 6) - 5(x - 7) = 24$

6 I think of a number x.
If I subtract the number 7 from it, I get the same answer as if I double it and add 3. Find the value of x.

7 Rope is sold for 85p per metre.
a Write an equation for the cost, £y, of x metres of rope.
b What are the cost of the following lengths of rope?
i 12 m   ii 22.5 m   iii 1500 m
c How much rope was bought if these were the prices paid?
i £4.25   ii £68   iii £6.38

8 EasiBuild sells and delivers bricks in bulk. The fixed delivery charge is £75 plus £200 per pallet of bricks ordered.
a Write an equation for the cost, £y, of ordering x pallets.
b If the cost of an order was £1675, how many pallets were ordered?
c Ted complains that his bill for £1900 cannot be correct. Explain how he knows this.

What next?

Score		
0 – 2	Your knowledge of this topic is still developing. To improve look at Formative test: 2B-10; MyMaths: 1154, 1182 and 1247
3 – 6	You are gaining a secure knowledge of this topic. To improve look at InvisiPen: 233, 234, 235, 236 and 237
7 – 8	You have mastered this topic. Well done, you are ready to progress!

 MyMaths.co.uk

Question commentary

Students should be encouraged to use the balance method. They should show all working clearly, working down the page.

Question 1 – Single step equations. Part **g** will confuse some students. Remind them that $\frac{x}{3}$ means 'x divided by 3'. A common incorrect answer may be 4.

Question 2 – For parts **e** to **h** the first step should be to subtract one of the terms involving x from both sides of the equation.

Question 3 – For part **a**, students can either expand the bracket or divide both sides of the equation by the number in front of it first. However, in parts **b**, **c** and **d**, it is best to expand the brackets and collect like terms first. In part **d**, students should take care with the negative in the second bracket.

Question 4 – Remind students that the answers could be negative.

Question 5 – Students sometimes divide terms the wrong way around. They should be encouraged to check their answers using back substitution.

Question 6 – Encourage students to form an equation to solve. It should be $x - 7 = 2x + 3$.

Questions 7 and **8** – These are practical applications of the work covered and students should be encouraged to check their answers for sense and magnitude.

Answers

1	a	33	b	21	c	29	d	8
	e	11	f	9	g	36	h	16
2	a	9	b	6	c	17	d	9
	e	6	f	9	g	12	h	5
3	a	4	b	8	c	1	d	13
4	a	-3	b	2	c	-1	d	-4
	e	0	f	-4				

5 a $\frac{1}{2}$ b $\frac{3}{2}$ c $\frac{5}{4}$ d $\frac{1}{3}$

6 -10

7 a $y = 0.85x$
  b i £10.20   ii £19.13   iii £1275
  c i 5 m   ii 7.5 m   iii 1500 m

8 a $y = 75 + 200x$ b 8
  c $1900 - 75 = 1825$ is not a multiple of 200.

10 MyPractice

1 Find the value of x in each of these balances.

a    b

2 Solve these equations by using inverse operations.

a $x + 3 = 7$ b $x - 3 = 7$ c $2x = 8$ d $\dfrac{x}{2} = 5$

e $4 + x = 6$ f $x - 4 = 1$ g $3x = 18$ h $\dfrac{x}{4} = 2$

3 Solve these equations. Each of them needs two steps.

a $2x + 4 = 14$ b $3x + 2 = 23$ c $2x - 1 = 11$

d $5x - 6 = 9$ e $\dfrac{x}{2} + 1 = 6$ f $\dfrac{x}{3} - 3 = 3$

4 Find the value of x in each of these balances.

a    b

5 Solve these equations. There are unknowns on both sides.

a $4x + 2 = 3x + 7$ b $6x + 1 = 5x + 13$ c $3x + 6 = x + 10$

d $7x + 2 = 4x + 8$ e $6x + 9 = x + 24$ f $7x = 3x + 20$

6 Solve these equations. Take care with the negative signs.

a $3x - 1 = 2x + 4$ b $7x - 2 = 5x + 6$ c $5x - 5 = 3x - 1$

d $8x - 11 = 5x - 2$ e $9x + 8 = 7x + 4$ f $6x + 14 = 3x + 5$

7 Sarah has six packets of Christmas cards and two loose cards. Her sister, Jane, has three similar packets of cards and seventeen loose cards. Each packet has x cards in it. When the sisters open all their boxes and count their cards, they find that they have the same total.

Write an equation and find the value of x.

8 a Think of a number, multiply it by 5 and then subtract 3. If you double the same number and add 15, you get the same answer. Find the number.

b This mobile is made from different shapes.

It can hang from the ceiling.

If the square shape has a mass of 60 grams, find the masses of all the other shapes.

9 Solve these equations.

a $2(3x + 4) = 20$ b $3(2x - 1) = 21$ c $5(x - 2) = 20$

d $3(4x + 1) = 123$ e $4(2x + 1) = 6(x + 2)$ f $5(3x + 2) = 4(3x + 4)$

10 Solve these equations by expanding the brackets and collecting like terms.

a $3(2x + 4) + 2(3x + 1) = 38$ b $5(2x + 1) + 2(x + 3) = 35$

c $4(x + 3) + 6(x + 1) = 28$ d $2(2x + 3) + 4(2x + 1) = 18$

e $3(5x + 1) + 2(1 - 6x) = 9$ f $5(x + 5) + 2(2x - 3) = 31$

11 I think of a number. I subtract it from 2 and then treble what is left. My final answer is 18. Find the number.

12 I think of a number x.

If I subtract the number from 16, I get the number itself.

Find the value of x.

13 I think of a number n.

If I double it and add 12, I get the same answer as if I treble it and add 2. Find the value of n.

14 In this triangle, the number in each square is found by adding the two numbers in the corner circles on either side of it.

a Find expressions to write in the two empty circles.

b Write an equation in x and find the value of x.

15 A taxi company charges £2.30 per journey plus 25 pence per mile.

a Write down an equation for the total cost, C, of the journey in terms of the number of miles, m.

b Work out the cost of my journey if I travel a total of 12 miles.

c How many miles will I have travelled if I am charged £6.05?

16 The equation used to convert pounds, x, into Euros, y, is $y = 1.162x$.

a Convert £400 into Euros.

b Convert £1500 into Euros.

c Convert €1000 into pounds.

d Convert €740 into pounds.

MyMaths.co.uk

Question commentary

Questions 1 and **2** – Simple one-step equations. These could be done orally or using mini-whiteboards.

Questions 3 to **6** – Students are expected to show each step in their working, working down the page. Care should be taken with negative signs and some answers may legitimately be negative or fractional.

Questions 5 and **6** – Students should be encouraged to form equations and show them using precise mathematical notation. Answers can be checked by back substituting into the original context.

Questions 9 and **10** – Students are expected to show each step of working and work down the page. Answers can be checked by back substitution.

Questions 11 to **14** – Students should be encouraged to form equations and show them using precise mathematical notation. Answers can be checked by substituting back into the original context.

Questions 15 and **16** – Questions in context. Check the equation formed in question **15** before students substitute. Calculators will be required for question **16**.

Answers

1   **a**   3   **b**   6

2   **a** $x = 4$ **b** $x = 10$ **c** $x = 4$ **d** $x = 10$
   e $x = 2$ **f** $x = 5$ **g** $x = 6$ **h** $x = 8$

3   **a** $x = 5$ **b** $x = 7$ **c** $x = 6$
   d $x = 3$ **e** $x = 10$ **f** $x = 18$

4   **a**   5   **b**   4

5   **a**   5   **b**   12   **c**   2
   d   2   **e**   3   **f**   5

6   **a**   5   **b**   4   **c**   2
   d   3   **e**   -2   **f**   -3

7   $6x + 2 = 3x + 17$
   $x = 5$

8   **a**   6
   b   Triangle 120 g, Hexagon 150 g, Circle 75 g, Star 165 g

9   **a**   2   **b**   4   **c**   6
   d   10   **e**   4   **f**   2

10 **a**   2   **b**   2   **c**   1
   d $\frac{2}{3}$ **e** $1\frac{1}{3}$ **f** $1\frac{1}{3}$

11   8

12   8

13   10

14 **a**   Left: $18 - x$ Right: $16 - x$
   b $(18 - x) + (16 - x) = 26$
     $x = 4$

15 **a** $C = 2.3 + 0.25m$ **b**   £5.30   **c**   15

16 **a**   €464.80   **b**   €1743   **c**   £861   **d**   £6.83

Learning outcomes

N4 Use the 4 operations, including formal written methods, applied to integers, decimals, proper and improper fractions, and mixed numbers, all both positive and negative (L5)

N5 Use conventional notation for the priority of operations, including brackets, powers, roots and reciprocals (L5)

N15 Use a calculator and other technologies to calculate results accurately and then interpret them appropriately (L6)

Introduction

The chapter starts by looking at written methods for addition, subtraction, multiplication and division (including decimal numbers) before a section focusing on the order of operations. The next two sections put these skills into context through a series of problem-solving exercises before the final section on calculator methods for solving complex problems.

The introduction discusses the different types of way in which cultures write. The right to left conventions of the Arabic and Hebrew cultures and the top to bottom conventions of the Chinese and Japanese mean that they have very different ways of setting out text. Obviously, since mathematics is a 'universal' language, we have to agree to a convention in which everyone follows the same method. The use of right to left conventions in setting out mathematical calculations, the use of BIDMAS and some of the standard methods are the same throughout the world.

However, different cultures still have different methods for carrying out calculations, many of which are as efficient as the ones we are used to using in a typical mathematical classroom. Chinese multiplication, for example, is a nice alternative to our standard method and can be used to show the students a different way.

http://www.youtube.com/watch?v=n97nmGGlBf4

Prior knowledge

Students should already know how to…

- Add, subtract, multiply and divide numbers using mental methods
- Add, subtract, multiply and divide whole numbers

Starter problem

The starter problem invites students to make up an 'amazing' story using a series of two sets of number facts, one about the masses of animals and one about the eating habits of people. Obviously, there is no right answer to this, but the information given can be used to stimulate discussion about scale or the relationships between numbers of different magnitudes, or in the case of the eating example, the value of calculating with complex information.

The first set of information tells us that the mass of a blue whale is $120 \div 7.5 = 16$ times that of an elephant whereas the elephant is $7500 \div 0.022 = 340\,909$ times that of a mouse. This makes the blue whale over 5 million times heavier than a mouse!

The second set of information tells us that the average meal weighs $9 \times 62 = 558$ grams and that it takes on average $19.3 \times 62 = 1197$ seconds (nearly 20 minutes) to eat, assuming that we just keep shovelling the food in without a break!

Resources

⊞ MyMaths

Add and subtract decimals	1007	Divide decimals by whole numbers	1008
Multiply decimals by whole numbers	1010	Multiply triple digits	1026
Long division	1041	Order of operations	1167
Word problems	1393		

Online assessment

Chapter test	2B–11
Formative test	2B–11
Summative test	2B–11

InvisiPen solutions

Order of operations	124	Written multiplication	126
Written division	127	Calculator methods	129
Adding and subtracting decimals			131
Written methods multiplying decimals			133
Written methods dividing decimals			134

Topic scheme

Teaching time = 7 lessons/3 weeks

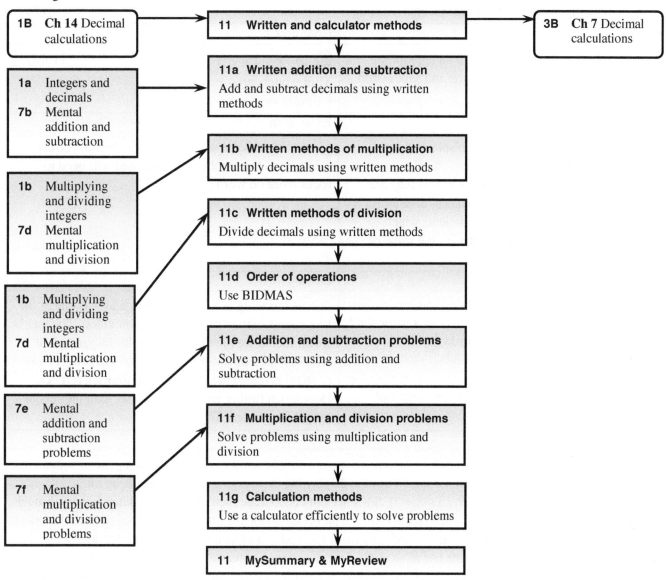

| 1B Ch 14 Decimal calculations |

| 1a Integers and decimals
7b Mental addition and subtraction |

| 1b Multiplying and dividing integers
7d Mental multiplication and division |

| 1b Multiplying and dividing integers
7d Mental multiplication and division |

| 7e Mental addition and subtraction problems |

| 7f Mental multiplication and division problems |

11 Written and calculator methods

11a Written addition and subtraction
Add and subtract decimals using written methods

11b Written methods of multiplication
Multiply decimals using written methods

11c Written methods of division
Divide decimals using written methods

11d Order of operations
Use BIDMAS

11e Addition and subtraction problems
Solve problems using addition and subtraction

11f Multiplication and division problems
Solve problems using multiplication and division

11g Calculation methods
Use a calculator efficiently to solve problems

11 MySummary & MyReview

| 3B Ch 7 Decimal calculations |

Differentiation

Student book 2A   206 –223

Written addition and subtraction
Written multiplication
Written division
Written arithmetic problems
Calculator skills
Interpreting the display

Student book 2B   190 – 209

Written addition and subtraction
Written methods of multiplication
Written methods of division
Order of operations
Addition and subtraction problems
Multiplication and division
                         problems
Calculation methods

Student book 2C   196 –215

Multiplication
Division
Calculator skills
Calculators in context
Order of operations
Written addition and subtraction
Multiplication and division
                         problems

11a Written addition and subtraction

Objectives

- Use efficient written methods to add and subtract integers and decimals of any size, including numbers with differing numbers of decimal places   (L5)

Key ideas	Resources
1 For students to be confident with an appropriate written approach for both addition and subtraction	Add and subtract decimals (1007) Mini whiteboards Calculators

Simplification	Extension
Common difficulties here will be misplacing digits. Some students persist in setting out a calculation horizontally, which works perfectly well if they are using a mental method but often leads to disaster for a written one. Discuss with weaker students which method they plan to use and emphasise the value of approximating first.	More able students will quickly achieve the correct solutions to the number problems and will need to focus more on word problems.

Literacy	Links
Common written methods for addition and subtraction vary. Check if your school has a policy of a particular one across all departments. The key is that 'the' method is both effective (correct) and efficient for any particular student. Check other vocabulary for the terms addition and subtraction.	Discus throwing is an ancient sport and was one of the five events in the original Greek pentathlon. The men's world record for the discus is held by Jürgen Schult (GDR) with a throw of 74.08 m. The women's record is 76.80 m and is held by Gabriele Reinsch (GDR). How much further are these distances than the school record in question **5**?

Alternative approach

Begin by reminding students of equivalent statements using a simple number statement and a general statement, so, $8 + 7 = 15$; and $p + q = 21$. Students should be able display the three rearranged statements on mini whiteboards ($7 + 8 = 15$; $15 - 7 = 8$; $15 - 8 = 7$). Students can consolidate their skills by working in pairs through a range of calculations, selected from Exercise **11a** .The pairs can divide the questions between them and work in three stages: estimate and calculate; lastly check and mark each other's calculation with a calculator. Encourage the checking procedure to involve the use of an equivalent statement or inverse. Discuss with the whole group the meaning of being effective and being efficient when calculating, sharing different approaches and asking some students to explain why they prefer their particular chosen approach. Note: some students will have been encouraged to change the order of values in addition problems from primary schools – starting with the largest value and working downwards.

Checkpoint

1   Ask that a student talks through completing an addition and a subtraction, including an initial estimate and a 'check' stage:

   a $24.78 + 143.5$ (Estimate ~165; calculate 168.28; agree with estimate or alternative)

   b $42.06 - 19.4$ (Estimate ~20; calculate 22.66; agree with estimate, or inverse)

Starter – Miss the multiples

Ask students to add up numbers you read out that are **not** multiples of 7.

For example, 16, 21, 3, 7, 28, 30, 15, 8, 35, 11, 5, 14, 12, 49, 17 (117).

Can be differentiated by choice of multiple and numbers.

Teaching notes

The worked examples in the unit stress the importance of correctly lining up the digits in written calculation as this causes many students to make errors. Draw particular attention to the extra zeros that have been added where necessary.

It is again worth emphasising that students should use an *appropriate* method of calculation, there is no *right* way and allow time for discussion of which method they will use and ask them to justify that decision.

Students should be advised to estimate a solution first as a strategy for self-checking both to build confidence and for support in taking increased responsibility for their own learning.

Plenary

Refer students back to the exercise and ask them to look at the questions where they were asked to choose an *appropriate* method. Ask them to justify the method they chose. Preferably work in pairs here, if possible pairing students who chose different methods.

Exercise commentary

Question 1 – Emphasise using the most appropriate method and that there is no 'right' method.

Questions 2 to 4 – Similar to the two examples. Ensure digits are lined up and encourage first making an estimate.

Question 5 – Word problems. Ask students to explain why they decided that their method of calculation was most appropriate.

Question 6 – Students may need to revisit inverse operations.

Answers

1	**a**	96.1	**b**	44.3	**c**	83.7	**d**	123.3
	e	54.2	**f**	104.1	**g**	11.5	**h**	6.5
	i	2.55	**j**	3.66	**k**	0.213	**l**	0.391
2	**a**	14.85	**b**	25.94	**c**	44.12	**d**	58.14
	e	43.66	**f**	73.29	**g**	4.71	**h**	28.02
	i	107.83	**j**	11.796	**k**	9.24	**l**	82.369
3	**a**	483.7	**b**	706.66	**c**	897.58	**d**	1112.34
	e	578.31	**f**	226.83	**g**	682.58	**h**	1267.47
	i	57134	**j**	76.089	**k**	539.069	**l**	901.8205
4	**a**	413.79	**b**	290.87	**c**	20.1	**d**	40.37
	e	497.8	**f**	504.65	**g**	16316.681		
5	**a**	52.24 km	**b**	100.233 kg	**c**	43.485 m		
6	**a**	8.72 kg			**b**	4.69 km		
	c	60.78 litres			**d**	4.39 tonnes		

Objectives

- Use efficient written methods for multiplication (and division) of integers and decimals   (L5)
- Understand where to position the decimal point by considering equivalent calculations   (L5)
- Make and justify estimates and approximations of calculations   (L5)

Key ideas	Resources	
1 For students to think of and be aware of the likely size of a resulting calculation 2 For students to be confident with an appropriate written approach for multiplication	Multiple triple digits Mini whiteboards Calculators	(1026)

Simplification	Extension
Where students struggle, spend time allowing them to work in pairs on an activity. Allow students to use the grid method if they are not ready to switch to a common written method.	Encourage more able students to create their own spider diagram to ensure that they have clarity of understanding of how calculations link together.

Literacy	Links
Common written methods for multiplication and division vary. Check if your school has a policy of a particular one across all departments. The key is that 'the' method is both effective (correct) and efficient for any particular student. Check other vocabulary for the terms multiplication.	A computer virus is an often malevolent program that can copy itself into other programs without the permission of the user. If a virus-infected email is sent to 10 people who each send it to 10 people who each send it to 10 more people, how many computers could become infected? (1000). There is more information at http://en.wikipedia.org/wiki/Computer_virus

Alternative approach

Begin by reminding students of equivalent statements using a simple number statement and a general statement, so, $8 \times 7 = 56$; and $p \times q = 21$. Students should be able display the three rearranged statements on mini whiteboards ($7 \times 8 = 56$; $56 \div 7 = 8$; $56 \div 8 = 7$). Students can consolidate their skills by working in pairs through a range of calculations, selected from Exercise **11b** .The pairs can divide the questions between them and work in three stages: estimate and calculate; lastly check and mark each other's calculation with a calculator. Encourage the checking procedure to involve the use of an equivalent statement or inverse. Discuss with the whole group the meaning of being effective and being efficient when calculating, sharing different approaches and asking some students to explain why they prefer their particular chosen approach.

Checkpoint

1 Ask that a student talks through completing a multiplication including an initial estimate, and a 'check' stage:

   4.56×27 (Estimate ~125; calculate 123.12; check with estimate or inverse with calculator)

Starter – Factor bingo

Ask students to draw a 3 × 3 grid and enter three factors of 24, three factors of 36 and three factors of 75.

Give possible answers (1, 2, 3, 4, 5, 6, 8, 9, 12, 15, 18, 24, 25, 36, 75).

Winner is the first student to cross out all their factors.

Can be differentiated by the choice of numbers.

Teaching notes

The worked examples in this unit emphasise the value of using approximation in the first instance to get an idea of what the answer to a calculation might be. This needs to be stressed to students, not only because of its usefulness as a checking mechanism here but also as a recap of rounding and the value of making sensible estimates in general.

There is scope to discuss how to choose the numbers to round to.

The use of using whole number calculations also helps to improve understanding of multiplication and division by 10 and 100.

The second example is especially useful in supporting links with literacy. Discuss as a whole class how the question should be analysed and identify what is the key information to be extracted.

Plenary

Refer students back to questions **6** and **7**. Ask them to choose one part of one of these questions and to explain how they did it to a friend.

Exercise commentary

Question 1 – Integers only. The mental approximations could all be made first as a whole-class activity.

Questions 2 to 5 – Routine practice. Similar to the first example.

Question 3 – Insist students first approximate and highlight how this helps to avoid careless errors.

Question 5 – Students can mark their work most effectively by initially comparing answers with their approximation and then with another student.

Question 6 – Word problems. Although the mathematics is no more challenging, some students will need support to analyse the text.

Question 7 – In part **b**, ask students why the answer is an estimate. This will link effectively to students' work on averages.

Question 8 – Ask students to explain their methods to each other. Talking through can clarify both understanding and any errors.

Answers

1. a 180 b 456 c 468 d 714
   e 1075 f 488 g 408 h 1986
   i 16 402 j 17 108 k 247 665 l 196 794
2. a 32.2 b 17.5 c 63.2 d 54.4
   e 47.7 f 36.8 g 27.9 h 140.4
   i 2041.2 j 4174.8 k 10 968.2 l 32 481.8
3. a 10.8 b 9.8 c 48.93 d 74.24
   e 48.87 f 30.72 g 25.02 h 45.45
4. a 70.2 b 38.4 c 39.9 d 281.2
   e 214.6 f 264 g 436.1 h 112
5. a 30.48 b 53.76 c 61.23 d 104.22
   e 262.86 f 304.5 g 373.32 h 759.05
   i 2362.36 j 1087.96 k 37 132.5 l 62 925.8
6. a £106 b £40.30
   c Megan, as Megan has run 374 m whereas Hayden has run 331.1 m
7. a 57.72 m b 166.17 cm
8. a 705 b 7.05 c 7050
   d Missing boxes are 15 × 4700, 15 × 47 000 and 15 × 4.7 (on top line), but many others are possible, e.g. 15 × 0.047
   e Several, for example 70.5 ÷ 15, 70.5 ÷ 1.5, and 70.5 × 4.7, 70.5 × 47, etc.

Objectives	
• Use efficient written methods for (multiplication and) division of integers and decimals	(L6)
• Make and justify estimates and approximations of calculations	(L5)

Key ideas	Resources	
1 For students to think of and be aware of the likely size of a resulting calculation 2 For students to be confident with an appropriate written approach for division	Long division Mini whiteboards Calculators	(1041)

Simplification	Extension
For students who may struggle with some of the strategies discussed in this unit, re-emphasise the importance of estimating an answer in the first instance. Offer word problems with a decrease in technical demand and complexity and an increase in familiarity.	More able students will need to increase their skills at a functional level by considering (word) problems with decreased familiarity and an increase in complexity and the level of independence required.

Literacy	Links
Common written methods for division vary. Check if your school has a policy of a particular one across all departments. The key is that 'the' method is both effective (correct) and efficient for any particular student. Check other vocabulary for the term division, as well as student understanding of the terms division by 'chunking'; long division and short division.	As a car moves it has to push air out of the way. This produces a force called air resistance, or drag, which slows down the car. The greater the drag, the more fuel is required to make the car drive the same distance. Sleek aerodynamic design reduces the drag and so improves the fuel economy. Other factors that affect fuel economy are mass and speed.

Alternative approach

Begin with an equivalent spider diagram using a central multiplication fact and encourage students to add legs. Remind them of the inverse operation for multiplication. Division is likely to be the most challenging written operation for the students. Students can consolidate their skills by working in pairs through a range of calculations, selected from Exercise **11c** . The pairs can divide the questions between them and work in three stages: estimate and calculate; lastly check and mark each other's calculation with a calculator. Encourage the checking procedure to involve the use of an equivalent statement or inverse. Reiterate the meaning of being effective and being efficient when calculating with the whole group, sharing different approaches and asking some students to explain why they prefer their particular chosen approach.

Checkpoint

1 Ask that a student talks through completing a division problem including an initial estimate, and a 'check' stage:

$58.6 \div 11$
              (Estimate ~ 6; calculate 5.327; relate to estimate or otherwise)

Starter – Double products

Draw a 4 × 4 table on the board.

Label the columns 9, 4, 18, 11 and the rows 3, 7, 14, 5.

Ask students to fill in the table with the products (no calculators). For example, the top row in the table would read 27, 12, 54, 33.

Hint: 18 is double 9 and 14 is double 7.

Can be differentiated by the choice of numbers.

Teaching notes

This topic, together with the preceding few, develops the key processes in number: in representing, where students need to identify the type of problem and the operations needed to solve it; in analysing, where it is important to visualise images, such as a number line to support mental methods; and in communicating and reflecting where students compare the efficiency of calculation procedures and discuss and reflect on different approaches to solving a numerical problem.

The worked examples are very helpful for clarifying methods and strategies Refer students back to these, when they get stuck, in order to encourage them to take responsibility for their learning. The greatest emphasis however needs to be on the development of the students' capacity to apply their skills in a functional setting. The word problems provided here strongly support this.

Plenary

Provide one word problem involving multiplication and one involving division and ask students to work in pairs to answer one each and to explain their working to each other. Encourage students to ask questions of each other for clarification. In addition to being a consolidation activity, this also offers the opportunity for students to provide constructive support and feedback to others.

Exercise commentary

Question 1 – Appropriate methods are short division or chunking; students should approximate first, whichever method they choose.

Question 2 – Discuss with students how they found their answers to parts **b** and **c**.

Question 3 – Encourage students to share their ideas about an 'appropriate' method. The decimals may be a stumbling block for some.

Question 4 – Remind students to work out 2 decimal places and then to round to 1 decimal place.

Question 5 – Extends question **4** to include decimals.

Question 6 – The functional setting will require analysis, and perhaps support, to tease out the mathematics to use.

Question 7 – Use this activity to strengthen the development of functional skills, emphasising the element of explanation and justification.

Answers

1	a	23	b	26	c	31	d	34
	e	15	f	16 r 1	g	24	h	21 r 3
2	a	27	b	21	c	18		
3	a	7.6	b	7.9	c	7.2	d	5.6
	e	5.4	f	6.3	g	7.1	h	6.6
4	a	6.9	b	2.9	c	5.8	d	5.1
	e	10.9	f	11.4	g	9.4	h	12.4
	i	328.1	j	463				
5	a	3.2	b	4.6	c	2.4	d	2.7
	e	2.5	f	2.5	g	2.6	h	2.6
	i	22.0	j	83.3	k	37.2	l	47.7

6   a   Devvon's, because Devvon's car travels 14.8 km per litre and Alec's travels 14.6 km per litre

    b   1 month = 31 × 24 hours = 744 hours, so she has been alive 1 month and 21 hours (assuming 31 days in a month). So, she is more than a month old.

    c   3.4 seconds

    d   28 trains

7   a   The blue packet.

    b   The blue packet costs the least per gram at 0.147p per gram.

Objectives

- Use the order of operations, including brackets, with more complex calculations (L5)
- Carry out more difficult calculations effectively and efficiently using the function key for powers (L5)
- Use brackets (L5)

Key ideas	Resources
1 Understand and apply the conventions of operation order 2 Improving effective and efficient use of the calculator	Order of operations (1167) Mini whiteboards Scientific calculators

Simplification	Extension
Provide three questions that have been answered with some errors included. Ask the students to mark the work and include feedback on the errors. Use this as a paired activity where errors are analysed without exposure of students' own weaknesses.	Ask students to generate a small set of questions involving the order of operations with true/false answers. A selection of these could be compiled into a starter activity for a future lesson.

Literacy	Links
Make sure that students realise that operation order is an agreed mathematical convention, ensuring that there is no confusion or doubt about communicating meaning. Check your school policy on the description order, for consistency across all staff (BIDMAS or BODMAS?). N.B. O in the latter for 'of' as in 'to the power of'	The order of operations can be described using the mnemonic BIDMAS. (Brackets, Indices or Powers, Division and Multiplication, Addition and Subtraction). A mnemonic is a memory aid which uses words and letters to jog the memory. Some well-known mnemonics are *Richard of York Gave Battle In Vain* (colours of the rainbow), and the rhyme beginning *Thirty Days hath September* (number of days in the months of the year). How many other mnemonics can the class remember?

Alternative approach

Begin with calculations that can be solved easily mentally, for example by using those in question **1** with students showing answers on mini whiteboards. This allows misconceptions to be exposed and corrected; asking neighbouring students to help or explain where appropriate. Encourage rough estimation when calculators are being used. Students will commonly interpret order with errors when solving problems such as those in questions **3** and **5**, either because they read or recognise the division sign only once and do not realise that the denominator implicitly requires brackets following the division. Request that students identify the numerator and denominator as a whole expression to help overcome this problem before meeting these questions.

Checkpoint

1 Given the problem $\dfrac{72 \times 3.4}{4.5 + 7.2}$

a student uses a calculator and enters: $72 \times 3.4 \div 4.5 + 7.2$.

  a Will this produce a correct result? Explain.   (No – the denominator needs brackets included)

  b Work out the correct answer.   (20.923... rounded to 3 dp)

Starter – Crazy clocks

One clock chimes every six minutes and a second every seven minutes.

The clocks chime together. How long before the clocks chime together again? (42 min)

What if a third clock chimes every half hour? (210 min)

Can be extended by asking how many times the clocks will chime together in 24 hours. (2 clocks 34 times, 3 clocks 6 times).

Teaching notes

The order of operations is a matter of convention, so students may differ on how to evaluate an expression. Use question 1 to identify different ways of interpreting expressions and to agree on an order of precedence. Introduce the BIDMAS acronym as a useful mnemonic and, for visual learners, the 'traffic light' diagram. Encourage students to refer back to these when applying the rules. Use examples of increasing complexity to reinforce the correct interpretation.

The efficient use of calculators relies on correctly using rules of precedence to obtain a unique/correct answer. Encourage students to check how a calculator works by doing simple 'toy calculations' for which they already know the answer. This may vary between calculators, as may the appearance of some of the keys.

The process skill of analysing, using appropriate mathematical procedures, is developed as students learn efficient use of the calculator.

Encourage students to work collaboratively in this spread, so that they can develop confidence in themselves and their contribution.

Plenary

Provide three calculations, of varying difficulty, which involve the correct order of operations. Ask students to choose one of these and write an annotated solution showing a step-by-step approach that would be useful for a classmate who had been absent and missed the work on this topic. Ask them to swap with someone who has answered a different question to check each other's work.

Exercise commentary

Question 1 – Similar to the first example.

Question 2 – Ask students to collaborate, taking turns to explain the right answer or account for the wrong answer in order to build confidence and encourage participation.

Question 3 – If necessary, remind students how to round.

Question 4 – Invite students to compare answers here as a checking strategy.

Question 5 – Similar to the second example. Ensure that weaker students are confident in using brackets on a calculator and, if necessary, discuss rounding to 2 decimal places.

Question 6 – This is a very useful activity to strengthen understanding of number operations. Ask students to work in pairs initially and then take whole class feedback.

Question 7 – A challenging puzzle which can be worked on collaboratively. It could also be set as a homework task.

Answers

1.
   a 29   b 9   c 22   d 20
   e 9   f 46   g 5   h 20
2.
   a X   b Y   c Y   d X
   e Y   f X   g Y
3.
   a 4   b 1.8   c 25   d 3.3
4.
   a $(8 + 5) \times 4 - 3 = 49$ b $8 + 5 \times (4 - 3) = 13$
   c $8 + 5 \times 4 - 3 = 25$ d $(7 + 3^2) \div 4 = 4$
   e $(7 + 3)^2 \div 4 = 25$ f $7 + 3^2 \div 4 = 9\frac{1}{4}$
5.
   a 1.11   b 22.44   c 21.66   d 45.5
   e 5.33   f 1.54   g 1   h 1
   i 1.36   j 8.79   k 0.19   l 0.81
6. $\frac{60}{3} \times \frac{1}{4} = \frac{60}{12} = 60 \div 12 = 5$

   but $\frac{60}{3} \times \frac{1}{4} = (60 \div 3) \div 4 = 5$
7. Rows from top:
   $9 \div 3 + 5 = 8$
   $6 + 1 + 7 = 14$
   $8 + 2 + 4 = 14$
   Columns from left:
   $9 \times 6 - 8 = 46$
   $3 - 1 \times 2 = 1$
   $5 \times 7 + 4 = 39$

11e Addition and subtraction problems

Objectives

- Use efficient written methods to add and subtract integers and decimals of any size, including numbers with differing numbers of decimal places   (L5)
- Select from a range of checking methods, including estimating in context and using inverse operations (L5)

Key ideas	Resources
1 Choose an appropriate approach for solving a problem 2 Make sure that resulting values make sense in the context of the problem	Add and subtract decimals (1007)

Simplification	Extension
If students experience difficulty here, it is likely to be due to the need to support their literacy skills. Scaffold their attempts to highlight and extract key information from word-based problems.	Invite more able students to research an area of interest from which they can construct their own written addition and/or subtraction problems.

Literacy	Links
Reading a problem with comprehension is essential. Encourage reading out loud; highlighting or underlining key pieces of information, and reviewing solutions in context.	To date over 120 US space shuttle flights have been made since the space shuttle Columbia made its first test flight into space in 1981. There is more information about the US space shuttle at http://www.nasa.gov/mission_pages/shuttle/main/index.html

Alternative approach

Differentiate problems in terms of level of challenge, either by labelling or using colour-coding, and group students appropriately, with the task of producing team solutions to each of their problems. Make it clear that presentation of solution with choice of approach is important to include and also encourage checking devices. Each student within a group may be given the lead role as: Reader; Checker; Explainer, for example.

Checkpoint

1   Johan has three part empty bottles of water, one containing 1.23 litres, one 0.96 litres and one 0.82 litres. He wishes to empty them all into a fourth bottle with a capacity of three litres. Will they all fit? Explain.

(No: the total of the three part bottles is 3.01 litres)

Starter – How many sweets?

Five students estimated the number of sweets in a jar.

Their estimates were: 41, 45, 49, 58, and 62.

The errors in their estimates, not necessarily in the same order, were: 2, 6, 7, 11 and 15.

Ask students how many sweets were in the jar. (56)

Can be extended by asking students to explain their strategies and making their own puzzles.

Teaching notes

Written addition and subtraction methods are consolidated here in a variety of real-life settings to support the development of functional skills in mathematics. Through the worked examples, students are shown the importance of lining up the digits in calculations and the outcomes of failing to do this correctly are illustrated.

Discussion of the examples should consider not only the processes for correct addition and subtraction but also the importance of using inverse operations for checking and, indeed, common sense.

Throughout, the mathematical problems are word-based and students are offered the opportunity to develop their skills in identifying key points from text and to ascertain the mathematical operation required to find a solution. These skills are equally as important as the actual mathematics itself and students build on the key processes in number, particularly representing, as they identify the type of problem and the operations needed to reach a solution.

Plenary

Ask students to revisit question **3** from the exercise and to write a different set of questions using the same map. Swap with a friend to complete and then swap back to mark.

Exercise commentary

Question 1 – This question helps to consolidate the importance of lining up the digits in the correct columns when using written methods. Students could break the additions down if this helps.

Question 2 – Students may find it helps to make their own simplified drawing and write in the various dimensions.

Question 3 – Encourage students to perform approximate calculations first to eliminate a number of possibilities before doing full calculations. Part **d** is related to the famous 'travelling salesman' problem.

Answers

1 Risotto   1621.936 g
   Spiced Rice   757.527 g
2 **a** 9.35 m   **b** 157 m
3 **a** Ayton → Isay → Hodear → Gewizzle→ Eckerslike
        47.453 km
   b Not necessarily. Depends on traffic conditions, road works, etc.
   c Multiple answers – check students' working
   d e.g. Ayton → Isay → Hodear → Flippineck → Gewizzle → Eckerslike → Drat → Crikey → Biheck → Ayton

Objectives	
• Use efficient written methods for multiplication and division of integers and decimals (L5)	
• Select from a range of checking methods, including estimating in context and using inverse operations (L5)	

Key ideas	Resources
1 Choose an appropriate approach for solving a problem 2 Make sure that resulting values make sense in the context of the problem	Divide decimals by whole numbers (1008) Multiply decimals by whole numbers (1010) Highlighters

Simplification	Extension
Where students experience difficulty, support them in the analysis of the questions. Offer highlighters to help pick out key points from (copies of) individual questions and encourage dialogue with other students.	More able students can be challenged to produce high quality explanations and justifications of their thinking that could be used as model strategies.

Literacy	Links
Reading a problem with comprehension is essential. Encourage reading out loud; highlighting or underlining key pieces of information, and reviewing solutions in context.	The division symbol ÷ is called an obelus. The symbol was originally used in manuscripts to mark passages containing errors but first appeared as a division symbol in a book called *Teutsche Algebra* by Johann Rahn in 1659. In Denmark, the obelus was used to represent subtraction.

Alternative approach

Differentiate problems in terms of level of challenge, either by labelling or using colour-coding, and group students appropriately, with the task of producing team solutions to each of their problems. Make it clear that presentation of solutions with choice of approach is important to include and also encourage checking devices. Each student within a group may be given the lead role as: Reader; Checker; Explainer, for example, and if this approach was used in the previous lesson, change the roles of each student.

Checkpoint

1 Oliver collects £2.41 per week for 7 weeks for recycling old drinks bottles.
   a How many bottles of drink can he now buy if each bottle costs £1.20? (14)
   b How much money will he have left? (7 pence)

Starter – Last minute?

Write the following list of times on the board:

3 days, 192 hours, 47 hours, 24 600 seconds, 8 days, 17 hours, 12 300 minutes, 1020 minutes, 169 200 seconds, 4320 minutes, 410 minutes, 205 hours.

Challenge students to match up six pairs in the shortest possible time.

Teaching notes

The main aim of the topic is to pose real-life problems to solve. These are presented in a fashion that invites the development of skill transferability, as students extract the mathematics from a situation. There is, however, thorough discussion of the worked examples, a review of methods of calculation and a reminder of the value of checking with inverse operations.

The key process of representing is central to the work here, as students identify the type of problem and the mathematics needed to reach a solution and break down more complex problems into a sequence of steps.

Where the opportunity is taken to use the questions in the exercise to develop purposeful mathematical discussion, students will take responsibility, showing confidence in themselves and their contribution.

Plenary

While students are working, identify some of the best interaction and high quality discussion. Invite a selection of students to present their working methods to the class.

Exercise commentary

Consider pairing students so that they can work together to extract the relevant information and discuss their methods for finding the solution.

Question 1 – Similar to the example.

Question 2 – In pairs, students could answer one part each and then explain to their partner how they arrived at their solution.

Question 3 – Again, an effective learning strategy is to share out the parts of the question, asking students to explain to each other and to account for their methods.

Question 4 – This multi-step problem will require students to work from miles per week to days to hours as the best strategy, rather than trying to work out the number of hours in two weeks first of all. Some may need guidance on how to start off.

Answers

1   a   14p   b   54p   c   £28.08
2   a   £7.20
    b   14.8 miles (assume that Louise walks the same distance each day)
3   a   £7.20 per hour
    b   £8.20 per hour
    c   £13.20 per hour
4   19.4 mph

Objectives

- Calculate accurately, selecting mental methods or calculating devices as appropriate   (L5)
- Carry out more difficult calculations effectively and efficiently   (L5)
- Estimate, approximate and check working   (L5)

Key ideas	Resources
1 Choosing an appropriate approach for solving a problem 2 Making sure that resulting values make sense in the context of the problem.	Divide decimals by whole numbers (1008) Multiply decimals by whole numbers (1010) Word problems (1393) Functional Skills past papers (AQA): http://www.aqa.org.uk/subjects/mathematics/functional-skills/functional-mathematics-4367-4368/past-papers-and-mark-schemes

Simplification	Extension
Students who are not confident here will learn most effectively through discussion and sharing ideas with others. Also, the opportunity to solve the same problem using more than one method will build confidence.	Challenge more able students with further opportunities to use mathematics to substantiate a point of view or a recommendation as in question **3**.

Literacy	Links
Reading a problem with comprehension is essential. Encourage reading out loud; highlighting or underlining key pieces of information, and reviewing solutions in context.	Before electronic calculators became widely available in around 1974, slide rules were used to perform multiplication and division calculations at school and in science and engineering. A slide rule is a mechanical calculator shaped like a large ruler with 2 or more scales that can slide against each other. Using a slide rule converted a multiplication or division into an addition or subtraction. There is more information about slide rules at http://en.wikipedia.org/wiki/Slide_rule and at http://www.sliderulemuseum.com/

Alternative approach

A variety of short calculations can be presented initially for students to consider and state whether they would use mental approaches, mental with jottings, a written approach, or a calculator. Students may challenge each other and disagree, with reasons which might be consider the 'ideal' approach. Problems can be presented to students on coloured card/paper, colour coded for one of three levels of challenge – low, medium, high challenge. Further sources of problems can be found from any past exam papers of functional mathematics, entry level 3 and level 1 are likely to be appropriate. Working with real contexts in problems will strengthen engagement. Groups of students may be formed after solving in order to share and discuss results of particular problems.

Checkpoint

1 Would you use a mental approach, mental with jottings, written or a calculator for each of these? (Explain your choice.) Work each answer out.

  a Three friends shared £411. How much did each friend get?

                                  (Mental approach, recognition of divisible by 3; £137)

  b The mass of an object is 0.312 kg and its volume is 0.12 m^3. Density is mass divided by volume. What is the density of the object?

                       (Calculator is acceptable here, though a written method may be a choice; 2.6kg/m^3)

Starter – Same digit

Ask students to find pairs of numbers that will give the same digit when one of the numbers is divided by the other, for example,

$385 \div 50 = 7.7$

$33 \div 6 = 5.5$

$3000 \div 9 = 333.33333...$

Can be extended by asking students to explain any methods they have used.

Teaching notes

The work here supports process skill development throughout. In terms of representing, students will be involved in choosing between mental, written and calculator methods; they will strengthen analysing skills as they develop routines for estimating, approximating and checking; and they will communicate and reflect as they discuss different approaches to solving numerical problems and compare the efficiency of calculation procedures.

Through collaborating and sharing thinking, students will question their own and others' assumptions and try out alternatives or new solutions and follow ideas through.

Students will be encouraged to feel successful here as there is no necessarily correct approach. The key focus is on the ability to explain and justify the method chosen and to be able to use a checking strategy to know whether a solution is likely to be right.

Plenary

Invite students to list good checking strategies and when they would use them. Take feedback and discuss as a class.

Exercise commentary

Question 1 – Similar to the example. Encourage students to explain which method of calculation they used and to say why they chose this method.

Question 2 – After completing this question, ask students to work with a friend to compare methods and solutions. Where they have used different strategies they should discuss the relative merits of each.

Question 3 – This question also supports developing skills in persuasive writing.

Answers

1 Packet   A : each biscuit costs 5.5p

                   B : each biscuit costs 5p

                   C : each biscuit costs 5.2p

So packet B is the best value

2   i   8.4 miles   ii   £4088.36

3   *By car* Jayne's driving distance is 110 km per day. So in 46 weeks, she drives 25 300 km (5 day week). This requires 2056.9 litres of petrol at a cost of £2342.82

Therefore, her cost of driving to work is

Petrol	2342.82
Insurance	280.45
Road tax	180.00
Servicing	390.00
MOT	50.63
Total	3243.90

Her daily travelling time is *1 hour 50 min.*

By train Jayne requires 11 monthly season tickets (excluding August) at a cost of £3138.19

Her daily travelling time is *2 hours 20 min.*

Jayne could save money by selling her car and travelling by train. However, her journey times would be longer and she would not have the convenience of the car for her holidays, shopping, etc. On the other hand using the car is worse for the environment.

Key outcomes	Quick check
Use standard written methods for addition, subtraction, multiplication and division. **L5**	Work out **a** 23.54 + 172.6 (196.14) **b** 323.81 − 47.84 (275.97) **c** 11.3 × 4.2 (47.46) **d** 875.3 ÷ 13 (answer to 2 dp) (67.33)
Use the order of operations. **L5**	Work out **a** $7 + 8 \times 4 - 5$ $\quad(34)$ **b** $\dfrac{3^2 + 4.5}{17 - 8.4}$ $\quad$ (1.57 (to 2 dp))
Solve problems using standard methods for addition, subtraction, multiplication and division. **L6**	**a** Six friends all have £8.26 to spend. A seventh friend joins them but has forgotten her money. They decide to share the total between all seven people. How much does each person get? (£7.08) **b** Alexander buys four textbooks each costing £4.56 and a calculator costing £7.63. How much change does he receive from £30? (£4.13)

⊞ MyMaths extra support

Lesson/online homework			Description
Adding in columns	1020	L3	Adding 2- and 3-digit numbers where carrying tens and hundreds is needed
Multiply double digits	1025	L4	Multiplying 2-digit numbers using the grid method
Subtraction columns	1028	L3	Subtracting 2- and 3-digit numbers where exchanging tens and hundreds is needed

MyReview

Check out

You should now be able to ...

Test it ➡
Questions

✓ Use standard written methods for addition, subtraction, multiplication and division.	(5)	1–5
✓ Use the order of operations.	(9)	6, 7
✓ Solve problems using standard methods for addition, subtraction, multiplication and division.	(9)	8–12

Language	Meaning	Example
Estimate	Simplify a calculation, by rounding the numbers, in order to have a value to check the full calculation against	$2 \times 3 = 6$ is an estimate for 1.87×3.251
Short division	A way of setting out workings when dividing by a single digit number	$1\ 8\ 9\ r\ 1$ $7\overline{)13^62^64}$
Long division	A way of setting out workings when dividing by a multi-digit number	$110\ r\ 4$ $12\overline{)1324}$ $\underline{12}$ 12 $\underline{12}$ 04
BIDMAS	A word which helps you to remember the order in which to carry out operations: **B**rackets, **I**ndices, **D**ivision and **M**ultiplication, **A**ddition and **S**ubtraction	$(9 \times 3 - 3) \div (2^2 + 2) - 4$ $= (27 - 3) \div (4 + 2) - 4$ $= 24 \div 6 - 4$ $= 4 - 4$ $= 0$
Long multiplication	A way of setting out workings when multiplying	317 $\times\ \ 51$ $\overline{15850}$ $+\ \overset{3}{3}17$ $\overline{16167}$ $\ \ _1$

1 Calculate these using a written method.
 a $54.3 + 16.9$ b $235.87 + 14.075$
 c $45.34 - 27.97$ d $821.4 - 67.09$

2 Calculate these using the standard written method.
 a 24×78 b 8×3.9
 c 39×4.7 d 72×3.81

3 Calculate these using an appropriate written method.
 a $243 \div 9$ b $322 \div 14$

4 What is the remainder when 515 is divided by 19?

5 Calculate these using an appropriate method. Give your answer as a decimal rounded to 1 decimal place.
 a $87 \div 9$ b $150 \div 8$
 c $47.6 \div 7$ d $205.38 \div 8$

6 Calculate these using the correct order of operations.
 a $13 + 2 \times 7$
 b $12 - 6 \div 2$
 c $(15 + 9) \times 4$
 d $34 - 2 \times (3 + 7)$
 e $4 \times 3^2 + 8 \div 2$
 f $\dfrac{(5 + 1)^2}{15 - 2 \times 3}$

7 Add brackets to these calculations to make them correct.
 a $4 + 8 \div 4 - 1 = 2$
 b $4 + 8 \div 4 - 1 = 4$
 c $6 - 3 \times 12 - 8 = 12$
 d $6 - 3 \times 12 - 8 = -6$

8 A family have the following weights
 Dad: 85.6 kg
 Mum: 58.4 kg
 Daughter: 37 kg
 Baby: 5.47 kg
 What is the total weight of the family?

9 Dillon buys 36 reams of paper.
 Each ream costs £3.82.
 What is the total cost of the paper?

10 Josh buys 18 burgers at a total cost of £22.32. What is the cost of one burger?

11 A family of 3 people budget £7.89 per person per day for food.
 What is their weekly budget for food?

12 A doctor works 6 hours a day for 5 days a week seeing patients. During this time she must see 99 patients. On average, how long can she spend with each patient? Give your answer to the nearest minute.

What next?

Score		
0 – 4		Your knowledge of this topic is still developing. To improve look at Formative test: 2B–11; MyMaths: 1007, 1026, 1041 and 1167
5 – 10		You are gaining a secure knowledge of this topic. To improve look at InvisiPen: 124, 126, 127, 129, 131, 133 and 134
11 – 12		You have mastered this topic. Well done, you are ready to progress!

Question commentary

Question 1 – Remind students, in particular with **b** and **d**, that the decimal points should be lined up in their working.

Question 2 – Students should ideally be using a standard long multiplication method but other methods will work effectively

Questions 3 to **5** – Students should ideally be using standard short division but any other appropriate method which gives the right answer should also be allowed.

Question 6 – Remind students to use BIDMAS and show intermediate stages in working where necessary.

Question 7 – Students should be asked to show working to justify their placement of brackets. This question can be set as a pairs challenge.

Question 8 – Students should be using a written method to add the weights, taking care with place value.

Questions 9 and **10** – Questions in context. Check the students are correctly selecting an operation and using a sensible method.

Question 11 – Students need to calculateo 3×7.89 $(23.67) \times 7$

Question 12 – Number of hours doctor seeing patients: 6×5 (30), convert to minutes: 30×60 (1800), $\div 99$ (18.1818...) then round.

Answers

1 a 71.2   b 249.945   c 17.37   d 754.31
2 a 1872   b 31.2   c 183.3   d 274.32
3 a 27   b 23
4 2
5 a 9.7   b 18.8   c 6.8   d 25.7
6 a 27   b 9   c 96   d 14
 e 40   f 4
7 a $(4 + 8) \div 4 - 1 = 2$
 b $(4 + 8) \div (4 - 1) = 4$
 c $(6 - 3) \times (12 - 8) = 12$
 d $6 - 3 \times (12 - 8) = -6$
8 186.47 kg
9 £137.32
10 £1.24
11 165.69
12 18 minutes

11 MyPractice

1 Calculate these using a written method.

a 257.3 − 67.9
b 540.87 + 55.9
c 45.79 + 753.4
d 1252.6 − 38.79
e 763.72 − 85.4
f 376.62 − 49.8
g 582.5 + 10.36
h 2476.2 − 78.67
i 1468.4 − 72.56
j 816.3 − 95.9
k 923.28 + 359
l 43.5 + 2186.39

2 Calculate these using the standard method.

a 15 × 6.5
b 35 × 2.7
c 16 × 4.8
d 43 × 8.5
e 39 × 9.2
f 57 × 6.7
g 38 × 7.6
h 88 × 7.7

3 Calculate these using the standard method.

a 19 × 3.68
b 27 × 4.18
c 46 × 5.53
d 62 × 7.26
e 49 × 5.69
f 74 × 8.57
g 79 × 8.37
h 99 × 9.99

4 Calculate these using an appropriate method. Give your answer as a decimal rounded to 1 decimal place where appropriate.

a 76 ÷ 8
b 40 ÷ 9
c 85 ÷ 6
d 99 ÷ 9
e 252 ÷ 18
f 314 ÷ 19
g 388 ÷ 21
h 404 ÷ 25

5 Calculate these using an appropriate method. Give your answer as a decimal rounded to 1 decimal place where appropriate.

a 36.7 ÷ 8
b 43.6 ÷ 7
c 25.6 ÷ 6
d 35.7 ÷ 9
e 50.4 ÷ 24
f 52.7 ÷ 39
g 91.6 ÷ 24
h 41.8 ÷ 17

6 Calculate

a $2 × 8 ÷ 4$
b $40 ÷ 2 ÷ 2$
c $3 × 16 − (7 − 3)$
d $216 ÷ 18 − (3^2 + 1)$
e $9 × 19 − (14 − 5)$
f $90 ÷ 50 − (5^2 − 4^2)$

7 Use a calculator to work out these calculations. Give your answers to 2 decimal places where appropriate.

a $(7 + 3.9) ÷ 5$
b $48 − 2.3^2 × 5$
c $9 × (7.2 − 1.9)^2$
d $(3 + 6.7) × 4$
e $\frac{8+5^2}{39−5^2}$
f $12^2 − 8^2$
g $\frac{256}{2^2 × 2^3}$
h $\frac{11+5^2}{7^2−13}$

Side tabs: 11a, 11b, 11c, 11d

8 An airline baggage handler has 1.35 tonnes of capacity left on a plane. Can she load all of the following packages?

car parts, 560 kg | cut flowers, 34.6 kg | a sack of letters 76 kg
two sacks of parcels 98 kg each | a crate of mangoes 425 kg

9 Darren is having trouble with his arithmetic. For each problem
i work out the correct answer
ii explain Darren's probable mistake.

a 346.95 + 564.32 — Darren's answer, 811.27
b 1.0046 − 0.045 — Darren's answer, 1.0001
c 627.43 − 451.62 — Darren's answer, 275.81
d 126.6 + 59.3 + 384.13 — Darren's answer, 4027.2

10 Fiona and Alison have part-time jobs

a Fiona gets paid £5.66 an hour and works for 12 hours. How much does she get paid?
b Alison works for 15.5 hours and earns £93.78. What is her hourly rate?
c Fiona is saving for a holiday and needs £500. How many more hours will she need to work?
d Tom works 7 hours a day for 5 days and gets paid £201.25. Is his hourly rate higher or lower than Fiona's hourly rate?

11 Depak is driving the 249 miles home from holiday.

a His average speed is 45 miles per hour. How long will it take him?
b His fuel consumption is 33 miles per gallon. How much fuel will he need?
c When full his petrol tank holds 14 gallons but at the start of this journey it is only five-eighths full. Can he make it home without having to fill up?
d Depak doesn't know it but his car has a leak, and it is losing 0.15 gallons of petrol every hour. Will he still make it home?

12 a Elliot is cooking an 8.5kg turkey for his family. The instructions say cook at a high heat for 5min per kg, then turn the heat down and cook for 25min per kg and finally cook for 30min at the high heat again. How long will it take to cook the turkey?

b After cooking the turkey must rest for 45min. It will take Elliot a further 20min to carve and serve. If Elliot wants to serve dinner at 4 o'clock in the afternoon, when should he put the turkey in the oven?

Side tabs: 11e, 11f, 11g

Question commentary

Questions 1 to **5** – Routine practice questions. Students should be encouraged to choose a method which they prefer (and get the correct answers using), rather than be directed to a specific method.

Questions 6 and **7** – Check the rules of BIDMAS are being correctly applied. If a student gets an answer wrong, encourage them to analyse where the error is.

Questions 8 to **12** – Questions in context. A mixed selection taking elements from all aspects of the chapter and encouraging students to show good comprehension skills to extract the required information before selecting an appropriate method to solve the problem. Discourage the use of calculators, although they could be used for checking answers at the end.

Answers

1	**a** 189.4	**b** 596.77	**c** 799.11	**d** 1213.81
	e 678.32	**f** 326.82	**g** 592.86	**h** 2397.53
	i 1395.84	**j** 720.4	**k** 1282.28	**l** 2229.89
2	**a** 97.5	**b** 94.5	**c** 76.8	**d** 365.5
	e 358.8	**f** 381.9	**g** 288.8	**h** 677.6
3	**a** 69.92	**b** 112.86	**c** 254.38	**d** 450.12
	e 278.81	**f** 634.18	**g** 661.23	**h** 989.01
4	**a** 9.5	**b** 4.4	**c** 14.2	**d** 11
	e 14	**f** 16.5	**g** 18.5	**h** 16.2
5	**a** 4.6	**b** 6.2	**c** 4.3	**d** 4.0
	e 2.1	**f** 1.4	**g** 3.8	**h** 2.5
6	**a** 4	**b** 10	**c** 44	
	d 2	**e** 162	**f** -7.2	
7	**a** 2.18	**b** 21.55	**c** 252.81	**d** 38.8
	e 2.36	**f** 80	**g** 8	**h** 1

8 Yes (1291.6 kg < 1.35 tonnes)

9 **a** **i** 911.27

     ii Failed to include the carry digit in 100s column

  b **i** 0.9596

     ii Misaligned digits (1.0046 – 0.0045)

  c **i** 175.81

     ii Failed to borrow from 100s column (3 + 5 + 1)

  d **i** 570.03

     ii Misaligned digits (126.6 + 59.3 + 384.13)

10 **a** £67.92

  b £6.05 per hour

  c 77 hours

  d Higher (£5.75)

11 **a** 5.5333... hrs = 5 hrs 32 min

  b 7.545454… gallons

  c Yes (8.75 > 7.55)

  d Yes (loss on full journey = 0.83 gallons and 0.83 + 7.55 < 8.75)

12 **a** 4 hrs 45 min

  b 10:10 am

Learning outcomes

G3 Draw and measure line segments and angles in geometric figures, including interpreting scale drawings
(L6)

G4 Derive and use the standard ruler and compass constructions (perpendicular bisector of a line segment, constructing a perpendicular to a given line from/at a given point, bisecting a given angle); recognise and use the perpendicular distance from a point to a line as the shortest distance to the line (L6)

Introduction	Prior knowledge
The chapter starts by using a ruler and protractor to construct triangles before developing a method that uses a pair of compasses. The construction of bisectors and perpendiculars are then covered before these constructions are contextualised through an introduction to loci. The final two sections cover scale drawing and bearings.	Students should already know how to… <ul><li>Measure lengths and angles using a ruler and protractor</li><li>Use a pair of compasses to draw circles and arcs</li></ul>

Introduction (continued)

The introduction discusses how supermarket companies make use of geometrical construction methods to find ideal sites to locate things like warehouses. For example, if there are three supermarkets located in a particular area, it would make sense for the distribution warehouse to be an equal distance from each one. This can be done by using a map (drawn to scale) and constructing the perpendicular bisectors of each pair of supermarkets. The rules of triangulation tell us that these three lines should cross at a single point and this should be our warehouse location.

The idea of triangulation as a method of location goes beyond this practical use. Map makers, navigators and the people who make mobile phone location apps and GPS all use triangulation methods to help them. In GPS, for example, the phone (or satnav) transmits a signal to three masts (or towers) or satellites, and the distance the signal travels to each one can be used to calculate (accurate to a few metres) the location of the device.

Starter problem

The starter problem requires the students to construct an equilateral triangle (using a protractor will probably be the easiest way) and then bisect each side to find the centre of the triangle. By finding the point where all if these bisectors meet, a circle can be drawn which fits exactly through the vertices of the triangle (the circumcircle, drawn using the circumcentre as the fixed point). This will be true irrespective of the type of triangle drawn and students can be invited to try the technique on a range of different triangles.

The idea of triangle 'centres' has fascinated mathematicians right back to the days of classical geometry in Ancient Greece. There are several different centres, all of which can be constructed using simple techniques.

The incentre is the meeting point of the angle bisectors of the triangle and a circle drawn using this centre as its fixed point will fit exactly inside the triangle (the incircle).

If each vertex of the triangle is joined to the midpoint of the opposite side you get what is called the centroid of the triangle, or the barycentre. This is the centre of mass of the triangle and if it was to be suspended from any point on its edge, the direct line to the ground would pass through this point.

Resources

MyMaths

Bearings	1086	Constructing shapes	1089	Constructing triangles	1090
Scale drawing	1117	Drawing loci	1147		

Online assessment		InvisiPen solutions			
Chapter test	2B–12	Constructing a triangle	371	Scale drawings	372
Formative test	2B–12	Constructing bisectors	373	Bearings	374
Summative test	2B–12	Loci	375		

Topic scheme

Teaching time = 7 lessons/3 weeks

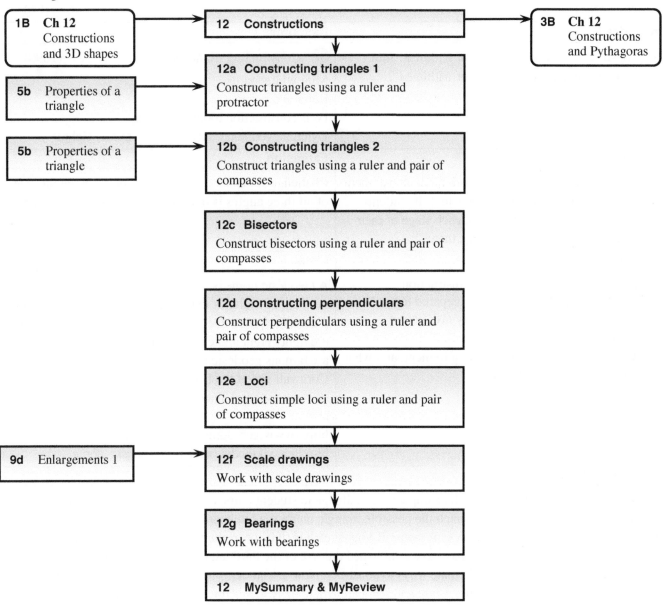

1B Ch 12
Constructions
and 3D shapes

5b Properties of a triangle

5b Properties of a triangle

9d Enlargements 1

12 Constructions

3B Ch 12
Constructions
and Pythagoras

12a Constructing triangles 1
Construct triangles using a ruler and protractor

12b Constructing triangles 2
Construct triangles using a ruler and pair of compasses

12c Bisectors
Construct bisectors using a ruler and pair of compasses

12d Constructing perpendiculars
Construct perpendiculars using a ruler and pair of compasses

12e Loci
Construct simple loci using a ruler and pair of compasses

12f Scale drawings
Work with scale drawings

12g Bearings
Work with bearings

12 MySummary & MyReview

Differentiation

Student book 2A   224 – 237

Lines and angles
Constructing a triangle 1
Constructing a triangle 2
Scale drawing

Student book 2B   210 – 229

Constructing triangles 1
Constructing triangles 2
Bisectors
Constructing perpendiculars
Loci
Scale drawings
Bearings

Student book 2C   216 – 233

Constructing triangles 1
Constructing triangles 2
Bisectors and perpendiculars
Scale drawings
Loci
Bearings

12a Constructing triangles 1

Objectives
• Construct a triangle, given two sides and the included angle (SAS) or two angles and the included side (ASA)   (L6)

Key ideas	Resources
1 Construct to an accurate level of within ±1 mm 2 Construct to an accurate level of within ±1°	Constructing triangles (1090) Mini whiteboards Ruler and protractor IWB construction tools for display Dynamic geometry software such as GeoGebra

Simplification	Extension
Where students are finding this work difficult ask them to follow the procedure given in the text. If students are paired together they can check each stage of their constructions as they work through them.	Challenge students to explain why being given the size of all three angles is insufficient to construct a triangle.

Literacy	Links
Tackle the difference between the instruction CONSTRUCT and SKETCH. Be prepared to encourage a sketch as a preliminary task before constructing. Draw attention to the 'included' requirement, and what the term means in this context.	A Geodesic dome is a structure comprised of a network of triangles that form a surface shaped like a piece of a sphere. Geodesic domes are very strong but are lightweight and can be built very quickly. There are famous geodesic domes at the Eden Project in Cornwall and at the Epcot Centre in Florida (a complete sphere) There are pictures of geodesic domes at http://www.geo-dome.co.uk/ and at http://en.wikipedia.org/wiki/Geodesic_dome

Alternative approach
Present the construction task of each example as a challenge to student pairs, using only the information (no diagram). Firstly ask students to sketch the possible triangle on mini whiteboards. Students should then compare their sketches. Raise the question does it matter if your sketch is 'left' or 'right handed? Are these shapes congruent? Why? Some students may have established the size of the third angle in the first example, which can provide further discussion, and alternate ways to construct. Now ask students to plan how they would construct their triangles, step by step. Discuss, share and compare where there are differences. Follow with all students carrying out the construction, and then checking by comparing the resulting sizes of the unknown aspects. Quick demonstrations of student suggested steps may help using your IWB tools, and/or dynamic geometry software.
It may be a helpful addition to tackle using a compass when marking a length on a line. Later in the lesson, ask students to consider whether it matters where the measure detail exits in order to establish the nature of SAS and ASA. Students can sketch triangles with the three pieces of information in different positions, compare and discuss which might be congruent or not, which can be constructed with ease, and so on.

Checkpoint
1 a If you have constructed a triangle with angles of 48°, 54°, and an included side of 5 cm, how might you check your accuracy?   (Use the third angle (78°) and measure for accuracy)   b Construct the triangle.   (Check students' constructions)

Starter – Estimating angles

Ask students to draw angles of different sizes without using a protractor, for example, 35°, 140°, 245°.

Students should then measure the angles and score points accordingly, for example, six points for an exact answer, four points for within 10° and two points for within 15°.

Teaching notes

Before starting, ensure that all students have the correct equipment and a sharp pencil.

Discuss with students the minimum amount of information required to draw a triangle without any ambiguity. Highlight the ASA and SAS cases.

Work through the ASA and SAS constructions, as a whole-class activity, taking the opportunity to check that students are following the instructions. Emphasis should be placed on the correct use of a protractor. A common error is to choose the scale that does not start at zero and thereby confuse, for example, 60° and 120°. Encourage students to consider whether the angle is acute or obtuse and whether their measurement makes sense.

Check the constructions by measuring the missing angles and sides: A = 50°, AC = 1.6 cm, AB = 4.3 cm; DF = 4.9 cm, D = 60° and F = 50°.

Plenary

Ask students to draw two different triangles, each with one right angle, one side 4 cm long and another 5 cm long. What length is the other side in each of the triangles? (3 cm, 6.4 cm) Can they explain why the triangles are different?

Exercise commentary

As an aid to checking the accuracy of constructions, ask students to measure the missing angles and lengths. Ideally angles should be accurate to ± 1° and lengths to ± 1 mm.

Question 1 – Similar to the first example. Remind students not to rub out any construction lines.

Question 2 – Similar to the second example.

Question 3 – AAS triangles: help students to realise that they will need to calculate the third angle in order to obtain an ASA triangle as in question **1**. In part **c**, check that students recognise the right angle symbol.

Question 4 – A practical example based on a scale drawing; check that students correctly convert lengths between real life and the drawing.

Question 5 – There are several ways to do this construction. Ask students to write a list of instructions explaining the process for drawing the parallelogram.

Answers

1 Check accuracy of constructions
   - **a** Isosceles   **b** Right-angled
   - **c** Equilateral
2 Check constructions. Missing lengths are
   - **a** 8 cm   **b** 9.1 cm   **c** 4.2 cm
3 **a** Third angle = 45°. Check accuracy of construction using ASA with 45°, 6 cm, 40°
   - **b** 110°. Check construction uses ASA with 43°, 5.5 cm, 110°
   - **c** 57°. Check construction uses ASA with 33°, 6.5 cm, 57°
   - **d** 70°. Check construction uses ASA with 70°, 5 cm, 70°
4 **a** Check construction of triangle using ASA with 40°, 5.5 cm, 105°
   - **b** 209.2 m
5 **a** Check accuracy of students' construction
   - **b** 9.4 cm and 3.9 cm

Objectives	
• Use straight edge and compasses to construct a triangle, given three sides (SSS) (L6)	

Key ideas	Resources
1 Introducing the use of compasses for length markers	Constructing triangles (1090) Ruler Protractor Compasses Scissors and sticky tape IWB construction tools for display Dynamic geometry software such as GeoGebra

Simplification	Extension
A number of students find using compasses difficult; allow them to draw some patterns using compasses to become more confident.	Invite students to make more elaborate constructions or to combine tetrahedra to make more complex shapes.

Literacy	Links
Establish and link back to previous work on the vocabulary congruent and similar. What is the same and what is different helps to establish and reinforce the meaning. Point out that, conventionally, construction lines and arcs are left in construction diagrams. They can provide useful guides and checking points.	A hexaflexagon is a flat hexagon-shaped paper toy that can be folded or flexed along its folds to reveal and conceal its faces alternately. It was invented in 1939 in the USA by Arthur Stone and its construction is based on equilateral triangles. There are instructions to make a hexaflexagon at http://www.flexagon.net/flexagons/hexahexaflexagon-c.pdf

Alternative approach

An approach similar to that of the previous section may be used, starting with a discussion with sketches of drawing triangles either with all three sides given or with all three angles given. Use the results to reinforce previous points about congruent shapes and similar shapes, thus establishing that 3 angles is insufficient information for accurate construction. Other points that arise may well include which length to choose as the start or base of the construction. There is common sense in choosing the longest given side for placement purposes, but discussing whether it really matters, and also if the 'left' or 'right' aspects of length matters. Use of dynamic software for quick comparisons of congruence is worthwhile. If this approach is used either leave out question 3, or use it as a checkpoint in the exercise.

Checkpoint

1 How would you use a compass to mark off a given length on a given line?
   (Appropriate responses, which should include marking a start point and the use of the ruler with the pair of compasses.)

2 Construct a triangle with side lengths 6 cm, 8 cm and 10 cm.
                              (Check students' constructions – angles should be 90°, 53° and 37°)

Starter – Take three

Ask students to make as many triangles as they can from six rods that are exactly 1 cm, 2 cm, 3 cm, 4 cm, 5 cm and 6 cm long (only one of each rod).

How many different triangles can they find? (7)

Which rod does not get used at all? (1 cm)

Can they explain why?

Teaching notes

Insist on the use of sharp pencils and do not allow students to draw with the pencil whilst in the compass. For best results, emphasise that the pencil point should be extended just longer than the point of the compass leg.

When measuring angles made with short lines it is difficult to read the size of the angle using a protractor. As an initial activity in the lesson ask students to draw two lines 4 cm long to make an angle. Ask them to measure that angle; ask, why it is difficult to measure. There are two good strategies here: either extend the length of the line so that it reaches the (circumference) edge of the protractor or use a ruler on top of the protractor to extend the line.

A useful way to demonstrate the SSS construction and to illustrate how to complete question **2** would be to construct a quadrilateral as a whole-class activity.

Plenary

The first two nets in question **5** were constructed from four equilateral triangles and both nets folded into a tetrahedron. How many different nets can students draw for these solids? A cube, a cuboid and an octahedron.

Exercise commentary

Question 1 – Similar to the example. Remind students to draw faint construction lines and not to rub them out. The measured angles provide a check of accuracy.

Question 2 – Drawing a quadrilateral using two SSS triangle constructions on a common base.

Question 3 – Take the opportunity to remind students of the difference between similar and congruent.

Question 4 – Do any students know what is the relationship between the lengths of the sides?

Question 5 – This question could be extended to include octahedrons and icosahedrons, etc., to make display items for the classroom.

Answers

1   Check accuracy of constructions
    Angles are   **a**   60°, 60°, 60°
                 b   34°, 34°, 112°
                 c   44°, 57°, 79°
2   Check constructions. Quadrilaterals are:
    kite, rhombus, parallelogram
3   The triangles can all be different sizes as no side was given. However, they are all similar
4   **a**   Check construction
    b   It is right-angled
5   **a**   Tetrahedron (triangular-based pyramid)
    b   Tetrahedron
    c   Square-based pyramid

Objectives

- Use straight edge and compasses to construct
  - the midpoint and perpendicular bisector of a line segment (L6)
  - the bisector of an angle (L6)

Key ideas	Resources
1 Understanding and constructing an angle bisector 2 Understanding and constructing a perpendicular bisector	Constructing shapes (1089) Compasses Ruler

Simplification	Extension
Group together the students who are finding construction difficult. This will allow you the opportunity to support their needs whilst other students work through other questions. In pairs ask one student to explain to the other how he or she is completing the bisection of the angle. The second student can make comments and highlight errors. Reverse the roles for constructing a perpendicular line.	Give students a reflex angle, can they construct an angle bisector? Using their answer to question **5** as a guide, can they explain why their construction works? Further challenges: construct an angle of 45°; 30° 15° without a protractor.

Literacy	Links
Compare the words bisect and dissect. Examine the prefixes 'bi-' and 'dis-'. Compare with words that also have these prefixes thus establishing 'dis' – meaning split/divide; 'bi' – meaning two equal parts. Remind students of the meaning of perpendicular, taking care that it is not associated with being vertical – a frequent misconception of some students.	Bring in some dictionaries for the class to use. 'Bi-' is a Latin prefix meaning 'two'. How many words can the class find that begin with 'bi-'? What is the connection with the number two?

Alternative approach

Ask students, in pairs, to try to work out how to construct a rhombus. You may add detail of a particular rhombus if/where the students are more comfortable with greater structure. Establish possible steps, so students can construct the rhombus. Request that they now explore the diagonals, and what effect the diagonal has on the interior angles. Now request that they use their findings to come up with steps for constructing angle bisectors. Check and share the results, probing understanding through questions such as would the diagonals of a parallelogram bisect. Perpendicular bisector construction may also be posed as a challenge.

Checkpoint

1 **a** Describe how you could construct an angle of 45° without using a protractor.
(Appropriate responses establishing constructing a perpendicular, hence 90°, then bisecting it.)

   b Construct a 45° angle. (Check by measurement)

Starter – Quad bingo

Ask students to draw a 3 × 3 grid and enter nine angles from the following list:

30°, 35°, 40°, 45°, 50°, 55°, 60°, 65°, 70°, 75°, 80°, 85°, 90°, 95°, 100°, 105°, 110°, 115°, 120°, 125°.

Ask questions, for example, one of the angles in a rhombus is 135°, what is the smallest angle? (45°)

Winner is the first student to cross out all nine angles.

Teaching notes

Construction often proves a difficult topic to share with students as some are very capable and others struggle. Rather than showing a construction stage by stage (with students copying) allow them to follow instructions such as in the examples in the student book. They are then able to work at their own speed. Students who are confident can either help those who struggle or complete a further example of their own. As a teacher you will have more time to help those who genuinely need it.

Plenary

In pairs, ask students to agree three or four tips on how to produce the most accurate work when using a compass. Take tips from each pair to share with the class.

Exercise commentary

Remind students that all construction lines should be left to be seen.

Questions 1 and **2** – The previous page models how to do these constructions.

Question 3 – Ensure that students do not guess at right angles but use a protractor at each corner to draw the initial rectangle. In an accurate diagram, the perpendicular bisectors of opposite sides should coincide to form the lines of symmetry.

Question 4 – If the construction is accurate the three bisectors will pass through a single point – the centre of the inscribed circle. The radius will have to be established by 'inspection'.

Question 5 – If the pairs of compasses are reset a kite and scalene triangles will result, otherwise a rhombus and isosceles triangles. Suggest that the mathematical explanation is given as a series of bullet points.

Question 6 – To draw the small circles, it is only necessary to bisect OA as OB, OC and OD are all the same length.

Question 7 – See **checkpoint** question. This can be extended to include constructing 30° angles (bisect the angle in an equilateral triangle) or angles of 22.5°, 15°, etc.

Answers

1   Check constructions
2   Check constructions
3   **a, b**   Check constructions
    c   The 2 lines of symmetry coincide with the perpendicular bisectors
4   Check constructions
5   **a**   *OACB* is a rhombus (but note that it could be a kite – this would still give the angle bisector.)
        As constructed, *OAC* and *OBC* are isosceles triangles
    b   Because the diagonals of a rhombus are lines of symmetry and therefore bisect the angles
6   Check constructions
7   Check constructions

Objectives	

• Use straight edge and compass to construct
   – the perpendicular from a point to a line
   – the perpendicular from a point on a line
	(L6)
	(L6)

Key ideas	Resources
1 Recognising the different nature of positioning a perpendicular to a line	Constructing shapes (1089) Ruler Compasses Protractor Squared paper Dynamic Geometry Software.

Simplification	Extension
Students who are unable to complete this construction should be given more practice at constructing triangles and quadrilaterals from given lengths and angles.	Ask students to draw a (scalene) triangle about 10 cm across, then construct the perpendiculars from each vertex to the opposite side. In an accurate construction all three lines will pass through a single point: the orthocentre. (If the triangle is obtuse, this will be outside the original triangle.) Students should be able to measure the 'altitudes' and find the area of the triangle in three different ways.

Literacy	Links
Make sure that students use the vocabulary correctly when describing the steps they take.	Perpendicular recording is a new technology that increases the storage capacity of hard drives. It is predicted that perpendicular recording will allow information densities of up to around 1000 Gb/in^2 compared with 100–200 Gb/in^2 using conventional technology. There is an amusing video describing perpendicular recording at http://www.hitachigst.com/hdd/research/recording_head/pr/PerpendicularAnimation.html

Alternative approach
Set the required constructions into an attractive design that needs to be replicated by the students. This can be done with dynamic geometry software for display purposes, and/or for printing off as references for the students. The design may also make use of some of the other techniques met earlier in the chapter.

Checkpoint
1 Describe how you would draw a perpendicular on a given line going through a given point. (Appropriate responses establishing equal arcs either side of the given point; setting compasses at a length > half, and marking arcs above or below the line, etc.) 2 ABC is a straight line such that AB = 3 cm and BC = 5 cm. Construct a perpendicular to the line ABC passing through B.   (Check students' constructions)

Starter – Clock angles

Ask students to give the angle between the hour and minute hands at the following times:

7:00, 4:00, 9:30, 1:30, 4:30 and 3:15

Hint: The hour hand moves as well as the minute hand! (Answers: 150° or 210°, 120°, 105°, 135°, 45° and 7.5°)

Teaching notes

If students have completed the previous topic they should be confident with the use of a pair of compasses. Organise students to work in pairs and set this challenge before they look in the textbook. Draw a diagonal line and mark a point about 5 cm away – can they find the shortest distance from this point to the line? At first, use a ruler only. Then explain that you need to develop a mathematical method to be exactly correct and they can use a ruler and compasses. Anticipate that at this point some will draw an arc that is approximately a tangent with the line; develop this work so that students are able to complete the construction as shown in the example. This method will allow for discussion and an understanding of constructing a perpendicular to a line from a point.

Note that, when constructing a perpendicular to a line, it is not strictly necessary to draw intersecting arcs both above and below the line as one pair and the point will suffice.

Plenary

Draw a triangle with perpendiculars drawn from two vertices to the opposite sides. Supply lengths for the sides of the triangle and one of the perpendiculars. Can the students work out the length (height) of the other perpendicular line? (Hint at the area of the triangle.) Can they say what the length of the third perpendicular line is?

Exercise commentary

Questions 1 and **2** – The previous page models how to do these constructions.

Question 3 – Use a 2 cm square grid to avoid a tiny diagram. As a further challenge, ask students to find the gradients of the two lines; do they notice anything?

Question 4 – In an accurate diagram AC = AD = 4.2 cm and BC = BD = 6.7 cm.

Question 5 – In an accurate diagram all three perpendiculars (which coincide with the angle bisectors) will pass through a single point, the centre of the inscribing and circumscribing circles.

Question 6 – The perpendiculars coincide at a single point. Encourage students to check each other's drawings.

Answers

1   Check construction. Angle $PXB = 90°$
2   Check construction
3   **a, b**   Check construction
    c   2.7 units
4   Check construction
    a   A kite
    b $A = 90°$, $B = 53°$, $C = D = 108.5°$
5   **a, b** Check constructions
    c   The lines of symmetry are the three perpendiculars constructed in **b**
6   The perpendiculars intersect at exactly one point

Objectives

- Find simple loci, both by reasoning and using ICT, to produce shapes and paths   (L6/7)

Key ideas	Resources
1 Understanding that loci is about exploring the paths traced by a moving point 2 Beginning to visualise possible resulting paths from simple conditions given	Drawing loci (1147) Metre rule; ruler; compasses Squared paper Mini whiteboards Short Problems: http://nrich.maths.org/9369 Rolling Around; and/or Rolling, rolling, rolling: http://nrich.maths.org/8486 Loci problems & demos, with GeoGebra: http://www.tes.co.uk/teaching-resource/Loci-6082780/ Visualisations on Loci: http://www.nationalstemcentre.org.uk/elibrary/resource/4628/teaching-mental-maths-from-level-five-geometry

Simplification	Extension
Where students are unable to construct the exact answer to the questions, allow them to sketch the answer. This will allow them to understand the concept of loci and, where appropriate, they can be referred back to the example in the previous exercises to copy the construction.	Give students two points 6 cm apart. Can they find all the positions which are within 4 cm of each point? Can they design other questions like this?

Literacy	Links
Both spelling and pronunciation of the word loci and its singular locus should be addressed. There tends to be two acceptable ways to pronounce loci, but you may need to check for consistent use within your own department or school.	Drinking rocking birds (or dippy ducks) are toys that rock backwards and forwards and appear to drink from a glass of water. The bird consists of two glass bulbs joined by a tube filled with a coloured liquid. There is a video of a drinking bird and an explanation of how it works at http://www.Icefoundry.org/how-the-drinking-bird-works.php

Alternative approach

This concept is quite a challenging one for many students, so it is helpful to take a practical approach and let students work in 2s or 3s to support each other. Begin by describing some very simple situations, such as those given in question 1, and encourage the students to trace what they think will be the paths in the air with their finger. Follow this up with sketching on mini whiteboards. People maths activities are very helpful. So also is the use of marking the positions of a moving point with counters. Different scenarios or problems can be given in card form for a student group to work on. A variety of strategies including people maths, counter marking/tracing and sketching can be applied using for example visualisations from Teaching Mental Mathematics.. Using a moving demonstration, for example, with GeoGebra, following discussion about each scenario will help to establish the concept.

Checkpoint

1 a When going on a walk, Ben steers himself between two trees so that his distance from one is equal to his distance from the other at all times. What does his path look like in relation to these two trees?

(A straight line)

 b How might this path be best described?   (As a perpendicular bisector of the line linking the two trees)

Ask students to find a triangle where all the angles are square numbers. (100°, 64°, 16°)

Can they find any quadrilaterals where all the angles are square numbers? (144°, 100°, 100°, 16° and others.)

Teaching notes

It is important for students to realise that a locus of points is actually a mathematical way of describing the path of a moving object and the examples given should be discussed. It is also vital that they are allowed to consider the answer before they draw it accurately and, where appropriate, students should be asked to sketch a solution in their books.

Plenary

Clear a space in your classroom – move a few desks – for a people maths activity.

- Have one person stand in the middle. Ask ten others to stand one metre away (they will make a circle of types)

- Have a 1 metre ruler – students have to stand one metre away from it – they can stand either side but they will also need to create semicircles around the end point

- Have two students stand 3 m apart – other students have to stand equal distances away from both – this creates a line of students across the middle.

Exercise commentary

Question 1 – Similar to the three illustrations. Give students 5 minutes to work in pairs and then discuss their answers, especially parts **d** and **e**.

Question 2 – The locus requires the angle bisector construction.

Question 3 – Similar to the second example.

Question 4 – Similar to the first example. Encourage students to pick a point, P, on the perpendicular bisector and measure the distances AP and PB.

Question 5 – The locus is a parallel line mid-way between those given. Accurate construction of the locus may prove challenging. It can be drawn by constructing a (mutually) perpendicular transversal and then its perpendicular bisector.

Question 6 – Ensure that the workings are tidy as the ladder will need to be drawn repeatedly. If the man was not at the centre of the ladder, an ellipse would result.

Question 7 – Students should be able to establish that it is a series of curves, each one starting and finishing when the stone 'hits' the ground.

Question 8 – Constructions of the perpendicular bisector of AB and the angle bisector of BAC will lead to a single common point.

Answers

1. **a** A vertical straight line
   b A circle
   c A vertical straight line
   d A series of straight lines and curves
   e A series of straight lines and curves
2. **a** Check students' drawing of angle
   b Check that the locus constructed is the angle bisector of angle AOB.
3. Check that the locus is a circle, centre the fixed point, radius 3 cm
4. Check that the locus constructed is the perpendicular bisector of AB
5. Another parallel line, 2 cm from both of the originals.
6. Discuss students' results. Should get a curve that is a circle radius half the length of the ladder.
7. Check students' drawings. The path should be a series of curves (cycloids) on a straight line. Discuss why path is not circular
8. With A the origin, P equidistant from AB and AC => P lies on line $y = x$. Hence $P = (3, 3)$.

Objectives	
• Make scale drawings	(L6)

Key ideas	Resources
1 Identify and use scale information as a scale factor 2 Draw simple scale drawings to a given scale	Scale drawing (1117) Ruler and protractor Photographic Enlargement ITP: http://www.nationalstemcentre.org.uk/elibrary/resource/4982/year-nine-proportional-reasoning-mini-pack

Simplification	Extension
Make this a real activity – students find it difficult to relate book work to real life. How would they draw a scale plan of the classroom on a piece of squared paper? If the dimensions of the classroom are 7 m × 6 m what would be a good scale to use (1 cm : 1 m or 1 cm : 50 cm?).	Give students a plan of the school (or part of it) – can they work out the scale factor reduction? Having found the scale for the plan can they work out the dimensions for some of the corridors/halls/rooms and check? It is likely that these will not be accurate, raising the question of how the plan could be improved.

Literacy	Links
Rehearse vocabulary linked with enlargement – similar and congruent, and connect the ideas of scale and scale factor. Scale notation needs adequate time spent on it, particularly as seen in commonly used maps. Examine the use made of the proportional reasoning notation involving ratio symbols. Students may well find this notation challenging, for example, 1 : 25 000 for an Explorer Map, but with support this can be translated into 1 cm represents 250 m.	Model railways are available in different gauges. OO gauge means that the model is built to a scale of 1 : 76, or 1 cm on the model represents a distance of 76 cm in real life. 1 cm on an N gauge model represents a distance of 146 cm. If an N gauge model locomotive is 5 cm long, how long is the real-life locomotive?

Alternative approach

If liaison takes place with geography, the OS maps can provide an initial and tangible example of scale drawings from which to generate further references from the students. Photographs make good sources of scale drawings, particularly as the edge lengths are clear. An interactive teaching programme looking at 3 photograph outlines provides a good demonstration and activity source (see Resources). Shadows are another good source, as well as any projection equipment, which is likely to be readily available in the classroom. Strengthen proportional reasoning by asking students to identify the multiplicative or scale factor from any given scales.

Checkpoint

1 The London Eye is 135 metres tall and has a diameter of 120 metres. On a scale drawing of the wheel, the radius of the circle is 3 cm.

    a What is the scale of the drawing?   (1 cm represents 20 m; or 1 : 2000)

    b How tall, in the drawing, would the London Eye be?   (6.75 cm)

Starter – Shape pairs

Write the following list of shapes, orders of rotation and line symmetries on the board: regular hexagon, isosceles triangle, rectangle, regular pentagon, equilateral triangle, square, order 1, 3 lines, 6 lines, order 2, 4 lines, order 5.

Challenge students to match up the pairs in the shortest possible time. Ask students which shapes out of the six will not tessellate. (Pentagon)

Teaching notes

As a whole-class introductory activity, ask students where they have seen scale factors used. Maps may be the common answer but scale factors are all around us: drawings in books, photographs, posters, toy/model cars, etc. It is important to highlight that all dimensions in scale factor reductions and enlargements are in proportion with the original.

As a practical activity for all, ask students to draw a scale factor reduction of their desk (table) – where students are sharing a table they should work together. To show this diagram in their book or on paper what would be a sensible scale to use? 1 cm for 10 cm? or 1 cm for 20 cm? or …? The scale drawing can then be used to 'predict' the length of the desk's diagonal; how accurate is their prediction compared to an actual measurement?

Plenary

Show a poster (or projection) of a real-life scene; it could be of buildings in New York or London. What do students think is the scale factor reduction? How can you work it out? How close was your estimate?

Exercise commentary

Question 1 – Similar to the example part **a**. Clarify the meanings of radius and diameter if necessary.

Question 2 – Similar to the example part **b**.

Question 3 – A point for discussion is how accurately to quote the answer. To the nearest metre is sensible but why? Could students give a more accurate answer based on their diagram? How accurately do they think 80 m and 50 m are measured?

Question 4 – Have a ready supply of heights for other tall buildings. What would be a sensible scale for the tallest skyscraper in the world? The Burj Khalifa in Dubai is 828 m tall. Students could be asked to research the history of tall buildings as a homework activity.

Answers

1

	Real life	Scale drawing
a	40 cm	2 cm
b	80 cm	4 cm
c	60 cm	3 cm
d	120 cm	6 cm
e	90 cm	4.5 cm

2 **a** 3.3 cm   **b** 3.3 m, 36°

3 **a** Check scale drawing. Lengths should be 8 cm and 5 cm

   b 94.3 m

4 Check heights are as follows:
   Blackpool Tower 3 cm
   The Shard 6 cm
   Chamberlain Clock 2 cm
   Sutton Coldfield Mast 5 cm
   Rotunda 1.6 cm

12g Bearings

Objectives	
• Use bearings to specify direction	(L6)

Key ideas	Resources
1 Know that all bearings are measured from North 2 Know that bearings are given as 3-figure/digit amounts of turn in a clockwise direction	Bearings (1086) 360° angle indicator Ruler Chippy's Journeys (NRICH) : http://nrich.maths.org/2813

Simplification	Extension
Use an enlarged version of the compass rose in question **2** so that students can measure the bearings with a protractor. As students gain confidence, add points that do not coincide with the cardinal directions before removing the compass rose altogether.	Use the map with question **1**, ask students to find the bearings of Church, College and Westwick farm from Beech Hill. Then set them the task of writing three questions on bearings using the map – with a partner exchange questions, answer them and discuss what makes a good question.

Literacy	Links
Convention and notation of bearings should be explicitly shared with students: namely the three figures, the North starting point and the clockwise direction. Refer to GPS locations and directions 'over the air' to planes and/or ships.	Live webcams for Mount Snowdon can be viewed at http://www.bbc.co.uk/wales/northwest/sites/webcams/pages/snowdon.shtml

Alternative approach
The resource Chippy's Journeys can provide a simple introduction. Students generally grasp the ideas in this section quite quickly, but may struggle when any journey includes more than one leg. Journeys of student to student in the classroom can help overcome the tendency for students to measure any bearing from the previous journey line rather than North. Some students may be familiar with the use compass bearings as a result of an interest in orienteering or camping. Explore if this is the case, and use their expertise. OS maps of the locality can be employed for tracing a route linking some familiar of important local features. There may be potential to liaise with Geography and link work here.

Checkpoint
1 In order to travel to a certain place, a journey requires a bearing of 165°.   When making the return journey, what bearing is required?   (345°)

Starter – Directions

Ask students to visualise the following shape:

A line 5 cm long towards N, then 4 cm in SE direction, then 4 cm in NE direction, finally 5 cm towards S.

Ask students to sketch what they have visualised. (The letter M)

Students can then make up their own direction puzzle.

Teaching notes

Using a 360° angle indicator is helpful as students are able to start at 0 and rotate the indicator (clockwise) to show the bearing. It is possible to use a protractor but when the bearing is more than 180°, students need to measure from the 180° line and add on the extra angle.

After explaining the conventions for measuring and quoting bearings, ask for a volunteer. Position the volunteer at the entrance to the classroom and define the front of the class as North. Go around the class asking students to give a series of bearings and number of paces for the volunteer to follow so that his or her route will take him or her to the student's desk.

Plenary

In pairs, ask students to, use the map in question **1**, to find the bearings from each of the places to the Middle School. For example, the bearing of College from Middle School is 100°; the bearing of Middle School from the College is 280°. When they have found all the bearings, ask students if they can find a quick way of working out the reverse bearings. Most think that you take away the original bearing from 360° – instead you need to add the original bearing on to 180° (modulo 360°).

Exercise commentary

Ensure that students measure angles in a clockwise direction, as opposed to the anticlockwise direction used for rotations.

Question 1 – Similar to the example. Ask students to write full answers: 'the bearing of the College is 100° from the Middle School'.

Question 2 – This can be related to geography. It can also be extended to include bearings such as NNE, ENE, etc. Check that students start the three-figure bearings with a 0 where necessary.

Question 3 – Suggest students look at their answers to question **1** to get an idea of the approximate directions of the bearings.

Question 4 – For part **c**, students may need to be reminded of parallel line theorems. You could challenge students to find Edensor which is on a bearing of 070° from Bakewell and 195° from Baslow.

Question 5 – Students will need to establish a new North line after constructing the first stage of the journey. Beware of students who construct the second part of the journey from the original start point.

Answers

1 a College   **b** Windmill   **c** Westwick Farm
   d Moss Farm   **e** Well   **f** Church
   g Camping barn   **h** Bus Station **i** Beech Hill
   j Youth Hostel

2

Direction	N	NE	E	SE
Bearing	360°	045°	090°	135°

Direction	S	SW	W	NW
Bearing	180°	225°	270°	315°

3 Check students' constructions
4   **a** Check scale drawing
    b 225°
    c Measuring from North gives the required bearing as 180° + 45° (alternate angle of 45°)
5   **a** Check scale drawing
    b **i** 17.2 km
      ii 102.7°

Key outcomes	Quick check
Construct triangles and quadrilaterals accurately. L6	Construct a triangle with side lengths 5 cm, 12 cm and 13 cm. (Check students' constructions – angles should be 90°, 23° and 67°)
Construct angle bisectors, perpendicular bisectors and perpendicular lines. L6	Draw a line *AB* 7 cm long. Construct **a** The perpendicular bisector of *AB* **b** A perpendicular line through *A* **c** The angle bisector of the resulting right angle at *A*. (Check students' constructions)
Describe the locus of a point and draw it accurately. L7	**a** Describe the locus of the point equidistant from two fixed points *C* and *D*. (Perpendicular bisector) **b** Describe the locus of points 4 cm from a fixed point *X*. (Circle, centred on *X*, radius 4 cm)
Use scale drawings to represent real-life objects. L6	A sports car is 4 m in length. A scale drawing shows the length as 20 cm. **a** What is the scale of the drawing? (1 : 20) **b** If the car is 4 cm tall in the drawing, how tall is it in real life? (0.8 m)
Use bearings to specify direction. L6	The bearing of Arcminster from Barcminster is 046°. What is the bearing from Barcminster to Arcminster? (226°)

⊞ MyMaths extra support

Lesson/online homework		Description
Measuring angles	1081 L5	Using a protractor to measure acute and obtuse angles
Map scales	1103 L5	Using ratio notation for map scales
Measuring lengths	1146 L3	An interactive ruler to test measuring skills

MyReview

Check out

You should now be able to ...

Test it ➡
Questions

✓	Construct triangles and quadrilaterals accurately.	1
✓	Construct angle bisectors, perpendicular bisectors and perpendicular lines.	2–5
✓	Describe the locus of a point and draw it accurately.	6, 7
✓	Use scale drawings to represent real life objects.	8
✓	Use bearings to specify direction.	9

Language	Meaning	Example
Construct	To draw a shape accurately using a ruler, protractor and pair of compasses	Drawing an SAS triangle is a construction
Perpendicular	At right angles	Horizontal and vertical lines are perpendicular
Bisect	To divide into two equally	The midpoint of a straight line bisects it
Locus (plural loci)	The locus of an object is its path.	A circle is the locus of points equidistant from a fixed point
Equidistant	The same distance from a given point	
Bearing	An angle, measured clockwise from north and quoted using three figures, used to describe a direction	East has a bearing 090° West has a bearing 270°
Scale drawing	A diagram which is used to accurately represent real life objects	Architects' plans are scale drawings of buildings

1 Construct these triangles.

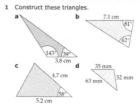

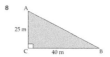

2 a Use your protractor to draw an angle of 130°.
  b Use a pair of compasses to construct the angle bisector.

3 a Draw a line AB, so that AB = 9 cm.
  b Using a pair of compasses, construct the perpendicular bisector of AB.

4 a Draw a line AB so that AB = 11 cm.
  b Mark the point P on AB so that AP = 4 cm.
  c Construct the perpendicular to AB passing through P.

5 Copy the diagram on square grid paper. Construct the perpendicular from the point (4, 2) to the line.

6 a Draw a line AB where AB = 5 cm.
  b Construct the locus of a point that is 2 cm from the line AB.

7 a Use your protractor to draw an angle AOB of 70°.

  b Construct the locus of a point that is equidistant from OA and OB.

8

  a Construct a scale drawing of this triangle using a scale of 1 cm to represent 5 m.
  b Calculate the real life length of AB to the nearest metre.

9 Draw bearings at
  a 042°   b 304°

What next?

Score		
0 – 3	Your knowledge of this topic is still developing. To improve look at Formative test: 2B-12; MyMaths: 1086, 1089, 1090, 1117 and 1147
4 – 7	You are gaining a secure knowledge of this topic. To improve look at InvisiPen: 371, 372, 373, 374 and 375
8 – 9	You have mastered this topic. Well done, you are ready to progress!

⠿ **MyMaths**.co.uk

Question commentary

Ensure students have a protractor, rule, a pair of compasses and a sharp pencil that fits into them. Allow ±1° and ±1 mm on all constructions.

Question 1 – Students will need to select the appropriate 'tools' for each construction and may need to carry out an initial calculation (part **b**).

Questions 2 to 7 – Standard constructions. Emphasise that construction lines should be left on the diagrams and that students will need to choose appropriate methods from those studied in the chapter. The diagram in question **5** may need enlarging as students copy it onto their paper.

Question 8 – Measurement on the diagram should be 9.4 cm so 9.4 × 5 (m) for the real-life measurement.

Question 9 – For part **b** either the acute or reflex angle could be labelled.

Answers

1   a   Check ASA 143°, 3.8 cm, 39°
   b   Check ASA 81°, 7.1 cm, 37°
   c   Check SAS 5.2 cm, 58°, 4.7 cm
   d   Check SSS 63 mm, 52 mm, 35 mm
2   a   Angle of 130°   b   Angle of 65°
3   a   Line of 9 cm, labelled AB
   b   Check 90° angle and 4.5 cm length along AB
4   a   Line of 11 cm, labelled AB
   b   Point P on AB so that AP = 4 cm
   c   Check 90° angle at P
5   Check students' diagrams. Perpendicular should bisect line at (2.5, 3.5)
6   a, b   Region bounded by two lines parallel to AB, one 2 cm above and the other 2 cm below AB
7   a   Angle of 70°   b   Bisected angle of 35°
8   a   Right-angled triangle, height 5 cm, length 8 cm
   b   47 m
9   a   An angle of 42°   b   An angle of 304°

12 MyPractice

1 Construct these triangles.
Measure the lengths of the sides and calculate the perimeter of each triangle.

a

64°   44°
7.5 cm

b

115°   8 cm
6.5 cm

c

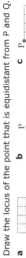

54°
5.5 cm

2 Construct these triangles, using ruler and compasses.
State the mathematical name of each triangle.

a

25 mm   35 mm
30 mm

b

3 cm   4.5 cm
3 cm

c

6.5 cm   6 cm
2.5 cm

3 a Draw a large triangle.
b Construct the perpendicular bisector for each of the three sides.
c Draw a circle passing through the vertices of the triangle, using the point of intersection as the centre.

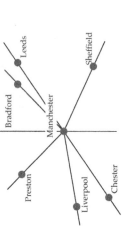

4 Copy this diagram.
Using compasses, construct a vertical wall through the dot to separate the giraffe from the person.

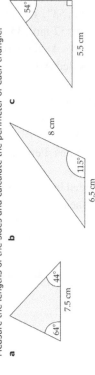

5 Copy the diagrams on square grid paper.
Draw the locus of the point that is equidistant from P and Q.

a

P
Q

b

P
Q

c

P
Q

> Equidistant means 'equal length'.

6 A sales brochure shows a scale drawing of a door.
The scale is 1 cm represents 50 cm.
Calculate
a the height
b the width
c the area of the real door.

4 cm
1.5 cm →
Scale: 1 cm represents 50 cm

7 Measure the three-figure bearings of these places from Manchester.

a Leeds   **b** Liverpool   **c** Sheffield
d Preston   **e** Bradford   **f** Chester

N
Bradford
Leeds
Manchester
Sheffield
Preston
Liverpool
Chester

Question commentary

Question 1 – Only protractor and ruler are required for each part but students will need to do an initial calculation for part **c**.

Question 2 – Emphasise that construction lines should be left on the diagrams and that a pair of compasses is required for this question.

Questions 3 to **5** – Standard constructions. Students should refer to the instructions in the chapter if they need reminding of the steps.

Question 6 – No scale drawing should be required. All of the given lengths can be converted using the scale provided.

Question 7 – A protractor is needed here. All of the bearings should be given in three-figure form. As an extension, the back-bearings could be asked for.

Answers

1 Check constructions
   a 5.5 cm, 7.1 cm, 20.1 cm
   b 12.3 cm, 26.8 cm
   c 4.0 cm, 6.8 cm, 16.3 cm
2 a Check construction Scalene
   b Check construction Isosceles
   c Check construction Right-angled
3 Check construction
4 Check that a perpendicular to the base line has been constructed from the dot
5 Check diagrams. In each case locus is the perpendicular bisector of PQ
6 a 2 m   b 0.75 m   c 1.5 m^2
7 a 055°   b 260°   c 115°
   d 315°   e 045°   f 235°

Related lessons		Resources	
Properties of a triangle	5b	Angle reasoning	(1080)
Properties of a quadrilateral	5d	Interior exterior angles	(1100)
Congruent shapes	5f	Examples of folded figures	
		Prepared squares of paper	
		Other examples of origami from books, etc.	
Simplification		**Extension**	
Prepared origami squares can be used to help students get started with the activities. Pre-folded templates can also be given to students.		Students could be challenged to make further origami shapes from instructions in books or found on the internet. Some students may already be able to make origami patterns and these students could be used as 'experts' to teach others.	
Links			

Links could be made to design technology, considering the practical uses of folding. For example, there has been much research on effective ways of folding a map so that adjacent sections can be made visible without unfolding the whole map and one such fold has been used with large solar panel arrays on satellites where the panel opens up once the satellite is in orbit. See:

http://math.serenevy.net/?page=Origami-ApplicationLinks

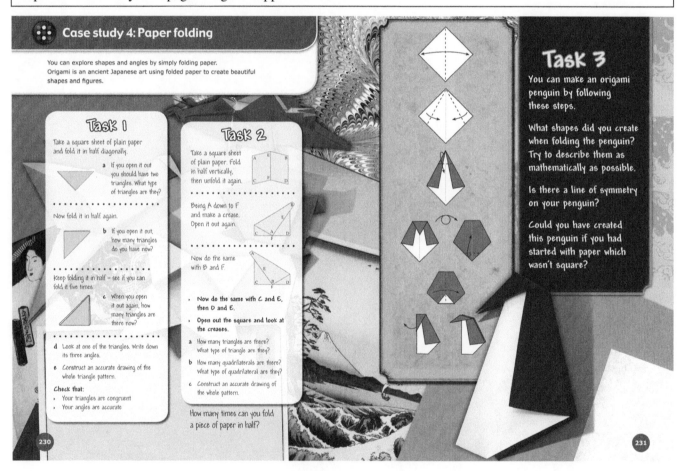

Teaching notes

Origami is the art of paper folding and has been practised in Japan since the 17th century. It uses a combination of folds and creases to produce designs from paper, without cutting or sticking. This case study looks at several such designs and gives students the opportunity to consider the shapes within them.

Task 1

Encourage students to fold their paper using sharp creases. This will mean that the triangles formed are easy to see. Can the students see other sizes of triangle as well as the small ones created from the repeated folding?

Task 2

Again, stress the importance of sharp folds. Students should be encouraged to compare their patterns with others to check the constructions and also to enable discussion of the end results.

Task 3

Look at the pictures showing how to make a penguin. Check that the students understand how they show the stages for folding the paper. Ask them to use the instructions to make a penguin, stressing the importance of making sharp folds. When they have made their penguins, ask them to answer the questions in the panel. To answer the last question, they might want to try folding a penguin from a rectangular piece of paper. When they have had sufficient time, discuss their answers.

Answers

1   a   Isosceles

    b   4

    c   32

    d   45°, 45°, 90°

    e   Students' own drawings

2   a   4; Isosceles

    b   8; Trapeziums

    c   Students' own drawings

3   Discuss task with students

MyAssessment 3

These questions will test you on your knowledge of the topics in chapters 9 to 12.
They give you practice in the types of questions that you may eventually be given in your
GCSE exams. There are 80 marks in total.

1 Copy this diagram onto square grid paper.

 a Draw the image of shape A after reflecting
   it in the x-axis. Label the image B. (2 marks)
 b Draw the image of shape B after
   rotating it through 180° clockwise
   about the point X. Label the image C. (2 marks)
 c Draw the image of the shape C after
   translating it 4 units up.
   Label the image D. (1 mark)
 d What is the connection between
   shape A and shape D? (2 marks)

2 Copy these shapes onto square
  grid paper.
 a Draw any lines of symmetry
   on each of the shapes. (3 marks)
 b State the order of rotational
   symmetry of each shape. (3 marks)

3 The quadrilateral ABCD is enlarged
  to give the quadrilateral A'B'C'D'
  Copy the diagram on square
  grid paper.
 a By drawing lines find the point of
   intersection and mark this point O.
 b Measure the lines OA and OA'
   and OB, OB' to determine the
   scale factor. (4 marks)

   (3 marks)

4 Solve these equations.
 a h + 12 = 32 (1 mark)
 b 12 = j + 11 (1 mark)
 c g/6 = 4 (1 mark)
 d 2x + 7 = x + 10 (1 mark)

5 Solve these equations by expanding the brackets.
 a 3(d + 2) = 18 (2 marks)
 b 6(4t − 1) = 42 (2 marks)
 c 5(r − 1) = 2r + 4 (3 marks)
 d 4(2w + 6) = 5(6w − 4) (4 marks)

6 One of the equations used to solve motion problems is 2s = t × (u + v)
  Work out the value of s if u = 4, v = 10 and t = 5. (4 marks)

7 Calculate these using a written method.
 a 9.34 + 3.6
 b 86.4 − 64.9
 c 62.76 + 12.09 + 49.3
 d 985.2 − 104.6 (4 marks)

8 Use the standard method to calculate these. Give an estimate first.
 a 8 × 4.65
 b 16 × 2.73 (4 marks)

9 Calculate these using an appropriate method. Where appropriate,
  give your answer to 1 decimal place. Give an estimate first.
 a 76.3 ÷ 9
 b 251 ÷ 15
 c 34.6 ÷ 4
 d 234.3 ÷ 21 (8 marks)

10 Use a calculator to work out these.
   Where appropriate, give your answer to 2dp.
 a 84 − 5.2² × 2
 b (5 + 2³)/(64 − 7²) (4 marks)

11 A scale drawing of the Nepalese flag
   is being made.

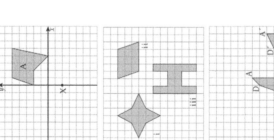

 a Construct an accurate copy
   using a ruler and a protractor. (4 marks)
 b Measure the length of the
   perimeter. (1 mark)

12 a Draw a line PQ so that
     PQ = 10cm
     Mark the point O on PQ so that PO = 4cm. (2 marks)
 b Construct the perpendicular bisector of PQ passing through O.
   Label this line RS and make OR = OS = 5cm. (3 marks)
 c Join the points P, R, Q, S to form a quadrilateral.
   What is the mathematical name given to this shape PRQS? (1 mark)
 d Measure the angles at P, Q, R and S. (4 marks)

13 A helicopter landing area (H) is being constructed 100m away
   from the entrance to the depot (D) and at a bearing of
   160° from the depot. There is an exclusion zone around the
   helicopter landing point of 20m.
 a Draw an accurate diagram to show the positions of H and D.
   Use a scale of 1cm = 10m. (2 marks)
 b Draw the locus of points that represents the helicopter
   exclusion zone. (2 marks)
 c A wall extends south from the depot for over 200m.
   What is the closest distance between this wall and the
   helicopter exclusion zone? (1 mark)

MyMaths.co.uk

Mark scheme

Questions 1 – 7 marks

a 2 Check students' drawings

b 2 Check students' drawings

c 1 Check students' drawings

d 2 The final shape is a reflection; in the *y*-axis; which acts as a mirror line

Questions 2 – 6 marks

a i 1 4 lines of symmetry

ii 1 no lines of symmetry

iii 1 2 lines of symmetry

b i 1 order 4 about centre of shape

ii 1 order 1 about centre of shape

iii 1 order 2 about centre of shape

Questions 3 – 7 marks

a 4 Check students' drawings. Lines should be drawn from all four corners; correct point of intersection; 4 left, 6 up from C; point marked as O

b 3 Scale factor 2

Questions 4 – 5 marks

a 1 $h = 20$

b 1 $j = 1$

c 1 $g = 24$

d 2 $x = 3$

Questions 5 – 11 marks

a 2 $d = 4$

b 2 $t = 2$

c 3 $r = 3$

d 4 $w = 2$

Questions 6 – 4 marks

4 $s = 35$; 1 mark 14 seen; 1 mark 70 seen;

Questions 7 – 4 marks

a 1 12.94

b 1 21.5

c 1 124.15

d 1 880.6

(all working must be shown)

Questions 8 – 4 marks

a 2 40; 37.2

b 2 45; 43.68

(all working must be shown)

Questions 9 – 8 marks

a 2 8; 8.5

b 2 13; 16.7

c 2 9; 8.7

d 2 10; 11.2

Questions 10 – 4 marks

a 2 29.92

b 2 0.87

Questions 11 – 5 marks

a 4 Check students' drawings

b 1 41.7 cm ± 0.3 cm

Questions 12 – 10 marks

a 2 Check students' drawings

b 3 Check students' drawings

c 1 Check accurate drawings of quadrilateral: kite

d 4 P = 102° ± 1°, Q = 80° ± 1°, R = S = 88° ± 1°

Questions 13 – 5 marks

a 2 Check students' scale drawing

b 2 Circle drawn accurately; 2 cm radius; centre H

c 1 1.6 cm on diagram = 16 m in real life

Learning outcomes

A14 Generate terms of a sequence from either a term-to-term or a position-to-term rule (L6)
A15 Recognise arithmetic sequences and find the *n*th term (L6)
A16 Recognise geometric sequences and appreciate other sequences that arise (L6)

Introduction	Prior knowledge

Prior knowledge

Students should already know how to...

- Recognise patterns in sequences of numbers

Introduction

The chapter starts by looking at the term-to-term and position-to-term rules for arithmetic and other sequences before looking at sequences in context. Recognising and working with geometric sequences is covered in the final section.

The introduction discusses the presence of sequences inside the human body, specifically related to the sequence of bases in DNA which determine the physical characteristics of each cell in the body. The use of DNA sequencing can help us to treat specific diseases and also in the solving of crimes by using DNA profiling of both the physical evidence and the suspects in the crime. This kind of profiling is known as DNA fingerprinting since each person has a unique genetic sequence in their DNA.

The study of the human genome has been a huge part of modern scientific research and scientists have spent many years developing their techniques to allow them to determine the sequence of chemical base pairs which make up human DNA. There are 3 billion bases of genetic information found in human cells and it has therefore been a massive undertaking. Information on the human genome project, its uses and future developments can be found at:

http://www.wellcome.ac.uk/Our-vision/Research-challenges/Genetics-and-genomics/index.htm?gclid=CMyQu9Xagr0CFerpwgod62cAOw

Starter problem

The starter problem considers a specific sequence of 'growth' of a 'dog' made up of coloured squares. Students should quickly recognise that the neck of the dog (coloured blue) grows by one square each evolution and that the legs of the dog (coloured red) both grow by one square each evolution. This should enable them to quickly draw the next one or two evolutions. The fourth evolution will have a neck three squares long and legs four squares long.

Students could be invited to come up with a simple rule (either written down or using mathematical language) which describes each evolution. They could also be invited to come up with their own 'mad scientist' design that has similar growth patterns.

The idea of evolution in sequences started with work done by John Conway in 1970. He developed a 'Game of Life' simulation in which successive iterations of an initial cellular structure (drawn on a square grid) evolved according to a very simple rule structure. An online applet showing how the 'Game of Life' works can be found at: http://www.bitstorm.org/gameoflife/

The rules which make up the 'Game of Life' are:

- For a space that is 'populated':
  Each cell with one or no neighbours dies, as if by loneliness.
  Each cell with four or more neighbours dies, as if by overpopulation.
  Each cell with two or three neighbours survives.
- For a space that is 'empty' or 'unpopulated':
  Each cell with three neighbours becomes populated.

Resources

MyMaths

Comparing fractions	1075	*n*th term	1165	Sequences	1173

Online assessment		InvisiPen solutions			
Chapter test	2B–13	Term-to-term rules	282	Position-to-term rules	283
Formative test	2B–13	Real-life sequences	285		
Summative test	2B–13				

Topic scheme

Teaching time = 4 lessons/2 weeks

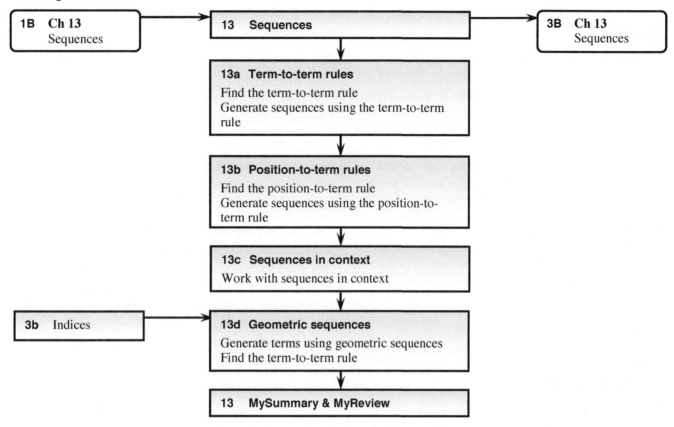

| 1B   Ch 13
Sequences | → | 13   Sequences | → | 3B   Ch 13
Sequences |

13a   Term-to-term rules

Find the term-to-term rule
Generate sequences using the term-to-term rule

13b   Position-to-term rules

Find the position-to-term rule
Generate sequences using the position-to-term rule

13c   Sequences in context

Work with sequences in context

| 3b   Indices | → | **13d   Geometric sequences** |

Generate terms using geometric sequences
Find the term-to-term rule

13   MySummary & MyReview

Differentiation

Student book 2A   242 – 255
Term-to-term rules Position-to-term rules Real-life sequences Triangular numbers

Student book 2B   234 – 247
Term-to-term rules Position-to-term rules Sequences in context Geometric sequences

Student book 2C   238 – 251
General term of a sequence Sequences in context Geometric sequences Recursive sequences

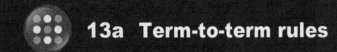
Objectives

• Describe integer sequences	(L5)
• Generate terms of a linear sequence using term-to-term (and position-to-term) rules	(L6)

Key ideas	Resources
1 Recognise, describe and use patterns in linear sequences 2 Begin to recognise links to a term's position term	Sequences (1173) Mini whiteboard Go Forth and Generalise (NRICH): http://nrich.maths.org/2338

Simplification	Extension
If students struggle at this point, offer more visual consolidation with sequences in diagrammatic form.	More able students can progress towards finding the nth term of a sequence.

Literacy	Links
Students are likely to be familiar with the key word sequence. Students should be encouraged to use term frequently and correctly. It might be helpful to discuss moving from term to term as a pattern.	The look-and-say sequence is a famous non-linear sequence that sometimes appears in puzzle books. The first eight terms are 1, 11, 21, 1211, 111221, 312211, 13112221, 1113213211. What is the rule for moving from one term to the next? (Describe the previous term in words and then write it in numbers, so one one; two ones; one two, two ones, etc.). Try starting the sequence with 2 or 3 instead of 1.

Alternative approach

Begin by giving students three terms of a number sequence: 1, 2, 4, … and ask them to find at least two different sequences with these three first terms. (Most obvious likely to be 1, 2, 4, 7, 11, 16…; or 1, 2, 4, 8, 16, …). Can student partners spot the pattern when they are given the fourth term? An alternative approach to this section and the following one is to take two lessons, exploring patterns and position-to-term rules in both, with growing levels of sophistication. Prepare a variety of sequences presented on separate cards, for students to group together, thus all the ones that involve, for example, 'adding 3', 'subtracting 2', 'doubling', 'multiplying by 10', where the initial terms are all different. Students can then be encouraged to identify the nature of 'linear' sequences, by being informed which are linear. Students can then be encouraged to examine a term's position to help establish rules for each linear sequence. The article and resources Go Forth and Generalise (NRICH) reminds us that students need to explore *why* a pattern works and its influence on the rule.

Checkpoint

1 You know that a sequence has the term-to-term rule of 'add three'.
   a Suggest at least two different possible sequences.   (Any correct responses such as 2, 5, 8, 11, …)
   b Explain why it is not possible to find the 10th term of the sequence.
   (Indication that the actual sequence is not known, or the first term is not known. There are an infinite number of possible sequences.)

Starter – Connections

If $x = -2$ and $y = 5$, ask students to write down 10 rules connecting x and y, for example,
$y = 5x + 15$, $y - x = 7$, $x + 2y = 8$ ...

Can be extended by changing the values of x and y.

Teaching notes

To make connections with students' prior learning, ensure that the vocabulary of this unit is understood. Ask students to write definitions of 'term', 'rule' and 'sequence' and take feedback.

When providing worked examples, place an emphasis on looking at how to get from one term to the next – this can often be linked to a diagrammatic representation. A useful technique is to look at first differences, which will be most useful for linear sequences such as occur in question **2** parts **a–f**.

Students often forget to state the first term of a sequence when giving a term-to-term rule. To help reinforce the need for this, give the partial rule 'add 5' and challenge students to give first terms that result in a sequence of odd numbers, even numbers, multiples of 4 and non-integer numbers.

Plenary

Ask students to generate sequences for a friend to find the rule. They could use both numbers and diagrams.

Exercise commentary

Question 1 – A visual approach to understanding sequences.

Question 2 – Similar to the example. Parts **a** to **f** are linear and looking at first differences should be encouraged. Parts **h** to **j** may benefit from whole-class discussion.

Question 3 – Applying a term-to-term rule.

Question 4 – Similar to the example. Students may need to be reminded to find the rule first and to use the next number on as a check if appropriate.

Question 5 – Here students are encouraged towards finding a position-to-term rule.

Answers

1 a ii 3, 6, 9, 12   iii Add 3
      iv 15, 18, 21
   b ii 4, 8, 12, 16   iii Add 4
      iv 20, 24, 28
   c ii 3, 5, 7, 9   iii Add 2
      iv 9, 11, 13
   d ii 6, 10, 14, 18   iii Add 4
      iv 18, 22, 26
   e ii 4, 7, 10, 13   iii Add 3
      iv 13, 16, 19
   f ii 8, 16, 24, 32   iii Add 8
      iv 32, 40, 48
2 a i add 3   ii 14, 17, 20
   b i add 5   ii 24, 29, 34
   c i add 4   ii 24, 28, 32
   d i subtract 4   ii 34, 30, 26
   e i subtract 3   ii 18, 15, 12
   f i add 11   ii 64, 75, 86
   g i × 2   ii 32, 64, 128
   h i double and add 1   ii 47, 95, 191
   i i double and add 1   ii 63, 127, 255
   j i × 3 and subtract 1   ii 203, 608, 1823
3 a 6, 10, 14, 18, 22, 26   b 8, 10, 12, 14, 16, 18
   c 60, 55, 50, 45, 40, 35   d 5, 11, 23, 47, 95, 191
   e 2, 8, 20, 44, 92, 188   f 100, 89, 78, 67, 56, 45
   g 1, 4, 13, 40, 121, 364   h 0, 2, 8, 26, 80, 242
4 a 40   b 21   c 15   d 12
   e 175   f 81   g 100   h 38
   i -21   j -8
5 50th term = 204
   No. Add 49 lots of 4 to 8, or multiply the position by 4 and add 4.
   9 hours after laying the first slab

Objectives

- Generate sequences from patterns or practical contexts and describe the general term in simple cases   (L6)
- Generate terms of a linear sequence using (term-to-term and) position-to-term rules   (L6)

Key ideas	Resources
1 Recognising the importance of a term's position in a sequence	nth term (1165) Tape measures

Simplification	Extension
Where students struggle with the later questions in the exercise, refer them back to the worked example and encourage the use of diagrams to represent the sequence in a more concrete way.	Encourage more able students to discuss how to write a formula for finding the nth term of a sequence which is of a simple quadratic style such as $2, 5, 10, 17, \ldots$

Literacy	Links
Most students will be able to verbalise aspects of a linear sequence but will find recording more challenging. Reminding students that multiplying is repeated addition (division – repeated subtraction) may help communication. Both *row* recording and *column* recording should be encouraged so that students do not wrongly assume only one of these approaches is correct. It may be helpful to use the words INPUT and OUTPUT as with function machines.	Chronophotography is the art of taking a series of photographs of a moving object at regular time intervals. The resulting photographs form a sequence, similar to a flip book. Chronophotography was made popular during Victorian times by photographers such as Étienne-Jules Marey and Georges Demeny. There are examples of chronophotography at http://www.sequences.org.uk/chrono1/0000.html and http://www.elearning-art.net/art-net_courses/Moving_Images_Workshop_(Eng)/1SHORTHISTORY/1Zoopraxinoscope.htm

Alternative approach

The need to include position is the key to helpful recording for students here. However, position and term is often sufficient, and is more likely to encourage the next step – pattern seeking – after recording. Comments may be added to tables say in a thought bubble, for example

Add 3

3 times table

Encourage students to include a large position value, such 20, in their table followed by n or equivalent for the variable position. This will help to support recording of the position-to-term rule. Always ask students to check their result by using substitution with a term that they know.

Checkpoint

1 A sequence is given as: $3, 5, 7, 9, 11, \ldots$
  a Find the 20th term.   (41)
  b Find the nth term. $(2n + 1)$

Starter – Match point!

Write the following coordinates of points on the board:
$(1, -1), (-1, 5), (-1, -3), (-1, 2), (-1, -4)$

Write the following equations of lines on the board:
$y = 4x + 1$, $y = 3x - 4$, $y = -4$, $y = 4 - x$, $y = 2(x + 2)$

Ask students which points lie on which lines and to give the coordinates of another point on each line.

Teaching notes

The key processes in algebra, particularly the development of analysing through using mathematical reasoning, are supported here where students are required to identify and describe numerical patterns.

The worked examples show the process that students need to use and offer clear visual representations which students can apply for themselves in other situations. The use of tables to organise thinking is especially important. When finding the value of any term from its position in the sequence, make links back to work on substitution.

Plenary

Use the plenary to link to the research students have done on the Fibonacci sequence. Discuss the golden ratio in nature and give tape measures to students to investigate their own height to belly button to floor ratio. Who is the 'most perfect' student? Or is their teacher perfect?

Exercise commentary

Question 1 – A structured investigation supported by a diagrammatic representation.

Question 2 – Similar to question 1 but with less scaffolding.

Question 3 – Similar to the example. Encourage students to draw their own diagrams and follow the procedure set out in the previous questions if appropriate.

Question 4 – Students may need guidance how to start this question. Once the general method has been established, further problems could be set or students could be challenged to come up with their own examples.

Question 5 – An opportunity to discuss the historical development of mathematics and how much harder arithmetic was before Arabic numerals. Some students may have read the book or seen the film 'The DaVinci Code' – link to this if appropriate.

Answers

1 a 3

b Check students' drawings. Diagram should have 4 squares and 14 circles

c

Position	1	2	3	4
Times table	3	6	9	12
Term (circles)	5	8	11	14

d Multiply the position by 3 then add 2

e 14 **f** 62

2 a i Check students' drawings

ii

Position	1	2	3	4
Times table	3	6	9	12
Term (circles)	3	6	9	12

iii Position to term rule is multiply the position by 3

iv 50th term = 150

b i Check students' drawings

ii

Position	1	2	3	4
Times table	2	4	6	8
Term (circles)	3	5	7	9

iii Rule is multiply the position by 2 and add 1

iv 50th term = 101

c i Check students' drawings

ii

Position	1	2	3	4
Times table	4	8	12	16
Term (circles)	5	9	13	17

iii Rule is multiply the position by 4 and add 1

iv 50th term = 201

d i Check students' drawings

ii

Position	1	2	3	4
Times table	2	4	6	8
Term (circles)	5	7	9	11

iii Rule is multiply the position by 2 and add 3

iv 50th term = 103

3 a × 3 and add 1 19, 151

b × 2 and subtract 1   11, 99

c × 4 and subtract 3   21, 197

d × 4 and add 2 26, 202

e × 3 and subtract 2   16, 148

f × 7 and add 1 43, 351

g × 8 and subtract 3   45, 397

h add 3 to the position   9, 53

4 a 79   **b** 15, 25, 35, …

5 Open ended

Objectives

- Use linear expressions to describe the *n*th term of a simple arithmetic sequence, justifying its form by referring to the activity or practical context from which it was generated   (L6)

Key ideas	Resources
1 Investigating a simple situation systematically recording, analysing observations, generalising and testing conclusions	*n*th term (1165)

Simplification	Extension
Encourage students having difficulty to make full use of diagrams and tables for structure.	More able students can be stretched with the investigation of a rule for triangular numbers (as in the handshakes investigation).

Literacy	Links
Quality of written communication, particularly of reasoning and testing, should be encouraged in this session. Students can work together and challenge each other as to whether points made are clear, results clearly presented in tables, diagrams used to illustrate or clarify, and so on.	All human cells contain DNA. DNA stands for Deoxyribonucleic Acid and DNA molecules hold the instructions for building living things. DNA molecules are made up of four building blocks called bases or nucleotides. The order or sequence of the bases along the molecule gives the genetic information for characteristics such as hair and eye colour.

Alternative approach

Students may work in pairs on an investigation which has the capability of resulting in linear relationships, and perhaps others. Match stick growth patterns are a good source, and these could be used as a starting activity to a full investigation such as Rotten Apples, where placement of one initial rotten apple can be varied for more complex rules. A simple starting point here is for the one to be placed in a corner:

Day 1 one apple; Day 2 three apples, Day 3 five apples…

Checkpoint

1 An investigation finds that on day 3 there are 11 rotten apples, on day 5 there are 19 rotten apples and on day 10 there are 39 rotten apples. How would you look for a rule for this sequence?

(Try day 4 has 15 rotten apples, so growing by 4 each day. Check and confirm with other values; establish $4n - 1$ as the total for day n, also checked.)

Starter – Strange sequences

Write the following sequences on the board:

50, 48, 44, 38, 30, …   J, F, M, A, M, …
3, -6, 12, -24, 48, …   2, 5, 10, 17, 26, …
S, M, T, W, T, …

Ask students for the next term in each sequence.

Answers: 20, J (June), -96 (multiply previous term by -2), 37, F (Friday).

Can be extended by students making their own 'strange sequences'.

Teaching notes

A focus in this unit is to demonstrate the use of sequences in a real-life context. Students can be encouraged to describe the rules with which they are working in words and using symbols. Collaborative approaches can be encouraged here in order to develop student confidence and to promote purposeful mathematical discussion.

Having initiated whole-class discussion through the worked example, invite students to discuss how sequences might appear in real-life contexts.

To become functional in mathematics, students need the confidence to use mathematics as a tool to investigate and solve problems, which leads to better understanding. For this reason, the link to real-life settings is most important.

Plenary

Challenge students to write a word-based sequence problem of their own, using the examples in the exercise as a model.

Exercise commentary

Question 1 – Invite students to suggest similar situations from nature where a sequence might arise.

Question 2 – Ask students how their answers would change if Wasim earned £10 a week or £12: can they see how this relates to their position-to-term rule?

Question 3 – Ensure that students know what are 'migrating geese'. Also the 'average' may need some explaining. Invite students to discuss how this will impact on the answer for day 30.

Question 4 – The classic 'handshakes' investigation which leads to identifying the sequence of triangular numbers. Part **e** will promote mathematical discussion.

Answers

1 a 9, 11
 b

Position (week)	1	2	3	4	5	
Times table	2	4	6	8	10	× 2
Term (leaves)	3	5	7	9	11	+ 1

Rule is × position by 2 and add 1
 c 25

2 a Add 8
 b 52, 60
 c

Position	1	2	3	4	
Times table	8	16	24	32	× 8
Term (£)	20	28	36	44	+ 12

Rule is × position by 8 and add 12
 d £332
 e £352 (as he already had £20 before he started work)

3 a 130, 150   **b** × 20 and add 30
 c 430   **d** 630

4 a 3   **b** 6, 10, 15   **c** 1, 3, 6, 10, 15, 21, …
 d Add 1 more than you added last time
 e The differences between successive terms are not constant so the term-to-term rule does not work. The position-to-term rule is not straightforward. It is

$$\tfrac{1}{2}n(n+1) = \sum_{r=1}^{n} r$$

Objectives	
• Recognise geometric sequences and appreciate other sequences that arise	(L6)

Key ideas	Resources
1 Describe the term-to-term rule for geometric sequences 2 Generate terms in a geometric sequence	Comparing fractions (1075)

Simplification	Extension
Most students will appreciate the pattern in simple geometric sequences but may struggle to get to grips with fractional or negative common ratios. These can be omitted to simplify this work.	Students could be asked to investigate geometric sequences for which the common ratio is between 1 and -1 and asked to look at the behaviour of the sequence as the number of terms gets larger. Do the sequences converge to a limiting value? If so what?

Literacy	Links
Students should be familiar now with most of the language of sequences. Geometric sequences, on the other hand, are new to the students and will need carefully defining. The phrase 'term-to-term rule' should be familiar but students should understand what it means in this specific context.	Exponential growth and decay are both real-life examples of geometric sequences and links can be made to both biology and physics where these phenomena are commonplace. Students may be familiar with radioactive decay or the exponential growth of bacteria through studying science.

Alternative approach
A real-life context could be used to stimulate discussion of geometric sequences. Consider, for example, a petri dish full of bacteria. The number of bacteria doubles each minute. How long ago was the dish half full? (1 minute: since the dish is now full, it was half full one minute ago so that when it doubled it is now full). This is a classic 'brainteaser' which shows the power of the geometric sequence. Another alternative could be to just give students some 'random' term-to-term rules and ask them to work out the sequence following a function machine approach similar to question **2**. These can be mixed arithmetic and geometric sequences and then the sequences can be split into two groups using observation of patterns and reference back to the original rules.

Checkpoint	
1 Find the next two terms in this sequence: 2, 6, 18, 54, ...	(162, 486)
2 A sequence starts with 7 and doubles each time. Write down the first four terms.	(7, 14, 28, 56)

Starter – Rice on a chessboard

A classic mathematical puzzle is where a single grain of rice is placed of the first square of a chessboard and then two, four, eight, etc. grains on the next squares. Challenge students to work out how many grains are on the 6th square, the 10th square, the 20th square, etc. or to find the total number of grains of rice on, say, the first five squares.

Teaching notes

The concept of a geometric sequence can be developed from the idea in the **starter**. The phrase 'common ratio' is not used but could be introduced if students become familiar with the principle of multiplicative sequences. Model the sequences in the introduction or develop the **starter** to show the pattern of simple sequences.

It is important that students appreciate that geometric sequences can be formed by dividing (multiplying by a *fractional* ratio) and also by multiplying by negative numbers (so the signs alternate +/-).

The contextual example about birds of prey is useful to discuss since it combines both a geometrical element and an arithmetical element.

Plenary

Consider: If the first term of a geometric sequence is 2 and the third term 8, how can you find out the term-to-term rule? (Square root the ratio of the given terms)

What about if you have a first term of 3 and a fourth term of 24? (Cube root the ratio of the given terms)

Can this pattern be used to develop a method for working out the answers to question **4** without writing all the terms out?

Exercise commentary

Question 1 – Continuation of sequences. Students may be less happy with the fractional ratios in parts **e** and **f**.

Question 2 – Students should pick up the pattern from these sequence descriptions. Multiplying by -2 or 2½ may cause some difficulties.

Question 3 – Students should follow the model from question **2** when writing down the sequence rules.

Question 4 – There is no shortcut to writing down all of the preceding terms here.

Question 5 – a practical application of geometric sequences. Option A is similar to the 'rice on a chessboard' problem from the **starter**.

Question 6 – Students may need a calculator here to continue the sequences with large numbers.

Question 7 – An opportunity to extend students' knowledge of similar types of sequence and to generate discussion. Pairs work could be used here.

Answers

1. **a** 96, 192   **b** 972, 2916 **c** 1944, 5832
   d 100 000, 1 000 000   **e** 31.25, 15.625
   f -1, -0.5
2. **a** 3, 6, 12, 24, 48   **b** 4, 20, 100, 500, 2500
   c 2, 16, 128, 1024, 8192   **d** -5, -15, -45, -135, -406
   e 8, -16, 32, -64, 128   **f** 32, 80, 200, 500, 1250
3. **a** Multiply by 5   **b** Multiply by 6
   c Multiply by 3   **d** Multiply by 4
   e Multiply by 1.5   **f** Multiply by -5
4. **a** 2560   **b** 7 812 500 **c** -524 288
   d -8   **e** -3072   **f** $\frac{5}{128}$
5. Option A since it pays £315 altogether, whereas Option B pays £300 altogether.
6. On the seventh term A is greater than B
7. **a** 1, 4, 9, 16, 25, ... The square numbers
   b 1, 8, 27, 64, 125, ... The cube numbers
   c **i** $1^7, 2^7, 3^7, 4^7, 5^7$
       ii 2 097 152

Key outcomes	Quick check
Find and use the term-to-term rule in a sequence. L6	Write down the term-to-term rule for these sequences and find the next two terms. **a** 2, 6, 10, 14, ... (Add four; 18, 22) **b** 3, 9, 27, 81, ... (Treble; 243, 729)
Find and use the position-to-term rule in a sequence. L6	Find the position-to-term rule for these sequences and find the 20th term. **a** 3, 5, 7, 9, ... $(2n + 1; 41)$ **b** 5, 2, -1, -4, ... $(-3n + 8; -52)$
Use sequences in context and in real life. L6	A scientist measures the length of a worm and finds it to be 5 cm long. If the worm grows an average of 5 mm per day, how long will it be after 8 days? (9 cm) How long will it be after n days? $(5 + 0.5n$ cm)
Recognise and describe geometric sequences. L6	For these geometric sequences, find the term-to-term rule and the next two terms. **a** 2, 6, 18, 54, ... (Treble; 162, 486) **b** 256, 64, 16, 4, ... (÷ by 4; 1, ¼)

 ## MyMaths extra support

Lesson/online homework	Description
Squares and triangles 1054 L4	Investigating square numbers and triangular numbers

MyReview

Check out
You should now be able to ...

Test it ➡
Questions

✓ Find and use the term-to-term rule in a sequence.		1–2
✓ Find and use the position-to-term rule in a sequence.		3–5
✓ Use sequences in context and in real life.		6
✓ Recognise and describe geometric sequences.		7

Language	Meaning	Example
Sequence	An ordered list of numbers, called *terms*, which often follow a pattern	2, 5, 8, 11, ... is a sequence
Position	A number that counts the terms, in order, starting from 1	The first term has position 1, the second term has position 2 etc.
Term-to-term rule	An instruction how to get from one term in a sequence to the next term	For the sequence above the rule is +3
Position-to-term rule	A rule which works out the value of any term from its position in the sequence	For the sequence above, the term in the nth position is given by $3n - 1$
Geometric sequence	A sequence in which the term-to-term rule is multiplied by a fixed number	2, 6, 18, 54, 162, ... each term is 3× the previous term

1 For each sequence
 i find the term-to-term rule
 ii write the next two terms.
 a 8 14 20 26 **b** 60 56 52 48
 c 2 4 8 16

2 Write the first 5 terms of these sequences.
 a Start with 9 and add 5
 b Start with 30 and subtract 3
 c Start with 1 and treble
 d Start with 5, double and subtract 2

3 This sequence of diagrams is formed by adding squares.
 a Draw the diagram for position 4.
 b Copy and complete this table, use the correct 'times table' for the middle row.

Position	1	2	3	4	5	6
Times table						
Term (squares)						

 c Find the position-to-term rule for the number of squares.
 d Find how many squares are in the 20th term of the sequence.

4 Find the position-to-term-rule for each of these sequences.
 a 9 12 15 18 21
 b 2 9 16 23 30

5 Find the 12th term of the sequences with these position-to-term rules.
 a Multiply the position by 3 then subtract 8
 b 5n + 6

6 Debbie bought 2 raffle tickets on Monday, 5 on Tuesday, 8 on Wednesday and so on for the whole week.
 a Write a term-to-term rule for the number of raffle tickets bought each day.
 b How many tickets did she buy on Saturday?
 c How many tickets did she buy altogether over the 7 days?
 d Copy and complete the table.

Position (day)	1	2	3	4	5	6	7
Times table							
Term (squares)							

 e Find the position-to-term rule.

7 For each geometric sequence
 i find the term-to-term rule
 ii write the next two terms.
 a 3 6 12 36
 b 128 64 32 16
 c 1 -3 9 -27

What next?

Score	0 – 3	Your knowledge of this topic is still developing. To improve look at Formative test: 2B-13; MyMaths: 1165 and 1173
	4 – 6	You are gaining a secure knowledge of this topic. To improve look at InvisiPen: 282, 283 and 285
	7	You have mastered this topic. Well done, you are ready to progress!

Question commentary

Questions 1 and 2 – Term-to-term rules: first finding the rule and then writing the sequences. Students could be caught out by question **1** part **c** if they only look at the first two terms.

Question 3 – Student can give the position-to-term rule using words or algebra. For part **d** the students should substitute 20 into their rule: $2 \times 20 + 1$.

Question 4 – Student can give the position-to-term rule using words or algebra. If necessary, they can draw tables as in question **3** to help them work it out.

Question 5 – Even students who are not confident writing the position-to-term rule algebraically, should be able to substitute into the rule given in part **b**.

Question 6 – Get students to write down the sequence 2, 5, 8, ... and work from there.

Question 7 – Students may need a prompt in part **c** that they can multiply by a negative common ratio.

Answers

1 **a** i Start with 8 and add 6 ii 32, 38
 b i Start with 60 and subtract 4 ii 44, 40
 c i Start with 2 and double ii 32, 64

2 **a** 9, 14, 19, 24, 29 **b** 30, 27, 24, 21, 18
 c 1, 3, 9, 27, 81 **d** 5, 8, 14, 26, 50

3 **a** 6 green squares going down, 3 blue across
 b

Position	1	2	3	4	5	6
Times table	2	4	6	8	10	12
Term (squares)	3	5	7	9	11	13

 c Multiply the position by 2 and add 1 or $2n + 1$
 d 41

4 **a** Multiply the position by 3 and add 6 or $3n + 6$
 b Multiply the position by 7 and subtract 5 or $7n - 5$

5 **a** 28 **b** 66

6 **a** Start with 4 and add 3 **b** 17 **c** 77
 d

Position (day)	1	2	3	4	5	6	7
Times table	3	6	9	12	15	18	21
Term (squares)	2	5	8	11	14	17	20

 e Multiply the position by 3 and subtract 2 or $3n - 2$

7 **a** i Start with 3 and multiply by 2 ii 72, 144
 b i Start with 128 and multiply by $\frac{1}{2}$ ii 8, 4
 c i Start with 1 and multiply by -3
   ii 81, -243

13A

1 This sequence is made using straws.

   a Draw the next diagram in the sequence.
   b Write the first four terms.
   c Find the term-to-term rule.
   d Write the next three terms.

2 For each of these sequences, find the term-to-term rule and write the next three terms of the sequence.

   a 2 6 10 14 ...   b 3 8 13 18 ...
   c 2 5 11 23 ...   d 30 27 24 21 ...

3 Write the first six terms of each of the sequences with these rules.

   a *Start with 5. Add 4.*   b *Start with 12. Add 6.*
   c *Start with 40. Subtract 6.* d *Start with 2. Double and add 1.*
   e *Start with 3. Double and subtract 2.*   f *Start with 100 and subtract 21.*

13B

4 This sequence of diagrams is made from triangles.

   Position 1   2   3   4

   a How many extra triangles are added to each position to make the next position?
   b Draw the diagram for position 5.
   c Copy and complete this table. Use the correct 'times table' for the middle row.

Position	1	2	3	4
Times table				
Term (No. of triangles)				

   d Find the position-to-term rule.
   e How many triangles are there in the 10th diagram of the sequence?

5 a Find the position-to-term rule for this sequence.

Sequence	4	7	10	13	16
Position →	1	2	3	4	5

   Find the next two terms of the sequence.

   b Find the position-to-term rule for each of these sequences.
   Also find the next term and the 20th term in the sequence.

   i 1 3 5 7 9   ii 3 6 9 12 15
   iii 7 12 17 22 27   iv 19 18 17 16 15

13C

6 Jamie bought three tins of cat food on the day he first owned some cats.
He then bought two tins every day after that.
The sequence for the total number of tins bought is 3   5   7   9   ...

Day 1   Day 2   Day 3

   a Find the term-to-term rule and the next two terms of this sequence.
   b Copy and complete this table and find the position-to-term rule.

Position (day)	1	2	3	4	5
Times table					
Term (tins)					

   c Find the 20th term of the sequence.
   d How many tins had he bought altogether by the 100th day?

7 Abbi and Gail both decide to start saving for a new car in January.
Abbi's parents give her £500 at the start of the year and at the end of the month she adds £60.
Gail is given no money but can save £100 at the end of each month.

   a Write out how much money each person has at the end of the first five months.
   b Find the position-to-term rule for each person.
   c Write out how much money each person has at the end of the first two years.
   d When will each person have saved £3000?

13D

8 Generate the first five terms of each sequence.

   a Start at 3, multiply by 3
   b Start at 2, multiply by 4
   c Start at 4, multiply by 5
   d Start at 16, multiply by $\frac{1}{2}$

9 Describe a term-to-term rule for each sequence.

   a 2, 6, 18, 54, 162, ...
   b 3, 6, 12, 24, 48, ...
   c 4, 16, 64, 256, 1024, ...
   d 3, −9, 27, −81, 243, ...

MyMaths.co.uk

Question commentary

Questions 1 to **3** – Practice at working with term-to-term rules. Make sure students recognise the non-linearity in question **2** part **c**.

Questions 4 and **5** – The tabular method used to scaffold question **4** can be used repeatedly for the sequences given in question **5**.

Questions 6 and **7** – Contextualised sequences. Students may need guidance extracting the information from the text and can use the tabular method to help find the position-to-term rules.

Questions 8 and **9** – Geometric sequences: first generating terms and then describing the sequences. Negative or fractional common ratios may confuse the students and they may need further examples.

Answers

1 a Check students' diagram. The next term in sequence should consist of 4 hexagons.

   b $6, 11, 16, 21$ **c** Add 5

   d $26, 31, 36$

2 a Add 4 $18, 22, 26$ **b** Add 5 $23, 28, 33$

   c Double the previous term and add 1
   $47, 95, 191$

   d Subtract 3 $18, 15, 12$

3 a $5, 9, 13, 17, 21, 25$ **b** $12, 18, 24, 30, 36, 42$

   c $40, 34, 28, 22, 16, 10$ **d** $2, 5, 11, 23, 47, 95$

   e $3, 4, 6, 10, 18, 34$ **f** $100, 79, 58, 37, 16, -5$

4 a 3

   b Check students' diagram. Position 5 should consist of 13 triangles.

   c

Position	1	2	3	4	
Times table	3	6	9	12	× 3
Term (triangles)	1	4	7	10	− 2

   d × position by 3 and subtract 2

   e 28

5 a × position by 3 and add 1
   $19, 22$

   b i × position by 2 and subtract 1; $11, 39$

   ii × position by 3; $18, 60$

   iii × position by 5 and add 2; $32, 102$

   iv Take position from 20; $14, 0$

6 a add 2; $11, 13$

   b

Position (day)	1	2	3	4	5
Times table	2	4	6	8	10
Term (tins)	3	5	7	9	11

   × position by 2 and add 1

   c 41   **d** 201

7 a Abbi: £800, Gail: £500

   b Abbi: $500 + 60n$ Gail: $100n$

   c Abbi: £1940   Gail: £2400

   d Abbi: 3 years 6 months
   Gail: 2 years 6 months

8 a $3, 9, 27, 81, 243$ **b** $2, 8, 32, 128, 512$

   c $4, 20, 100, 500, 2500$ **d** $16, 8, 4, 2, 1$

9 a Multiply by 3   **b** Multiply by 2

   c Multiply by 4   **d** Multiply by -3

Learning outcomes

G1 Derive and apply formulae to calculate and solve problems involving: perimeter and area of triangles, parallelograms, trapezia, volume of cuboids (including cubes) and other prisms (including cylinders) (L6)

G15 Use the properties of faces, surfaces, edges and vertices of cubes, cuboids, prisms, cylinders, pyramids, cones and spheres to solve problems in 3D (L5)

Introduction

The chapter starts by looking at 3D shapes in general: naming the shapes and looking at the number of faces, edges and vertices that each shape has. The second section covers plans and elevations of 3D shapes. Surface area and volume of a cuboid are then covered before the final section which looks at the volume of prisms.

The introduction discusses how companies use an appreciation of surface area and volume to design environmentally-friendly packaging for their products. If you look around the supermarket, you can see packaging designed as cubes, cuboids, cylinders and other prisms, each of which is designed to suit the purpose of the packaging and also to add some aesthetic value while being only as big as necessary to safely package the goods. The use of efficient packaging can also help companies to reduce costs, since customers do not buy the products for the packaging alone. The cost incurred from the packaging is a 'throw away' cost to the company since the packaging is rarely useful to the consumer and almost always gets thrown away or at best recycled.

Higher level mathematics can help companies solve what are referred to as 'optimisation' problems. Mathematicians use what is called differential calculus to find the minimum surface area for a given volume, or to solve similar problems. This type of mathematics will be covered in A level.

Prior knowledge

Students should already know how to...

- Carry out simple arithmetic
- Work out the areas and perimeters of plane figures, including compound shapes

Starter problem

The starter problem requires students to work with the volume of a cuboid formula in order to reduce the surface area of a given package, for the fixed volume stated. Trial-and-improvement is clearly going to be the method of choice for most students and they should easily be able to determine that a package measuring 10 cm by 6 cm by 6 cm will work. Here the surface area is $4 \times 10 \times 6 + 2 \times 6 \times 6 = 312$ cm^2 as opposed to the original of $2 \times 12 \times 6 + 2 \times 12 \times 5 + 2 \times 6 \times 5 = 324$ cm^2.

There is an interesting link to prime factorisation (section **1d**). There are many possible (whole number) combinations of side length for the cuboid and some will be better than the original and some worse. By finding the prime factorisation of 360 we can actually work out how many combinations there will be and also what these combinations are. We *could* therefore try them all.

$360 = 2^3 \times 3^2 \times 5$ so if we split this prime factorisation into three parts, lots of different ways, we can find all the combinations. The one given in the question is $2 \times 2 \times 3, 2 \times 3$ and 5. The one stated above is 2×5, 2×3 and 2×3. An alternative could be $2 \times 2 \times 2$, 3×5 and 3 and more able students could be invited to come up with others and check their surface areas.

Resources

MyMaths

3D shapes	1078	Plans elevations	1098	Nets of 3D shapes	1106
Nets, surface area	1107	Volume of cuboids	1137	Volume of prisms	1139

Online assessment

Chapter test	2B–14
Formative test	2B–14
Summative test	2B–14

InvisiPen solutions

Properties of 3D shapes	321	Surface area of cuboid	322
Volume of shapes made from cuboids			323
Nets of simple 3D shapes			325
2D representations of 3D solids			326
Prisms	327		

Topic scheme

Teaching time = 5 lessons/2 weeks

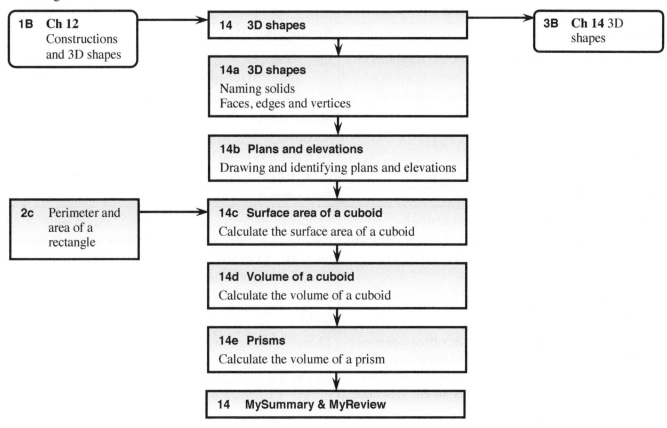

Differentiation

Student book 2A 256 – 271	**Student book 2B** 248 – 263
3D shapes	3D shapes
Isometric drawings	Plans and elevations
Nets of 3D shapes	Surface area of a cuboid
Surface area of a cuboid	Volume of a cuboid
Volume of a cuboid	Prisms

Student book 2C   252 – 265

3D shapes
Plans and elevations
Surface area of a prism
Volume of a prism

Objectives

- Use 2D representations to visualise 3D shapes and deduce some of their properties   (L5)
- Visualise 3D shapes from their nets   (L6)

Key ideas	Resources
1 Read, understand and begin to use 2D diagrams of 3D shapes 2 Begin to link a 3D shape with its possible net.	3D shapes (1078) Nets of 3D shapes (1106) Isometric paper – dotty and/or lined Squared paper Scissors IWB displays using three very different cuboids – one close to a cube, one tall, thin, and one flattish

Simplification	Extension
Wherever possible have 3D solids available for students to compare with the nets in the book. This will also help with counting faces, vertices and edges.	Challenge students to make the net of a solid with eight faces so that each face is a regular shape. What is the name of this solid? Can they make other solids using only regular shapes with different numbers of faces?

Literacy	Links
The words pyramid and prism are important categories of 3D shapes, but students may well have particular shape perceptions associated with each and therefore this needs to be fully exposed and explored. That cube and cuboids are also prisms, may well not be appreciated by many students. However, students may well bring knowledge of other 3D shape terms with them, such as octahedron and so on. Celebrate and share their knowledge.	There is a collection of nets for paper models of more complex solids at http://www.korthalsaltes.com/index.html

Alternative approach

If there is a set of 3D shapes in your department, use these with groups of three students. Label them and circulate them for student groups to examine carefully, decide whether the shape is a prism, pyramid or other, name it if possible and record the number of faces, edges and vertices. This activity can be carried out with a collection of cardboard cartons of a variety of shapes. Share and discuss the students' results fully. Cardboard cartons can be used for a different task where students are required to 'undo' the carton in order to sketch its net. Alternative use can be made from constructions using for example polydron, ATM MATs, or geomag to support visualisations.

Checkpoint

1 Prepared slides are useful for this checkpoint using three very different cuboids – one close to a cube, one tall and thin, and one flattish. Display an isometric drawing of a particular cuboid.

   a Which of the three particular cuboids is represented? How do you know?

   (Appropriate selection; length observations correctly described)

   b Which of the three nets belongs to each shape?   (Appropriate selection)

Starter – How many angles?

Two lines meet exactly at a point. Excluding reflex angles, one angle is made.

Ask students how many non-reflex angles will be made if three lines meet at a point. (3)

What if four lines meet at a point? (6) Five lines? (10) [n lines, $n(n-1)/2$ angles]

Teaching notes

Nets seen in a book do not always give the impression of a plan that will fold into a solid shape. It is important that students are able to identify this relationship and the challenge as a teacher is to make this exercise a real constructional activity for all students. Where possible have a number of nets available that can be easily folded into a 3D solid.

In addition to making students aware of nets, it is also desirable to practise drawing solids on isometric paper.

As a whole-class activity it may be helpful to complete the example on the introductory page; make sure that the isometric paper is the right way round!

Plenary

Using squared paper, challenge students to draw three nets for a cube: one should have four square faces in a row, one should have no more than three square faces in a row and one should have no more than two square faces in a row.

Exercise commentary

Question 1 – Students could work in pairs. Ask them to put their results in a table and to see if they can spot a relationship: Euler's formula is $F + V - E = 2$.

Question 2 – Similar to the example. Check that students orient the isometric paper so as to have vertical (not horizontal) lines. Having drawn one face it may help to draw the matching back face faintly to make it easier to join the parallel edges. Students may need reminding how to calculate the surface area.

Question 3 – It will help to have available copies of the net so that students can see how it fits together.

Question 4 – Encourage students to draw a net, using the example as a model, and mark the coloured faces as an aid to visualisation.

Question 5 – Two solutions are possible: square pyramid (5 vertices, 8 edges), triangular prism (6 vertices and 9 edges). Challenge students to find both.

Question 6 – Encourage students to hold their cube in the same orientation as one of the diagrams and to copy over the three images, then move on to the next diagram. The orientation of the symbols should be correct.

Answers

1. **a** **i** Cuboid
       ii 6 faces, 8 vertices, 12 edges
   b **i** Cube
       ii 6 faces, 8 vertices, 12 edges
   c **i** Square-based pyramid
       ii 5 faces, 5 vertices, 8 edges
   d **i** Tetrahedron (triangular-based pyramid)
       ii 4 faces, 4 vertices, 6 edges
   e **i** Tetrahedron
       ii 4 faces, 4 vertices, 6 edges
   f **i** Triangular prism
       ii 5 faces, 6 vertices, 9 edges
   g **i** Hexagonal prism
       ii 8 faces, 12 vertices, 18 edge
   h **i** Hexagonal pyramid
       ii 7 faces, 7 vertices, 12 edges
2. **a, b** Check students' drawings
   c 80 cm^2
3. **a, b** Check students' drawings
4. **a** 4   **b** 8   **c** 0
5. **a** Check students' drawings
   b Depends on shape drawn
6. **a, b** Check students' drawings
   c times   is opposite   oval
       diamond   is opposite   spade
       heart   is opposite   club

Objectives

- Use geometric properties of cuboids and shapes made from cuboids   (L6)
- Use simple plans and elevations   (L6)

Key ideas	Resources
1 Being able to match a 2D diagram to the corresponding 3D shape 2 Understanding the aspects of elevations and plans	Plans elevation (1098) Isometric dotty and/or lined paper Squared paper Multilink cubes Representing 3D Shapes (SS6 Improving Learning in Mathematics, Standards Unit): http://www.nationalstemcentre.org.uk/elibrary/collecti on/492/mostly-shape-and-space-materials Set of plans & elevations for the IWB

Simplification	Extension
Make available multilink cubes for all the questions. If possible, actual 3D solids that can be handled will also help with visualisation.	Give students the challenge of drawing three different solids on isometric paper that will have the same plan view, which they should also draw. How different can they make the solids?

Literacy	Links
Relate the word elevation to the height or rise of a building/shape to help nail the vocabulary. Plan can be related to top or bottom view, or even 'bird's eye view'.	Engineers and architects use drawings showing plan and elevation views of parts, products and buildings. Traditionally, drawings were produced by hand but computers have revolutionised the process and most drawings are now produced using computer-aided design (CAD). There is an example of an engineering drawing showing plan and elevation views at http://en.wikipedia.org/wiki/Image:Schneckengetriebe. png

Alternative approach

The Standards Unit resources, including the software, Build, provide a strong alternative and active approach to this section. A further approach could be to set up pairs of students to build, draw plans and elevations, and challenge another pair to recreate their shape from the plans. This can also be set up as a team 'collective memory' game, where one student from the group is allowed to view the shape for a short amount of time, and then reports back to the group. The group challenge is to produce a set of plans and elevations for the 'hidden' shape based on the team's observations and feedback.

Checkpoint

1 Ask questions such as 'if the width of the side elevation is doubled, how are the 3D shape, the plan and the elevation altered?'

(Recognition that the 'depth' of the shape is doubled, that the front elevation will remain the same, but that the plan will need to be appropriately adjusted)

Starter – Faceless

Ask students questions involving the numbers of faces, edges and vertices of 3D shapes, for example,

The sum of faces on a cuboid and vertices on a triangular prism. (12)

The product of edges on a cube and faces on a square-based pyramid. (60)

The difference between vertices on a cuboid and edges on a pentagonal pyramid. (2)

Teaching notes

The use of multi-link cubes in the classroom is challenging. Start with a short exercise to help introduce views and elevations. Show the class four cubes in an L-shape: ask them (in pairs) to draw the front elevation, the side elevation and the plan view. This is similar to the example given. It will allow you to highlight the language and also the need for bold lines where the level of cubes changes.

Plenary

Give students four or five multi-link cubes each. Projected or drawn on paper show them a front elevation, for example, two squares as a rectangle. What could the shape be? Show them the side elevation, for example, again two squares as a rectangle, what could the shape be? Show them the plan view, for example, this could be four squares as a 2×2 square. At each stage they should make the solid they think is being represented. Other shapes could be an L-shape using three cubes, a T-shape using five cubes, or be more adventurous! To plan this, make the shape yourself using cubes and then draw the views.

Exercise commentary

Question 1 – Similar to the first example. Check that students show 'bold' lines where appropriate.

Question 2 – Check the orientation of the isometric paper. It may help to first draw the solid including the shaded cube and then to remove it. Part **ii** is similar to the first example.

Question 3 – Similar to the second example. Remind students to pay attention to the 'bold' lines.

Question 4 – Insist on correct and full mathematical names: for example triangular prism, not just prism.

Question 5 – For part **c**, there is a whole family of various sized cubes but encourage other solutions such as '3D crosses'.

Answers

1 **a–d**   Check students' drawings
2 **a–d**   Check students' drawings
3 **a**   Check students' drawings
  b   4
4 **a**   A ⬌ H, B ⬌ G, C ⬌ E, D ⬌ F
  b   A triangular prism   B cube   C square pyramid   D cylinder
5 **a**   2 by 2 by 2 cube
  b   Check students' drawings
  c   Discuss students' answers

Objectives	
• Visualise 3D shapes from their nets	(L6)
• Calculate (volumes and) surface areas of cuboids and shapes made from cuboids	(L6)

Key ideas	Resources	
1 Be able to visualise all the faces of a cuboid	Nets, surface area	(1066)
2 Understand how to find the surface area of a cuboid	A cuboid and its net Multi-link cube models	

Simplification	Extension
Where students find question **3** difficult, it may help to draw the net of the cuboid in each case. Alternatively, use a model that students can trace dimensions on physically, for example, which lengths are 3 cm; how many; and so on.	Ask questions such as, if the height and width of a cuboid are the same (whole centimetre) length and the area of one face is 12 cm², what could be the dimensions of the cuboid? Ask students to make up similar questions of their own.

Literacy	Links
Students often work confidently with area, but do not always transfer their understanding to that of surface area. Stress both words and take students back to the definition of each. Make links with the units to help emphasise the definitions.	Human skin accounts for between 15% and 20% of the total weight of the human body and helps to protect the body from the environment. It helps keep body fluids in and water and germs out and constantly renews itself. Over 90% of common house dust is made up of dead skin cells.

Alternative approach
It can be helpful to initially discuss all the measures of a cuboid – length, area and volume – establishing and rehearsing the key features of each, before deepening the work on surface area. Multi-link cube models can be helpful, as not only is each cube about 1 cm long, they can be readily counted, if necessary. 'Missing' dimensions is often a sticking point for students when working with surface area, so make sure every length of any cuboid is linked to its measure, while stressing unit links of length (cm), area (cm²) and volume (cm³). Placing model cuboids that correspond together can open up some interesting student dialogue about the changes to surface area that result, with reasoning.

Checkpoint
1 Find the surface area of a cuboid that has dimensions of 3 cm, 4 cm and 5 cm, showing your steps. (94 cm²; with any appropriate stages, such as three different surface areas summed and doubled)

Starter – Area pairs

Write the following three lists on the board.

Triangle bases and heights in cm: 6 and 8, 9 and 12, 7 and 7. Rectangle lengths and widths in cm: 12 and 8, 14 and 2.5, 9 and 7. Areas in cm^2: 96, 54, 63, 24, 24.5, 35.

Ask students to match up the shapes and areas, and calculate the perimeters of the three rectangles.

Teaching notes

As an introduction to the lesson, show a cuboid and ask students 'What is the surface area of this cuboid?' 'How would they work out this area?' Give students time to discuss with each other and then take feedback. This will lead to a discussion around finding the area of each face and adding them together. This will lead to the introduction of nets and finding the area of each face.

Plenary

If the challenge has been completed by most in the classroom, ask students to work in pairs with this problem – if the area of one of the faces of a cuboid is 24 cm^2 and another is 40 cm^2, what could the area of the other face be if it was not 15 cm^2? There are a number of similar questions possible here, for example, area A = 48 cm^2, area B = 24 cm^2, find possible values for area face C. Ask students to sketch the cuboids.

Exercise commentary

Check that units are given with all answers.

Question 1 – Encourage students to multiply the lengths of the sides of the component rectangles rather than count the squares. Highlight the fact that, as the rectangles come in equal pairs, you can double the area of one to find the area of both.

Question 2 – A structured approach to calculating the total surface area, similar to the first example. Students may need to be reminded to double the areas of the three coloured rectangles.

Question 3 – Refer students back to question **2** for scaffolding.

Question 4 – A special case where the total surface area = 6 × area of one face.

Question 5 – Similar to the second example.

Question 6 – Suggest students work in pairs to find the (prime) factors of the areas. Challenge those who find the question easy to write their own question.

Answers

1	a	16 cm^2	b	22 cm^2	c	32 cm^2	d	22 cm^2
2	a	40 cm^2	b	48 cm^2	c	30 cm^2	d	236 cm^2
3	a	72 cm^2	b	250 mm^2	c	58 m^2		
4	a	150 mm^2	b	486 m^2	c	1350 cm^2		
5	a	10 cm	b	8 cm	c	1.5 cm		
6	8 cm × 5 cm × 3 cm							

14d Volume of a cuboid

Objectives	
• Know and use a formula for volume of a cuboid	(L6)
• Calculate volumes (and surface areas) of cuboids and shapes made from cuboids	(L6)

Key ideas	Resources	
1 Correctly find the volume of any cuboid **2** Explain how to find any cuboid's volume	Volume of cuboids Calculator Isometric paper Squared paper Cubes	(1137)

Simplification	Extension
It will help students who find volume difficult to be able to see cuboids. Make the cuboids with small cubes so that the problem can be broken down to: how many layers? How many rows in each layer? How many cubes in each row? This allows students to appreciate $L \times W \times H$. Sketching a layer can also be encouraged. Where appropriate a calculator should be used.	In question **5**, imagine that the box was placed on its side so that the height was 15 cm. What height would the sand be now? Ask students how else the box could be placed.

Literacy	Links
Make sure that the units are stated clearly by students, particularly the 'cubic' or 'cubed' emphasising the nature of volume.	The largest building in the world by volume is the Boeing aircraft factory at Everett, Washington state in the USA. The volume of the building is 13.3 million m³ and it has a floor area of 398,000 m² or 98 acres. There is more information about the factory at http://www.boeing.com/commercial/facilities/index.html

Alternative approach
It may be more helpful to develop a formula for cuboid volume as 'base area' multiplied by height – matching the modelling with layers, and also noting that a cuboid is a member of the set of prisms. Students can struggle with associating the dimensions of length, width and height to a diagram and more so when there is no diagram given. It is worth encouraging them to find out that this does not matter, reminding them that multiplication is commutative, and that a cuboid can be arranged in (how many?) different ways. It may help students to recognise that the dimensions radiate out from any vertex of the cuboid.

Checkpoint		
1 **a** Can a cuboid be made up of 30 cubes?		(Yes)
b If so, suggest possible dimensions.	($1 \times 3 \times 10$; $2 \times 3 \times 5$; $1 \times 2 \times 15$; $1 \times 1 \times 30$; $6 \times 5 \times 1$)	
c Without calculating, which of these is likely to have the smallest surface area?		
	($2 \times 3 \times 5$ because it is the most compact)	

Starter – Costly solids

A face costs 5p, an edge costs 8p and a vertex costs 10p.

Ask students to find the cost of different solids, for example, a cuboid, a square-based pyramid, a triangular prism, a pentagonal prism.

(Answers: £2.06, £1.39, £1.57 and £2.55)

Can be differentiated by the choice of costs.

Teaching notes

It is important to show students the reasoning why we multiply $L \times W \times H$ to find the volume of cuboids. Use cubes to make the example cuboid, $2 \times 4 \times 3$ units in size. You can show this to be 3 layers of 2×4. That is 3 layers of 8 cubes, 3×8 is 24 cubes.

Plenary

Give students the information that the volume of a cuboid is 24 cm³. What could be the dimensions of the cuboid? Take some answers and then give further information. It looks like a long stick, or the height is half the length. Ask for further answers. Continue with a similar question such as the volume of a cuboid is 60 cm³. The width and length are the same. What are the dimensions? Now ask students, in pairs, to write their own problem. They should share with another pair and exchange questions. You could collect in the questions and put them together for homework!

Exercise commentary

Check that all answers have appropriate units.

Question 1 – Similar to the discussion. Students can work in pairs to agree on the best answers.

Question 2 – Similar to the example.

Question 3 – A special case where volume = length³. If a calculator is used, ask students to first write down an estimated volume: $8 < 2.5^3 < 27$.

Question 4 – Remind students to think which lengths (numbers) they need to multiply to find the volume.

Question 5 – In part **c**, if students used a method similar to that in question **4**, ask them to calculate $\frac{3}{4}$ of the height: why does this give the same answer?

Question 6 – Make available small cubes for students to experiment with but also encourage students to think about the prime factor decomposition of $20 = 2^2 \times 5$.

Answers

1	**a**	cm³	**b**	mm³	**c**	cm³
	d	m³	**e**	cm³	**f**	mm³

2   **a**   36 m³   **b**   240 cm³   **c**   30 m³

3   15.625 cm³

4   **a**   2 cm   **b**   6 cm   **c**   0.5 m   **d**   2.78 m

5   **a**   6000 cm³   **b**   4500 cm³   **c**   12 cm

6

Possible cuboids	Surface area
$20 \times 1 \times 1$	82
$10 \times 2 \times 1$	64
$5 \times 4 \times 1$	58
$5 \times 2 \times 2$	48 ← smallest

Objectives
- Calculate the volume of right prisms (L6)

Key ideas	Resources
1 Recognise and name prisms 2 Calculate the volume of prisms using the standard formula	Volume of prisms (1139) Examples of prisms Mini whiteboards

Simplification	Extension
Students should focus on applying the formula for the volume of a prism rather than working through problems in reverse. Further examples can be given to the students who might struggle to pick up the ideas, including further cuboid questions that link back to the previous section **14d**.	Question **6** introduces the idea of the surface area of a prism since it uses a right-angled triangle cross-section with the value of the hypotenuse shown. This can be developed by providing the students with the value of the hypotenuse in question **2** part **c** (10.63 cm) or through the use of other right-angled triangle cross-sections such as one with base = 12 cm, height = 5 cm and hypotenuse = 13 cm.

Literacy	Links
The word 'prism' may be familiar to students from previous work but if not, it is important to give a precise definition using the correct mathematical vocabulary. Students can add the name of common prisms to a glossary of key terms and provide their own definitions as appropriate.	A link can be made to science since students may have met the idea of a prism being used to split light beams into their composite colours (effectively creating a rainbow). Students could also link to work on nets from **14a** and actually make some prisms of their own. There is a collection of nets for paper models of more complex solids at http://www.korthalsaltes.com/index.html

Alternative approach

Models of prisms can be used to generate initial discussion about what it is to be 'a prism'. Students could be invited to think up their own examples from experience (triangular prism chocolate boxes, for example) and asked to come up with an informal definition of what a prism is. Develop this into the standard definition with reference to a constant cross-section and highlight special cases such as the cuboid and cylinder.

Checkpoint

1 A triangular prism has length 12 cm. If the triangular cross-section has a base of 4 cm and a perpendicular height of 3 cm, find the volume. (72 cm^3)
2 A prism has volume 1200 mm^3. If the length is 10 cm, find the area of the cross-section. (12 mm^2)

Starter – Speed quiz

10 questions, all of which are either area of rectangle or area of triangle.

Give the students 3 seconds per question and use mini whiteboards to record all answers (rather than writing and wiping after each one).

Example questions:

'Rectangle, base 6 cm, height 3 cm'

'Triangle, base 4 cm, height 2 cm'

Teaching notes

Construct a cuboid from multi-link cubes. How can the number of cubes be found without having to count every single one? Establish that multiplication can find the area on the end 'slice' of the cuboid, and a final multiplication by the number of 'slices' can find the number of cubes. This develops work from **14d** and can be generalised to show volume = area of the cross section × length for a rectangular prism.

Look at the volume of a right-angled triangular prism. Can its volume be found in a similar way to that of the cuboid? Visualisation of two prisms joining together to form a cuboid could be used here. So if the volume of the prism is half that of the cuboid, can we work from the formula for the area of a triangle (half of the rectangle) instead? Show that half base times height times length works fine.

Establish that the cross-section can be of any shape, as long as it is continuous (same size and shape all the way along) to produce a prism and generalise to the formula volume of a prism = area of the cross section × length.

Model examples where the students have to work backwards as well (questions **4** and **5**).

Plenary

Quick-fire questioning on this work using mini whiteboards will enable effective assessment of progress. Mix up the questions to include ones where the cross-section area and volume are given. This should ensure students listen carefully to the information.

Exercise commentary

Question 1 – Students should recognise and be able to name these prisms quickly.

Question 2 – Emphasise in part **c** that the triangle is right-angled.

Question 3 – Students might need help extracting the information from the word problem since no diagram is given.

Question 4 – Students should work with the formula in reverse to find the length of the prisms. In parts **b** and **c** they will also need to work out the area of the triangular face.

Question 5 – Students might need help extracting the information from the word problem since no diagram is given.

Question 6 – Part **a** should hold no problems for the students. Part **b** links to work on surface area and they may benefit from a net of the prism to see the five faces clearly.

Answers

1 **a** Cuboid/rectangular prism
   b Pentagonal prism
   c Right-angled triangular prism
2 **a** 30 cm^3 **b** 100 cm^3 **c** 252 cm^3
3 180 cm^3
4 **a** 8 cm **b** 15 cm **c** 3.5 cm
5 1.5 cm
6 **a** 48 cm^3 **b** 108 cm^2

14 3D shapes – MySummary

Key outcomes	Quick check
Recognise and name 3D solids and recognise their nets. L6	**a** A 3D solid has six rectangular faces. Name the solid. (Cuboid) **b** Write down the number of edges and vertices the solid has. (12, 8)
Use isometric paper and draw plans and elevations of 3D shapes. L6	A model is made from a base of three cubes in a line with two cubes placed on top, one at each end. **a** Draw the model on isometric paper. (Check students' drawings) **b** Draw the plan view and the front and side elevations. (Check students' drawings)
Calculate the surface area and volume of cuboids. L6	Calculate the volume and surface area of a cuboid with edge lengths 10 cm, 5 cm and 2 cm. (100 cm^3, 160 cm^2)
Calculate the volume of a prism. L6	Calculate the volume of a prism with cross section area equal to 24 cm^2 and length 6 cm. (144 cm^3)

⊞ MyMaths extra support

Lesson/online homework	Description
2D and 3D shapes 1229 L2	Names and properties of 2D and 3D shapes

MyReview

Check out
You should now be able to ...

✓ Recognise and name 3D solids and recognise their nets.	1–3
✓ Use isometric paper and draw plans and elevations of 3D shapes.	4–5
✓ Calculate the surface area and volume of cuboids.	6–9
✓ Calculate the volume of a prism.	10, 11

Language	Meaning	Example
Solid	A shape formed in three dimensions.	Cubes, spheres and cones are solids
Face	A flat surface of a solid	Vertex, Edge, Face
Edge	The line where two faces meet	
Vertex	The point where three or more edges meet	
Net	A 2D shape that can be folded to form a solid	An opened out cardboard box forms a net
Surface area	The total area of all the faces of a solid shape	The surface area of a cube is six times the area of one square face
Volume	The amount of space inside a 3D shape	The volume of a cube is its side length cubed
Prism	A 3D shape with a constant cross-section	A cuboid could be called a rectangular prism, and a cylinder is a circular prism
Cross-section	The 2D shape made when a 3D solid is cut along its length	Cross-sections of a cylinder include circles and rectangles

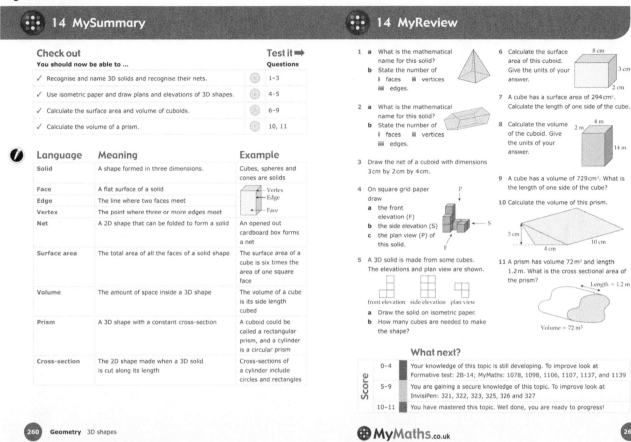

1 a What is the mathematical name of this solid?
   b State the number of
     i faces   ii vertices
     iii edges.

2 a What is the mathematical name for this solid?
   b State the number of
     i faces   ii vertices
     iii edges.

3 Draw the net of a cuboid with dimensions 3cm by 2cm by 4cm.

4 On square grid paper draw
   a the front elevation (F)
   b the side elevation (S)
   c the plan view (P) of this solid.

5 A 3D solid is made from some cubes. The elevations and plan view are shown.

   front elevation   side elevation   plan view
   a Draw the solid on isometric paper.
   b How many cubes are needed to make the shape?

6 Calculate the surface area of this cuboid. Give the units of your answer.

7 A cube has a surface area of 294cm². Calculate the length of one side of the cube.

8 Calculate the volume of the cuboid. Give the units of your answer.

9 A cube has a volume of 729cm³. What is the length of one side of the cube?

10 Calculate the volume of this prism.

11 A prism has volume 72m³ and length 1.2m. What is the cross sectional area of the prism?

Volume = 72 m³

What next?

	0–4	Your knowledge of this topic is still developing. To improve look at Formative test: 2B-14; MyMaths: 1078, 1098, 1106, 1107, 1137, and 1139
Score	5–9	You are gaining a secure knowledge of this topic. To improve look at InvisiPen: 321, 322, 323, 325, 326 and 327
	10–11	You have mastered this topic. Well done, you are ready to progress!

Question commentary

Questions 1 and **2** – Students should be able to describe the difference between a pyramid and a prism.

Question 3 – Check that their diagram is a possible net of the cuboid.

Question 4 – Diagrams should be drawn accurately with no attempt to make them look 3D.

Question 5 – Remind students to turn their isometric paper so straight lines are vertical.

Questions 6 and **7** – Students often forget about faces or confuse volume with surface area (incorrect answers are 48 and 6.6).

Questions 8 and **9** – Note that units are metres in question **8**. For question **9**, suggest students find a suitable button on their calculators to help (cube root).

Question 10 – Students may need reminding of the formula for the area of a triangle. The perpendicular height given outside the triangle may also confuse some.

Question 11 – Students work backwards. Note the dimensions are in metres.

Answers

1 a Square-based pyramid
   b i 5   ii 5   iii 8
2 a Pentagonal prism
   b i 7   ii 15   iii 10
3 Check two 3×2, two 2×4 and two 3×4 rectangles
4 a, b, c Check students' drawings
5 a Check students' drawings
   b 7
6 92 cm²
7 7 cm
8 112 m³
9 9 cm
10 60 cm³
11 60 m²

14 MyPractice

1 A prism is shown.

a State the number of
  i faces
  ii vertices
  iii edges.

b Draw the solid on isometric paper.

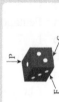

2 cm 2 cm 3 cm

2 a Draw a shape with six faces and ten edges.
How many vertices does the shape have?

b Draw a shape with nine edges and six vertices.
How many faces does the shape have?

3 Sketch the front elevation (F), the side elevation (S) and the plan view (P) of this dice.

P S F

Front elevation   Side elevation   Plan

4 A 3D shape is made from cubes.
The elevations and plan view are shown.

a Draw the solid on isometric paper.

b How many cubes are needed to make the solid?

5 Calculate the surface area of these cuboids.

a   9 cm   3 cm   3 cm

b   7 cm   6 cm   3 cm

c   10 cm   8 cm   4 cm

6 Calculate the length of one side of the cube, if the surface area of the cube is

a 294 cm²   b 1536 cm²   c 235.5 cm²

7 A cuboid has three faces with areas 54 m², 48 m² and 72 m². What are the dimensions of the cuboid?

Area = 72 m²   Area = 48 m²   Area = 54 m²   length

8 Copy and complete the table for the cuboids.

width   length   height

	Length	Width	Height	Volume
a	9 m	8 m	8 m	
b	15 mm	10 mm	20 mm	
c	2.5 cm	2 cm	8 cm	
d	5 m	3.5 m	3.2 m	
e	6 cm	2 cm		42 cm³
f	4 m	4 m		48 m³
g	7 cm		20 cm	280 cm³
h	9 cm		32 cm	288 cm³

9 A cube has volume 91.125 mm³.
What is the length of the cube's edge?

10 Find the volumes of these prisms.

a   Area = 20 cm²   14 cm

b   5 cm   4 cm   13 cm

c   6 cm   7 cm   25 cm

11 Find the area of the cross section of these prisms.

a   Volume = 360 cm³   12 cm

b   Volume = 97.5 m³   7.5 m

Question commentary

Questions 1 and **2** – Students will need to carefully visualise the shapes in these questions.

Question 3 – Make sure students are drawing the dots in the correct orientation.

Question 4 – Students could be provided with cubes and asked to make the shape before drawing the isometric view.

Question 5 – Check that all six faces are included in the students' calculations.

Question 6 – Students should divide by six before square rooting.

Question 7 – Students may need guidance investigating the (prime) factors of the areas of the faces. Paired discussion could be used here.

Question 8 – Students must work backwards in parts **e** to **h**. Emphasise that it does not matter *which* of the sides are missing.

Question 9 – Suggest students use a button on their calculator (the cube root key) to work this out quickly.

Question 10 – Students may need reminding of the formula for the area of a triangle in part **c**.

Question 11 – Working backwards. Note that part **b** has units in metres.

Answers

1 a i 8   **ii** 12   **iii** 18
  b Check students' drawings

2 a Check students' drawings
    6 vertices (unless the student has drawn a very strange shape)
  b Check students' drawings
    5 faces (unless the student has drawn a very strange shape)

3

4 a Check students' drawings
  b 6

5 a 126 cm^2 **b** 162 cm^2 **c** 304 cm^2

6 a 7 cm   **b** 16 cm   **c** 6.26 cm

7 a 9 cm × 6 cm × 8 cm

8

	Length	Width	Height	Volume
a	9 m	8 m	8 m	576 m^3
b	15 mm	10 mm	20 mm	3000 mm^3
c	2.5 cm	2 cm	8 cm	40 cm^3
d	5 m	3.5 cm	3.2 cm	56 m^3
e	6 cm	2 cm	3.5 cm	42 cm^3
f	4 m	4 m	3 m	48 m^3
g	7 cm	2 cm	20 cm	280 cm^3
h	9 cm	1 cm	32 cm	288 cm^3

9 4.5 mm

10 a 280 cm^3 **b** 260 cm^3 **c** 525 cm^3

11 a 30 cm^2 **b** 13 m^2

Case study 5: Perspective

Related lessons		Resources	
3D shapes	14a	3D shapes	(1078)
Enlargements 1	9d	Enlarging shapes	(1099)
		Cubes and cuboids	
		Old newspapers or magazines	

Simplification	Extension
Prepared templates could be used for task **2**. Encourage students to complete one very good drawing rather than trying to complete too many of the tasks in the time available.	Students could look in old magazines or newspapers for examples of pictures that show single or two point perspective. They could draw guidelines on the pictures to find their vanishing points and eye-lines. Whilst searching for these, ask them to look out for pictures that seem to have more than two vanishing points. They might come across some such as looking upwards at an edge on a skyscraper that show tapering of the vertical edges as well as the horizontal ones.
	Students could also research the use of reverse perspective, where the exact opposite of perspective happens and the vanishing point would be behind or on the person viewing the picture rather than its more natural position in the distance away from the viewer.

Links
Design and technology uses perspective drawing when creating designs for objects to be manufactured. Links can be made to other types of technical drawing and the rationale behind them. Consider the need for such drawing techniques. http://en.wikipedia.org/wiki/Technical_drawing

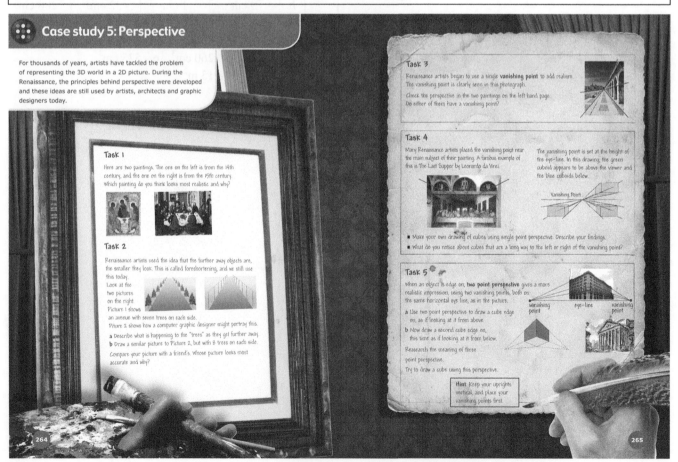

Teaching notes

During the Renaissance period (from the 14th century to the 17th century), artists strived to produce paintings that gave a more realistic representation of the world than had been the case in many paintings prior to the Renaissance period. In the Renaissance, artists became interested in using perspective to represent 3D objects in a 2D picture in a way that showed them as they were seen in the real world.

Talk about the Renaissance period and look together at the two paintings shown on the left hand page. Remind students that both pictures are painted on a flat 2D surface and are trying to show a 3D world. Ask them which one they think is more realistic and how this realism is created.

Task 1

Discuss angles in the pictures. In the right hand picture, lines that lie along the sight line and would be parallel in the real world are shown converging to a common point. In the left hand picture, the angle of the seat and the platforms under the feet are tapering in an unnatural looking manner, as are some parts of the building in the background. Discuss how sizes are used to create depth in the right hand picture. People in the foreground are shown slightly larger than those further away, windows that are closer are taller than those that are further away, etc. In comparison, the left hand picture looks almost flat, even though there are things in the background.

Task 2

Students will need to create the 'framework' onto which to put their trees. They should ensure that they consider the vanishing point along the sight lines.

Task 3

Talk about the vanishing point and look again at the original two paintings to see if either of those have a vanishing point (you should find that the right hand painting does). Discuss how the vanishing point is on the eye-line and how the angles converge from above for things that are above the eye-line and from below for things below the eye-line.

Task 4

Look at the diagram of cuboids and discuss with the students how to draw diagrams with single point perspective. Establish that, to draw a cube, you would set an eye-line and vanishing point and then draw the front face as a square. Then you would draw guidelines from the corners of this face to the vanishing point and use these to help construct the diagram. Give students time to draw their own diagram of cubes, positioning at least one above the eye-line

and using different amounts of horizontal offset either side of the vanishing point.

Task 5

Discuss how, when the building is viewed edge on, the two walls either side of the edge appear to taper away in different directions to form two vanishing points that lie on the same eye-line. Discuss how you would use two point perspective to draw a cube edge on and give the students some time to make their own drawings as described.

Answers

1 The 15th century painting looks more realistic. The people in the foreground look larger than the people in the background.

2 **a** The trees get smaller

   b Students' own answers

3 Yes, the right hand one

4 Students' own answers

5 Students' own answers

15 Ratio and proportion

Learning outcomes

R2	Use scale factors, scale diagrams and maps	(L5)
R3	Express one quantity as a fraction of another, where the fraction is less than 1 and greater than 1	(L5)
R4	Use ratio notation, including reduction to simplest form	(L5)
R5	Divide a given quantity in two parts in a given part : part or part : whole ratio; express the division of a quantity into two parts as a ratio	(L6)
R7	Understand that a multiplicative relationship between two quantities can be expressed as a ratio or a fraction	(L6)
R8	Solve problems involving percentage change, including: percentage increase, decrease and original value problems and simple interest in financial mathematics	(L6)

Introduction

This chapter builds on ratio and proportion work done in Phase 1 and the FDP work done in Chapter 4. Students learn to: simplify ratios, including those with mixed units; solve ratio problems, such as scale drawings, by scaling both sides by a common factor; divide a quantity in a given ratio; solve direct proportion problems using the unitary method; and solve problems that mix ratio and proportion. The chapter moves on to looking at percentage increase and decrease problems and comparing proportions as fractions or percentages.

The idea of creating things which are in proportion is vital to art and architecture. However there is one number, called the 'Golden Proportion', which is supposed to be the most pleasing to the eye.

The Golden Proportion relates to a rectangle whose ratio of length to width is 1.6180339887 : 1. There is evidence that the ancient Greeks and Egyptians used this proportion in the design of many of their buildings, and Renaissance artists used it commonly in their paintings.

Prior knowledge

Students should already know how to…
- Identify factors and multiples
- Convert between common units of time, length and mass
- Convert between fractions, decimals and percentages
- Calculate simple percentages of an amount

Starter problem

Students should be encouraged to collect their own data on height and head circumference as well as the sizes of other body parts (which could link to work in statistics). This data can then be used to quantify various ratios and proportions. Opportunities can be taken to emphasise the need to use common units and how to draw scale drawings. Posing the question 'In an accurate 10 cm tall model of an adult, how big should the head be?' allows a discussion of dividing in a given ratio. Similar modelling questions can be used to introduce direct proportion.

Students could investigate the age dependence of measurements. What are the percentage changes in the size of body parts as people grow? How should you compare relative proportions? At birth a baby is about four heads tall but only $7\frac{1}{2}$ heads tall as an adult.

The theory of art contains several examples of the ideal proportions for bodies and faces. How do you quantify these proportions and how realistic are they? One famous example is da Vinci's version of Vitruvian man. Manga comics illustrate the effect of modifying ratios.

Resources

MyMaths

Proportion unitary method	1036	Ratio dividing 1	1038	Ratio dividing 2	1039
Comparing fractions	1075	Change as a percentage	1302		

Online assessment

Chapter test	2B–15
Formative test	2B–15
Summative test	2B–15

InvisiPen solutions

Simplify and use ratio	191	Simple ratio and proportion	192
Ratio and proportion	193	Comparing proportions	194
Direct proportion and unitary method			195

Topic scheme

Teaching time = 6 lessons/2 weeks

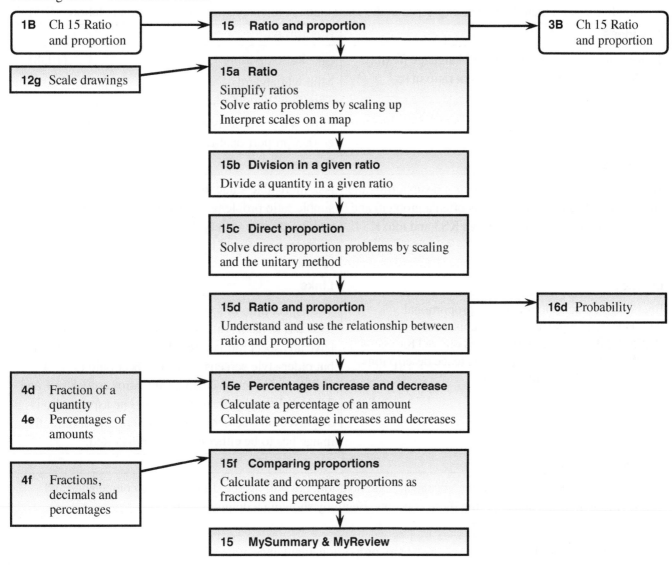

1B Ch 15 Ratio and proportion

15 Ratio and proportion

3B Ch 15 Ratio and proportion

12g Scale drawings

15a Ratio
Simplify ratios
Solve ratio problems by scaling up
Interpret scales on a map

15b Division in a given ratio
Divide a quantity in a given ratio

15c Direct proportion
Solve direct proportion problems by scaling and the unitary method

15d Ratio and proportion
Understand and use the relationship between ratio and proportion

16d Probability

4d Fraction of a quantity
4e Percentages of amounts

15e Percentages increase and decrease
Calculate a percentage of an amount
Calculate percentage increases and decreases

4f Fractions, decimals and percentages

15f Comparing proportions
Calculate and compare proportions as fractions and percentages

15 MySummary & MyReview

Differentiation

Student book 2A   274 – 293
Simplifying ratios
Dividing into ratios
Proportion
Proportion problems
Ratio and proportion problems
Comparing proportions
Calculations involving money

Student book 2B   266 – 283
Ratio
Division in a given ratio
Direct proportion
Ratio and proportion
Percentage increase and decrease
Comparing proportions

Student book 2C   268 – 285
Ratio
Division in a given ratio
Direct proportion
Ratio and proportion
Comparing proportions
Algebra and proportion

Objectives

- Solve simple problems involving ratio and proportion using informal strategies   (L5)
- Simplify a ratio, including those expressed in different units, recognising links with fraction notation   (L5)

Key ideas	Resources
1 Recognise and use proportional language flexibly 2 Understand what is expected of a ratio in its simplest form	Ratio dividing 1 (1038) Mini whiteboards Thinking Proportionally: Y8 lessons & resources: http://www.nationalstemcentre.org.uk/elibrary/resource/5005/proportional-reasoning-transition-lessons

Simplification	Extension
Where students have difficulty, focus on supporting the analysis of word problems. This is often a problem and will be a focus for learning through KS3 and into KS4.	Ask more able students to design a worksheet of some simple ratio problems around mixing colours or making bead jewellery that could be used in a year 6 classroom as part of a transition package with feeder schools.

Literacy	Links
Encourage students to use all the proportional language, with equivalent statements, such as 'half/0.5/50% are red' and 'there is one red for every one blue'. Encourage complete sentence descriptions in order to establish full meaning.	The aspect ratio of a screen or an image is the ratio of its width to its height. HD televisions and monitors have an aspect ratio of 16 : 9 (also known as 1.78 : 1) but older-style screens have an aspect ratio of 4 : 3 (1.33 : 1). Common cinema film ratios are 1.85 : 1 and 2.35 : 1. When an image filmed in one aspect ratio is displayed on a screen with a different aspect ratio, the image has to be either cropped or distorted.

Alternative approach

Students should be familiar with the vocabulary and notation, but will need to fully develop competence and confidence with using and applying these concepts. Begin by showing a diagram such as:

Ask students to describe what they see, using any proportional language, e.g. 3/7 of the bar is white; white area is 75% of grey; the ratio of white to grey squares is 3 : 4; and so on. Gather, share and explore as many of these statements as is sensible. Equivalent proportion card sorting can also be used to widen students' appreciation of variety. Resources such as those found in the Y8 Thinking Proportionally by DFES, may be used here. Equivalent spider diagrams can also be developed by pairs of students, and may include equivalent ratios, simplest form as well as amounts with units.

Checkpoint

1 Two thirds of a drink of squash is water. If the actual drink is 300 ml, how much water was needed? (200 ml)

2 At a mathematics master class the ratio of boys to girls is 5 : 4. If there are 80 girls there, how many students are there altogether?   (180)

Starter – Amazing digits

Ask students to think of a three-digit number (3 different digits), for example, 451.

Ask them to reverse the digits (154).

Subtract the smaller number from the larger number (451 – 154 = 297).

Add the answer digits together until a single digit is obtained (2 + 9 + 7 = 18, 1 + 8 = 9).

Repeat with another three-digit number.

Ask students what they notice. (Always 9)

Teaching notes

Students can be encouraged to make explicit links here between fractions and ratios in terms of cancelling and simplifying. Stress the importance of both parts of the ratio being in the same units, as in the introductory example.

To facilitate assessment of students' prior knowledge at an early stage, use question **1** as a class activity using mini whiteboards.

In the first worked example, for those students who appear uncertain, focus on looking for how many lots of 7 there are in 175 to find the multiplier.

The example involving scales on maps can be linked to work elsewhere in the curriculum such as geography or scale drawing in design and technology. Invite students to suggest other examples. This work provides opportunities for students to demonstrate their capacity to transfer mathematical skills to other contexts, supporting their development as functional mathematicians.

Plenary

Invite students to think of how they use ratio in real life: Food technology? Recipes? Art? Mixing colours?

Exercise commentary

Question 1 – Make links here with fractions and cancelling. Possibly use this as a whole-class mini whiteboard activity.

Question 2 – Here students will need to rewrite the questions in the same units first before cancelling. Refer students back to the introduction if necessary.

Question 3 – This example provides the opportunity for students to practise rewriting text-based problems in mathematical form before simplifying. The units may catch some students out in part **c**.

Question 4 – Similar to the two examples: word problems to solve in a real-life context to develop functional skills.

Question 5 – It may help students to write the ratio in the form $n : 1$.

Answers

1	**a**	2 : 7	**b**	2 : 3	**c**	3 : 5	**d**	2 : 3
	e	8 : 5	**f**	5 : 8	**g**	8 : 5	**h**	8 : 7
	i	11 : 7	**j**	1 : 2	**k**	1 : 3	**l**	1 : 3
	m	16 : 1	**n**	7 : 2				
2	**a**	2 : 5	**b**	9 : 20	**c**	5 : 8	**d**	3 : 10
	e	8 : 5	**f**	3 : 4	**g**	9 : 2	**h**	4 : 9
	i	1 : 8	**j**	1 : 36	**k**	2 : 9	**l**	2 : 15
	m	12 : 25	**n**	3 : 1				
3	**a**	3 : 2	**b**	5 : 22	**c**	1 : 25		
4	**a**	39	**b**	480 g	**c i**	30 m	**ii**	20 cm
	d	1.5 m						
5	**a**	3 : 1	**b**	11 : 7	**c**	The ratio gets closer to 1		

Objectives	
• Divide a quantity into two (or more) parts in a given ratio	(L6)
• Use the unitary method to solve simple problems involving ratio and direct proportion	(L6)

Key ideas	Resources
1 Dividing into given ratios with any appropriate method 2 Begin to consider more efficient ways of solving proportional problems	Ratio dividing 2 (1039) Mini whiteboards Calculators

Simplification	Extension
Support students who are experiencing difficulty with word problems by guiding them in underlining or highlighting the key information needed to solve the problem. Use block diagrams to represent values of each section, to aid informal method building.	Challenge more able students to develop real-life word-based problems that could be used in an assessment for a parallel group. They must provide a mark scheme.

Literacy	Links
Check the quality of the students' reading of any problems, by encouraging reading out loud. Check also that answers are completed fully, and include appropriate units. Commonly, students will offer answers such as '20 : 30' for question 1a, for example, rather than '£20 and £30'.	The Golden Ratio occurs in mathematics, art and in nature and is calculated as 1 : 1.618 (to 3 dp). It can be used to divide an object into two parts so that the ratio of the smaller part to the larger part is the same as the ratio of the larger part to the whole object. The ratio is used in architecture to produce buildings of aesthetically pleasing proportions.

Alternative approach
Students can be grouped into threes, and presented with a scenario that three people have jointly won £367 425 with a lottery ticket that they all contributed to. If they decided to share the money fairly, based on their contributions to the £1 ticket, find what they might receive for, say, three different situations. It is likely that students will begin with proportions that are likely to be solved with informal methods. Suggested further situations can be suggested and shared – with differentiation – and efficient use of a calculator explored.

Checkpoint
1 The angles of a triangle are in the ratio of 5 : 6 : 7. What are their sizes and explain how you know? (50°; 60°; 70°; recognise total of 180°; multiplicative factor of 10 produces result)
2 1 inch is 2.54 cm. How many inches would 20 cm be? (7.87 inches)

Starter – Countdown

Ask students for six numbers: five between 1 and 10, and one from 25, 50 and 100.

Write the numbers on the board.

Throw a dice three times to generate a three-digit target number.

Challenge students to calculate this target number (or get as close as possible to it) using the six numbers and any operations.

Teaching notes

The worked example emphasises the value of a simple checking strategy and students should be encouraged to use this for themselves. This is a means of developing key processes in number through considering the appropriateness and accuracy of numerical results and also, as a paired activity, as a means of assessing themselves and others and reviewing progress.

The real-life, everyday settings used in the worked examples and in the word-based problems in the exercise fully support the embedding of functional skills in the curriculum, where the focus is on students learning to access their 'mathematical toolbox' to find the appropriate skill to solve a problem and then to understand how to check a solution so that they know they have a reasonable answer.

Plenary

Ask students to reflect on the word problems they have been working on and to vote on which was most challenging. Discuss this as a whole class.

Exercise commentary

Take opportunities to use the real-life scenarios in this exercise to develop the students as functional mathematicians.

Question 1 – Simple calculations that can be done mentally.

Questions 2 and 3 – Similar to the example.

Question 4 – If students struggle here, support them in identifying key information.

Question 5 – This question highlights the value of the simple checking strategy promoted in the discussion and emphasises the importance of explaining thinking. Students could compare their reasoning with a partner.

Question 6 – Here students investigate links between ratio and fractions of areas.

Answers

1   **a**   £20 : £30   **b**   25 cm : 35 cm   **c**   32 MB : 40 MB
    d   15 p : 75 p   **e**   45 : 75 seconds   **f**   £150 : £90

2   **a**   Students' diagram to show apples are divided by 5
    b   9

3   **a**   Students' diagram to show money is divided by 8
    b   £25

4   **a**   36   **b**   £24

5   **a**   Correct. If the ratio is 2 : 3 from 25 then each part of the ratio represents 5 pieces of equipment and so $2 \times 5 = 10 : 3 \times 5 = 15$ is the correct number of funnels and beakers.

    b   Incorrect $\frac{65}{4+9} = 5$ $5 \times 4 = 20$ $9 \times 5 = 45$

      Jack receives £20 and Oprah receives £45.

6   **a**   Answers will vary. Check students' drawings
    b   Similar to the rectangle above but with slightly different dimensions.
    c   If their lengths are easily divisible by 8.

Objectives

- Use direct proportion in simple contexts   (L5)
- Use the unitary method to solve simple problems involving ratio and direct proportion   (L6)

Key ideas	Resources
1 Recognise when a problem involves direct proportion 2 Begin to spot the multiplicative relationship or scale factor in a direct proportion problem	Proportion unitary method (1036) Y8 multiplicative relationships: http://www.nationalstemcentre.org.uk/elibrary/resource/4981/year-eight-multiplicative-relationships-mini-pack

Simplification	Extension
Use spider diagrams to illustrate how some values can be easily calculated to increase confidence and make links with fractions and percentages.	Encourage more able students to look for just one multiplicative relationship, equivalent to two stages in the unitary method. Invite more able students to apply their skills to investigate value for money between various mobile phone packages.

Literacy	Links
Emphasise units and context of problems, and that these are reflected in both recorded work and verbally.	As part of the design process for a product, manufacturers draw up a list of all the components incorporated in the assembled product. This is called a parts list. The manufacturer decides how many of the product he is going to build, and then orders the number of parts required. The number he needs is in direct proportion to the number on the parts list.

Alternative approach

Use vertical bars to represent values in problems, for example in the given examples:

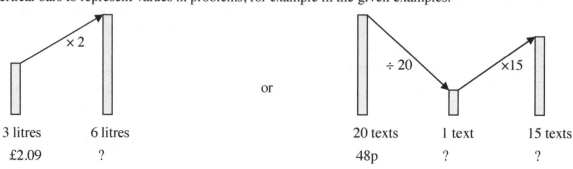

3 litres	6 litres		20 texts	1 text	15 texts
£2.09	?		48p	?	?

This helps to secure the intuitive approach that students may have when they recognise a simple 'scale factor', and develops a visual approach to using the unitary method. Students will have varying recognition of proportional facts that they may apply, which needs to be encouraged. Some students, for example, may well spot that in example 2 '× ¾' is an effective and an efficient way to the solution, though they may not recognise this as an application of the unitary method extended to a multiplicative relationship. Further direct proportion problems including card sorts and vertical bar/line resource sheets can be found in the Y8 Multiplicative Relationships mini pack.

Checkpoint

1   10 gallons is equivalent to 45.5 litres.
    a   What is equivalent to 5 gallons?   (22.75 litres)
    b   What is equivalent to 12 gallons?   (54.6 litres)

Starter – Granddad Bob

Bob wanted to share £5500 between his 4 grandchildren. He decided to give the money in the ratio of their ages. Simon was 16, Lucy and Jo were both 12 and Steven was 10.

Ask students how much money each grandchild received. (£1760, £1320, £1320, £1100)

Can be extended by students making up their own ratio problems.

Teaching notes

The material throughout this topic is related to real-life everyday application of the mathematics being learned. Students can be encouraged to look for examples of their own from everyday experience and equally to identify cases where increases are not in direct proportion.

The unitary method of solving problems will need to be supported for some students, although all will be able to use doubling and halving strategies. It may be helpful to use the spider diagram approach to illustrate which values are easy to calculate for any given example. Students will be familiar with this strategy from previous work on fractions and percentages and this may help to make connections.

To embed functional skills, discuss how this work can be used to make comparisons of such things as nutritional value or value for money.

Plenary

Link to real-life situations and invite students to suggest examples where two quantities may not increase in direct proportion. For example, with special offers on food, drinks, text message costs, etc. Why would this happen?

Exercise commentary

Question 1 – This question could be used as a whole-class activity.

Question 2 – The explanation of how students find their answers is particularly important.

Questions 3 and **4** – Real-life settings for word problems. Students may need to be reminded to use the unitary method where appropriate. Looking for short-cuts is also a good strategy.

Question 5 – Ask students to explain the strategy they used to decide which parts of the table to complete first.

Answers

1   **a**   £5.52   **b**   £2.76   **c**   23p
    d   £1.15   **e**   £11.50   **f**   £1.38

2   D-Mobile and Codaphone

3   **a**   £2.76   **b**   21 g   **c**   100 cals
    d   **i**   875 g   **ii**   1625 g

4   **a**   **i**   £3.33   **ii**   £2.96   **b**   24.5 litres   **c**   84p
    d   225 Chinese Yuan   **e**   £43.60   **f**   525 g

5

kg	lb
1	2.2
1.8	4
5	11
10	22
12	50.6
50	110

2.2 lb = 1 kg   0.45kg = 1 lb

Objectives	
• Understand the relationship between ratio and proportion	(L5)
• Apply understanding of the relationship between ratio and proportion	(L6)

Key ideas	Resources
1 Recognise that proportion is equality of ratios 2 Solving simple ratio and proportion problems	Proportion unitary method (1036) Ratio dividing 2 (1039) What is a fraction? (Chapters 4 and 5) http://www.nationalstemcentre.org.uk/elibrary/resourc e/4651/what-is-a-fraction

Simplification	Extension
Make further use of diagrams to offer visual clues, as in the first question of the exercise, to support students who struggle with this work.	Involve more able students in a mini project using these skills, possibly involving some aspect of school life, such as comparing exam results for boys and girls.

Literacy	Links
The definition of proportion as an equality of ratios is important to communicate in order to give a clear and useable sense of the concept to the students. Use illustrations from across the curriculum and from other areas of mathematics, such as similarity, enlargement.	Proportional representation is a system of election where the number of seats given to a particular party is proportional to the number of votes that it receives. In an election in the UK, only the winning candidate in each constituency becomes a Member of Parliament. Smaller parties might win a sizeable proportion of the vote without winning any seats.

Alternative approach
The key idea is not an easy one, so students need to explore and practise application fully. An alternative approach is to tackle this section after section **15e** and directly followed by section **15f**, so that the ideas can be consolidated more firmly. Useful ideas and activities for students can be found in the booklet 'What is a fraction?' Chapters 4 and 5, which cover the themes for both section **15d** and section **15f**.

Checkpoint
1 3/7 of the pets at a vet's waiting room are dogs, and the rest are cats. What is the ratio of cats to dogs? (4 : 3)
2 The ratio of fiction to non-fiction books in a particular library is 8 : 3. What fraction of the books is fiction?   (8/11)

Starter – Emergency!

Ask students to arrange the digits 1 to 9 to make three 3-digit numbers that will add up to 999. Challenge students to see who can find the greatest number of different ways this can be done.

(One possible way is 498 + 375 + 126 = 999)

Teaching notes

This topic clarifies the terms ratio and proportion providing illustration through worked examples. The emphasis in the topic is on real-life use of this learning and students can be encouraged to look for or generate examples of their own to provide further illustration and to develop increasing responsibility for their learning.

Students can be encouraged to work collaboratively here and share ideas to clarify understanding. This also provides the opportunity to explore issues or problems from different perspectives and to generate ideas and explore possibilities.

Again, emphasise connections with students' knowledge of fractions throughout.

Plenary

Take whole-class feedback on the challenge activity to discuss examples that students have generated in pairs.

Exercise commentary

Question 1 – Similar to the initial discussion. The diagrams should support understanding and clarify the distinction between ratio and proportion.

Questions 2 and **3** – Similar to the first example.

Question 4 – Similar to the second example. Students may need to be reminded that they may need to change the units in parts **e** and **f**.

Question 5 – Students will need to recognise that the proportions are out of the *total*.

Question 6 – Two real-life examples. Encourage students to discuss their methods and check each other's solutions.

Question 7 – Use this question to develop student dialogue around misunderstandings. Tell students that some said the answer to part **a** was 3 : 5. Is this correct?

Question 8 – A triple ratio problem from real life. Ask students to add some challenges of their own and share these with a partner.

Answers

1 **a i** 4 : 1 **ii** $\frac{4}{5}$

   iii red section = 4 × yellow section
   yellow section = $\frac{1}{4}$ × red section

 b i 3 : 1 **ii** $\frac{3}{4}$

   iii red section = 3 × yellow section
   yellow section = $\frac{1}{3}$ × red section

 c i 5 : 1 **ii** $\frac{5}{6}$

   iii red section = 5 × yellow section
   yellow section = $\frac{1}{5}$ × red section

2 **a** 12 : 20   **b** $\frac{20}{32}$

3 **a** 20 : 25   **b** $\frac{20}{45}$

4 **a** 24 kg : 16 kg   **b** £20 : £100
 c 160° : 200°   **d** 75 : 105 cats
 e £1.50 : £2.50   **f** 3.5 m : 2.5 m

5 **a** B   **b** C   **c** A

6 **a** 16   **b i** 42   **ii** 12

7 **a** 2 : 3   **b** £48

8 Margarine 210 g
 Sugar 350 g

Objectives

- Use the equivalence of fractions, decimals and percentages to compare proportions   (L6)
- Calculate percentages and find the outcome of a given percentage increase or decrease   (L6)

Key ideas	Resources
1 Be able to find percentages of amounts 2 Begin to consider percentage increase and decrease as a one stage problem	Change as a percentage (1302) Mini whiteboards Calculators

Simplification	Extension
Support students experiencing difficulty here to consolidate mental methods using spider diagrams and involving simple quantities of which to calculate percentages.	Encourage more able students to use a calculator with more complex calculations to find and use a multiplier for calculating percentage increase and decrease.

Literacy	Links
Remind students that the word 'of' is another way of expressing the multiplication operation. Students frequently wrongly attribute percentage of with division, so this will help to dispel this notion.	What two factors could cause the proportion of people of pensionable age to increase in an area? (More people over the state pension age move into the area, perhaps to retire, or younger people leave the area, perhaps to find work elsewhere.)

Alternative approach

This section can be done immediately after section **15c**, as it continues and rehearses the concepts of multiplicative relationships. Use mini whiteboards for initial mental calculations finding percentages of amounts. Student pairs may also work on spider diagrams with a range of percentages as legs, and with a central value. Include legs of value 100% and values of more than 100% in such diagrams. Increasing and decreasing by percentages is unlikely to be too challenging for most students. Encourage deeper exploration of such problems by posing a challenge such as one person increases £50 by 20% by finding 20% then adding it to £50. Another produces the answer by multiplying £50 by 1.2. Will it give the right answer? Can you explain why? What difference would occur in these methods if the amount was decreased by 20%? Equivalent multiplicative relationships for percentage increases and decreases can be explored with mini whiteboards. Not all students will be comfortable to apply one stage calculations at this stage so allow completion of Exercise **12e** with whatever methods they are confident with.

Checkpoint

1 In a sale, a pair of jeans that originally cost £40 is reduced by 20%. What is the sale price of the jeans? (£32)

2 If an amount is to be decreased by 10% what would I need to multiply that amount by to find the new value?   (0.9)

Starter – Percentage pairs

Write the following list of percentage calculations on the board:

50% of 28, 30% of 75, 15% of 70, 90% of 25, 20% of 75, 10% of 350, 56% of 25, 40% of 30, 25% of 60, 100% of 35, 10% of 120, 25% of 42.

Challenge students to match up the pairs in the shortest possible time. Hint: 90% of 25 = 25% of 90.

Can be differentiated by the choice of percentages.

Teaching notes

The worked examples here illustrate a variety of methods that students should discuss in order to support learning. The mental method will be worth particular attention as students need to have a solid grasp of this in order to fully develop understanding.

Explicit links are made throughout to the equivalence of fractions, decimals and percentages and these links need to be highlighted to students. This particularly supports the key processes in number, encouraging analysis through the use of appropriate mathematical procedures.

The work in which students are engaged and the suggested approaches foster opportunities for the exploration of issues or problems from different perspectives, and there are also opportunities to collaborate with others to work towards common goals.

The work in this exercise focuses on skills that strongly support the students in becoming functional mathematicians.

Plenary

Ask students to write three word problems involving percentage increase and decrease and to swap with a friend. They need to know the answers so that they can swap back for marking. By observation collect a few of the most interesting examples for use as a starter activity next lesson.

Exercise commentary

Question 1 – Practice at finding equivalent fractions, decimals and percentages.

Question 2 – If necessary use spider diagrams to remind students how to calculate simple percentages. In part **e**, N stands for Newton, the SI unit of force.

Question 3 – Some of these percentage calculations are more challenging than in question **2** but it is best to persist with mental strategies as far as possible because of the embedding of understanding that this promotes.

Question 4 – Again students should use mental methods to find the change. They may need to be reminded to add on or subtract this change. In part **h**, J stands for Joule the SI unit of energy.

Question 5 – Similar to the two examples. You could ask students to work in pairs and to explain their approach to each other for each scenario.

Question 6 – A practical scenario that guides students towards an efficient way of calculating using a single multiplier.

Question 7 – Students should test their thoughts using the example (and possibly other) amounts rather than just assuming it will stay the same.

Answers

1	a	D	b	C	c	B	d	A
2	a	8	b	£12	c	9 g	d	£45
	e	128 N	f	40 mm	g	£1540	h	57.20%
	i	£6.12	j	6.48 kg				
3	a	£6.50	b	28.14	c	43 kg	d	$3.84
	e	£16.65	f	14 km	g	£149.50	h	18.24 kg
4	a	£57.50	b	£42.50	c	200 m	d	324°
	e	63 kg	f	£1479	g	£348	h	153.6 J
5	a	62 930	b	197.6 kB	c	644 ml		

6   a   TV £15.80

      Games consul £67.15

      Rug £3.95

      Computer £71.10

      Chair £2.37

   b   Multiply by 0.79

   c   Discuss student's ideas as a class.

7   £396: 10% of £440 is greater than 10% of £400, hence we reduce the price overall

Objectives	
• Use the equivalence of fractions, decimals and percentages to compare proportions	(L6)

Key ideas	Resources
1 Recognising and using equivalence of fractions, decimals and percentage 2 Supporting the concept that proportion is an equality of ratio	Comparing fractions (1075) Mini whiteboards What is a fraction?:(Chapters 4 & 5) http://www.nationalstemcentre.org.uk/elibrary/resource/4651/what-is-a-fraction Teaching and Learning Functional Mathematics: Section 2 Problem Solving: http://archive.excellencegateway.org.uk/pdf/T%20%26%20L%20Maths%20Apr%202009.pdf

Simplification	Extension
Where students experience difficulty, scaffold understanding with additional examples that can be supported with diagrams as in question **2** of the exercise.	Support learning in more able students through use of investigations such as in question **5**. For example, invite students to look at their own test results.

Literacy	Links
Continue to encourage students to use the correct terms when stating which proportional language they are using, as well as making sure that units and contexts are reflected in their solutions, both verbally and in writing.	For every 100 girls born in the UK, there are around 105 boys. What ratio is this of male to female? What percentage of all babies born in the UK are boys? In 2011 the population of the UK was 31 million males and 32.2 million females. What percentage of the population is male? Why is this different to the percentage at birth? (Life expectancy for females is longer than for males.)

Alternative approach	
As suggested earlier, use this section directly after that of **15d** in order to consolidate the concepts more firmly. Useful ideas and activities for students can be found in the booklet 'What is a Fraction?' Chapters 4 and 5, which cover the themes for both section **15d** and section **15f**. Also draw on examples from across the school's curriculum, as well as using sources of real-life contexts. Section 2 on Problem solving from the referenced resource provides several appropriate problems.	

Checkpoint	
1 A supermarket stocks two different boxes of the same breakfast cereal. They charge £1.20 for 300 g or £1.50 for 400 g. Which is the best value for money? Why might it not be best to buy this box? (400 g box; discuss why the alternative may be a better choice – for instance, if being used for a short-term visitor, if storage might be an issue, and so on.)	

Starter – Paper round

Sam earns £20 each week doing a paper round. As a bonus Sam was offered a choice of three options:

> an extra lump sum of £8 for one week
> an extra £2 each week for four weeks
> a pay rise of 50% for one week followed by a pay cut of 50% the following week.

Ask students what choice Sam should make and why?

See also the plenary of lesson **15e**.

Teaching notes

The worked examples in this unit make explicit the links between fractions, decimals and percentages and their place in comparing proportions, thereby supporting the development of the process skills in number, representing, where knowledge of equivalent forms is essential.

Students should always be encouraged to explain and justify their thinking, both to the teacher and to each other. The development of student dialogue and purposeful mathematical talk fosters confidence in all abilities of students and facilitates learning effectively.

Comparison of proportions is a vital skill in becoming functional in mathematics. Encourage students to take ownership and responsibility for their own learning through inviting them to suggest examples from their own life experiences where this skill is needed.

Plenary

Refer students back to question **5** in the exercise and initiate whole-class discussion around explaining how to tackle this activity. Allow students to listen to each other's' justifications and to contribute to a whole-class 'best answer'.

Exercise commentary

Question 1 – Practice in converting fractions to percentages: a suitable method is used in the discussion. Invite comments as to which ones are most efficiently converted without a calculator.

Question 2 – Similar to the introduction.

Question 3 – Similar to question **2** but with the removal of the visual scaffolding.

Question 4 – Two real-life examples to develop students' functional mathematics. The key element of the question is 'how do you know?'

Question 5 – Students may need their attention drawn to the fact that the marks are out of different totals for each subject. The explanation and justification of answers is very important.

Answers

1	**a**	70%	**b**	46%	**c**	56%	**d**	125%
	e	42.5%	**f**	41.7%	**g**	94.3%	**h**	71.4%
	i	80%	**j**	65%	**k**	12.5%	**l**	16.7%

2 a i $\frac{2}{5}$ **ii** 40%   **b i** $\frac{8}{15}$ **ii** 53.3%

  c i $\frac{2}{3}$ **ii** 66.7%   **d i** $\frac{9}{16}$ **ii** 56.3%

3 a i $\frac{7}{10}$ **ii** 70%   **b i** $\frac{4}{11}$ **ii** 36.4%

4 a Hilary scores 65.7% of the time, whereas Jodie scores 69.0% of the time, so Jodie is the better goal scorer

  b Tina got 6.7% whereas Harriet got 7.8%. So Harriet got the better rate

5 Marks in percentages are:

Name	History	Geography	RS	Best subject
Zak	40%	42.9%	41.3%	Geography
Wilson	33.3%	20%	20%	History
Yvonne	75%	71.4%	65%	History
Ulf	91.7%	91.4%	91.3%	History
Veronica	50%	54.3%	41.3%	Geography

Key outcomes	Quick check
Simplify and use ratios including dividing a quantity in a given ratio. L5	**a** Simplify the ratio 45 : 30 (3 : 2) **b** Divide £450 in the ratio 7 : 3 (£315; £135)
Solve problems involving direct proportion. L6	A box of 24 packets of biscuits costs £15.60 **a** How much does 8 packets cost? (£5.20) **b** How much does 20 packets cost? (£13.00)
Understand and use the relationship between ratio and proportion. L6	In a particular school year, boys and girls are in the ratio 7 : 6. What proportion of the year are boys? ($\frac{7}{13}$)
Calculate a percentage of an amount. L6	Work out **a** 45% of 90 (40.5) **b** 13% of 650 (84.5)
Calculate a percentage increase or decrease. L6	**a** Increase £320 by 15% (£368) **b** Decrease 720 kg by 22% (561.6 kg)
Use fractions, decimals and percentages to compare simple proportions and solve problems. L6	Amy scored 72 out of 80 and John scored 55 out of 60. Who did better? Justify your answer. (John: 91.66…% compared to Amy: 90%)

⊞ MyMaths extra support

Lesson/online homework		Description
Fractions of amounts	1018 L5	Investigating fractions, finding fractions of whole numbers
Percentages of amounts 2	1031 L5	Finding harder percentages and finding simple percentage discounts
Proportion	1037 L5	An introduction to simple proportion problems
Ratio introduction	1052 L4	Describing patterns and simplifying ratios
Best buys and value for money	1243 L5	Finding the best value when prices are given for different amounts

MyReview

Check out

You should now be able to ...

Test it ➡
Questions

✓	Simplify and use ratios including dividing a quantity in a given ratio.	1–4
✓	Solve problems involving direct proportion.	5, 6
✓	Understand and use the relationship between ratio and proportion.	7, 8
✓	Calculate a percentage of an amount.	9
✓	Calculate a percentage increase or decrease.	10, 11
✓	Use fractions, decimals and percentages to compare simple proportions and solve problems.	12, 13

Language	Meaning	Example
Ratio	The relationship between parts of a whole	red : yellow $= 1 : 2$ is the ratio of colours used to make light orange
Proportion	The relationship between one part and the whole	The proportion of red in light orange is $\frac{1}{3}$
Unitary Method	The method for dividing into a given ratio or proportion using the value of one equal share	To divide £20 in the ratio 2 : 3 1 share is $20 \div (2 + 3) = £4$ 2 shares are $2 \times 4 = £8$ and 3 shares are $3 \times 4 = £12$
Direct proportion	Quantities are in direct proportion if when you increase one the other increases in the same proportion	The perimeter of a square is directly proportional to the length of one side: doubling the length of a side doubles the perimeter

1 Write each of these ratios in its simplest form.
  a 15 : 45   b 30 : 24
  c 95 cm : 2 m   d £3 : 84p

2 A scale drawing is made with a scale of 1 : 50.
  a What is the distance in real life of a measurement of 9 cm on the drawing?
  b What length on the drawing would be needed to represent a distance of 8 m?

3 Divide
  a £90 in the ratio 2 : 3
  b 117 g in the ratio 8 : 1

4 In a choir, the ratio of men to women is 4 : 7. If there are 12 men, how many women are there?

5 A recipe for four people requires 360 g of pasta. How much pasta will be needed for six people?

6 100 g of brioche contains 345 calories. A slice of brioche is about 30 g. Approximately how many calories does it contain?

7 A farm has 28 cows and 42 sheep.
  a What is the ratio of cows to sheep?
  b What proportion of the animals are cows?

8
  a What proportion of the pentagon is yellow?
  b What is the ratio of yellow to blue?

9 Calculate these percentages using a suitable method.
  a 35% of 120
  b 78% of 59

10 Increase 88 kg by 12.5%

11 Decrease £6500 by 65%

12 Convert these fractions into percentages.
  a $\frac{18}{25}$ b $\frac{28}{35}$ c $\frac{14}{17}$

13 Medication A cured 78 out of 94 patients and medication B cured 86 out of 109. Which is the most effective medicine?

What next?

Score		
	0 – 5	Your knowledge of this topic is still developing. To improve look at Formative test: 2B–15; MyMaths: 1036, 1038, 1039 and 1302
	6 – 10	You are gaining a secure knowledge of this topic. To improve look at InvisiPen: 152, 192, 193 and 194
	11 – 13	You have mastered this topic. Well done, you are ready to progress!

⊙ MyMaths.co.uk

Question commentary

Question 1 – Encourage students to look for the HCF of the two parts of the ratio.

Question 2 – Check that students convert distances appropriately.

Question 3 – Students could check their solutions to by adding their answers.

Question 4 – Students can check their solution by seeing if the ratio simplifies to 4 : 7.

Question 5 – Can be done easily without a calculator by working out the amount of pasta needed for 1 person (90 g) and multiplying by 6, or by finding the amount for 2 people and adding to the original amount.

Question 6 – Students could use a calculator here. They could find how many calories in 1g then × 30.

Question 7 – Students should simplify the ratio 28 : 42 fully. 14 : 21 would be a likely solution which is a correct ratio but not fully simplified.

Question 8 – The ratio must be the correct way around and should be simplified.

Questions 9 to 11 – Percentage calculations: calculators could be used.

Question 12 – Students should not need a calculator for parts **a** and **b**. For part **b** simplify the fraction first.

Question 13 – A: 83%, B: 79%

Answers

1 a 1 : 3   b 5 : 4   c 19 : 40   d 25 : 7
2 a 4.5 m   b 16 cm
3 a £36, £54   b 104 g, 13 g
4 21
5 540 g
6 103.5 calories
7 a 2 : 3   b $\frac{2}{5}$ or 40%
8 a $\frac{3}{5}$ or 60%   b   3 : 2
9 a 42   b 46.02
10 99 kg
11 £2275
12 a 72%   b 80%   c 82.4%
13 A, working must also been seen.

15 MyPractice

15A 1 Write each of these ratios in its simplest form.
a 6:18
b 5:15
c 8:12
d 6:15
e 35:28
f 32:56
g 63:90
h 70:60
i 24:100
j 24:104
k 128:256
l 64:176

2 Write each of these ratios in its simplest form.
a 20cm:3m
b 50p:£4
c 65mm:8cm
d 70cl:2 litres
e 7km:700m
f 1900g:4kg
g 1hr 20 mins:80 mins
h 70p:£1.70
i 18 inches:2 feet

3 Solve these problems.
a In a fishing club, the ratio of men to women is 7:2. There are 84 men in the club. How many women are there?
b In a school, the ratio of boys to girls is 8:9. If there are 624 boys at the school, how many girls are there?
c A map has a scale of 1:10 000.
  i What is the distance in real life of a measurement of 3cm on the map?
  ii What is the distance on the map of a measurement of 5km in real life?

15B 4 Divide these quantities in the ratios given.
a Divide 65 km in the ratio 6:7
b Divide £225 in the ratio 8:7
c Divide 256 MB in the ratio 3:5
d Divide 4500 N in the ratio 4:5
e Divide 3 minutes in the ratio 4:5
f Divide £2 in the ratio 7:13

5 Solve these problems.
a In a running club, the ratio of boys to girls is 5:3. There are 96 children in total at the club. How many girls are there?
b Sam and Siobhan share £2400 in the ratio 7:5. How much money does Sam receive?
c A pizza is made with dough and toppings in the ratio 3:5. The total weight of the pizza is 320g. What weight of dough has been used to make the pizza?

15C 6 Here are three offers for different types of bread. In which of these offers are the numbers in direct proportion? In each case explain and justify your answers.

a Wholemeal loaves

Weight of bread	Cost
300g	£0.45
400g	£0.60
800g	£1.20

b Croissants

Weight of bread	Cost
50g	£0.32
125g	£0.75
200g	£1.25

c Currant teacakes

Weight of bread	Cost
40g	£0.24
100g	£0.60
240g	£1.44

Number Ratio and proportion

15C 7 Use direct proportion to solve each of these problems.
a Five pears cost 82p. What is the cost of 15 pears?
b 150g of crisps contain 240 calories. How many calories are there in 50g of crisps?
c A recipe for six people uses 420g of flour.
  i What weight of flour is needed for seven people?
  ii How much flour is needed for three people?
d Five litres of water costs £1.45.
  i What is the cost of seven litres of water?
  ii What is the cost of 17 litres of water?

15D 8 a Steve and Jenny break a 120g chocolate bar into two pieces. Steve has $\frac{3}{8}$ of the bar and Jenny has the rest. What is the ratio of Jenny's piece of the bar to Steve's piece of the bar?
b $\frac{8}{9}$ of the people who attended a cricket match were men. What was the ratio of men to women at the cricket match?
c Shirley and Hanif share some money. Shirley receives $\frac{2}{5}$ of the money and Hanif receives £66. How much money did Shirley and Hanif share?

15E 9 a Increase £30 by 10%
b Decrease 700 euros by 5%
c Increase 8miles by 20%
d Decrease 180° by 15%
e Increase 280kg by 25%
f Decrease £100 000 by 3%
g Increase 250 rabbits by 30%
h Decrease 2500kJ by 22%
i Increase 70g by 9%
j Decrease £1.80 by 35%

10 a Chelski football stadium has 71440 seats. It is rebuilt with an increased seating of 15%. How many seats are there at the new stadium?
b A jar of jam holds 370g. It is increased in capacity by 23%. What is the new capacity of the jar? (Give your answer to the nearest gram.)
c A memory stick normally costs £36. It is reduced in price in a sale by 17.5%. What is the sale price of the memory stick?

15F 11 a Dan scores 62% in his Maths exam, $\frac{37}{60}$ in his Science exam and $\frac{29}{50}$ in his English exam. In which subject did Dan do the best?
b Megan and Jane play tennis. Last week Megan played seven matches and won five of them. Last month Jane played 20 matches and won 14 of them. Who is the better tennis player? Explain and justify your answer.

 MyMaths.co.uk

Question commentary

Questions 1 to **5** – A large array of ratio questions, many of which can be done using mini whiteboards. Check for inconsistent units. For the word problems, ensure students are extracting the correct information and explaining their methods.

Question 6 – This question directs students to explain and justify their answers. Make sure they are showing clear working and giving clear reasons.

Question 7 – Several examples where the unitary method works well. However, encourage students to find short-cut methods where they can.

Question 8 – Students can check their answers by looking at alternative representations of the proportions, ratios and amounts in each part.

Question 9 – Can be done without a calculator. Encourage efficient methods such as working with 10% or 5% rather than always going via 1%.

Question 10 – Calculators will be required for these applied questions.

Question 11 – Students should fully justify their answers in both cases.

Answers

1 **a** 1 : 3 **b** 1 : 3 **c** 2 : 3 **d** 2 : 5
  e 5 : 4 **f** 4 : 7 **g** 7 : 10 **h** 7 : 6
  i 6 : 25 **j** 3 : 13 **k** 1 : 2 **l** 4 : 11

2 **a** 1 : 15 **b** 1 : 8 **c** 13 : 16 **d** 7 : 20
  e 10 : 1 **f** 19 : 40 **g** 1 : 1 **h** 7 : 17
  i 3 : 4

3 **a** 24 **b** 702 **c** **i** 300 m **ii** 50 cm

4 **a** 30 km : 35 km **b** £120 : £105
  c 96 MB : 160MB **d** 2000 N : 2500 N
  e 80 s : 100 s **f** 70p : £1.30

5 **a** 36 **b** £1400 **c** 120 g

6 **a** Yes, the cost increases by 15p with every extra 100 g.
  b No, the cost changes at a different rate than the weight.
  c Yes, the cost increases at the same rate as the weight.

7 **a** £2.46 **b** 80 cals **c** **i** 490 g **ii** 210 g
  d **i** £2.03 **ii** £4.93

8 **a** 5 : 3 **b** 8 : 1 **c** £110

9 **a** £33 **b** €665 **c** 9.6 miles **d** 153°
  e 350 kg **f** £97 000 **g** 325 rabbits
  h 1950 kJ **i** 76.3 g **j** £1.17

10 **a** 82 156 **b** 455 g **c** £29.70

11 **a** Maths
  b Megan won 71.4% of her matches, whereas Jane won 70% of hers. This suggests Megan is the better player although her results are based on a small sample and it depends on the quality of the opposition in each case.

Learning outcomes

P1 Record, describe and analyse the frequency of outcomes of simple probability experiments involving randomness, fairness, equally and unequally likely outcomes, using appropriate language and the 0–1 probability scale (L6)

P2 Understand that the probabilities of all possible outcomes sum to 1 (L6)

P3 Enumerate sets and unions/intersections of sets systematically, using tables, grids and Venn diagrams (L6)

P4 Generate theoretical sample spaces for single and combined events with equally likely, mutually exclusive outcomes and use these to calculate theoretical probabilities (L6)

Introduction	Prior knowledge
The chapter starts by looking at how outcomes can be listed using sample space diagrams and tree diagrams. The language and scale of probability is then covered before experimental and theoretical probabilities. The final section looks at sets and Venn diagrams.	Students should already know how to… • Work with simple fractions and/or decimals • Understand simple probability

Introduction (continued)

The introduction discusses the use of probability in clinical trials for things like new drugs. The idea of giving a 'control group' a placebo in order to measure the effect of the real drug on the other patients relies heavily on the idea of probability. What is the probability, for example, of the drug failing to work on a patient who has the disease being looked at? What is the probability of the patient who takes the placebo actually recovering from the illness being tested on despite not getting the real drug?

Mathematicians can help the scientists and doctors solve these kinds of problems by working out the chances of 'false positives' and errors in the trial. This kind of statistical analysis goes way beyond Key Stage 3 mathematics, but the fundamentals are important to understand at this level by analysing the probabilities of single events and looking at the effect of combining probabilities into two or more sequential or related events.

Starter problem

The starter problem looks at the probability of getting a five when you roll a number of dice. The first situation, a single dice, has simple probability equal to 1/6. How does this change when you roll two dice?

You could now get a five on *either* dice (or both) and we will have to look in more detail at the possible outcomes – here a sample space diagram might be useful. It turns out that there are 11 ways of rolling the two dice so that at least one of them shows a five, giving the overall probability of rolling a five as 11/36 (just under 1/3).

The simple answer to the question posed at the end of the starter problem is 'yes'. To analyse this further, and work out *how* it changes would require students to list large numbers of outcomes (216 for 3 dice) or draw (construct?) 3D sample spaces. The discussion might instead be focussed on trying to find a logical argument for working out the number of ways it can be done on three dice.

Resources

MyMaths

Listing outcomes	1199	Probability intro	1209	Relative frequency	1211

Online assessment

Chapter test	2B–16
Formative test	2B–16
Summative test	2B–16

InvisiPen solutions

Finding probabilities	452	Probabilities add to one	453
Experimental and theoretical probability			461
Outcomes	462		

Topic scheme

Teaching time = 5 lessons/2 weeks

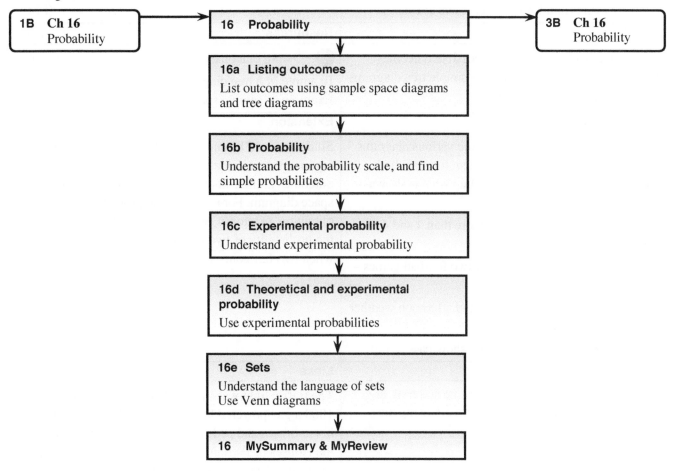

1B   Ch 16
Probability

16   Probability

3B   Ch 16
Probability

16a Listing outcomes
List outcomes using sample space diagrams and tree diagrams

16b Probability
Understand the probability scale, and find simple probabilities

16c Experimental probability
Understand experimental probability

16d Theoretical and experimental probability
Use experimental probabilities

16e Sets
Understand the language of sets
Use Venn diagrams

16   MySummary & MyReview

Differentiation

Student book 2A   294 – 309
Likelihood and chance
The probability scale
Equally likely outcomes
Experimental probability
Venn diagrams

Student book 2B   284 – 299
Listing outcomes
Probability
Experimental probability
Theoretical and experimental probability
Sets

Student book 2C   286 – 305
Two or more events
Tree diagrams
Mutually exclusive outcomes
Experimental probability
Comparing experimental and theoretical probability
Simulating experimental data
Venn diagrams and probability

Objectives	
• Use diagrams and tables to record in a systematic way all possible mutually exclusive outcomes for single events and for two successive events (L6)	

Key ideas	Resources
1 Systematically recording all possible outcomes 2 Being able to interpret and use simple tree diagrams and sample space diagrams	 Listing outcomes (1199) Example of a tree diagram Example of sample space diagram

Simplification	Extension
Students' understanding of what the various diagrams show can be clarified by giving them four labelled examples and asking them to explain what is shown. For example, Tree diagram: one dice – show more than 4 and 4 or less. Sample space diagram: results of two football games – show win, draw and loss. Sample space diagram: morning and afternoon weather – show sunny, cloudy and rainy. Tree diagram: driving test result – show pass or fail.	Students could be encouraged to use simple counting arguments to calculate probabilities based on the list of outcomes at the end of a tree diagram or in a sample space diagram. For example, the probability of obtaining a factor of twelve on the roll of a fair dice or the probability of two heads or one head and one tail when two fair coins are tossed.

Literacy	Links
Refer to the key words event, outcome and trial, and encourage students to discuss their work using the words accurately.	The traffic light was invented before the motor car. In 1868 a gas-powered lantern was used to control the horse-drawn and pedestrian traffic at a junction outside the Houses of Parliament in London. The lantern had rotating red and green lamps which were turned manually to face the oncoming traffic. The lantern exploded on January 2, 1869 injuring its operator.

Alternative approach
Begin by posing one or two Always/Sometimes/Never true statements such as 'the probability of a football club winning a match is 1/3 because they can either win, draw or lose'; 'The probability of having two boys in a family of two children is ¼'. Students should discuss these in pairs then some key points shared with the whole group. Display an example of a tree diagram, and ask students to explain what it is about, and what information it can give. Similarly, display a sample space diagram, of for example male/female and left/right handed, for discussion.

Checkpoint
1 How would you record the outcomes of rolling two dice and summing for a total? <div align="right">(Sample space diagram most efficient; though tree diagram is acceptable)</div> 2 How can you check that you have recorded all possible outcomes? <div align="right">(Appropriate responses such as being systematic)</div> 3 Draw the sample space diagram for rolling two dice and summing for a total. <div align="right">(6 × 6 grid with row/column totals going '2, 3, 4, 5, 6, 7' and '3, 4, 5, 6, 7, 8', etc.)</div>

Starter – Ice cream

Ask students how many different combinations of ice cream they could make choosing two different flavours from the following six flavours: vanilla, strawberry, toffee, mint choc, pistachio and banana. (15)

What if they had seven flavours to choose from? (21)

Teaching notes

Ask students, what is the probability of getting a head and a tail when two coins are tossed? Expect answers of $\frac{1}{3}$ and $\frac{1}{2}$ (HT and TH are different and both contribute). Ask students how they reached their answers. Guide them to the need to list all possible outcomes and count the number that contain a head and a tail so that they can apply the formula in lesson **16b**. Can students suggest ways to systematically list all the outcomes from one or two events?

For the two coins, show how to construct the sample space diagram (also known as a two-way table) and the tree diagram. In the tree diagram emphasise the need to label the 'First' and 'Second' set of branches and to label individual 'H' and 'T' outcomes at the end of the branches. When many branches are involved it may help to draw the outside branches first and then fill in the middle branches.

Counting arguments work for calculating probabilities with these diagrams if each outcome is equally likely.

Plenary

Develop question **2**: suppose Danni likes to give her cat meat one day and fish the next – can the students show this in either a tree diagram or a sample space diagram?

Exercise commentary

Questions 1 and **2** – Simple one-stage tree diagrams.

Question 3 – Drawing two-stage tree and sample space diagrams. Check that students correctly label their diagrams.

Questions 4 and **5** – Converting between sample space and two-stage tree diagrams. Students could compare their answers as a way of checking they have completed these conversions correctly.

Question 6 – This could be done in pairs. Students could be asked to draw actual diagrams to show the outcomes of tossing one, two or three coins. A 'cuboidal' sample space drawing might be possible using perspective or colours but is unlikely to be practical.

Answers

1 **a, b** Check students' diagrams
2 **b** Check students' diagrams
3 **a i** Check students' diagrams
   ii

		Second throw	
		Hit	**Miss**
First throw	**Hit**	Hit Hit	Hit Miss
	Miss	Miss Hit	Miss Miss

b i Check students' diagrams
   ii

		Second Test	
		Pass	**Fail**
First Test	**Pass**	Pass Pass	Pass Fail
	Fail	Fail Pass	Fail Fail

c i Check students' diagrams
   ii

		2nd Match		
		W	**D**	**L**
1st Match	**W**	(W, W)	(W, D)	(W,L)
	D	(D,W)	(D,D)	(D,L)
	L	(L,W)	(L,D)	(L,L)

4 Check students' diagrams
5

		2nd day		
		P	**L**	**A**
1st day	**P**	(P,P)	(P,L)	(P,A)
	L	(L,P)	(L,L)	(L,A)
	A	(A,P)	(A,L)	(A,A)

6 A tree diagram

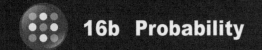

Objectives

- Understand and use the probability scale from 0 to 1 (L5)
- Find and justify probabilities based on equally likely outcomes in simple contexts (L5)
- Know that if the probability of an event occurring is p then the probability of it not occurring is $1 - p$ (L5)

Key ideas	Resources
1 Knowing that probability is expressed as a value between 0 to 1 2 Understanding that the probability of all possible events must add to one.	Probability intro (1209) A large horizontal probability line on display (marked 0.1, 10%, 1/10, etc.). 'Probable' words on cards; events on cards; smaller probability scales

Simplification	Extension
In questions **2** and **5**, use only fractions.	Ask students (in pairs) to write a set of probability questions for an octahedral dice (a dice with eight faces numbered from 1 to 8) with each face equally likely to be thrown. Ask pairs to exchange questions, discuss the answers and the difficulty.

Literacy	Links
Students sometimes have interesting and differing interpretations of words such as 'likely'. Explore this fully. Make sure that the vocabulary of probability is that of proportion. Some students will introduce betting terms such as '2 to 1', and when this occurs correct the response with a full explanation (2/3 or 1/3).	Snow can still fall even when the air temperature is above freezing. As snowflakes fall, they gain heat from the surrounding air by conduction but they also lose heat by evaporation. If the flakes lose more heat than they gain, the flakes will remain frozen. The rate of evaporation is greatest in dry air, so whether the snowflakes melt or not depends on both the temperature of the surrounding air and on the relative humidity.

Alternative approach

Ask students to work in small groups with a probability scale and a range of cards. Firstly, ask them to decide where to position probable words such as likely, maybe, rarely, probably, definitely, never, evens cards. Secondly, they can decide where to place the events on the scale. Finally, the groups may want to estimate the values of some of these cards using either decimal or vulgar fractions. Share key points that have arisen during the activity with the whole group. This activity can replace questions **1** and **2** of the exercise.

Checkpoint

1 What is the probability of getting an even number when rolling a dice? (1/2 or 0.5)
2 The probability of being right-handed is 3/5. What is the probability of being left-handed? (2/5)

Starter – Dice bingo

Ask students to draw a 3 × 3 grid and enter nine numbers from 2 to 12 inclusive, duplicates allowed.

Throw two dice. Students add the scores and cross out the total if they have it in their grid (only one number at a time).

The winner is the first student to cross out all their numbers.

Teaching notes

As an introduction to probability, students could be given statements on large cards to read out and then stand at the appropriate point on the probability line. For example, 'I will get my maths correct', 'I will arrive at school on time tomorrow', 'the head of year will come in the room this lesson', 'there will be someone away in class tomorrow', 'it will be sunny at the end of school', 'there will be a fire alarm in school today', etc.

Probability is described in several ways and students need to be aware of this. In words, only 'certain', 'equally likely/evens' and 'impossible/certain not to happen' have definite meanings, words such as 'likely', etc. are subjective. Using numbers gives definite meaning but they can be expressed in one of three ways: decimals, percentages or fractions. Students may need reminding how to simplify fractions and recognise common FDP equivalences.

Working through a problem, such as that in the example, will show students how to apply the probability formula and to calculate the probability of a complementary event.

Plenary

Give pairs of students a small piece of card showing a percentage or fraction written on, for example, 1/4 or 20%. Ask each pair to write a statement that they feel would fit the probability they have been given. Allow four or five pairs to get together to discuss and agree their statements and place on a probability line.

Exercise commentary

Question 1 – Students could be asked to work in pairs to discuss the most appropriate placement. If the statements are written on pieces of paper it will be easier to rearrange them and help avoid unduly messy answers.

Question 2 – This question also provides good opportunities for discussion among students.

Question 3 – Students could be asked to explain how they reached their answers.

Question 4 – Applications of P(not A) = 1 – P(A).

Question 5 – Similar to question 3. Again, students could be asked to explain how they reached their answers.

Question 6 – This could be done in small groups. Ask students to give two or three arguments to explain whether 2/7 is a sensible answer. Can they think of a practical way to measure the probability?

Question 7 – Check students do not think that 1 is a prime number. Ideas of bias can form the basis of extensive class discussion.

Answers

1   Very unlikely ————————————————→ show at $\frac{1}{10}$

       Likely ————————————————→ show at $\frac{7}{10}$

    Almost certain ————————————→ show at $\frac{9}{10}$

      Certain————————————————→ show at 1

2   Various answers possible, e.g.

a	Unlikely	0.1	(Depends on time of year and location)
b	Very likely	0.9	(Some will be 11)
c	Very likely	0.9	(Could be half-term!)
d	Evens	0.5	(Provided dice is unbiased)

3   **a** $\frac{1}{6}$ **b** $\frac{1}{3}$ **c** $\frac{1}{2}$ **d** 0

4   **a** 0.7   **b** 55%   **c** $\frac{9}{16}$

5   **a** 0.1   **b** 0.5   **c** 0.2   **d** 0
    e 0.4

6   No. The 7 days of the week do not have equal chances of being chosen, as the teenagers will probably be at work or school from Monday to Friday.

7   **a** 0.5 (assuming the dice is fair)
    b The expected number of eggs in a month is about 15 so it is likely that the dice is not fair

Objectives	
• Estimate probabilities by collecting data from a simple experiment	(L5)
• Recognise that increasing the number of times an experiment is repeated generally leads to better estimates of probability	(L5)

Key ideas	Resources	
1 Understand that experimental results can provide an indication of probability	Relative frequency	(1211)
2 Begin to recognise the importance of the size of data and the validity of the conclusions	Calculator Coins/two-sided tokens	

Simplification	Extension
A few students will find changing fractions into percentages a challenge, allow them to leave their answers as fractions. If there is time, work with them (or allow a competent student time) to show them how to change their fraction answers into percentages.	Ask students to construct a three-stage tree diagram for the results of tossing three coins and hence calculate P(HHT) from the introductory example. Develop question **3**: the athletes receive a gold, silver, or bronze medal or a certificate depending on how many points they score. What would be suitable boundaries for each of these awards? Note, there should be fewer gold medals than silver and bronze with most receiving a certificate.

Literacy	Links
Experimental probability should be discussed with students in order to give them a clear idea that most of the probability in our daily life comes from 'experimental' data or simply from the data collections of events past.	Dutch Elm disease has affected millions of trees in Britain since the late 1960s. It is caused by a fungus which is spread by the elm bark beetle. By the late 1990s, over 25 million of the UK's 30 million elm trees had died due to the disease. What fraction of the trees died?

Alternative approach
Pose the question: what is the probability of being left-handed? Students may want to estimate answers to this and share thoughts on it, before a simple experiment on this takes place. Ask students who are left-handed, and then use this information to suggest what the probability is from the class data. Now ask students to consider its validity. Ask how the result might be improved. Share discussion thoroughly with the group before informing them that it that it is generally 12% of males and 10% of females that are found to be left-handed. So overall there is a probability of 0.1 to 0.12 of being left-handed.

Checkpoint
1 In ten throws of a six-sided dice, 4 resulted in a score of 6. Do you think this indicates that the dice is unfair or biased?   (Responses indicating that it is a high occurrence, but with only 10 throws it is not conclusive)

Starter – Higher or lower

Using either a set of playing cards or a set of numbered cards, show students the first card and ask whether they think the next card will be higher or lower. Repeat several times.

This can be extended by being more specific, for example, the chance of the next card being a square number. (If using playing cards, the naming and numerical value of face cards may need to be explained.)

Teaching notes

Give groups of students three coins and ask them what do they think is the probability of getting two heads and one tail when they are tossed. Ask them to repeatedly toss the coins and create a tally chart for the possible outcomes (HHH, HHT, TTH, TTT). Show how each group's results can be used to calculate an estimate for P(HHT) (= 3/8 = 0.375) using the formula. Do they all agree? How could they get a better estimate? Combine all the groups' results to obtain a better estimate.

Probabilities can be given as fractions, decimals or percentages. You should clarify which form you prefer for an answer (decimals/percentages make comparisons easier) and if necessary how to convert between them, possibly using a calculator.

Question 5 can be organised as a **think, pair and share** activity. Give students two minutes to **think** about the problem themselves – what information would Tara need? Then give students, in **pairs**, time to agree and list the data they would require. Then put two pairs together to **share** their ideas and agree how best Tara could work out the probability.

Plenary

Display the table for question **2** on a whiteboard. On one day the buses are on strike: four students who normally catch a bus don't get to school, three cycle, two walk and the rest come by car. In pairs, ask students to work out the different probabilities for coming to school. Compare these percentages with those when buses were running. Why have they all increased? What is their total?

Exercise commentary

Question 1 – Similar to the example. Check how students set out their answer. Should it be given as a percentage?

Question 2 – Requires students to add up the total number of student journeys.

Question 3 – Requires students to identify and count 'successful' outcomes from the list.

Question 4 – Requires students to extract the appropriate information from a two-way table and appreciate the significance of the total number of trials. Ask the class if knowing the conditions used in the two experiments would affect their answers.

Question 5 – Will it snow on Christmas day in London next year? Students are asked to consider what information they need to be able to work out this as a probability.

Question 6 – An opportunity for a 'bit of fun' at the end of the lesson with students trying this for themselves.

Answers

1 $\frac{5}{28}$

2 a $\frac{6}{23}$ b $\frac{29}{69}$ c $\frac{55}{69}$

3 $\frac{13}{20}$

4 a $\frac{32}{50} = \frac{16}{25}$ or 0.64

   b $\frac{58}{100} = \frac{29}{50}$ or 0.58

   c Ben's, as he did double the number of trials.

5 One way would be to look at the Christmas Day weather records for London for the past 100 years and see on what proportion of these days snow was recorded.

6 $\frac{5}{12}$

Objectives	
• Compare estimated experimental probabilities with theoretical probabilities	(L5)
• Recognise that if an experiment is repeated the outcome may, and usually will, be different	(L5)

Key ideas	Resources	
1 Understand the similarities and the difference between theory and experiment in probability 2 Repeating experiments, while perhaps resulting in similar outcomes, may not be identical	Relative frequency Calculator A4 envelope Small coloured cards (red, blue, green, yellow) Stiff cardboard pentagons Spreadsheet	(1211)

Simplification	Extension
Question **4** can be made into a practical activity using an envelope with coloured cards (4 red, 3 green, 2 blue, 1 yellow). Discuss with students what they may expect and then allow them to complete the experiment (if there are two groups then both sets of data can be combined). Discuss the outcomes.	Make a biased spinner, for example, by cutting across two neighbouring sections of a five-sided spinner to make into one. After working out the theoretical probabilities, estimate how many of each score should be obtained in 40 spins. Do 40 spins and work out the experimental probabilities. Discuss how the answers compare.

Literacy	Links
Students can perceive theoretical probability as the only accurate or 'correct' probability, so using many real contexts to show the validity and relevance of experimental probability is important. Ask students to consider how the best medical treatments are established, or how localities provide adequate housing or transport.	Dice that are deliberately biased are called crooked or loaded dice. Dice can be loaded by adding a small amount of metal to one side or by manufacturing the dice with a hollow gap inside so that one side is lighter than the others. One way of testing for a loaded dice is to drop it several times into a glass of water. If it is hollow it will float with the hollow side uppermost; if it is weighted, it will sink with the same number always facing down.

Alternative approach
Use a simple experiment with the whole class, modelling and recording the data on a spreadsheet. For example, have a closed bag of 10 counters/cubes made up of 2 colours. Pose the question what is the probability of picking a red one? Draw out and replace a counter 10 times asking students to suggest probabilities, then enter the results on a spreadsheet showing frequency bar chart of the two colours. A second spreadsheet can show the trials as a scale in 10s against an estimated probability. Now add a further 10 trials – perhaps done by two of the students, and so on. The second chart will show clearly how there is a tendency to a consistent result the more trials take place. A randomly generated simulation can be set up on a spreadsheet to replicate the experiment in order to speed the trials up.

Checkpoint

1 Two experiments were carried out in order to estimate a probability. Experiment A involved 100 trials and experiment B involved 1000 trials.
   a Which experiment do you think might would be more reliable and why?
 (Experiment B because there were 10 times as many trials involved.)
   b If experiment B produced 642 successful outcomes, estimate the probability of success.
 (642/1000 = 0.642)

Starter – Probability jumble

Write a list of anagrams on the board and ask students to unscramble them. Possible anagrams are

ANCHEC, COMETOU, TEENV, LIRAT, NAMDOR, SLIPSOMBIE, KELLIY, TRAINCE

(Chance, outcome, event, trial, random, impossible, likely, certain)

Can be extended by asking students to make a probability word search.

Teaching notes

As students enter the lesson ask them, without looking, to pick one of four coloured cards from an envelope, remember the colour, then replace it. Record the results on a tally chart (use student helpers if necessary) and use them to calculate the probabilities of obtaining each colour. This set of data is analogous to that discussed in the first example; can students explain the similarities and any differences (is the spinner biased)?

Ensure that students appreciate that results obtained by repeating exactly the same experiment may differ from one another and from the theoretical probability. It is also important that they can clearly explain why, for example, an experiment may be biased.

Question **1** can be used to make sure that students explain their thinking in well-constructed statements. Allow a few minutes to complete the question then ask students to exchange their work with their neighbour – who should write a positive comment and a developmental comment (how the work could be better explained) in pencil on the book. Allow paired discussion after this with a small time for feedback.

Plenary

In an envelope have 2 red, 2 blue and 1 green card. Split the class into teams and explain that the envelope contains five cards. Draw out a card, show it and replace it. After 5, 7, 9, 11, 13 and 15 repeats, ask the teams to guess the colours of the five cards. Is any team's final guess correct? What strategies were used for 'best' guesses at each stage? Why is after five cards not a good time to have a guess?

The exercise can be repeated, say, using 1 red, 3 blue and 1 green or 2 red and 3 green cards.

Exercise commentary

Question 1 – A structured question similar to the second example. It encourages students to assess the reliability of their results.

Question 2 – This question requires students to think about an estimate's reliability/accuracy.

Question 3 – Again students can discuss the reliability of the experiment, the conditions it has been carried out in, etc.

Question 4 – This question requires students to realise that experimental results naturally vary and (usually) will not match the theoretical probabilities.

Question 5 – Suggest working in pairs. Students could perform their own dice-rolling experiments. Ask pairs to agree and list three reasons why it would be a good idea to combine results. These reasons can be shared with another pair and the best ideas fed back to the whole class.

Answers

1   a   80   b $P(H) = \frac{31}{80}$ $P(T) = \frac{49}{80}$

    c   It does not appear to be fair as $P(H)$ is less than $P(T)$.

    d   Increase number of trials.

2   a $P(H) \approx P(T)$ so it is likely the coin is fair

3   a $\frac{62}{77}$

    b $\frac{62}{77} < \frac{23}{28}$ (suggesting those on the second are more likely to pass) but only by a small amount and the sample size is small so we cannot make a definitive conclusion

4   a   Green $\frac{3}{10}$

Objectives
• Enumerate sets and unions/intersections of sets systematically, using tables, grids and Venn diagrams   (L6)

Key ideas	Resources
1 List elements in sets, understand the language of sets and understand the notation associated with sets **2** Work with sets and Venn diagrams to calculate probabilities	Cards for writing facts about sets Copies of Venn diagram puzzles

Simplification	Extension
Some students may have trouble understanding the set notation and the associated links to the Venn diagrams, so encourage them to use words and/or lists rather than focusing on the notation. Question **4** can be omitted as a general simplification.	Ask students to come up with their own problem similar to Ella's puzzle in question **4**. Can they give *just enough* information so that a partner can solve the Venn diagram?

Literacy	Links
The language of sets and Venn diagrams contains many words that may be unfamiliar to students such as 'union' and 'intersection'. Encourage students to write a glossary of terms as each new word or phrase is introduced.	Students may be familiar with these classic 2-circle Venn diagrams but can they come up with a way of representing three 'events'? What about four, or even five events? A quick search on the Internet will provide students with some pretty amazing Venn diagrams for these situations. The Wikipedia page for Venn diagrams with several of these on is at http://en.wikipedia.org/wiki/Venn_diagram

Alternative approach
A two-way table provides a good way to link work on sample spaces, etc. with this work on Venn diagrams. For example, consider a two-way table showing two types of chocolate split into 'like' and 'dislike':

	Like B	Dislike B
Like A	18	6
Dislike A	12	15

How can this information be translated into a Venn diagram? Students should be able to see that the four numbers in the table match the four regions in the Venn diagram and they can use this to complete the diagram. Follow-up questions can then be used such as 'What is the probability that…?'

Checkpoint
1 A set P comprises the first 10 whole numbers. A set Q contains the factors of 12. Which elements are common to both sets? $(1, 2, 3, 4, 6)$

Starter – How many people?

In a recent survey, 18 people said they liked rugby, 13 people said they liked hockey and 5 people said they liked both. 4 people said they liked neither. How many people were asked? (30)

Similar logic problems can be given like this and the level of challenge varied accordingly. For example, you might have no-one who liked both, or no-one who liked neither.

Teaching notes

Students need to be able to comprehend the general language of sets and the structure of the Venn diagram and explain, in words, what each region represents. Encourage them to do this first rather than diving straight into the questions. They can produce a glossary of terms since much of the language will be unfamiliar.

Walk the students through the first and second examples to illustrate the key points before giving them time to work through questions **1** and **2**.

In question **3a**, encourage students to link all their work together and provide a full written explanation of what they are doing.

Plenary

Return to the starter problem. Can the students now draw a Venn diagram to illustrate the results of the survey? Questions can also be asked such as 'What is the probability that a person chosen at random likes hockey?' (13/30)

Exercise commentary

Question 1 – Students may need help deciphering the language of sets used. Part **a** could be modelled to get them started.

Question 2 – Students could be asked to describe, in words, what each of the regions in the Venn diagram represent before answering the questions.

Question 3 – Encourage fully explained solutions to develop mathematical communication.

Question 4 – Encourage students to work systematically through the information. Working from the 'inside out' is the generally accepted method.

Answers

1 **a** **i** $3, 6, 9, 12$ **ii** $1, 2, 4, 5, 7, 8, 10, 11$
     iii $1, 2, 4, 5, 6, 8, 12$ **iv** $3, 9$
     v $3, 6, 7, 9, 10, 11, 12$ **vi** $6, 12$
  b **i** $1, 2, 3, 5, 8, 13$ **ii** $21, 34, 55$
     iii $5, 13, 21, 34, 55$ **iv** $1, 2, 3, 8$
     v $1, 2, 3, 5, 8, 13$ **vi** $5, 13$
  c **i** $1, 3, 5, 7, 9, 11, 13, 15$
     ii $2, 4, 6, 8, 10, 12, 14, 16$
     iii $1, 4, 6, 8, 10, 12, 14, 15, 16$
     iv $3, 5, 7, 11, 13$
     v $2, 3, 5, 7, 11, 13$
     vi $1, 9, 15$

2 **a** $\frac{14}{25}$ **b** $\frac{7}{25}$ **c** $\frac{10}{25}$ **d** $\frac{22}{25}$

3 **a** 8
  b 4 outside of the circles, 16 in the waterpark circle, 11 in the beach circle and 9 in the intersection of the circles

4   2 outside, 4 solely in A, 6 in $A \cap B$, 8 solely in B

Key outcomes	Quick check
Use diagrams and tables to record mutually exclusive outcomes. L6	Draw a tree diagram to show the outcomes on rolling a standard four-sided dice. (Four branches, numbered 1–4)
Find probabilities based on equally likely outcomes. L6	A fair eight-sided octahedral dice is rolled. **a** What is the probability of rolling an even number? (1/2) **b** What is the probability of rolling a multiple of three? (1/4)
Calculate the probability that an event does not occur from the probability that it does occur. L6	The probability of rolling a five on a fair six-sided dice is 1/6. What is the probability of not rolling a five? (5/6)
Estimate probabilities by collecting data from an experiment. L6	Julian was tossing a biased coin. He tossed it 200 times and it came down heads 140 times. Estimate the probability of his coin showing heads. (140/200 = 7/10)
Compare experimental probabilities with theoretical probabilities. L6	Nadia was rolling a dice. She rolled the dice 60 times and it landed on a three 18 times. By comparing the experimental and theoretical probabilities, do you think Nadia's dice is biased? (3/10 compared to 1/6 – 30% compared to approximately 17% – evidence suggests it *could* be biased.)
Use the language of sets and use sets to calculate probabilities. L6	Ω = {whole numbers from 1 to 10}. A = {prime numbers}, B = {square numbers}. Find the probability that a randomly chosen number is in the set **a** A (4/10 = 2/5) **b** B (3/10) **c** A $\cap$ B (1/10) **d** A′ $\cap$ B′ (3/10)

⊞ MyMaths extra support

Simple probability 1210 L5	Introducing some simple rules of probability

Check out

You should now be able to ...

		Test it ➡
		Questions
✓	Use diagrams and tables to record mutually exclusive outcomes.	1, 2
✓	Find probabilities based on equally likely outcomes.	3
✓	Calculate the probability that an event does not occur from the probability that it does occur.	4
✓	Estimate probabilities by collecting data from an experiment.	5
✓	Compare experimental probabilities with theoretical probabilities.	6
✓	Use the language of sets and use sets to calculate probabilities.	7

Language	Meaning	Example
Trial	An experiment with an uncertain outcome	Throwing a dice to see which number is on top
Outcome	A possible result of a trial	For a dice the possible outcomes are 1, 2, 3, 4, 5 and 6
Event	A collection of outcomes	The event an even number consists of the outcomes 2, 4 and 6
Tree diagram	A diagram which uses branches to record possible outcomes	See page 286
Sample space diagram	A diagram which uses a table to record possible outcomes	See page 286
Experiment	A series of trials which can be used to estimate a probability	Rolling a dice 600 times to see if it is biased is an experiment
Biased	A trial in which all the individual outcomes are *not* equally likely	A coin which shows heads twice as often as tails is biased

1 Dave picks a card from a pack of red and black cards, and records if it is black or red. He replaces it then selects another and again records the colour.
 a Draw a tree diagram to show the possible outcomes.
 b Draw a sample space diagram to show the possible outcomes.

2 This sample space diagram shows the possible lunch choices of a student.

		Food		
		Chicken	**Fish**	**Veg**
Drink	**Water**	(W,C)	(W,F)	(W,V)
	Squash	(S,C)	(S,F)	(S,V)

Draw a tree diagram to represent the same set of information.

3 A bag contains three white and five red counters. What is the probability that a randomly chosen counter will be
 a white
 b blue?

4 The probability that a person chosen at random from a doctor's waiting room will be a child is 0.3. What is the probability of choosing an adult?

5 The test results of 20 students are

14	12	15	12	18
20	17	15	11	9
12	14	16	17	19
8	10	13	17	16

A mark of 14 or more is needed to pass. Estimate the probability that a student chosen at random has passed the test.

6 Jen rolled a dice and recorded whether or not it showed a six. The results are in the table.

Six	**Not a six**
150	450

 a How many trials did Jen carry out?
 b Estimate the probability of getting a six with this dice.
 c Explain whether you think the dice was fair.

7 Ω = {whole numbers from 1 to 16},
 A = {multiples of 3} and
 B = {prime numbers}

 For the following sets
 i list the elements in the set
 ii give the probability that a randomly selected number is in the set.
 a A   b A′   c B′
 d A ∩ B   e A ∪ B   f A ∩ B′

What next?

	Score	
0 – 3		Your knowledge of this topic is still developing. To improve look at Formative test: 2B-16; MyMaths: 1199, 1209 and 1211
4 – 6		You are gaining a secure knowledge of this topic. To improve look at InvisiPen: 452, 453, 461 and 462
7		You have mastered this topic. Well done, you are ready to progress!

 MyMaths.co.uk

Question commentary

Questions 1 and **2** – Discuss when a sample space diagram might be better than a tree diagram, i.e. when there are lots of possible outcomes. Question **2** is about as big a tree diagram as students should ever need to be drawing.

Question 3 – Students should not put $\frac{0}{8}$ for **b**.

Question 4 – Use the fact that if the probability of an event occurring is p then the probability of it not occurring is $1 - p$.

Question 5 – 12 students out of 20 passed the test so $12 \div 20$. Remind students it is normal to use decimals or percentages for experimental probability.

Question 6 – Discuss how the sample size can affect the reliability of the experimental probability.

Question 7 – Students could draw a Venn diagram showing the numbers in each region before answering the questions.

Answers

1 a Check students' diagrams
 b

		Second card	
		Black	**Red**
First	**Black**	(B, B)	(B, R)
card	**Red**	(R, B)	(R, R)

2 Check students' diagrams

3 a $\frac{3}{8}$ b 0

4 0.7

5 0.6 or 60%

6 a 600   b 0.25 or 25%
 c Unfair, would expect probability near 0.17

7 a i A = {3, 6, 9, 12, 15}   ii P(A) = $\frac{5}{16}$
 b i A′ = {1, 2, 4, 5, 7, 8, 10, 11, 13, 14, 16}
  ii P(A′) = $\frac{11}{16}$
 c i B′ = {1, 4, 6, 8, 9, 10, 12, 13, 14, 15, 16}
  ii P(B′) = $\frac{11}{16}$
 d i A ∩ B = {3}
  ii P(A ∩ B) = $\frac{1}{16}$
 e i A ∪ B = {2, 3, 5, 6, 7, 9, 11, 12, 13, 15, 16}
  ii P(A ∪ B) = $\frac{11}{16}$
 f i A ∩ B′ = {6, 9, 12, 15}
  ii P(A ∩ B′) = $\frac{1}{4}$

1 Draw a tree diagram for each of these situations.

a An ordinary dice is rolled, and the score is noted; then a coin is spun, and the result is recorded.

b An experimenter rolls an ordinary dice, and notes whether the score is odd or even; then a coin is spun, and the result is recorded.

c A coin is spun, and the result is written down; then the experimenter rolls a dice and records whether or not the result is a multiple of 3.

2 Draw a sample space diagram for each of these situations.

a A player turns up two cards from a pack of playing cards, and notes the suits.

Hearts   Diamonds   Clubs   Spades

b A player picks two letters from a bag of letter tiles. Each tile has a vowel or a consonant.

c A shopper picks two cans of cat food from a shelf. The flavours available are chicken, beef and fish.

3 A computer is used to choose a random whole number between 1 and 100 (inclusive). Find the probability that the chosen number is

a exactly 13   b even
c a multiple of 10   d a multiple of 7
e less than 25 or greater than 85   f not a multiple of 7

4 Here are the scores obtained by a sample of people who carried out a safety test.

15 17 13 18 19 20 19 13 14 19
20 11 12 16 18 17 20 14 18 13

a A score of 15 or more is needed to pass the test. Estimate the experimental probability of passing the test.

b If 500 people took the test, how many would you expect to pass? Explain your answer.

5 Alexa and Bella each carried out an experiment to see how likely a seed was to germinate if it wasn't watered. The table shows their results.

	Alexa	Bella
Germinated	18	50
Failed	32	70

a Estimate the probability of germination for Alexa and Bella.

b Explain whose results are more reliable and why.

c What is the best estimate of the probability of germination based on these results?

6 In an experiment a dice was rolled several times to see if it was fair. The table shows the number of times an even or an odd number was obtained.

Even	Odd
36	54

a Calculate the theoretical probabilities of obtaining an even or an odd number for a fair dice.

b Estimate the probabilities of obtaining an even or an odd number using the experimental data.

c Explain whether you think the dice is biased or not.

7 Max put 25 blue counters, 50 red counters and 25 yellow counters into a bag.

He shook the bag, picked a counter without looking, recorded the colour and returned the counter to the bag. He did this 200 times altogether.

a Calculate the theoretical probability of choosing each colour.

b Max actually obtained 61 blues, 108 reds and 31 yellows. Estimate the experimental probability of obtaining each colour.

c Max thought that the theoretical and experimental probabilities were different. Give an example of a factor that could have caused this difference.

8 Sasha surveyed the students in his class to see who had participated in athletics or cricket in the previous week. He put his results into a Venn diagram.

Find

a P(A)   b P(C)   c P(A')
d P(C')   e P(A ∪ C)   f P(A ∩ C)

A
8   6   12
6

A = {Athletics}
C = {Cricket}

9 Jenny sorts 24 elements into two sets X and Y. She writes four fact cards.

$$P(X \cap Y) = \frac{1}{4}$$ $$P(Y) = \frac{5}{12}$$

$$P(X') = \frac{1}{2}$$ $$P(X \cup Y) = \frac{2}{3}$$

Complete Jenny's Venn diagram showing the number of elements in each region.

X   Y
... ...
...

MyMaths.co.uk

Question commentary

Questions 1 and **2** – Tree diagrams and sample space diagrams are often interchangeable but it is worth discussing when one is more appropriate than the other.

Question 3 – Students should try and find systematic ways of counting the 'successful' outcomes, rather than listing all the numbers.

Questions 4 to **7** – Lots of opportunities to discuss the principles of experimental probability, the need for a large number of trials and the principle of bias.

Question 8 – Students should read the numbers directly from the Venn diagram but may need reminding to find the total number of people first as the denominator of each fraction. Fractions could be simplified.

Question 9 – Students will need to perform arithmetic with fractions to 'unpick' the information given. Encourage them to work systematically 'outwards' from the intersection.

Answers

1 **a-c** Check students' diagrams

2 **a**

		2nd card			
		H	**C**	**D**	**S**
1st card	**H**	(H,H)	(H,C)	(H,D)	(H,S)
	C	(C,H)	(C,C)	(C,D)	(C,S)
	D	(D,H)	(D,C)	(D,D)	(D,S)
	S	(S,H)	(S,C)	(S,D)	(S,S)

b

		2nd letter	
		V	**C**
1st letter	**V**	(V,V)	(V,C)
	C	(C,V)	(C,C)

c

		2nd can		
		C	**B**	**F**
1st can	**C**	(C,C)	(C,B)	(C,F)
	B	(B,C)	(B,B)	(B,F)
	F	(F,C)	(F,B)	(F,F)

3 **a** $\frac{13}{100}$ **b** $\frac{1}{2}$ **c** $\frac{1}{10}$ **d** $\frac{7}{50}$

 e $\frac{40}{100} = \frac{2}{5}$ **f** $\frac{86}{100} = \frac{43}{50}$

4 **a** $\frac{13}{20}$ **b** $325 = \frac{13}{20} \times 500$

5 **a** Alexa: $\frac{18}{50} = \frac{9}{25}$ Bella: $\frac{50}{120} = \frac{5}{12}$

 b Bella's as her sample size is greater

 c $\frac{18+50}{50+120} = \frac{2}{5}$

6 **a** $\frac{1}{2}$

 b P(Even) $= \frac{36}{90} = \frac{2}{5}$ P(Odd) $= \frac{54}{90} = \frac{3}{5}$

 c It is likely that the dice is biased since we do not agree with the theoretical calculation even with a sample of 90 trials

7 **a** $P(B) = \frac{25}{100} = 0.25$ $P(R) = \frac{50}{100} = 0.5$

 $P(Y) = \frac{25}{100} = 0.25$

 b $P(B) = \frac{61}{200} = 0.305$ $P(R) = \frac{108}{200} = 0.54$

 $P(Y) = \frac{31}{200} = 0.155$

 c Various answers possible, e.g. he may not have shaken the bag or the counters may not all be the same size (anything that prevents each counter having an equal chance of being chosen on each occasion).

8 **a** $\frac{7}{16}$ **b** $\frac{9}{16}$ **c** $\frac{9}{16}$ **d** $\frac{7}{16}$

 e $\frac{13}{16}$ **f** $\frac{3}{16}$

9 6 in X, 6 in $X \cap Y$, 4 in Y, 8 outside

Related lessons		Resources	
Multiplication and division problems	11f	Divide decimals by whole numbers	(1008)
Scale drawings	12f	Multiply decimals by whole numbers	(1010)
Direct proportion	15c	Scale drawing	(1117)
		Proportion unitary method	(1036)
		Examples of food packaging with 'free range', 'fair trade' or 'organic' labels	

Simplification	Extension
Concentrate on just the outside area in task **1**. In task **2**, encourage students to work together to find possible areas before proceeding to plan the layout. Tasks **3** and **4** involve proportion and could be simplified by reducing the number of parts or changing some of the values.	Allowing students to assume that caged and free-range hens lay the same amount of eggs per day and that farmers would be able to sell all the eggs they produced regardless of type, students could explore each of the free-range farms and calculate the number of caged hens the farmer could keep to make more profit than they do selling their eggs as free-range.

Links
Students could look at the various rules for other produce labelled as 'free-range', 'fair trade' or 'organic'. Lots of information on this and other ethical foodstuffs can be found on the internet. An example can be found at http://www.co-operativefood.co.uk/food-ethics/ and a quick search in Google will throw up lots of other examples. Students could also keep a diary of their eating to record when they eat products that are labelled as ethical.

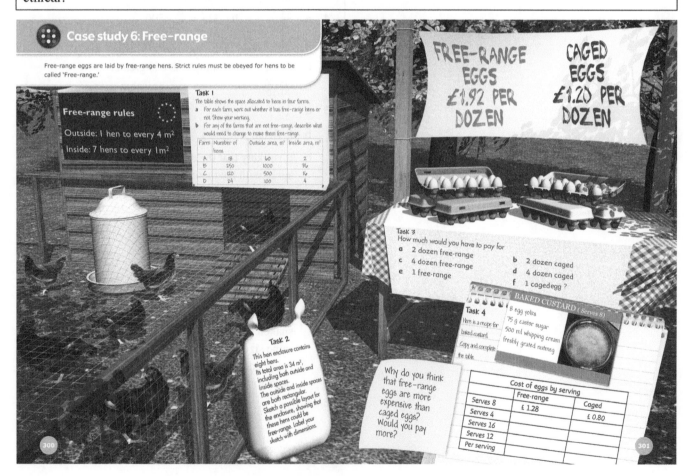

Teaching notes

Many students are interested in animal welfare and how animals farmed for produce are kept. Mathematics can be used to explore some of these issues by considering the extra cost of free-range eggs versus eggs from caged hens. Not only can students explore the legislation that enables a farmer to label their eggs as free-range, they can compare costs and discuss the reasons why people may choose to pay more for free-range eggs.

Ask students whether they have heard of free-range eggs and what their understanding of the term is. Explain that there are rules in place to determine whether a farmer can sell their eggs as free-range.

Task 1

Ask students how big they think 4 m^2 is. Consider the size of the classroom to get a feel for relative size. Look at farms A to D. Discuss with the students how to decide whether they are free-range. Make sure they take account of both the outside and inside dimensions.

Task 2

Look at the farm in the picture and the dimensions given on the feed bag. Ask students to plan with a partner a possible layout of the farm pen so they can consider the hens to be free-range.

Task 3

Now look at the costs of the different types of eggs. Ask students to find the answers to questions **a** to **f**. Discuss the different strategies used.

Task 4

Ask students to spend a few minutes looking at the baked custard recipe with a partner. How would you calculate the cost of the eggs for the different amounts of the pudding? Share ideas then ask students to complete the recipe card.

Answers

1. **a** A: No; B: Yes; C: No; D: Yes

   b A: Outside area to 72 m^2, inside to 2.57 m^2

   C: Inside area to 17.14 m^2

2. Check students' drawings

3. **a** £3.84

   b £7.68

   c 16 pence

   d £2.40

   e £4.80

   f 10 pence

4. 64 pence/40 pence

   £2.56/£1.60

   £1.92/£1.20

   16 pence/12 pence

These questions will test you on your knowledge of the topics in chapters 13 to 16. They give you practice in the types of questions that you may eventually be given in your GCSE exams. There are 85 marks in total.

1 For these sequences

 i find the term-to-term rules in the form 'start with …. and ….' (3 marks)

 ii write the next three terms in the sequence. (3 marks)

 a 3, 10, 17, 24, …   **b** 18, 13, 8, 3, …   **c** 2, 4, 10, 22, …

2 For these sequences

 i find the term-to-term rules (3 marks)

 ii find the position-to-term rules in the form 'multiply the position by … and then …' (3 marks)

 iii write these position-to-term rules in terms of the nth term (3 marks)

 iv use the nth term to find the 50th term of each sequence. (3 marks)

 a 1, 3, 5, 7, …   **b** 4, 8, 12, 16, …   **c** 11, 18, 25, 32, …

3 A farmer is building a fence around his field using pieces of wood as shown in the diagram.

 a Construct a sequence to show for each fence the number of pieces of wood used. (2 marks)

 b What is the term-to-term rule? (2 marks)

 c Write the position-to-term rule in terms of n. (2 marks)

 d To complete the fence the farmer requires wood up to the 40th term. How many pieces does he need? (1 mark)

4 A cuboid is 2 cm wide, 3 cm high and 5 cm long.

 a Draw the net of the cuboid on square grid paper. (2 marks)

 b How many faces, vertices and edges does it have? (2 marks)

 c Calculate the area of the cuboid. (3 marks)

 d Calculate the volume of the cuboid. (3 marks)

5 This solid is made from four cubes.

 a On square grid paper, draw

  i the front elevation (F)

  ii the side elevation (S)

  iii the plan view (P). (3 marks)

 b Draw the solid using isometric paper. (3 marks)

6 a What is the mathematical name for this solid? (1 mark)

 b How many faces, vertices and edges does it have? (2 marks)

 c On square grid paper draw the net of this solid. (2 marks)

 d Calculate the surface area of this solid. (2 marks)

 e Calculate the volume of this solid. (2 marks)

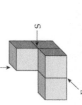

7 Write these ratios in their simplest form. (4 marks)

 a 4 litres : 300ml   **b** 600g : 2kg   **c** 16h : 1 day   **d** 5km : 300m

8 a Share £126 in the ratio 5 : 4. (2 marks)

 b Share 72g of chocolate in the ratio 3 : 5. (2 marks)

9 a Three tins of paint costs £31.11. What is the cost of (4 marks)

  i 2 tins of paint   **ii** 5 tins of paint?

 b 18 litres of diesel fuel costs £25. What is the cost of (4 marks)

  i 20 litres of fuel   **ii** 45 litres of fuel?

10 Calculate these using a suitable method.

 a A new car depreciated (lost value) by 27% after one year. If it was bought for £17 500, how much is it worth after one year? (2 marks)

 b A computer's memory was increased from 2MB to 3MB. What was the percentage increase in memory? (2 marks)

11 A bag contains 18 counters: five red, four blue and nine yellow. A counter is taken out of the bag at random.

 a Draw a tree diagram to show this event. (2 marks)

 b What is the probability of choosing (3 marks)

  i a yellow counter   **ii** a red counter   **iii** a red or blue counter?

12 Electrical appliances were being checked in a school and the table shows the results of these checks.

	Pass	Fail
	153	21

 a Use these results to estimate the probability that an appliance chosen at random would pass the test. (2 marks)

 b The following year another check was made and out of 193 appliances, 24 failed. Which year were the appliances more reliable? Give a reason for your answer. (3 marks)

13 A bag contains 7 red counters and 5 blue counters. One counter is taken out of the bag and then returned. This is done 50 times and the colour noted.

Red	37
Blue	13

 a Estimate the probability of a red counter being picked from the bag. (2 marks)

 b What is the theoretical probability of a red counter being picked? (1 mark)

 c If the experiment was repeated 500 times how often would you expect a blue counter to be chosen? (2 marks)

 MyMaths.co.uk

Mark scheme

Questions 1 – 6 marks

a **i** 1 start with 3 and + 7   **ii** 1   31, 38, 45

b **i** 1 start with 18 and − 5   **ii** 1   -2, -7, -12

c **i** 1 start with 2, double and + 2

   ii 1 46, 94, 190

Questions 2 – 12 marks

a **i** 1 start with 1 and + 2

   ii 1 multiply the position by 2 and − 1

   iii 1 $2n − 1$

   iv 1 99

b **i** 1 start with 4 and + 4

   ii 1 multiply the position by 4

   iii 1 $4n$

   iv 1 200

c **i** 1 start with 11 and + 7

   ii 1 multiply the position by 7 and + 4

   iii 1 $7n + 4$

   iv 1 354

Questions 3 – 7 marks

a 2 fence 1: 4, fence 2: 7, fence 3: 10

b 2 start with 4 and + 3

c 2 multiply by 3 and + 1; $3n + 1$

d 1 $n = 40$ gives 121 pieces

Questions 4 – 10 marks

a 2 Check students' drawings: correct net and size

b 3 6 faces, 12 edges, 8 vertices

c 3 62 cm^2

d 2 30 cm^3

Questions 5 – 6 marks

a 3 3 squares seen in each elevation

b 3 Check students' drawings

Questions 6 – 9 marks

a 1 Triangular prism

b 2 5 faces, 9 edges, 6 vertices

c 2 Check students' drawings

d 2 152 cm^2

e 2 96 cm^3

Questions 7 – 4 marks

a 1 40 : 3   **b** 1   3 : 10

c 1 2 : 3   **d** 1   50 : 3

Questions 8 – 4 marks

a 2 £70 : £56

b 2 27 g : 45 g

Questions 9 – 8 marks

a i 2 £20.74; £10.37 seen for 1 mark

   ii 2 £51.85

b i 2 £27.78; £1.39 seen for 1 mark

   ii 2 £62.50

Questions 10 – 4 marks

a 2 £12 775; 0.73 seen for 1 mark

b 2 50%; ½ × 100% seen for 1 mark

Questions 11 – 5 marks

a 2 Check students drawings: correct tree diagram showing 3 branches and labelled

b **i** 1 $\frac{9}{18}$ or $\frac{1}{2}$ **ii** 1 $\frac{5}{18}$ **iii** 1 $\frac{9}{18}$ or $\frac{1}{2}$

Questions 12 – 5 marks

a 2 0.88 or 88%; accept 87.9%, 153/174

b 3 Pass rate is 0.87 or 87%. This difference is not significant, so the appliances weren't more reliable in either year.

Questions 13 – 5 marks

a 2 $\frac{37}{50}$ or 0.74 or 74%

b 1 $\frac{7}{12}$ or 0.58 or 58%

c 2 $\frac{5}{12} \times 500 = 208$

Learning outcomes

DF2 Select and use appropriate calculation strategies to solve increasingly complex problems (L6)

DF3 Use algebra to generalise the structure of arithmetic, including to formulate mathematical relationship (L6)

DF5 Move freely between different numerical, algebraic, graphical and diagrammatic representations (for example, equivalent fractions, fractions and decimals, and equations and graphs) (L6)

DF7 Use language and properties precisely to analyse numbers, algebraic expressions, 2D and 3D shapes, probability and statistics (L6)

RM2 Extend and formalise their knowledge of ratio and proportion in working with measures and geometry, and in formulating proportional relations algebraically (L6)

RM6 Interpret when the structure of a numerical problem requires additive, multiplicative or proportional reasoning (L6)

RM7 Explore what can and cannot be inferred in statistical and probabilistic settings, and begin to express their arguments formally (L6)

SP1 Develop their mathematical knowledge, in part through solving problems and evaluating the outcomes, including multi-step problems (L6)

SP2 Develop their use of formal mathematical knowledge to interpret and solve problems, including in financial mathematics (L6)

SP4 Select appropriate concepts, methods and techniques to apply to unfamiliar and non-routine problems (L6)

Introduction	Prior knowledge
The chapter consists of a sequence of five spreads based on the theme of a school trip to France. This allows questions to cover a wide range of topics taken from algebra, statistics, geometry and number. The questions are word-based and often do not directly indicate what type of mathematics is involved. Therefore students will need to work to identify the relevant mathematics and in several instances which of a variety of methods to apply before commencing. This approach is rather different from the previous topic based spreads and students may require additional support in this aspect of functional maths.	The chapter covers many topics; lessons which contain directly related material include • 2d, 2e • 3e, 3f • 4d, 4e • 5a, 5c • 7a, 7e, 7f • 8c, 8e, 8f • 9a • 10d • 11e, 11f • 12f, 12g

Using mathematics

The student book start of chapter suggests three areas of everyday life where aspects of the ability to apply mathematical ideas prove highly valuable.

Fluency: If you run a small business you need to be able to do your accounts. Are you making a profit? Is the money you make from sales bigger than all your overheads – wages, rent, materials…? People often use spreadsheet type programs to help them to do their accounts. However, should you trust what they say? It helps if you have a 'feel' for what the right answer should be and if you can quickly do simpler versions of the calculations yourself as checks.

Mathematical reasoning: Sometimes finding the answer to a mathematical problem is the easy part. The hardest part can be convincing other people that your solution is the right one. One way to help persuade other people is by choosing the best graph to show your results. You also need to be able to back up your results with carefully reasoned explanations.

Problem solving: Controlling a robot is surprisingly complex. It requires breaking down into smaller tasks in order to be manageable. Each of these smaller tasks might need skills from several different areas of mathematics. To control a robot's movements you will need to use geometry, coordinates and algebra to represent instructions.

Topic scheme

Teaching time = 5 lessons/2 weeks

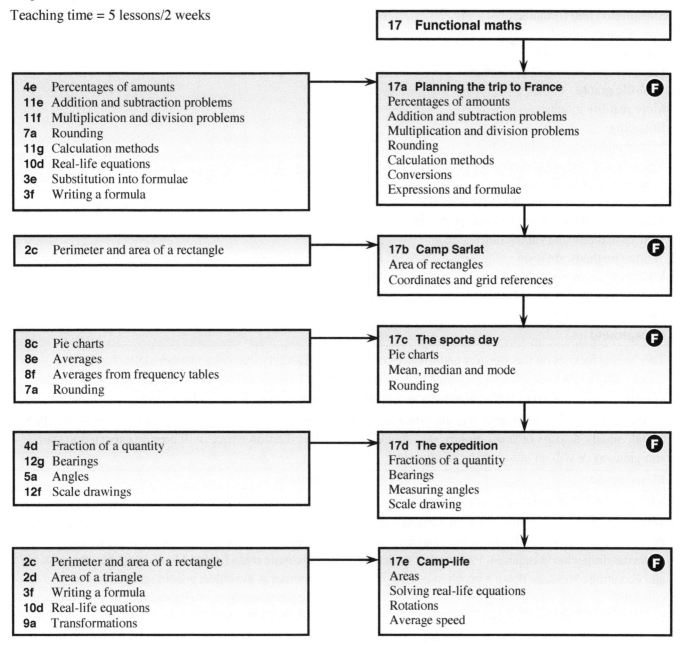

17   Functional maths

4e Percentages of amounts	**17a Planning the trip to France** (F)
11e Addition and subtraction problems	Percentages of amounts
11f Multiplication and division problems	Addition and subtraction problems
7a Rounding	Multiplication and division problems
11g Calculation methods	Rounding
10d Real-life equations	Calculation methods
3e Substitution into formulae	Conversions
3f Writing a formula	Expressions and formulae

2c Perimeter and area of a rectangle	**17b Camp Sarlat** (F)
	Area of rectangles
	Coordinates and grid references

8c Pie charts	**17c The sports day** (F)
8e Averages	Pie charts
8f Averages from frequency tables	Mean, median and mode
7a Rounding	Rounding

4d Fraction of a quantity	**17d The expedition** (F)
12g Bearings	Fractions of a quantity
5a Angles	Bearings
12f Scale drawings	Measuring angles
	Scale drawing

2c Perimeter and area of a rectangle	**17e Camp-life** (F)
2d Area of a triangle	Areas
3f Writing a formula	Solving real-life equations
10d Real-life equations	Rotations
9a Transformations	Average speed

Related lessons		Resources
Substitution into formulae	3e	Calculators
Constructing formulae	3f	Travel brochures
Percentages of amounts	4e	
Fractions, decimals and percentages	4f	
Real-life graphs	6d	
More real-life graphs	6e	
Rounding	7a	
Mental addition and subtraction	7b	
Multiply and divide by powers of 10	7c	
Mental multiplication and division	7d	
Mental addition and subtraction problems	7e	
Mental multiplication and division problems	7f	
Written addition and subtraction	11a	
Written methods: division	11c	
Written addition and subtraction	11e	
Written multiplication and division	11f	
Calculation methods	11g	

Background

This spread focuses on the logistics and finances of the trip and largely exercises number skills. Issues surrounding costs, deposits and exchange rates may be familiar to some students from family holidays and this knowledge can be used to both enliven discussion and provide a source of illustrative examples.

As the first spread in the chapter it is important to establish how the students should approach the work, whether as individuals, as pairs or small groups, etc., should they work at their own pace, will they be expected to start straightaway or will an introduction be given, etc.

Simplification

The questions in this spread involve straightforward arithmetic (discourage falling back on a calculator), the difficulties are likely to arise from the language and understanding what is required. Pair weaker students and encourage breaking down a problem using a checklist:

1) Understand the problem/question
2) Underline/copy important information
3) Decide which operation is necessary
4) Make an approximation
5) Work out the answer
6) Check that the answer is sensible

Extension

Provide students with a holiday brochure and ask them to calculate an approximate cost for two adults and two children to go on holiday. Ask them to include approximate costs for food, activities, etc. If access to the internet is available, encourage students to investigate total costs of flights including insurance and all surcharges etc.

Links

Planning a trip of any kind takes a lot of organisation and links can be drawn to both school trips and family holidays. It is also a good opportunity to discuss with students the idea of planning any kind of expenditure such as saving to buy a new games console, shopping on the high street and working out if you have enough money to buy your food and drink in the local café.

Teaching notes

Invite pairs of students to imagine that they are a teacher planning a school trip and ask them to suggest what they need to consider. Focus on the costs involved: how should they calculate deposits, deal with exchange rates, etc. The student book can be used as a prompt. The subsequent discussion should concentrate on generic approaches, what is required and a suitable method, rather than specific details.

Supply students with some example calculations and ask them to explain how they would complete them. Total cost £3782, 20 students: cost per student, 15% deposit, £435 to be paid in Euros at £1= €1.28. Ask how they decide whether to use mental, written or calculator methods: can they give two pros and two cons for each method? Also ask how they would go about checking their answers (against an approximation, using an inverse operation, is it reasonable, is it to an appropriate degree of accuracy?)

Ask students if they can supply some handy hints for doing calculations, especial using mental methods. These can be collected on the board as a reminder for students as they work through the spread.

Exercise commentary

Question 1 – Initially avoid using a calculator and encourage the use of 'tricks' supported by workings; can students see an equivalent decimal multiplication? For example, 15% of = 1/10 + ½ × 1/10 = 0.15

Question 2 – In part **a**, check that students line their calculation up on the decimal point. In part **b**, ask, is there an easy way to do the division?
(÷ 50 = × 2 ÷ 100)

Question 3 – In part **a**, ask, how does 'rounding up' differ from 'rounding'? In part **b**, check that the rounded-up deposit is subtracted.

Question 4 – Encourage students to check that the total cost is £9476. In part **a**, ask if it is possible to speed up the calculations using the memory function. (store 100 ÷ 9476)

Question 5 – A slightly simpler formula to use is $e = 12 \times p /10$. Can students spot any errors without doing a calculation? (€2040 > €1770 but £1475 < £1770) Ask students to try and explain how the errors happened and how they might try to avoid making such mistakes themselves.

Question 6 – It should not be necessary to use a calculator. Does it make sense to round the price of the trainers?

Answers

1. **a** accommodation: £147·50 **b** coach: £519·00
   c activities: £425·00 **d** ferry berths: £175
   e insurance: £64·50
2. **a** £1331·00
   b £27·00 Ms. Perry has rounded the money to the nearest £1·00 or, £30·00 rounded to the nearest £10·00
3. **a** £190 to the nearest £10
   b £190·00 – answer to question **2b**
   c £16·30 per week or more sensibly, £16·00 per week
4. **a** coach: 37%   ferry berths: 9%
      accommodation: 16%   food: 15%
      insurance: 5%   activities 18%
   b Should be 100%
5. **a** Those properly converted are: Coach
   b The two confused companies are: The Active Company and the Camp Company
6. **a** €3·00 = £2·50 €2.40 = £2·00 €45·00 = £37·50
      €19·99 = £99·99 (£100·00)

Related lessons		Resources
Perimeter and area of a rectangle	2c	Local area map
Drawing straight-line graphs	6a	Small name cards

Background

This spread takes up the theme of the school trip and arriving at the camp where they have to organise the accommodation and familiarise themselves with the campsite. The mathematics involves areas of rectangles, arithmetic with decimals, the use of coordinates (with direct cross-curricular links to geography) and logical reasoning.

Simplification	Extension
In question **1**, the decimals may cause difficulty. Suggest, for example, that students think about the area of a 2 × 2 tent and a 22 × 15 tent. Encourage students to think this through rather than simply use a calculator. For question **2**, provide cards with the five names on to allow students to experiment with their order.	Supply students with a scale for the map, the large squares are 10 m × 10 m, and ask them to determine the sizes of various features. How long is the football pitch? What is its area? If the swimming pool is 1.5 m deep, what is its volume?

Links

Working out areas from plans forms a link to design subjects and to architecture and town planning in the real world. Work on maps, coordinates and grid references link directly to geography and navigation in the wider sense.

Teaching notes

The first question involves the multiplication and division of decimals. It will be useful revision to ask students to explain how to do this and how to check their answer. Test their understanding by asking them to calculate the area of a rectangular tent. Ask how they think this is related to how many people the tent will comfortably sleep. Is the ground area the only thing that needs to be considered? What about the tent's shape?

Question **2** is likely to be new to the students in the context of mathematics. It may help to provide a similar example and ask students to provide a 'method' for solving the puzzle and for verifying any solution.

Questions **3** to **6** involve interpreting a map and finding locations. Using a local area map, ask students to specify the positions of local landmarks. Can they do this is such a way that they don't refer to other locations on the map? This may be familiar from geography and the method used in the questions is easily tied in with the use of coordinates in mathematics. The map is also a scale drawing and students could be asked to think about how they could calculate real-life distances based on either the local area or campsite maps. One way to approach this is by asking students to say how they would go about creating an accurate map of the school.

Exercise commentary

Question 1 – Calculators are not necessary. It will be important to check the size of the answers using approximate integer calculations; inverse operations can be used for part **c**. Check that units are given.

What is the area per person for the three tents?

Question 2 – This is a new type of question; students will need to be systematic in their reasoning and be careful to use each piece of information given.

Questions 3 – Check that students can read the scales and find coordinates in the first two quadrants. The postcard on the previous page may help with interpreting the map.

Questions 4 and 5 – Check that students are reading the scales to sufficient accuracy. It may help to accurately copy the sub-scale onto a piece of paper which students can use instead of a ruler to measure distances on the map. In question **5**, some help might be needed to find all the bins and taps.

Question 6 – As a first step, check that students have correctly identified and oriented the grid squares. Ask them to make a sketch and label the coordinates of the bottom-left corner and show the directions of the coordinate axes. For example, part **a** shows the grid square (2, 1) containing tent T rotated through 160°.

Answers

1 **a** $3 \cdot 3 \, \text{m}^2$ **b** $5 \cdot 25 \, \text{m}^2$ **c** $2.5 \, \text{m}$

2 Tent A: John Tent B: Carl Tent C: Magnus
   Tent D: Cherry Tent E: Kadeja

3 **a** **i** $(0 \cdot 5, 2 \cdot 7)$: Pool   **ii** $(2 \cdot 2, 3 \cdot 3)$: Sports Hall
      iii $(-2 \cdot 5, 2 \cdot 8)$: Pitch   **iv** $(-0 \cdot 4, 2 \cdot 1)$: Shop
      v $(-1 \cdot 5, 2 \cdot 0)$: Play Area
   b **i** $(1 \cdot 4, 0 \cdot 6)$: Tent N   **ii** $(3 \cdot 0, 1 \cdot 8)$: Tent U
      iii $(-2 \cdot 3, 0 \cdot 4)$: Tent A   **iv** $(-1 \cdot 0, 1 \cdot 2)$: Tent H
      v $(-1 \cdot 6, 0 \cdot 5)$: Tent C
   c Office

4 $(-1 \cdot 8, 2 \cdot 8)$

5 **a** $(-2.6, 2 \cdot 0)$ **b** $(-1 \cdot 8, 1 \cdot 7)$ **c** $(0 \cdot 4, 0 \cdot 7)$
   d $(1 \cdot 1, 0 \cdot 4)$ **e** $(2.7, 2 \cdot 8)$ **w** $(2.1, 1 \cdot 0)$
   x $(0.4, 1 \cdot 0)$ **y** $(1 \cdot 0, 1 \cdot 5)$ **z** $(3 \cdot 1, 1 \cdot 5)$

6 **a** **i** $(2, 1)$ **ii** $(1, 2)$ **iii** $(-3, 2)$
   b **i** $(2.6, 1 \cdot 7)$ **ii** $(1 \cdot 6, 2 \cdot 3)$ **iii** $(-2.2, 2 \cdot 3)$

17c The sports day

Related lessons		Resources
Constructing formulae	3f	Large copies of question 2 table
Ordering decimals	4a	
Rounding	7a	
Mental addition and subtraction	7b	
Mental addition and subtraction problems	7e	
Collecting data	8b	
Pie charts	8c	
Averages	8f	
Averages from frequency tables	8g	
Solving equations	10a	
Multi-step equations	10b	
More equations	10c	
Written addition and subtraction	11a	
Written addition and subtraction	11e	

Background

The sports day theme can be made even more real for the students if data from sports competitions in which they are involved can be used as illustrations or to replace numeric values in the questions.

A large range of mathematics is encountered in this spread broadly on the theme of statistics, including: interpreting pie charts, collating data and finding summary statistics, solving 'algebraic' problems, rounding, and making and justifying decisions.

Simplification

The wide variety of topics in this spread may prove discouraging to a student. At the same time it presents an opportunity to find questions with which they feel more comfortable, allowing them to build confidence. It will also help to organise students into small groups to share ideas and work together; this will be most helpful for questions **2** and **3**. For question **2**, provide students with a large version of the table and, working one team at a time, enter tallies of games' results and goals scored. In a second stage these can be added up and entered into the final table.

Extension

A number of checks are available for question **2c**. Ask students to investigate the following questions. Does the total number of won games have to equal the total number of lost games? Can the total number of drawn games be odd? How does the total number of won, drawn and lost games relate to the total number played? What is the difference between the total number of goals for and total number of goals against? How does this relate to the answer in part **a**?

Links

Sports and the results from sports may be of interest to a large number of students who regularly follow a local football team or athletics events. A league table from the newspaper could be used to provide a contrast to that given in question **2**, while results from events at the Olympics could be analysed in discussion with other questions.

Check out http://espn.go.com/olympics/summer/2012/results for a full list of all results from London 2012.

Teaching notes

Given the breadth of knowledge being tested here it will be most useful to focus attention on those areas that are likely to cause the students most difficulty, rather than try to address all potential issues.

A majority of the class is likely to be familiar with scoring in football. Using results from the school or an international competition will allow several of the issues associated with question **2** to be discussed. In particular, cover how to systematically collate the raw results into the summary table.

Put students into groups and pose a question similar to **3**. Ask students for their ideas on how to go about solving it; did they get it right? How do they know? Several approaches are possible and it will be instructive to get students to compare their relative merits.

Exercise commentary

Question 1 – One student = 7.2° so angles are only needed to this accuracy; can they be estimated? Ask students to measure the angles and calculate the numbers to check their answers.

Question 2 – In part **b**, encourage students to write down an ordered list of the number of goals scored per match and also to calculate the median. In part **c** students need to be very careful, what checks can be made? In part **d**, ask which is the more representative average, the mode, the median or the mean?

Question 3 – Encourage abstracting four equations: $B + R + 2G = 23$, $2B + R + G = 17$, $4R = 20$, $2B + 2G = 20$. The third target gives $R = 5$ and hence $B + 2G = 18$ and $2B + G = 12$. Possible approaches are: trial-and-improvement, algebraic or graphical – encourage trying out more than one.

Question 4 – In part **b**, check times go from smallest (fastest) to largest (slowest).

Question 5 – In part **b**, how can the answers from part **a** help? Do they need to divide by 3 to rank the competitors?

Question 6 – Encourage students to set up an equation rather than use an *ad hoc* method or trial-and-improvement.

Answers

1. **a** **i** Tennis
   ii $\frac{1}{2}$ of the students played football
   b **i** Archery
   ii Approximately 12 people
   c Football
2. **a** Total of goals in the competition = 37
   b The modal score per game is 2 goals
   c Check students' tables completed correctly
   d 3.7 goals
   e The team who scored most goals wins
3. **a** **i** Red → 5   **ii** Blue → 2   **iii** Gold
   b The mean is 20
4. **a** **i** 16.4 s   **ii** 14.4 s   **iii** 17.3 s
   iv 15.1 s   **v** 14.6 s
   b 14.4 14.6 15.1 16.4 17.3
5. **a** Carl, Darren, Hussain, Reece, Hamed
   b Carl, Darren, Hussain and (with the same score) Reece and Hamed
5. 7.5 m

Related lessons		Resources
Fraction of a quantity	4d	Protractor
Angles	5a	Ruler
Mental addition and subtraction	7b	Enlargement of map and cliff face
Mental addition and subtraction problems	7e	OS maps
Averages	8f	
Written addition and subtraction	11a	
Written addition and subtraction	11e	
Bearings	12f	
Scale drawings	12g	

Background

Students who are involved in the Duke of Edinburgh award scheme, Boy Scouts, Girl Guides, Woodcraft Folk, Combined Cadet Force, etc. may have direct experience of going on expeditions. Sailors and orienteerers may also have knowledge of navigation. These students' experiences of how mathematics can be applied should be used to enliven and inform classroom discussion.

The mathematics in this spread is broadly on the theme of geometry and includes giving compass bearings, measuring angles and measuring distances on scale drawings, as well as averages, time scales and finding proportions. There are direct links to the geography syllabus.

Simplification

Measuring some of the angles may prove awkward. Provide students with an enlarged copy of the map/cliff face or advise laying a ruler over the top of the protractor to make reading the scale easier. Using a 360° protractor should make measuring the reflex angles in question **4c** easier. (Enlarged diagrams should not be used for measuring distances.)

Extension

Supply students with an OS map and ask them to plan a walk between given points. To begin they should specify the route as a list of directions/bearings and distances read off the map. They should then give timings for the journey assuming a typical walking pace of 15mins/km on even, level ground. This could be refined to take account of the type of terrain, any altitude changes (allow 10 min/100 m climbed) and any rest stops.

Links

Route finding and planning can link into many different aspects of real life from walking to the shops to driving to a destination far away. Curriculum links to geography are very clear to see and other scenarios can be envisaged where map reading and calculating with angles is necessary in real life.

http://www.ordnancesurvey.co.uk/ is a good place to start exploring maps and the principles of mapping.

A link to history is provided by question **3**.

Teaching notes

In question **1c**, the mean can be thought of as a 'balance point' for the distribution of students' weights. This provides a means of checking the answer: the sum of the differences between individual students' weights and the mean should be zero. This provides a more formal definition of 'it should be in the middle'.

Question **2** has obvious links to geography with directions being specified by compass points, whilst in question **4**, angles are measured in degrees. The approaches can be combined to give directions as three-figure bearings.

A further option is to show how locations can be 'triangulated': what place is on a bearing 045° as seen from point A and 030° as seen from point B? (Cave/grotto) Can students provide their own examples, perhaps using a different base-line that requires larger angles to be measured? This could even be used as a challenge: can students produce an accurate scale drawing given the line AB and pairs of bearings for other locations? Distance can then be measured with a ruler and converted into a real-life distance using a scale; this skill is required for question **5**.

The first part of question **3** is likely to cause trouble due to the lack of a year zero – which some students might not appreciate. This is most easily clarified using small values and a number line.

Exercise commentary

Question 1 – A calculator is not necessary ($\frac{1}{5} = \frac{2}{10}$) especially if rounded answers are given. In part **c**, how does the mean compare to the median? Which is more representative?

Question 2 – Aim for ±1 mm accuracies in measurements. Students could be asked to give three-figure bearings as well as compass directions.

Question 3 – In part **a**, link BC dates to negative numbers. Explain the numbering 2 BC, 1 BC, 1 AD, 2 AD (no year zero). Encourage students to test their calculation with smaller numbers that can be shown on a 'number/time line'. In part **b**, what is a sensible accuracy for the answer?

Question 4 – Aim for ±1° accuracy. Encourage students to make estimates of the angles first (at least to the level acute, obtuse, reflex) to help to choose the correct scale to read. In parts **a** and **b**, can the obtuse angles be calculated by subtraction? How does this relate to the reflex angles in part **c**?

Question 5 – If 1 cm represents 1 m and you want answers accurate to 0.5 m, how accurately do you have to measure the lines with your ruler?

Answers

1 a Delica: 9 kg   Lau It: 7 kg   Ahmed: 14 kg
       Eddy: 8 kg   Dan: 12·2 kg   Maggie: 10 kg

   b 21 kg

   c Maggie

2 a i B to C, 500 m North East

      ii C to D, 250 m South East

      iii D to E, 500 m North

      iv E to F, 250 m South West

      v F to G, 100 m South

   b Anticlockwise

   c Clockwise 90°

3 a 100 years

   b 2010 years plus current year (e.g. if 2015, then 2010 + 2015 = 4025 years)

4 a i 120°   **ii** 45°   **iii** 50°   **iv** 95°

   b i 155°   **ii** 90°   **iii** 105°

   c i 250°   **ii** 235°   **iii** 255°

5 a i 5 m   **ii** 3 m   **iii** 5.5 m   **iv** 4.5 m

   b 12 m

Related lessons		Resources
Perimeter and area of a rectangle	2c	Graph paper
Area of a triangle	2d	Tracing paper
Real-life graphs	6d	
More real-life graphs	6e	
Rounding	7a	
Transformations	9a	
Solving equations	10a	
Multi-step equations	10b	
More equations	10c	

Background

The spread has a loose focus on incidents that occur in the life of Miss Perry and the students. It allows a breadth of mathematics to be covered including: finding areas, applying algebra, rotations, using systematic approaches to problem solving and the speed–distance–time relationship.

An aspect of camp life is giving awards for various types of achievement. This could be mirrored in this final spread with, for example, bronze, silver and gold awards being given to students in recognition of their 'effort', 'achievement' and 'support to others'. This ties in with a suggestion for an **extension** activity.

Simplification	Extension
Each question in this spread focuses on a different aspect of mathematics. In the first instance, direct students to questions on topics that they feel more comfortable with and are most likely to succeed. Allow students to work in small groups and do the questions collectively; as well as providing mutual support it is important that they discuss and share their approaches.	If it was decided to run an awards scheme students could be charged with collating class members' marks in the various categories, ranking them and deciding appropriate boundaries for gold, silver and bronze awards.
	This can be developed further with students producing pie charts and other graphs showing, for example, the differences between boys' and girls' achievements.

Links

There are lots of problem-solving type questions and puzzles similar to the ones here that can be provided to students as 'end-of-term' activities, enrichment puzzles and maths club activities.

Some examples of number puzzles can be found at http://www.mathsisfun.com/puzzles/number-puzzles-index.html and a quick google search will certainly turn up more puzzles from other strands of mathematics.

Teaching notes

Question **1** involves finding areas. It may be instructive to ask students to explain where the formula for the area of a triangle comes from. Can they use this argument to simplify calculating the area of the two triangles?

Question **2** should be tackled using algebra. Supply a similar question, for example $12a + 2 = 6a + 20$, and ask students to explain how they would solve this equation. Also ask how they could check that their answer is correct.

Question **3** may prove confusing to students given the apparent diagonal axes. It will be useful to get students to explain their methods for how to rotate a shape, drawn on a grid, through a right angle. Do they get the same result if the same problem were posed but with the axes in a different orientation? In fact, are axes required at all?

Question **4** requires students to work systematically through the possible combination of weights. Ask students to explain their methods for listing and testing the various possibilities

Question **5** involves the relationship between speed, distance and time, which students have not previously encountered. This can be left for students to reason through what is required using common sense and experience or a simple example could be discussed to demonstrate how they should proceed.

Exercise commentary

Question 1 – In part **a**, check that the slope height of the triangles is not used. Could the two triangles be made into a rectangle?

Question 2 – Whilst part **a** can be done using a pictorial balancing approach, suggest setting up equations, $5C + B = 3C + 11B$, and collecting like terms to give, $2C = 10B$ or $C = 5B$. To simplify further you could replace 11B by 11 etc. Part **b ii** gives a fractional answer.

Question 3 – In part **a**, a counting squares approach could be used instead of tracing paper. Ask, are the 45° lines relevant? Are you allowed to first turn the paper through 45° and then do the rotations? In part **b**, can students see the relationship between a +270° rotation and a -90° rotation?

Question 4 – Ask students to explain their strategies. Are they sure their answer is unique?

Question 5 – Challenge students to give their answer in hours and minutes without using a calculator: $550 \div 100 = 55 \div 10 = 5\ \frac{1}{2} = 5\ 30/60 = 5$ hrs 30 min. An intuitive approach based on flying 100 miles in an hour may prove helpful.

Answers

1. **a** $26\,\text{m}^2$ **b** $16\,\text{m}^2$
2. **a** 5 litres
   b i 3 litres   **ii** 4. litres
3. **a** Teacher to visually check
   b Teacher to visually check
4. $9\,\text{kg} + 13\,\text{kg} + 9\,\text{kg}$
5. 5.5 hours